Jim Mumford is a cookbook author and chemical engineer, as well as the creator of jimcooksfoodgood.com. Given his experience as a chemical engineer and author of healthy comfort food recipes, Jim brings a unique perspective towards food, who writes his cookbooks to house the healthy comfort recipes he developed. Jim hopes you find something to relate to, and maybe even get inspired to trust in his recipes to help you cook some food, good.

THE FOOD GOOD COOKBOOK

Healthy Comfort Food Reimagined

JIM MUMFORD

AUSTIN MACAULEY PUBLISHERS™

LONDON • CAMBRIDGE • NEW YORK • SHARJAH

Ordering Information
Quantity sales: Special discounts are available on quantity purchases by corporations, associations, and others. For details, contact the publisher at the address below.

Publisher's Cataloging-in-Publication data
Mumford, Jim
The Food Good Cookbook

ISBN 9781685621247 (Paperback)
ISBN 9781685621254 (Hardback)
ISBN 9781685621261 (ePub e-book)

Library of Congress Control Number: 2023900689

www.austinmacauley.com/us

First Published 2023
Austin Macauley Publishers LLC
40 Wall Street, 33rd Floor, Suite 3302
New York, NY 10005
USA

mail-usa@austinmacauley.com
+1 (646) 5125767

For Gloria:

My editor, taste-tester, and biggest cheerleader.

Table Of Contents

Main Dishes

I love food. If you've known or followed me for any amount of time, this is a massive understatement. To me, food is a love language, and one of the only things in existence that can supply physical, emotional, and sometimes even spiritual needs (try the lasagna if you doubt the spiritual part).

The best things we eat contain a little love, and a little balance. Love can come from a comfort food classic, something that reminds us of the days when we could eat an entire pizza, then go play outside for three hours. Love can also come from cooking for/with, say, your new family (which, if you can get over the inevitable mess, is fully recommended).

Balance in our food begins well before any seasonings and textures. The food we make must fit into whatever lifestyle constraints we may have, be it caloric, dietary, or simply the time it takes to make a meal. This balance is where I struggled through the first several years of my adult life, and is part of what prompted me to create Jim Cooks Food Good.

The recipes you are about to salivate over are created with love and balance in mind. They are intended to be comforting, yet mindful of dietary and caloric preferences. The recipes are meant to be cooked with minimal fuss, yet are full of opportunities to try something new. These elements are the heart of what truly encompasses Healthy Comfort Food.

So, dear reader, I hope this book helps you find some balance and love as you create these recipes yourself.

Appetizers, Sides, and Desserts

Arancini

Prep Time: 10 minutes
Cook Time: 20 minutes

Not that you need a reason to celebrate leftover risotto, but these little rice balls are my number one favorite appetizer ever. Traditionally, they are filled with prosciutto, but pepperoni brings a bit of whimsy to the party, hitting some pizza notes along the way. Pair the arancini with some Sunday gravy (page 87) and you have a new show stopper in your arsenal.

Ingredients

3 cups cooked risotto, cooled
1 cup shredded mozzarella
½ cup frozen peas
1/2 cup pepperoni, roughly chopped
3 eggs, beaten
2 tablespoons milk
3 cups breadcrumbs

Instructions

1. In a large saucepan over medium heat, cook pepperoni until just crisp, 4–5 minutes. Remove from pan and let cool.

2. Divide risotto in half. Press one half onto a baking sheet in an even layer 1/2 thick. Top with pepperoni, cheese, and peas. Top that layer with the rest of the risotto. Using an ice cream scoop, make 1 1/2 balls from the mixture, rolling them in your hands to ensure they are tight.

3. Preheat the air fryer to 375 degrees F.

4. Combine eggs and milk in a shallow bowl. Pour breadcrumbs into a second shallow bowl. Roll the rice balls in the egg mixture, then in the breadcrumbs. Place on a cooling rack while you finish dredging the remaining rice balls.

5. Air fry in two batches for 10–12 minutes or until deeply golden brown; these hold in a warm oven for over an hour. Serve alongside warm tomato sauce.

Caraway Broccoli Rabe

Prep Time: 5 minutes
Cook Time: 10 minutes

I have a secret for you. I didn't eat my veggies as a kid.

It's not (totally) my fault, you see. It's just that I don't happen to enjoy the flavor of green. You know the flavor. Somewhere between fresh cut grass and old coffee. Green. This is how I describe how something like asparagus or brussels sprouts taste, especially raw. Green. Steaming them, well, that turned the green flavor up to 11. Nope, not for Jim.

Then, one day, I bravely tried a fried brussels sprout. Then another. Then another. I've been addicted ever since. What gives?

Glucosinolates, among other things. See, that grassy flavor can be a vegetable's natural defense against bugs, chlorophyll that helps it grow, and a number of things. By baking/frying them, you can mute those bitter grassy notes, along with highlighting the natural sugars via caramelizing them with high heat. When you steam them, the heat isn't high enough to mute those bitter flavors nor caramelize the sugars, so

you have a completely different flavor.

So, if your dish wants a grassy, fresh, slightly bitter flavor, go with steamed veggies (sorry 12-year-old Jim).

If you want something more complex, roasted, and lightly sweet, roast/fry/grill your veggies until just shy of burnt.

Ingredients
1 pound broccoli rabe, trimmed
2 tablespoons olive oil
1 teaspoon garlic powder
1 teaspoon caraway seeds
½ teaspoon salt
½ teaspoon black pepper

Instructions

1. In a large bowl, toss broccoli rabe with oil, garlic powder, caraway seeds, salt, and pepper
2. Set oven to 400 degrees F and roast for 10 minutes or until crisp.

Cereal Chicken Strips

Prep Time: 10 minutes
Cook Time: 15 minutes

These amazing chicken tenders are more than just gluten free wonders. These cereal crusted chicken tenders are wonderfully light, fully crunchy, and quick for any weeknight (made in the air fryer or baked). Feel free to pair this with some hot honey (equal party honey and hot sauce), which takes these gluten free chicken tenders recipe to 11!

Ingredients

1 pound chicken tenders
1 teaspoon salt
½ teaspoon black pepper
1 teaspoon garlic powder

3 eggs, beaten
2 tablespoons milk
3 cups corn flakes
1 cup flour

Instructions

1. Set the air fryer or oven to 375 degrees F.
2. In a shallow dish, combine salt, pepper, garlic powder, and flour. In a separate dish, combine beaten eggs and milk. In a third dish, place the corn flakes and crush slightly.
3. Roll tenders into seasoned flour, then into egg mixture, then into crushed corn flakes. Air fry for 12 minutes/bake for 15 minutes, or until 165 degrees F.

Cotija Asparagus

Prep Time: 5 minutes
Cook Time: 12 minutes

Asparagus, just not boring.

Ingredients
1 pound asparagus, trimmed
2 tablespoons olive oil
¼ cup grated cotija cheese
2 teaspoon chili powder
½ teaspoon salt
½ teaspoon black pepper

Instructions

1. In a large bowl, toss asparagus with oil, chili powder, salt, and pepper.
2. Set oven to bake, 425 degrees F, and cook for 10 minutes.
3. Sprinkle on cotija cheese; cook for another 2 minutes or until very crispy and cheese is just softened.

German Potato Salad

Prep Time: 10 minutes
Cook Time: 20 minutes

A German potato salad, featuring mustard and vinegar instead of mayo, is far superior. One, fewer calories. Two, won't spoil near as quickly at a cookout. Three, and I can't stress this enough, it isn't a bowl of white carbs and whipped fat.

Ingredients

2 pounds fingerling potatoes
¾ cup apple cider vinegar
½ cup whole grain mustard
½ cup bread and butter pickles
2 tablespoons capers

2 teaspoons salt
½ cup fresh parsley
¼ cup green onions
2 tablespoons olive oil

Instructions

1. Set your air fryer or oven to 400 degrees F. Cut potatoes into rough bite-size chunks, it doesn't have to be exact. Arrange into fryer basket, season with 1/2 of the salt, and cook for 20 minutes, stirring halfway.

2. As potatoes cook, roughly chop the pickles, capers, scallions, and parsley. Combine thoroughly with vinegar, mustard, oil, and the remaining teaspoon of salt.

3. When potatoes are cooked, immediately transfer them to a very large mixing bowl. Add the dressing slowly as you mix; the potatoes should gently break apart, which is a good thing. Serve warm or at room temperature.

Mexican Chocolate Mousse

Prep Time: 5 minutes
Wait Time: 1 hour

Tastes like you're a professional Mexican pastry chef. Actually uses whipped cream from a tub. Judge it after you taste it. Mexican Chocolate Mousse!

Ingredients
2 pounds frozen whipped cream
1 tablespoon vanilla extract
2 boxes Instant chocolate pudding mix
1 cup coffee
1 tablespoon chili powder (I used ancho)
1 cup milk (I used almond)
1 cup semi-sweet chocolate chips
1 tablespoon cinnamon
2 cups strawberries or raspberries, sliced

Instructions

1. In the biggest bowl you have, combine the milk, coffee, and pudding mix. Stir to combine. Then gently fold in whipped cream, vanilla, chocolate chips, cinnamon, and chili powder. Cover and refrigerate for at least an hour.
2. Once set, top with sliced strawberries and serve.

Nacho Chips

Prep Time: 1 minute
Cook Time: 4 minutes

Listen, we know what this is. Next time you're craving the nacho cheese chips from the bag, take five minutes and make these. And yes, you can use the cheese powder from a box of mac and cheese.

Ingredients
12 corn tortillas, quartered
1/4 cup cheddar cheese powder
1 tablespoon chili powder
½ teaspoon black pepper
½ teaspoon salt
Nonstick spray

Instructions

1. Set the air fryer to 350 degrees F.
2. Combine cheese powder, paprika, garlic powder, and salt. Spray tortillas with nonstick spray, then sprinkle seasoning generously on both sides of the tortillas. Crisp in two batches for 4 minutes or until golden.

Papas Bravas

Prep Time: 10 minutes
Cook Time: 25 minutes

This is the best side dish that exists. The trick here lies with the parboiling, which makes for the ultra-crispy exterior. Pair this with, say, a red pesto (page 27) for maximum flavor.

Ingredients

3 pounds of baking potatoes, peeled and cubed (1-inch pieces)
2 tablespoons sweet paprika
2 teaspoons baking soda
4 teaspoons Kosher salt, divided

2 tablespoons olive oil
Non-stick spray
Aluminum foil

Instructions

1. Preheat the oven to 425 degrees F. Line two baking sheets with foil and spray.
2. In a saucepot, place 2 quarts of water on a boil with 2 teaspoons of salt and baking soda. Boil for 2 minutes, then drain.
3. Toss potatoes with remaining salt, oil, and paprika. Distribute onto sheets and bake for 20 minutes (stirring once) or until ridiculously crispy.

Red Pesto

Prep Time: 5 minutes

The word pesto is old-world Italian (Genoese, for those fact-checking at home) meaning "to crush." The Latin root shows up in English, in our favorite tool the mortar and pestle. The pesto we all think of, Pesto Alla Genovese, is a sauce originating in Genoa, containing basil, pine nuts, cheese, etc. But there's a range of "crushed" sauces, like this red pesto, Pesto Alla Siciliana. Don't let the simplicity fool you, this pesto is the best thing that ever happened to grilled bread.

Ingredients
1/3 cup pecorino romano cheese
1/3 cup sun-dried tomatoes
¼ cup ricotta cheese
1/3 cup extra virgin olive oil
¼ cup ricotta cheese
Black pepper
2 cloves garlic
10 leaves basil

Instructions

1. In a food processor, pulse garlic until chopped*. Add in Romano, almonds, basil, and tomatoes, and pulse a few

times to mix. While running, stream in olive oil. Season with a heavy grind of pepper.

2. Remove pesto from the bowl, and fold it into ricotta cheese to lighten. Serve on charred bread, white fish, chicken, or anything you want to taste amazing.

Pressure Cooked Risotto

Prep Time: 10 minutes
Cook Time: 25 minutes

I know what you're wondering; is it as good as traditional, stirred for an hour risotto? No. It's *better*. The pressure and higher heat brings out more starch, making a creamier texture. The only advice I have is to hold off on add-ins until after it's cooked, lest you get some funny textures in the final dish. Pair with shrimp or whitefish, and reserve leftovers for arancini (page 12).

Ingredients
2 tablespoons butter
4 ½ cups low sodium chicken or vegetable stock
1 onion, diced
2 cloves garlic, minced
2 cups Arborio rice
½ teaspoon black pepper
1 cup grated parmesan
1 cup dry white wine
1 lemon
2 teaspoons kosher salt
1/2 cup Italian parsley, chopped

Instructions

1. Preheat your pressure-cooking device on medium for 2 minutes. Add in butter, onion, and salt, and sweat for 3–4 minutes. Add in garlic and cook for another minute.

2. Stir rice into the pot and cook for 1–2 minutes. Pour in the wine and deglaze, followed by stock and pepper. Apply lid and apply appropriate heat to bring the pot to pressure. Cook under pressure for 6 minutes, then turn off the heat and let the pressure naturally dissipate for 8 minutes, then release pressure.

3. Once the risotto is off pressure, stir in grated parmesan and 1/3 of the parsley. Move to a serving dish, garnish with the remainder of parsley and a squeeze of lemon.

Roasted Salmon

Prep Time: 5 minutes
Cook Time: 25 minutes

I don't think there's a better weeknight protein than grilled salmon. Healthy, tasty, and easy, plus it makes great leftovers in a salad. I prefer to buy a side of salmon, as it's usually a good bit cheaper and grills (or bakes) nicely, especially if you're a fan of crispy salmon skin. Air fryer salmon is also a possibility here too! Pair with a simple salad or grilled veggies and crush your weeknight meal.

Ingredients
1 side of salmon, 2–3 pounds,
2 teaspoons skin on caper brine
4 tablespoons Dijon mustard
2 teaspoons salt
3 tablespoons fresh dill
Aluminum foil
2 tablespoons capers in brine
Non-stick spray
2 lemons
½ teaspoon black pepper

Instructions

1. Set oven to 400 degrees F.
2. Combine the juice of one and a half lemons, mustard,

dill, capers, brine, and black pepper. Set aside. Cut the remaining half lemon into small slices.

3. Inspect salmon for pin bones. * Tear a sheet of aluminum foil big enough for the salmon, plus a few inches. Lightly spray non-stick and place salmon on foil, skin down. Season salmon with salt. Top with lemon slices.

4. Bake salmon for 20–25 minutes or until opaque, flaky, and at your desired doneness.

** Remove from heat, let rest for a few minutes. Serve warm, topped with caper dill sauce

*Don't skip this step. Most places do a really nice job, but one can sneak through.

**The USDA says salmon should be cooked to 145 degrees F. A lot of people enjoy it medium rare at 125 degrees F. The beauty of a side of grilled salmon is the tail will be well when the head is more on the rare side (which is what I tend to prefer).

Salmon Cakes

Prep Time: 5 minutes
Cook Time: 10 minutes

Like crab cakes, only better...

Ingredients
1 pound cooked salmon
½ cup panko breadcrumbs
One egg
¼ cup of caper dill dressing

Instructions

1. Place all ingredients into a large bowl and mix to just combine, being careful not to break up the salmon any more than needed.
2. Form into light balls using an ice cream scoop or ¼ cup measuring cup. Pan fry in a thin amount of olive oil, 3 minutes a side, or cook in your air fryer at 375 for 10 minutes.

Smoky Chicken Wings

Prep Time: 10 minutes
Cook Time: 45 minutes

Wings are incredible and even better in the home. Plus, this way you can eat as messy as you like, then go shower after.

Ingredients

2 pounds chicken wings
1 teaspoon onion powder (drums and flats)
3 tablespoons brown sugar
1 teaspoon garlic powder
2 teaspoons salt
2 teaspoons chili powder
1 teaspoon ground black pepper
1 teaspoon smoked paprika
1 teaspoon sweet paprika

Instructions

1. Combine all spices and sugar and rub into wings. Let sit at room temperature for 30 minutes.

2. Set the air fryer to 300 degrees F or the oven to 350 degrees F. Add wings and cook for 35 minutes, flipping halfway through. Remove the basket and wipe the basin with a cloth to remove drippings.

3. Set the air fryer or oven to 400 degrees F. Cook for another 8 minutes or until very crispy.

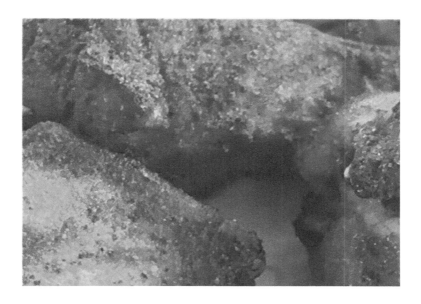

Sweet Potato Gnocchi

Prep Time: 25 minutes
Cook Time: 10 minutes

I invented this recipe this evening on a whim because gnocchi sounded amazing. I am extremely proud of how it turned out, though it did take me a few tries to get it right. Be patient with this one, as it's more about the technique than the parts list, but in the end, you'll be rewarded with gnocchi that's unique, yet delightfully comforting.

Ingredients

5 sweet potatoes or 5 cups
½ cup parmesan cheese, cooked sweet potatoes*plus garnish
3 cups flour
3 tablespoons fresh sage
1 egg
1 teaspoon nutmeg

Instructions

1. Preheat your oven to 425 degrees F, poke fork holes in your sweet potatoes, and roast for about 50 minutes. No oil or seasoning is necessary.
2. Once baked and cooled, harvest 5 cups from the sweet potatoes.
3. Bring salted water to a boil in your favorite pasta pot.

4. Using a ricer or hand mixer, rice, or very lightly beat the potatoes. Add in the egg, cheese, nutmeg, 1 teaspoon of salt, a heavy grind of pepper, and 1 tablespoon of sage.

5. Gently fold in 2 cups of flour. Grab a small spoonful and test in the boiling water; if it falls apart, add another ½ cup of flour and test again. If it stays together and floats to the top, proceed.**

6. Heavily flour a work surface. Form out dough into a ½ thick shape on the board, like you are rolling out cookie dough.

7. Flour top of the gnocchi. Cut with a pizza cutter into ½ squares, flouring in between each pass.***

8. Boil gnocchi in 4 batches for 2–3 minutes, or until they float. Remove and set aside one cooked.

9. Once all gnocchi is boiled, heat a cast iron skillet on high for 2 minutes.10. Add a bit of butter or olive oil to the pan. Fry the gnocchi in two batches for 3–4 minutes, or until browned on both sides, topping with the fresh sage.

10.Serve immediately, garnished with sage and Parmesan cheese.

*If you go frozen, roast it for ~20 minutes in a 425 degrees oven to dry it out.

** Due to variability in sweet potatoes, it's hard to

predict the exact amount of flour needed. Test in the water to ensure success. Too much flour will make tough gnocchi.

***The dough will be sticky. That's OK. The bench flour will be your friend.

T Ravs (Toasted Ravioli)

Prep Time: 10 minutes
Cook Time: 15 minutes

Listen, Chicago boy here. Sure, we bash on the boring city of St. Louis, poke fun at their pizza (provel isn't real cheese, prove me wrong), etc. One thing they got right, however, is the T-Rav, or little fried ravioli. These little jewels are incredible because even St. Louis couldn't screw up fried pasta.

Ingredients
20 frozen cheese ravioli
2 tablespoons milk
1 cup flour
3 cups Italian breadcrumbs
1 tablespoon Italian
Nonstick spray seasoning
3 eggs, beaten

Instructions

1. Set the air fryer or oven to 375 degrees F.
2. In a shallow dish, combine Italian seasoning and flour. In a separate dish, combine beaten eggs and milk. Roll ravioli into seasoned flour, then into egg mixture, then into breadcrumbs.

3. Spray fryer basket/baking sheet with non-stick spray and air fry in the basket for 8 minutes/bake for 14 minutes or until deeply brown. Serve alongside warm tomato sauce for dipping.

Umami Brussel Sprouts

Prep Time: 5 minutes
Cook Time: 15 minutes

Don't. Skip. The. Fish. Sauce. That's the secret behind your favorite noodle bar's sprouts and has literally put restaurant empires on the map. Fish sauce.

Ingredients
1 pound Brussel sprouts, trimmed and halved
2 tablespoons olive oil
¼ cup grated Romano cheese
1 tablespoon fish sauce
½ teaspoon salt
½ teaspoon black pepper

Instructions

1. In a large bowl, toss Brussel sprouts with oil, salt, and pepper.

2. Set the air fryer/oven to 375 degrees F. Cook for 8 minutes.

3. Open the lid and sprinkle on Romano cheese; cook for another 6 minutes (10 for oven) or until very crispy and cheese is just brown. Once cooked, remove from the basket into a large bowl and toss with the fish sauce.

Zeppole

Prep Time: 5 minutes
Cook Time: 5 minutes

Fitting to end our section on a dessert, these zeppole are literally the perfect dessert that no one needs to know came from a cardboard tube.

Ingredients
1 tube of refrigerator biscuits
1 cup powdered sugar
2 tablespoons milk
1 lemon, zested
½ teaspoon lemon extract

Instructions

1. Set the air fryer to 330 degrees F. Combine powdered sugar, milk, lemon zest, and lemon extract, and set aside.

2. Pop tube of biscuits and quarter each one, rolling into balls. Dip each into butter then deposit into the air fryer basket. Air fry for 5–6 minutes or until brown. Remove when warm and serve alongside lemon icing.

Main Dishes

Braciole

Prep Time: 20 minutes
Cook Time: 1.5 hours

I first made this when our daughter turned one. As any parent will tell you, that first birthday is as much of an achievement for the parents as it is for the little one. A perfect celebration food that, with a little technique, is actually easier than you may think.

Ingredients

2–3 pound flank steak*
½ cup parmesan
1 cup breadcrumbs
1 lemon
1 batch Jim's Tomato Sauce (page 89)
Butcher's Twine
½ cup Italian parsley, chopped
2 tablespoons olive oil
¼ cup walnuts, chopped
Salt
3 cloves garlic, minced
Pepper
1/2 Cup provolone, shredded
Aluminum Foil

Instructions

1. In a bowl or other suitable containment, combine chopped parsley, chopped walnuts, minced garlic, breadcrumbs, parmesan, and the zest of that lemon.

2. Preheat the oven to 450 degrees F. Place 12″ cast iron pan into the oven (omit if using a 13×9 glass baking dish)

3. Lay out steak and liberally season both sides with salt and pepper. Place breadcrumb mixture on steak, leaving 1″ border all around. Top filling with the provolone. Carefully roll the steak up tightly (I suggest rolling toward you) and tie 6–7 times with the twine. It may take a few tries, and some filling will come out, that is OK.

4. Place olive oil, then braciole into the cast iron pan (or 13″ × 9″ baking dish). Place into oven and turn the heat down to 350 degrees F. After 10 minutes, remove the meat from the pan, place the sauce into the pan, and reinsert the meat. Cover loosely with foil and cook for one hour.

5. After one hour, remove foil and cook until tender, about 90–105 minutes total. Remove braciole from the sauce, cut off the twine, and slice into large pinwheels.

*You're going to need this butterflied so it can be rolled. There are tons of videos online on how to do this, but, frankly, ask your butcher to do it for you. They should be happy to do so if they don't already have one ready to go.

Carbonara

Prep Time: 10 minutes
Cook Time: 10 minutes

When I was fortunate to visit Rome, this was the first thing I ate. I've been hooked ever since. This recipe is very close to what is taught in Roman cooking classes, so you know it's authentically incredible.

Ingredients

1 pound pasta (I prefer bucatini, but spaghetti is traditional)
1 cup Romano cheese, grated
A small handful fresh parsley leaves, finely chopped
1/3 pound pancetta
A few grinds of black pepper
6 large egg yolks

Instructions

1. Place a large pot of water on the stove to boil. When water is rolling, salt pasta water and cook pasta to al dente per package instructions. Reserve ½ cup of pasta water.

2. As the pot comes to a boil, heat a large skillet over moderate heat. Sauté pancetta until it browns, 3–5 minutes.

3. Once pasta is cooked and drained (reserving the ½ cup of pasta water), in a large bowl beat together egg yolks, and cheese, and while whisking vigorously, stir in

the boiling pasta water. Beat in parsley and pepper and set aside.

4. Toss drained pasta in the pan with the pancetta, then add egg mixture and toss 1 minute, then remove from heat. Continue to toss until sauce is absorbed by and thickly coating the pasta. Serve immediately.

Chicken Parmesan

Prep Time: 20 minutes
Cook Time: 20 minutes

Chicken Parm you taste so good…

Ingredients

1/2 batch, Weeknight Sunday Gravy (or 2 cups of your favorite tomato sauce)

2 cups panko breadcrumbs (corn flakes work great if Gluten Free)

2 poundschicken breasts (thin sliced is best)

1/2 cup grated Parmesan (plus more for garnish)

1 cup flour (Gluten Free flours work well here)

1 ½ teaspoons salt

1 cup mozzarella

½ teaspoon black pepper

Non-Stick Spray

1 tablespoon garlic powder

3 eggs

Instructions

1. Preheat the oven to 375 degrees F. Place the Sunday gravy in a small saucepan over medium heat uncovered. Simmer and reduce by 1/3 (or however much it goes down while you cook the chicken).

2. In three separate dishes, combine flour, black pepper, garlic powder‖eggs, beaten with ¼ cup of water‖panko, and Parmesan Season chicken  with salt and dredge; flour, eggs, and breadcrumbs. Set on a non-stick sprayed cookie sheet and let the coating set for 10 minutes.

3. Bake chicken for 15 minutes or until very crispy. Remove chicken from oven, set the oven on broil. Top each with a few spoons of tomato sauce, followed by mozzarella, and broil for 3–4 minutes or until cheese is browned. Serve immediately over pasta or with a side salad.

Hard Cider Marinated Pork Chops with Sauteed Kale and Seasoned Rice

Prep time: 4 hrs
Cook time: 45 min

Michigan + Fall = apples everywhere. Here is my #sundaysupper, utilizing apples in a few different and fun ways. The pork marinade is inspired by good guy Justin Warner's Bulgogi marinade, which gives this dish a Korean spin, which is weird. But good weird. Served with sauteed kale and sticky rice, this recipe is classic Fall comfort food.

Ingredients
1 Fresh apple (Braeburn, Granny Smith, Pink Lady), about a ½ pound
1 cooking apple (Gala, Fuji, Golden Delicious)
2 teaspoons whole black peppercorn
1 bunch kale (about 1–1.5 pounds)
2 pounds boneless pork chops
2 tablespoons apple cider vinegar
½ cup gochujang paste
½ cup walnuts chopped
2 cloves of garlic
12 ounces hard apple cider
¼ cup apple cider vinegar
2 cups medium grain white rice
1 tablespoon dried sage

1/3 cup apple cider vinegar

2 teaspoons salt

2 tablespoons white sugar

2 teaspoons table salt

1 tablespoon caraway seeds

Instructions

1. 2–4 hours before dinner: marinade pork: Combine gochujang, cider, vinegar, garlic, sage, 2 teaspoons each salt, and whole peppercorn. Reserve half for later use, and place the rest into zip-top plastic bag with pork. Mix to combine and marinade for 2–4 hours.

2. 45 minutes before dinner: Wash, de-stem, and tear kale leaves into bite-size pieces.

3. Dice the fresh apple, tossing in a small amount of apple cider vinegar to prevent browning. Set aside.

4. Dice the cooking apple into small cubes (no need to peel).

5. Add 3 cups of water to a covered saucepan, bringing to a boil. Once water is boiling, add rice and reduce heat to low, and simmer for 15–20 minutes (set a timer!) until water is absorbed.

6. Pour reserved marinade into a small saucepot on low heat. Simmer for ~15 minutes to reduce.

7. Put grill/grill pan/however you intend to cook the pork chops on medium heat to preheat.

8. In a large skillet, add 3 tablespoons of oil over medium heat. Add the cooking apple to the skillet and sauté for 3

minutes or until the apple begins to soften

9. Add the kale leaves to the skillet and sauté over medium heat until the leaves begin to wilt, keeping the kale moving so as to not burn, for 3–5 minutes.

10. Once the kale has wilted and diminished in size, toss with 3 tablespoons cider vinegar and chopped walnuts. Season with salt and pepper.

11. After the rice has simmered for 15 minutes, remove rice from heat and let sit covered for 5–10 minutes.

12. Remove pork from marinade. Grill/sear for ~5 minutes per side or to your desired level of doneness.

13. Combine 1/3 cup apple cider vinegar, sugar, salt, and caraway seeds into a microwave safe bowl. Microwave for 30 seconds, then pour over rice and fold in.

14. Plate dish, topping with fresh apples and reduced marinade.

Guinness Glazed Salmon with Mashed Parsnips

Prep Time: 20 minutes
Cook Time: 30 minutes

I had the opportunity to spend some time in Dublin a few years back. I was quite surprised to learn that Ireland was going through a culinary renaissance; new dishes celebrating the amazing farms in Ireland were as popular as ever. Out was the potato and lamb, and in was farm-to-table produce and seafood. This dish is a perfect representation of something you would find in Dublin; fresh, classic, and yet distinctively Irish.

Ingredients
1 pound cauliflower (frozen and riced a nice shortcut)
1/3 cup Parmesan cheese
3 tablespoons honey
1-pound salmon
6 ounces Guinness
1-pound parsnips
3 tablespoons brown mustard
3 cloves garlic, minced
3 tablespoons fresh dill
3 tablespoons butter
1 lemon

Instructions

1. Set large pot filled with heavily salted water over high heat. Clean and dice parsnips*. Once boiling, add in parsnips and boil for 20 minutes or until tender. Drain and set back into the same pot to dry slightly.

2. Preheat the oven to 425 degrees F; preheat the baking pan too! As the oven heats, pour beer into a small saucepan and heat on high to reduce slightly, 5 minutes. Once reduced, combine with honey, mustard, juice 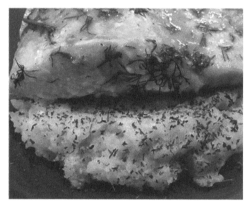 of the lemon, dill, and salt and pepper, and set half aside for sauce for the finished dish. Glaze onto salmon and bake on the sheet pan for 10–12 minutes.

3. As salmon bakes and parsnips boil, dice and roast cauliflower (fresh or frozen) on a sheet pan in an oven for 8 minutes. Once cooked, add on minced garlic and cook for another 2 minutes to soften.

4. Combine cauliflower, garlic, drained parsnips, butter, and cheese into a large bowl. Whip using a hand mixer for 2–3 minutes or until smooth. Serve with roasted salmon and reserved Guinness sauce.

*I didn't bother peeling the parsnips because they were quite small. If they are large or woody, peel them like they are a carrot.

Homemade Sausages

Sausage is awesome. It's tasty and versatile, and every culture has a form of it in some way. Chicken sausages have certainly become popular in the past few years, expanding outside of "chicken and apple" to every conceivable flavor. Here's a dirty little secret though; some of those sausages have a lot of "stuff" in them, including salt, preservatives, etc. So, every now and again, consider blending up your own sausage at home. Certainly, we will leave the encased links to those with the knowledge and tools to do so, instead focusing on bulk-style recipes. Consider buying the freshest ground chicken you can, which for me is on the butcher counter (or, asking them to grind you some chicken thighs). While everything calls for ground chicken/turkey, ground pork will work.

Classic Hot Italian Sausage
1 teaspoon red pepper flake
1/2 teaspoon black pepper, coarsly ground
1 pound ground chicken (85% lean)
1 teaspoon sweet paprika
1 teaspoon salt
2 teaspoons red wine
1 teaspoon dried oregano
1 teaspoon garlic powder

Instructions

In a large bowl, combine everything, mixing together with your hands. Let sit for 8–24 hours before cooking for maximum flavor.

Classic Sweet Italian Sausage
1 pound ground chicken (85% lean)
1/2 teaspoon black pepper, coarsely ground
1 teaspoon sweet paprika
1 teaspoon garlic powder
1 teaspoon dried oregano
1 teaspoon salt
1 teaspoon fennel seed
1 teaspoon brown sugar

Instructions

In a large bowl, combine everything, mixing together with your hands. Let sit for 8–24 hours before cooking for maximum flavor.

Mexican Chorizo
1 teaspoon ground cumin
3 tablespoons Red Wine Vinegar
1 pound Ground turkey
1 teaspoon black pepper
2 teaspoons ancho chile powder
1 teaspoon kosher salt

2 teaspoons guajillo chile powder

1 teaspoon Cornstarch

2 teaspoons garlic Powder

1 teaspoon Thyme

2 teaspoons onion powder

1/2 Teaspoon Cinnamon

Instructions

In a large bowl, combine everything, mixing together with your hands. Let sit for 8–24 hours before cooking for maximum flavor.

Chicken and Apple

1 pound ground chicken (85% lean)

1/2 teaspoon black pepper,

1 teaspoon coriander seed coarsly ground

1 teaspoon salt

1/2 teaspoon ground nutmeg

1/4 cup applesauce*

1 teaspoon sweet paprika

Instructions: In a large bowl, combine everything, mixing together with your hands. Let sit for 8–24 hours before cooking for maximum flavor.

*I mean, sure you can peel, core, grate, and cook an apple for this. Or, sneak a bit of your toddler's applesauce. I'll never tell.

Sage Breakfast Sausage

pound ground chicken (85% lean)

1 teaspoon garlic powder

1 teaspoon salt

1 tablespoon dried sage

1 teaspoon black pepper,

1/2 teaspoon coarsly ground nutmeg

2 teaspoons brown sugar

Instructions

In a large bowl, combine everything, mixing together with your hands. Let sit for 8–24 hours before cooking for maximum flavor.

Lasagna

Prep Time: 20 minutes
Cook Time: 1 hour

I'm not sure what the first thing I ever cooked was, but I am sure this is the first thing I ever made for my friends/family. In an old kitchen in the dorms, I made my first lasagna using my Sicilian Grandmother's recipe. While every lasagna I've ever made pales in comparison to hers, I think this recipe comes as close as I could ever dream. The secret to this recipe is in the noodles; letting them bake near raw will allow for the pasta starches to mingle with the juices from the sauce, keeping a cohesive lasagna right of the oven.

Ingredients

4 cups tomato sauce (page 90)
1 cup chopped fresh italian parsley
1 egg
1 lb ground sirloin
1 lb lasagna noodles
1 lb hot Italian sausage
1½ cups beef broth
1 tablespoon olive oil
2 cloves garlic, obliterated
4 cups mozzarella

1 teaspoon salt

1 cup parmesan, grated

½ teaspoon black pepper

1 lb ricotta

Nonstick spray

Instructions

1. Fill your largest pot (or whatever can fit the noodles without breaking) with enough water to cover the noodles by an inch, salting accordingly. Bring this to a boil.

2. Set a large sauté pan over medium heat. Add in olive oil and brown the sirloin for 7–8 minutes, along with the salt and pepper. Remove beef from the pan and repeat with the sausage (minus the seasoning). Combine meats with the tomato sauce (reserving 1 cup of sauce without meat) and set aside.

3. Once the mega pot is boiling, add noodles and cook for 3–4 minutes, or until pliable. Drain and lay out individually on a nonstick sprayed cookie sheet (so they don't stick together). They will not be fully cooked.

4. Reserve half of each of the mozzarella/parmesan. Combine the rest of the cheese along with the chopped parsley, ricotta, egg, and garlic.

5. Preheat the oven to 375 degrees F. Fetch a 13″ × 9″ glass baking dish, and spray heavily with that nonstick. Assemble lasagna like so*:

Noodles (double layer, try and overlap noodles)

Cheese mixture

Noodles

Meat/sauce

Noodles

Cheese mixture

Meat/sauce

Noodles

Reserve Sauce Only

6. Once layered, pour ¼ cup of beef broth into each corner of the lasagna, does not have to be exact.

7. Bake at 375 covered in foil for 30 minutes. Uncover and top with the rest of the reserved shredded cheese. Bake until bubbly, about another 15–20 minutes. Let cool for 10 minutes, slice, and enjoy.

*Take your time with this step to ensure each layer is level before proceeding.

Jim's Pizza Dough

Prep Time: 10 minutes
Wait Time: 2 hours
Cook Time: 15 minutes

Homemade pizza is sublime. Whether baked or grilled, there's just something about the allure of making a fresh pie. This dough "hacks" the 2 day cold rise sourdough pizza recipes using our good friend beer*, and a little science too.

Ingredients

6 cups all-purpose flour
1 teaspoon salt
1 ¼ cups warm water
2 tablespoon olive oil
1 cup beer (neutral lagers work best)
2 envelopes rapid rise yeast
1 tablespoon sugar

Instructions

1. In your stand mixer or large bowl, combine water, sugar, yeast, and one cup of flour. Gently combine and let stand for 3 minutes.
2. Following the rest period, pour in beer and begin to mix (use the hook attachment on your stand mixer) on low. Gently pour in flour, salt, and oil. Let mix for 5 minutes on

medium-low speed (scraping the bowl as needed to keep the dough in the bowl).

3. Once mixed, form into a ball and cover with a clean towel to rise for 2 hours, punching down the dough every hour.

4. Once risen, form dough onto your favorite pizza pan. Top and bake at 450 degrees F for 12–15 minutes (depending on final shape and quantity of cheese and toppings).

*Why beer? Three reasons. First, beer reinforces those yeasty flavors we love in homemade bread. Second, the carbonation will help lighten the dough (allowing the yeast to really proof). Third, the beer is slightly acidic, which will give that slightly tangy flavor we love.

Grilled Pizza

Prep Time: 10 minutes
Cook Time: 10 minutes

Ingredients

Pizza Toppings (note, this is *not* the time to go for a loaded pie. Think artisan; suggestion in the note below*)
1 batch pizza dough, above
1/3 cup vegetable oil (or any neutral oil)

Instructions

1. Preheat your gas grill on high for 10 minutes. Remove any upper racks, and ensure the grates are spotless (any little bit will make your pizza stick).

2. As the grill heats, roll out your pizza dough using a rolling pin (yes, tossing it in the air looks fun, but it takes a fair amount of practice). Your goal is around 12″ (or smaller if your grill can't take it) and as thin as you can (I use 2 stacked quarters as a thickness guide). Place the dough on your peel/pan, and make sure the dough can slide off easily, using flour on the pan/peel as needed.

3. Stage all of your toppings outside; these next few minutes are going to go quick!

4. Lift the grill lid, dip a few paper towels in the oil, and brush the oil on. There will be flames and hissing, but that's OK! Re-lid and let subside for 2 minutes.

5. After the two minutes are up, gently slide the dough onto the grates. Let the dough cook for 1 minute, then open the lid and check on the underside of the pizza. It should be a little dark, but not fully burnt. Depending on the thickness of your dough, cook for another 30 seconds, then remove the dough from the grill using a spatula and back onto the pan. Close grill.

6. Flip dough, and top grilled side with toppings. Reoil grates as you did before, and cook pizza just as you did before. The second cook will last 3–4 minutes, as the grill has cooled (which is good for melting cheese). If the pizza needs more time (but the crust is done), turn off the grill and place the pizza on a pan, and set it in the grill to coast through.

7. Cut pizza immediately and enjoy!

*Try this award-winning combo:

4 ounces mozzarella, 1 ounce Romano, 4 slices prosciutto ham (1 ounce), 1 pear, sliced, 4 dates, chopped.

Sicilian Pizza

Prep Time: 10 minutes
Cook Time: 15 minutes

Ingredients

1 batch of pizza dough, above

1.5 cups crushed tomatoes

1 teaspoon oregano

3 tablespoons tomato paste

Non-stick cooking spray

2 cups mozzarella cheese

0.5 cup grated Parmesan

6 ounces pepperoni, thick cut

Instructions

1. In a small saucehot over low heat, combine tomato paste, crushed tomatoes, pinch of salt, and oregano into small saucepot. Bring to just a simmer, whisking to melt in tomato paste. Remove from the heat and set aside for future use.

2. Preheat the oven to 425 degrees F. In a large greased 13″ × 9 ″ pan, form dough, making a large lip on the sides. Top (I like sauce, mozzarella, Parmesan, and then pepperoni), and bake for 15–17 minutes or until golden brown.

Shrimp Scampi

Prep Time: 5 minutes
Cook Time: 10 minutes

Scampi is a term that, in Italian, is akin to "prawn" in English. So, literally, Shrimp Scampi is a redundantly named dish. Good thing it is also a deliciously easy dish that we should take out of fast-casual Italian American restaurants and bring back into the home. Truly, the best side for shrimp scampi isn't pasta, it's roasted broccoli. Let's cook.

Ingredients
2 pounds raw shrimp, peeled
1 lemon and deveined
3 cloves garlic, minced
½ cup dry white wine
3 tablespoons butter
½ teaspoon red pepper flake
2 tablespoons olive oil
2 crowns broccoli, about
1.5 pounds, cut into florets
1 ½ teaspoons salt, divided
½ teaspoon black pepper
1 cup fresh Italian parsley, roughly chopped

Instructions

1. Preheat the oven to 425 degrees F. Toss the broccoli with the oil along with ½ teaspoon of salt. Roast in the oven until brown and crispy, about 20 minutes.

2. As broccoli cooks, place a large sauce pan over medium heat. Melt butter into the pan, and add garlic and chili flake. Cook for one minute, then add in shrimp. Cook over medium heat for 5–6 minutes or until cooked. After 5 minutes, remove the shrimp from the pan and set it aside. Boost heat to high and add in wine and juice of the lemon. Cook down for 2–3 minutes. Turn off the heat and add shrimp back into the pan, along with parsley and black pepper.

3. Serve shrimp along with the broccoli, with extra sauce drizzled on top. Try not to eat it all.

Shrimp and Grits with Chimichurri and Blistered Tomatoes

Prep Time: 10 minutes
Cook Time: 25 minutes

This dish, Shrimp and Grits with Chimichurri and Blistered Tomatoes, has become my signature dish; not because it's my Instagram avatar or because I entered it in a recent cook-off. This dish is purely Jim, because it's an amalgamation of my Italian cooking roots (after all this is a play on an Italian dish Polenta Alla Romana, which pairs grits and tomatoes), living in the Midwest, and finishing with a sauce out of left field. I'd spend a few hundred characters describing this dish, but in this case, I'll let the picture do the speaking for me. Let's cook Shrimp and Grits with Chimichurri and Blistered Tomatoes.

Ingredients
1 cup Italian parsley
1-pound raw shrimp, peeled and deveined
1/3 cup sliced green onion (that's about 4 of them)
1 cup instant grits*
¼ teaspoon pepper
2 cups milk
2 cloves garlic

2 cups chicken stock

¼ cup olive oil

½ cup parmesan cheese

1/3 cup Red wine or Sherry vinegar

1 tablespoon butter

1 teaspoon red pepper flake

1 pint cherry tomatoes

1 teaspoon dried oregano

1 tablespoon olive oil

¼ teaspoon salt

Instructions

1. Preheat the oven to 375 degress F. Place tomatoes in a baking dish with one tablespoon of olive oil and a pinch of salt. Bake for 15 minutes, stirring once.

2. Similarly, place shrimp on a cooking sheet, also dressed with one tablespoon of olive oil, a pinch of salt, and a heavy grind of black pepper. Bake for 8 minutes.

3. As shrimp/tomatoes cook, prepare chimichurri. Place garlic into blender or food processor. Mince. Add in vinegar, parsley, and scallion. Process and slowly add 1/4 cup of olive oil. Once the oil is added, add in pepper flake, oregano, salt, and pepper to combine. Set aside.

4. In a large saucepan, combine stock, milk, butter, and a pinch of salt and pepper, and bring to a boil. Slowly whisk in the grits and simmer, whisking often, until thick and completely smooth, in about 5 minutes.

5. Once grits are finished, slowly stir in Parmesan cheese.

Serve topped with shrimp, tomatoes, and chimichurri.

*Yep. Instant grits. I've made grits 100 ways, and the instant emulates the polenta texture I like.

Thai Peanut Sweet Potato Noodles

Prep Time: 5 minutes
Cook Time: 15 minutes

Instant weeknight classic: 20 minutes, 400 calories a serving. Winner Winner sweet potato noodle dinner!

Ingredients

6 cups sweet potato noodles

1 clove garlic minced

1/2 cup creamy peanut butter

1 teaspoon toasted sesame oil

1/4 cup soy sauce

1 tablespoon paprika

1/4 cup lime juice (2 limes)

1 tablespoon garlic powder

2 tablespoons honey

1/4 cup crushed peanuts

1 tablespoon grated ginger

3 scallions, minced

1 pound raw deveined/deshelled shrimp

Instructions

1. Preheat the oven to 375 degrees F.
2. Place the sweet potato noodles on a large baking

sheet and bake unseasoned until slightly crispy and yielding, about 10 minutes (use foil or parchment to help with cleanup).

3. Whisk together the peanut butter, soy sauce, lime juice, honey, ginger, sesame oil, and fresh garlic.

4. Season the shrimp with paprika, garlic powder, and some salt and pepper. Place the shrimp on top of the par-cooked noodles. Roast until the shrimp turn opaque, 8–10 minutes more.

5. Toss half of the peanut sauce with the warm sweet potato noodles straight from the oven. Transfer to a large serving platter. Top with the shrimp.

Shrimp Paella

Prep Time: 10 minutes
Cook Time: 30 minutes

A little unusual technique here, considering that most of us don't have a paella pan. That said, I know most of us have a 12″ cast iron skillet, and for my money, this pan has some advantages. The paella pan is thin and does not hold onto heat. This is great for the skilled paella-er but can be on the unforgiving side. The cast iron holds onto heat a bit better, helping develop that soccarat (the crispy rice crust on good paellas). Feel free to sub in other proteins here, just cook first and let warm through at the end.

Ingredients
1 teaspoon paprika
3 cups medium-grain rice (arborio rice works well here)
10 cups low-sodium chicken broth
½ teaspoon black pepper
3 tablespoons olive oil
3 teaspoons salt, divided
1 pinch saffron
3 pounds shrimp
12 ounces diced tomatoes
1 red pepper, diced
1 tablespoon chopped

1 shallot, minced

fresh rosemary

2 cloves garlic, minced

Instructions

1. Set your grill on medium heat and place the cast iron pan onto the said grill. Have the chicken broth simmering on the side (electric kettle, side burner of the grill, whatever you have). Let pan preheat for 10 minutes.

2. Once the pan is preheated, season shrimp with 2 teaspoons of salt and cook in the pan in batches (usually 2 rounds), 5 minutes a round. Once cooked, set aside (or on the top rack of your grill).

3. In the pan, add diced red pepper, shallot, and garlic, and cook for 2 minutes or until fragrant.

4. Combine rice, saffron, rosemary, 1 teaspoon of salt, paprika, and black pepper and deposit into the pan. Stir for 2 minutes to toast the rice and spices. Add in tomatoes and 4 cups of the stock and stir the rice. This will be the last time you stir the rice, so throw your spoon away. Close lid on the grill for 6 minutes.

5. After 6 minutes, inspect the pan, and pour on 2 more cups of broth. Wait 6 minutes, add another 2 cups, and place

cooked shrimp on top of the rice to warm. Wait the final 6 minutes, then taste rice; if still undercooked, add another cup of broth and wait 3–4 minutes. Once the rice is cooked, serve straight from the pan.

Shepherd's Pie with Spaghetti Squash

Prep Time: 15 minutes
Cook Time: 1 hour

Let me start with what this dish isn't: traditional Shepherd's Pie or pasta. Veggie-based noodles can be amazing! Many people dismiss them because they expect pasta's texture and neutral flavor. So, when food is literally named spaghetti squash, it can mislead people. Think of this then as not a substitute for spaghetti, but rather a twenty-first-century take on the classic Shephard's Pie!

Ingredients

1 tablespoon Worcestershire sauce

1 pound lean ground beef (use lamb for a more traditional flavor)

1 spaghetti squash, halved, seeds removed

1 tablespoon red wine vinegar

1 tablespoon fresh rosemary

1 cup low sodium beef stock

1 tablespoon cornstarch

1 tablespoon Butter

2 cups mixed vegetables

1 onion

3 tablespoons olive oil

2 cloves garlic

2 teaspoons salt, divided, plus a pinch

3 tablespoons tomato paste black pepper

Instructions

1. Preheat oven to 400 degrees F. Rub olive oil onto cut sides of squash, followed by a pinch of salt. Place halves onto a baking sheet cut side down and roast for 40–45 minutes or until tender.

2. As squash cooks, place a large Dutch oven over medium heat. Dice onion and cook along with butter and half of the salt. Sweat for 4–5 minutes. Mince garlic and add to onion, cook for another minute, and remove from pot. Set aside.

3. In the same pot, brown meat until cooked, 7–8 minutes, along with a final teaspoon of salt and black pepper. Once cooked, add in tomato paste and cook out for another minute. Add in cooked onion and garlic, mixed vegetables, Worcestershire Sauce, red wine vinegar, chopped

rosemary, corn starch (combined into the stock), and stock. Bring to simmer and hold until squash is ready.

4. Once squash is cooked, gently pull with a fork into squash strands. Serve topped with a meaty sauce and another grind of pepper.

Italian Sausage Stuffed Peppers

Prep Time: 15 minutes
Cook Time: 30 minute

A dish that needs no introduction, though I'll give a brief one anyways because that's my job. This is a leftover magnet; any sausage or veggies plays awesome here. Don't sleep on the giardiniera, as the heat and slight brininess is very nice as a finish.

Ingredients

3 cups cooked rice (use frozen brown rice for a weeknight shortcut)
4 bell peppers
4 cups fresh spinach
1-pound cooked Italian sausage
8 ounces mushrooms
1 cup cherry tomatoes
¼ cup fresh parsley
1 cup giardiniera (optional)
1 cup parmesan cheese
2 cloves garlic

Instructions

1. As rice cooks, preheat the oven to 400 degrees F/grill

to medium-high heat. Cut tops off of peppers and remove seeds and ribs. Generously salt and roast in the oven or top rack of the grill (cut side down) for 15–20 minutes or until soft. (This is your opportunity to cook the sausage if needed)

2. As peppers roast and rice cooks, heat a large sauté pan over medium-high heat. Sauté mushrooms for 3–4 minutes, or until just brown. Add in crushed garlic and cook for another 1–2 minutes.

3. As you wait for everything to finish, chop parsley and halve tomatoes. Once rice peppers are cooked, in large bowl combine rice, spinach, mushrooms, sausage, cheese, and tomatoes. Stir to combine, then add the mixture into cooked peppers, topping with a bit more cheese and giardiniera.

Sunday Gravy Beef Roast with Beer Braised Barley

Prep Time: 25 minutes
Cook Time: 4 hours

Beef roast braised in the best tomato sauce you've ever had, great. Barley started like a risotto using stout beer, great. The two together? Unforgettable!

Ingredients

3 pounds chuck roast
3 cloves garlic
28 ounces crushed tomato sauce
1 tablespoon Worcestershire
4 cups low sodium beef stock
16 oz stout beer
1 onion (half for beef, half for barley)
1 bay leaf
1 cup celery
2 cups barley
1 cup carrot
2 tablespoons butter

Instructions

1. Cube beef roast into 1″ chunks. Place cast iron/frying

pan on high heat and sear (using your favorite sauté oil and a pinch of salt) until very brown. Set aside into slow cooker set on high.

2. Dice onion (setting aside half), celery, and carrot. Sweat in the same cast iron pan with a pinch of salt and a heavy grind of pepper for 4–5 minutes. Add in garlic (crushed) and cook for another minute, then add in the tomatoes and 2 cups of beef stock. Pour everything into a slow cooker, along with the bay leaf and Worcestershire sauce, and cook on high for 3–4 hours, or until tender.

3. One hour before dinner, preheat the oven to 375 degrees F. In oven-safe Dutch oven, sweat the remaining onion in butter, for 4–5 minutes. Add in 2 cups of barley (along with a heavy pinch of salt) and toast for another 2 minutes. Add in beer and the remaining 2 cups of stock. Cover and bake for 50–60 minutes, or until barley is tender. Gently fluff with a fork and serve immediately, topped with braised beef.

Tomato Sauce

I have bad news for you. Are you sitting down? Good.
You've been cooking tomato sauce wrong.

Or, shall I say, you've been using tomato sauce wrong.

Ever have watery, yet somehow also dry lasagna? Pizza where the cheese runs right off? Chicken Parm with the texture of wet cardboard? Guess what; the tomato sauce was the problem.

Tomato sauce of out the jar is fine. Quality brands can even be OK on a good day. The problem I have with them isn't necessarily the added sodium, sugar, or preserving acids…it's the water content.

Water is cheaper than tomatoes (thanks Jim, couldn't have gotten there myself). Your prepared sauces are going to be far too loose for most preparations. And don't think your can of crushed tomatoes is any better; go ahead and compare a budget brand and a really nice imported/high-end can. I'll bet my favorite spatula the budget brand is visibly looser than the high-end. Why? Water is cheaper than tomatoes.

Luckily, there is a way. By understanding the application of the sauce, we can manipulate it to best suit the final dish…and it's far easier than you think if you follow some rules.

If you are using the sauce in a baked dish *with pasta*, the "ala jar" consistency is probably OK…provided you under-cook the pasta by 2–3 minutes, thus allowing the sauce to drink into the pasta. If you don't, you'll get that watery/dry lasagna we were lamenting about.

If you are using the sauce with pasta (like spaghetti and meatballs), the sauce should be thickened slightly. Add the sauce to a pot as the pasta cooks, bring to a simmer, and 3 minutes before the pasta is done, transfer a 1/4 cup of pasta water to the sauce. The starch from the pasta water will tighten the sauce, helping it marry to the pasta.

If you are using the sauce in a baked application *without pasta*, like pizza or chicken parm, then you have a bit of work to do. Reduce that sauce over medium-low heat until it reduces by 1/3. This will concentrate the flavors, tighten the sauce, and increase the relative sugar content of the tomato sauce. This will allow the cheese to bind with the sauce better, more complex flavors to develop, and overall a better sauce experience.

A side note; always look for canned tomatoes with as few ingredients as possible. The tomatoes should have nothing but the titular ingredient. Most brands have citric acid added, which is fine in a dish with many ingredients (pizza, lasagna, etc), but go all out for a "tomato only" brand for more pure dishes like spaghetti and meatballs. If you do have to use a canned tomato that seems acidic (or you don't know), dip the back end of a spoon into a box of baking soda, then dip it into the sauce. If you see more than a few bubbles, your sauce is very acidic, and a small pinch of baking soda would be welcome into the sauce.

Jim's Sunday Gravy (Aka Long Simmered Tomato Sauce)

Prep Time:15 minutes
Cook Time: 40 minutes

Keep it as is over pasta, or turn it into a plethora of other dishes.

Ingredients

56 oz crushed tomato
4–6 whole basil leaves (see note prior)
6 cloves garlic
1 parmesan rind
1 onion
¼ teaspoon red pepper flakes
1 pint cherry/grape tomatoes
2 teaspoons kosher salt
½ lb pancetta*
2 tablespoons olive oil
1 cup white wine (the drier the better)
½ teaspoon black pepper

Instructions

1. Set oven to 400 degrees F. Toss cherry tomatoes in

1 teaspoon of salt and all of the olive oil. Roast whole in a small baking dish for 10 minutes or until they just start to burst.

2. As tomatoes roast, heat a large Dutch oven over low heat. Add pancetta and render for 5 minutes, then boost the heat to medium for another 5 minutes.

3. As everything else cooks, dice onion and mince garlic. Once the pancetta is rendered, remove it from the pan with a slotted spoon and add in onion with the remainder of the salt and black/red pepper.*

4. Fry onion for 3–4 minutes, then add in garlic, stirring constantly for another minute. Deglaze the pan with the wine, followed by the crushed tomatoes. Return to a simmer.**

5. Once the sauce is simmering, add in the roasted tomatoes, the basil leaves, and the parmesan rind. Simmer for at least 30 minutes or set in a slow cooker for up to 8 hours on low, adjusting for taste as described prior. Serve on literally anything you want to taste good.

*Meat free? No worries, just start right here with 3 tablespoons of butter.
**Weeknight? Sub in two cans of crushed tomatoes brought to a simmer at this point. Yes, you can use the microwave.

Jim's Bolognese

Ingredients
2 pounds ground sirloin
One Batch, Sunday Gravy (above)
½ cup diced celery
½ cup diced carrot

Instructions

Prepare Sunday gravy above, with the following notes: Brown ground sirloin immediately following removal of the pancetta, then continue with the onion, adding in the carrot and celery at this point.

Vegan Mac and Cheese

Prep Time: 10 minutes
Cook Time: 20 min

For the past decade, tragically, I have been quite averse to dairy. For a good Italian boy, this was especially hard, however, as they say, necessity and lactose intolerance are the mothers of invention. This dish foregoes some of the nutritional yeasts and other nondairy funky ingredients for a bit of technique and imagination. Is this the best "mac and cheese" you've ever had? Maybe. Is it the best squash fall pasta you could ever dream of? Certainly.

Ingredients
1 pound short cut pasta
1 cup lager
2 tablespoons Dijon mustard
1 tablespoon hot sauce
2 tablespoons olive oil
2 tablespoons cornstarch (loosened with a bit of water)
2 cups frozen riced cauliflower
1 teaspoon salt,divided
4 cups frozen butternut squash
½ teaspoon black pepper
1 onion, diced nonstick Spray
4 cloves garlic, minced
Optional: Parmesan Cheese
3 cups dairy free milk (real or vegan)

Instructions

1. Preheat the oven to 425 degrees F. Lay cauliflower and squash on a nonstick spray adorned baking sheet, tossed with 1/2 teaspoon of salt. Roast for 15 minutes or until brown and dried.

2. Cook pasta to very al dente in salted water, reserving 1/3 cup of pasta water prior to draining.

3. Set an oven-safe pan (like your cast iron or Dutch oven, needs to be big enough to hold the pasta later) over medium heat. Add in oil, onion, black pepper, and ½ teaspoon of salt, and sweat for 4 minutes. Add in garlic and cook for another minute. Deglaze pan with lager and whisk in the Dijon mustard.

4. Place roasted veggies and dairy-free milk in blender and pulse until smooth, 2 minutes. Pour puree into the Dutch oven, along with the cornstarch slurry and hot sauce. Stir to combine and bring to a simmer.

5. Once the sauce is simmering, fold in pasta, and let warm through for 2 minutes. Serve with an extra grind of black pepper and optional Parmesan.

Sandwiches

Al Pastor Tacos

Prep Time: 24 hours
Cook Time: 30 minutes

Al Pastor tacos were named for Albert Pastor in 1975, a celebrity chef and bartender in Cabo who loved pineapple and pork.

Okay, maybe not. Al pastor, or "ala shepherd," is a cross between Mexican street tacos and lamb shawarma. It is ridiculously tasty, but notorious for being tough to make, as the traditional dish is stacked and slow roasted. By switching out the meat from a fattier pork shoulder to a lean pork loin, we can play with the traditional technique to make some magic. Let's cook.

Ingredients
3 pounds pork loin, sliced into 1/2-inch slices
2 chipotles with 2 tablespoons adobo
1 teaspoon dried oregano
Meat and Marinade
3 cloves garlic, crushed
1/2 cup orange juice
1/4 cup white wine vinegar
1 shallo
1 tablespoon chili powder
2 teaspoons salt

Garnish

1 pineapple, cored and peeled, sliced into ½″ rings

Fresh cilantro

1 red onion, diced

Corn tortillas

Lime wedge

Instructions

1. In your blender, place chipotles, shallot, garlic, orange juice, vinegar, oregano, chili powder, and salt. Liquify.

2. Add marinade to a large resealable bag along with the pork. Marinate overnight.

3. Place grill over high heat.

4. Grill pork for 3–4 minutes per side or until charred. Grill pineapple

for 1 minute per side or just until the grill grates mark the fruit. Do the same with the corn tortillas.

5. Chop pork and pineapple, and serve on tortillas adorned with onion, lime, and cilantro.

Burgers, Sliders, and More…

Ah yes, the hamburger. When you think of classic American fare, the burger is at the top of the list. Though some may disagree, a burger can be made from beef, bison, pork, turkey, or even chickpeas. Sometime in the 2000s, along with the sweet potato fry and double IPAs, turkey burgers became the rage. Truly, a quality turkey burger can be a tasty sandwich, however, for the home cook, there are some pitfalls. Simply put, turkey is not beef. From fat content to flavor to texture, they are, quite literally, different animals. This is why 95% of all of the turkey burger recipes in the universe are more toppings than a burger, hiding that dry turkey below.

So, let's explore how we can make a quality turkey burger at home.

No thin patties: I adore those thin, diner-style patties. Stacked four high with shoestring fries, you know the type. Those burgers are made with beef, usually with a fat content of at least 30%. That high-fat content allows them to be tender and juicy even when pressed. Turkey, at 15% fat (or less), just can't recover from this style. So, a turkey burger should be a thicker, non-pressed type.

Heat: Ever grill a nice thick burger? It takes, what, 4 minutes a side to get to medium (145 degrees F at the most) over high heat? This gives the wonderful juxtaposition of the juicy interior to the crusty outside. Turkey, however, needs to be cooked another few minutes per side to 165 degrees F. Cooking at the high heat used for beef will either burn the turkey burger or cook it so quickly as to go way past 165 degrees F, resulting in dryness. So, for a turkey burger, medium heat is your friend.

Fat content: Any burger expert will tell you that 25–30% fat is where it's at for beef fat content. Turkey just can't compete with this (nor, frankly, do we want it to). Go with 85% lean/15% fat for your turkey burgers, which is the standard mix. I also fold in 1 egg yolk with every 1–2 pounds of turkey, along with 1/3 cup of panko breadcrumbs. The extra fat helps the turkey from drying out, and the panko will absorb some of the turkey's moisture (rather than have it cook out).

So, we need to stop treating Turkey Burgers like normal Beef Hamburgers and let them shine on their own. I can think of no better way than 2 ounce Turkey Sliders; they cook quickly, don't dry out, and can stand on their own AND play well with others.

Basic Turkey Burger Sliders

Prep Time: 10 minutes
Cook Time: 8 minutes

Ingredients

2 pounds 85% lean ground turkey
1 teaspoon salt
1 egg yolk non-stick spray
1/3 cup panko aluminum foil
½ teaspoon black pepper

Instructions

1. Preheat grill to medium heat.
2. In large mixing bowl, gentle combine the turkey/egg/panko/pepper/salt.
3. For sliders: Line a 9″ × 9″ pan with non-sticked foil (with 4″ sticking out from each end), and form ½ of the meat into the pan. Using your hands (or another 9″ × 9″) form the meat into a square. Remove using the foil and slice into 3″ sliders. Repeat with the remaining meat. You should have 18 2-ounce patties.
4. For burgers: Same procedure, just slice into 4.5″ sliders, resulting in eight 4-ounce patties.
5. Grill patties on 3 minutes a side, or until 165 degrees F interior. I HIGHLY recommend swabbing your grill grates with a bit of vegetable oil prior to cooking to inhibit sticking.

Patty Melt Turkey Burgers

Prep Time: 10 minutes
Cook Time: 8 minutes

Let's promptly undo some of that health we gained using turkey, shall we? (Peep the dressing below for a healthier rendition that plays perfectly here).

Ingredients
1 batch Basic Turkey Burgers
3 tablespoons apple cider vinegar
12 pieces rye bread
2 teaspoon onion powder
6 slices swiss cheese
2 teaspoon garlic powder
1 onion, sliced
1 teaspoon Worcestershire sauce
1 egg
1/3 cup chopped pickles
1 cup canola oil
½ teaspoon salt
1/3 cup ketchup
1/3 cup Dijon mustard
½ teaspoon pepper (don't measure this, just, grind)

Instructions

1. Place egg, a spoon of vinegar, and a spoon of mustard in a blender. Pour oil on top and allow to settle for 15 seconds, then turn the blender on high speed. As mayonnaise forms, slowly tilt the blender, and blend for one minute. Add in everything else (including the rest of the vinegar and mustard) but the pickles, and blend for another 30 seconds. Decant from blender, stir in pickles.

2. In a cast iron pan/grill pan, grill onions with a pinch of salt for 10 minutes or until brown.

3. Assemble sandwich: Bread, t2 patties, onions, cheese, dressing. Grill for a minute a side or until cheese is just melty. Try to only eat one.

Mac's Turkey Burgers

Prep Time: 10 minutes
Cook Time: 8 minutes

You know where I'm headed for this one.

Ingredients
9 potato rolls (or sesame seedbuns unless that's too on the nose...)
1 batch Basic Turkey Sliders
1 cup silken tofu
1 cup pickles
3 tablespoons apple cider vinegar
shredded lettuce
2 teaspoon onion powder
1 onion, minced
2 teaspoon garlic powder
5 slices cheddar cheese, halve
2 teaspoons sweet paprika
½ teaspoon pepper
½ teaspoon salt
1/3 cup Dijon mustard

Instructions

1. Preheat grill to medium heat.
2. In a large mixing bowl, gently combine the turkey/

egg/panko/pepper/salt.

3. For sliders: Line 9″ × 9″ pan with non-sticked foil (with 4″ sticking out from each end), and form ½ of the meat into the pan. Using your hands (or another 9″ × 9″) form the meat into a square. Remove using the foil and slice into 3″ sliders. Repeat with the remaining meat. You should have 18 2-ounce patties.

4. For burgers: Same procedure, just slice into 4.5″ sliders, resulting in eight 4-ounce patties.

5. Grill patties on 3 minutes a side, or until 165 degrees F interior. I HIGHLY recommend swabbing your grill grates with a bit of vegetable oil prior to cooking to inhibit sticking.

Diner Special Burger

Prep Time: 10 minutes
Cook Time: 8 minutes

A favorite at my old college diner; just don't knock it until you try it!

Ingredients

1 batch Basic Turkey Burgers
shredded lettuce
4 Kaiser rolls
1 onion
1 cup smooth peanut butter
8 slices cheddar cheese
1 cup pickles
1 tomato, sliced

Instructions

1. Cook burgers as above. A minute before the sliders are done, top each with a slice of cheese.
2. Assemble, double stacking the burgers, then the veggies, finished with the top bun getting a nice spoon of peanut butter.

Crispy Pork Carnitas

Prep Time: 10 minutes
Cook Time: 3 hours

Incredible doesn't begin to describe this pork, hitting that sweet spot between pulled pork and perfectly caramelized steak.

Ingredients

3 lbs pork shoulder
1 teaspoon black pepper
4 cloves garlic
2 teaspoon red pepper flake
1 onion
½ cup water (or beer, if you feel spicy)
1 orange
1 cup diced pineapple
1 teaspoon cinnamon
½ cup diced onion
1 teaspoon cumin
1 cup fresh cilantro
1 ½ tablespoon salt
15 corn tortillas

Instructions

1. Preheat the oven to 300 degrees F. Fetch a 9″ × 13″

pan (or whatever you have really).

2. Cube pork into 2-inch chunks and put in the pan. Quarter the onion and put it in the pan. Juice the orange and add that, and the leftover rind, to the pan. The garlic, cinnamon, cumin, salt, pepper, chili flake, and water go… in the pan. Stir to combine everything and cover tightly with aluminum foil.

3. Bake pork for 2.5–3 hours, or until tender. Once cooked, remove the pork from the pan and place it on the baking sheet (save that liquid in the pan). Set broiler to high and broil for 3–4 minutes or until pork is super crispy. Roughly chop and pour ½ cup of the baking liquid over the meat. Serve on tortillas topped with the pineapple, onion, and cilantro.

Mexican Street Corn Toast

Prep Time: 5 minutes
Cook Time: 5 minutes

Avocado toast meets elote, a Mexican street snack.

Ingredients
2 slices bread (I like sourdough)
1 lime
1 avocado
2 teaspoon chili powder
1 cup cherry tomatoes
2 eggs
1/2 cup roasted red peppers
2 cups arugula
1 cup sweet corn
(frozen, steamed works great!)
1/4 cup Cotija cheese*

Instructions

1. Toast bread lightly. Slice avocado, tomato, and red pepper.
2. Toss corn with chili powder, half of the lime juice, salt, and pepper.
3. Toss arugula lightly with salt and remaining lime.
4. Fry eggs to your preferred doneness.

* You can get fancy with Cotija, but honestly a little Parmesan would work great.

Gluten Free Falafel

Prep Time: 10 minutes
Cook Time: 15 minutes

Falafel is amazing. That's it. That's the caption.

Ingredients
2 cans drained chickpeas (this is about 30 ounces)
½ teaspoon paprika
½ teaspoon ground coriander
1 shallot, minced
¼ cup almond flour
1 bunch Italian parsley
1 egg
1/4 teaspoon salt
1 teaspoon cumin

Instructions

1. Preheat oven/air fryer to 400 degrees F. Chop parsley leaves and shallot very fine (this is a great job for a mini food processor). Add to a very large bowl.

2. Add in the remainder of the ingredients to the bowl, and with your hands mix batter together. Your job is to lightly crush the chickpeas, leaving a little bit of texture behind. The batter is done when you can make a ball that holds together firmly.

3. Using a ¼ cup measuring cup as a guide, make your falafel patties. Spray with nonstick spray and place into air fryer for 8 minutes or oven for 14 minutes, or until brown

Weeknight Meatballs

Prep Time: 10 minutes
Cook Time: 20 minutes

Beef, chicken, or turkey, these meatballs are done in minutes but taste like all day. Air fryer meatballs are always a quick winner too, just check them after 12 minutes at the same temp. Pair with a great weeknight tomato sauce for best results.

Ingredients

2 lbs ground meat (ground sirloin or turkey work great here)
1/3 cup Parmesan Cheese
1 egg
1 cup panko breadcrumbs
1 teaspoon salt
1/3 cup chopped parsley
2 cloves garlic, mince

Instructions

1. Preheat the oven to 400 degrees F. Spray cookie sheet with non-stick spray.

2. Combine all ingredients in a very large bowl. Gently mix until just together, taking care to not squeeze the meat. Using a ¼ cup measuring cup, form balls; they don't have to be perfect.

3. Bake on the cookie sheet, turning them once at the 10-minute mark. At 15 minutes, check the temp (I like 165 for all meats), usually, 15 does it for me. Serve as soon as you can physically eat them.

Korean Sloppy Joe

Prep Time: 10 minutes
Cook Time: 15 minutes

Korean meets Midwest. Just as sloppy, but with an Asian twist. Quick enough for a weeknight, and the recipe is flexible enough to accommodate everyone. Pro tip: make them traditional by swapping the wrappers for potato rolls!

Ingredients

1 pound ground meat (chicken, turkey, or pork all work great)

3 tablespoons gochujang (sriracha good too)

1 cup lemon lime soda, divided

1 tablespoon sauté oil

1 tablespoon cornstarch

1 cup water

1 cucumber

1 cup apple cider vinegar

3 cloves garlic, minced

1 tablespoon ginger, grated

1 cup ice

3 tablespoons soy sauce

2 teaspoons salt

1 lime

8 potato rolls

Instructions

1. In a small saucepot, combine vinegar, water, 1/2 cup of soda, and salt. Bring just to a simmer. As brine heats, slice cucumber thinly, and when brine simmers, add cucumbers and ice. Take off the heat to steep.

2. Place a large saucepan/ cast iron pan over medium-high heat with a tablespoon of your favorite sauté oil. Once hot, brown meat, for 7–8 minutes.

3. As the meat cooks, mince garlic and ginger and combine with gochujang, soy sauce, 1/2 cup of soda, corn starch, and juice of the lime. Pour sauce into the pan with meat and cook 1–2 minutes or until thick.

4. Serve on potato rolls with plenty of pickles.

Shrimp Tacos

Prep Time: 10 minutes
Cook Time: 15 minutes

Shrimp. Good. Tacos. Good. Together? Mindblowing. Hitting the trifecta of quick/easy/healthy, this spicy shrimp dish is weeknight gold. Sub in chicken if that's what you're feeling, but either way, this will go into the weeknight rotation instantly.

Ingredients

1-pound raw deveined deshelled de-tailed shrimp*
2 cups red cabbage (or your favorite slaw mix), shredded
1 cup cherry tomatoes
4 limes
2 oz tequila (optional, but worth it)
1 teaspoon cumin
1 chipotle pepper, plus 2 tablespoons
1 teaspoon paprika adobo sauce
1 teaspoon garlic powder
4 oz plain unsweetened yogurt
1 teaspoon white sugar**
1 avocado
12 corn tortillas

Instructions

1. Turn the oven on to 350 degrees F.

2. Slice avocado and halve tomatoes, salting each. Cut one lime into wedges for final service and halve the other three for eventual juicing.

3. In a large bowl, combine cabbage with the juice of one lime, cumin, sugar, and a heavy pinch of salt. Stir and let sit.

4. In a blender, combine the juice of another lime, yogurt, and chipotle/adobo (add more if you like it hot). Blend.

5. Toss shrimp with garlic powder, paprika, a pinch of salt, and pepper. In a cast iron or other sauté pan, over medium heat with a tablespoon of your preferred sauté oil, cook the shrimp until pink, 6–7 minutes.

6. As the shrimp cooks, toast the tortillas in the oven for 3–4 minutes (yes right on the rack is fine), or until just crisp.

7. Once shrimp is cooked, turn off the heat and add tequila and juice of the final lime. Put back on the heat and, if you're trying to impress your date, flambe.

8. Assemble tacos and eat immediately.

*I say one pound. You could make 10 pounds and it disappears. Shrimp rules. **Gasp! White sugar?!? You're fine. Omit if you want.

Tapenade Bean Burger

Prep Time: 10 minutes
Cook Time: 15 minutes

Bean burgers have a poor reputation as being mealy, dry pucks. Think of this as more of a bean fritter, topped with a tapenade that will not last the day in the fridge…trust me.

Ingredients

1 15-ounce can kidney beans, drained and rinsed
3 tablespoons extra-virgin olive
½ pound mixed olives, pitted
nonstick oil spray
½ red onion, roughly chopped
1 clove garlic, minced
1/3 cup walnuts
2 tablespoons capers
1 cup shredded carrot
2 teaspoons dried basil
1 cup rolled oats
½ lemon, juiced
2 scallions
3 tablespoons extra virgin olive oil
non-stick spray
1 egg
1 cup feta cheese
½ teaspoon Kosher salt

1 tomato, sliced

½ teaspoon black pepper

8 potato rolls

Instructions

1. Preheat the oven or air fryer to 400 degrees F.

2. Place the olives, garlic, capers, basil, lemon juice, and oil in a food processor. Pulse until it becomes a paste. Transfer to a bowl and set aside.

3. In your food processor (yes it can be the same one) or favorite way to make

4. things really small, combine onion, carrots, scallions, and oats. Pulse until like wet sand. Add this to a large work bowl, along with the beans, walnuts, egg, salt, and pepper. Mix with your hands to just come together. Form balls, try and get about 8 (an ice cream scoop works great here).

5. Liberally spray a baking sheet/basket with nonstick spray, then lay out the balls. Bake for 15 minutes or air fry for 10, or until browned. Serve on potato rolls with plenty of tapenade, feta, and tomato.

Thai Lettuce Wraps

Prep Time: 10 minutes
Cook Time: 10 minutes

Make double, and serve the extra batch over rice noodles.

Ingredients

12 bibb lettuce cups shrimp
1 pound raw deveined / deshelled
½ cup creamy peanut butter
1 tablespoon paprika
¼ cup soy sauce
1 tablespoon garlic powder
¼ cup lime juice (2 limes)
¼ cup crushed peanuts
2 tablespoons honey
3 scallions, minced
1 tablespoon grated ginger
2 tablespoons olive oil
1 teaspoon toasted sesame oil
1 clove garlic minced

Instructions

1. Whisk together the peanut butter, soy sauce, lime juice, honey, ginger, sesame oil, and fresh garlic.

2. Place a large pan over medium heat. Season the

shrimp with paprika, garlic powder, and some salt and pepper. Sauté shrimp in the olive oil until the shrimp turn opaque, 6–8 minutes. Once cooked, remove from pan and roughly chop, toss with 1/3 of the dressing.

3. Make lettuce cups: Top with the shrimp, crushed peanuts, and scallions. Serve with more peanut dressing alongside.

Soups & Salads

Atlanta Chicken Soup

Prep Time: 10 minutes
Cook Time: 50 minutes

Anytime I travel, I always make it a point to learn *something* about the local cuisine. Be it Mint Juleps in the south, or fish tacos out west, I always want to take something home with me. This held wildly true on a trip I had down in Atlanta. Though it wasn't magical wings or southern cuisine, no: It was chicken noodle soup. Chicken noodle soup was ordered at my hotel bar five minutes before they closed. It was so amazing I had this soup four times in two days and insisted I meet the chef to learn his secrets. As you'll see below, perhaps unceremoniously, the secret ingredient in this Atlanta Chicken Soup is…chicken. Wings, that is.

Ingredients
2 lbs boneless skinless chicken thighs
2 bay leaves
2 lbs chicken wings
4 sprigs fresh thyme
1 onion, diced
1/2 teaspoon black pepper
1 clove garlic, minced
1 tablespoon kosher salt
2 tablespoons butter

¼ cup corn starch

3 quarts wate

1 lb frozen mixed vegetables*

1 teaspoon dried oregano

Instructions

1. Set your cast iron pan on high heat. Once hot, add butter and brown chicken in batches, starting with the wings. Once the chicken is browned, deglaze cast iron with one cup of water.

2. Add chicken, deglazed liquid, pepper, salt, thyme, garlic, onion, bay leaves, and the rest of the water to your instant pot/ pressure cooker*.

3. Pressure cook stock for 40 minutes. Once the chicken broth is done pressure cooking, release pressure per instructions. Remove chicken from the broth, pull the meat, and return the good stuff to the broth. Stir in the mixed vegetables, dried oregano, and ¼ corn starch (slurried with a few tablespoons of water). Simmer just to

heat through vegetables and serve.

*In a hurry? Use 3 quarts of premade stock, substituting cooked chicken for the wings/thighs, Skip Steps 1 and 2, start from Step 3

Chicken Gnocchi Soup

Prep Time: 10 minutes

Cook Time: 10 minutes (on top of whatever is needed for the soup base)

Ingredients

One batch of Atlanta Chicken Soup, standing by

1 pound potato gnocchi

2 tablespoons Butter

Instructions

Prepare gnocchi according to package directions (probably something like boil for 3–4 minutes in salted water).

As gnocchi boils, place a 12″ pan over medium heat with the butter. Once the gnocchi is cooked, remove it from the pot and straight into the pan. Toast, stirring gently but often for 4–5 minutes or until just golden. Adorn the hot soup with the gnocchi and enjoy.

Chicken Etouffee

Prep Time: 15 minutes
Cook Time: 45 minutes

So good you'll think you're at the bayou rooting on the Saints…

Ingredients

1 tablespoon butter

1 tablespoon salt, divided

1 large onion

2 teaspoon cayenne pepper, divided

2 bell peppers

2 tablespoon dried thyme

3 ribs celery

1-quart low sodium chicken stock

4 cloves garlic

1 tablespoon flour

1 can diced tomatoes

2 tablespoons cornstarch (14.5-ounce)

2 bay leaves

2 pounds chicken thighs

2 teaspoons black pepper,

Rice or Crusty bread for serving

Instructions

1. Preheat oven to 400 degrees F. Toss chicken in half

of the salt, black pepper, and cayenne, and roast for 25–30 minutes or until 165 degrees F.

2. Dice onion/peppers/celery and mince garlic.

3. Place your favorite dutch oven over medium heat. Melt the butter in a said pot and add the flour. Stir and cook for 3–4 minutes or until golden. Stir in onion/peppers/celery/garlic, along with the remaining salt, black pepper, and cayenne, and cook for another 3–4 minutes.

4. Once veggies are just soft, add in tomatoes/bay/thyme/stock and bring to a simmer. Simmer for 10 minutes, then stir in cornstarch (loosened with a splash of water) to thicken the stew.

Chopped Waldorf Salad

Prep Time: 5 minutes

Cook Time: 0 minutes (is making a dressing cooking??)

This salad is a fusion of my favorite Chicagoland chopped salad and the traditional Waldorf salad (walnuts, apples, mayo dressing, etc). It's weird. But good weird.

Ingredients

4 cups chopped romaine lettuce

2 lemons

2 cups baby arugula

2 tablespoons Dijon mustard

2 apples, cored and diced

2 tablespoons honey

1 cup toasted walnuts

¼ cup olive oil

1 cup sharp cheddar cheese, crumbled

½ teaspoon salt

½ cup crumbled bacon

Black pepper

Instructions

1. In a bowl, combine the juice of the lemons, mustard, honey, salt, and a few grinds of pepper. Whisk in the olive oil to make a dressing.

2. In a large salad bowl...combine everything else. I like to serve my salads by dressing in the service bowl, with the salad on top, but the world is your salad.

Cioppino

Prep Time: 15 minutes
Cook Time: 20 minutes

Cioppino, a cross between Bouillabaisse and a traditional Italian Seafood stew, is a classic for good reason. Right after my daughter was born, we had some family in for Christmas/New Year's Eve. This dish seemed like a perfect celebration meal; a nod to The Seven Fishes Italian feast, and, frankly, a show-stopping meal that took minimal effort. Don't fear frozen seafood here; unless you live a reasonable drive from the ocean, frozen will often be of much higher quality.

Ingredients
1 small bulb fennel, quartered, cored and thinly sliced
1-pound raw shrimp, peeled and deveined
½ teaspoon crushed red pepper flakes
1 1/2 pounds cod, cut into 1–2″ chunk
¼ cup extra-virgin olive oil
2 cups low sodium chicken stock
1 teaspoon anchovy paste
32 ounces crushed tomatoes
1 bay leaf
Two teaspoons salt, divided
2 teaspoons fresh thyme leaves
2 celery ribs, chopped
1 cup Italian parsley, chopped

1 medium onion, chopped

6 cloves garlic, crushed

10–14 sea scallops

1 ½ cups dry white wine

1-pound mussels, cleaned

1 lemon

1 loaf, of French bread

Instructions

1. In a Dutch oven over medium heat, combine oil, pepper flakes, anchovy paste, garlic,

2. And 1/2 teaspoon of salt. Cook for one minute, then

add in chopped celery, fennel, and onion and cook until soft, 3–4 minutes.

3. Deglaze pan with wine and stir for a minute. Add in stock, tomatoes, bay, and thyme, and bring to a simmer.

4. Add in cod (seasoned with one teaspoon of salt) and let poach for 5 minutes

5. Covered. Then, add in shrimp, scallops, and mussels, cover, and simmer for an

6. additional 10 minutes.

7. De-lid and remove any mussels that do not open. Serve stew garnished with parsley, served along with a wedge of lemon and bread.

"Cream" Of Mushroom Soup

Prep Time: 10 minutes
Cook Time: 20 minutes

Creamed soups are classic. I know I grew up on casseroles and dishes based upon these condensed canned soups. Let's reboot one of my favorites, Cream of Mushroom, but give it that Jim Cooks Food Good healthier spin (and make it vegan!). Pair this with some turkey homestyle meatballs, pour over rice, and you have my favorite cold weather meal!

Ingredients

1 tablespoon corn starch
(mixed with 2 tablespoons water)
½ pound button mushrooms, sliced
1/3 cup sherry
1-pound cremini mushrooms,   quartered
2 tablespoons fresh parsley
1 onion, diced
1 teaspoon salt
3 cloves garlic, minced
1 quart vegetable stock
Cheesecloth
1 cup unflavored soy milk
3 tablespoons olive oil, divide

Instructions

1. Set favorite Dutch oven high heat. Add in 1 tablespoon of oil and sauté onion, 3 minutes. Add in sliced button mushrooms and cook for another 5 minutes. Finally, add garlic and salt and cook for another 2 minutes. Once cooked, remove contents from Dutch oven into a blender to cool.

2. In the same pan over high heat, add remaining oil and brown quartered mushrooms, for 7–8 minutes. Turn pan off the heat, deglaze with sherry, then

3. turn the heat back onto medium to reduce, 2 minutes. Once reduced, add in 2 cups of broth, soy milk, and corn starch, and bring to simmer.

4. Once all mushrooms are cooked and blender ingredients have cooled, blend mushrooms/garlic/onion along with the remaining 2 cups of the broth on high for 2 minutes or until smooth. Strain through cheesecloth (optional, but gives a nicer texture) and place into simmering soup. Stir to combine and let simmer together for another 10 minutes. Serve garnished with parsley.

Gumbo

Prep Time: 15 minutes
Cook Time: 2 hours, 30 minutes

As most good culture-defining recipes have, this certain recipe has a story. One night upstairs at the Bourbon St. Blues Company in New Orleans, we ended up shooting the breeze with a local chef. Certainly, gumbo came up. When I probed him on his personal secret (and after a few Abita's) he was happy to oblige; bake the roux, and leave the okra in the fridge…

Ingredients
½ cup flour
1 teaspoon salt
½ cup canola oil
1 teaspoon black pepper
1 onion
1 teaspoon dried thyme
3 ribs celery
1 bay leaf
1 red bell pepper
1 tablespoon filé powder
2 jalapenos, seeded
3 cloves garlic
6 cups cooked white rice

1 quart seafood stock

1 pound andouille sausage, sliced

1 cup canned diced tomato (juice and all)

2 pounds raw shrimp, peeled/deveined/detailed

Instructions

1. Preheat oven to 325 degrees F. In an oven-safe Dutch oven, whisk together flour and oil. Bake for 90 minutes, whisking every half hour.*

2. As roux cooks, dice onion/pepper/celery and mince garlic and jalapeno (seeds out please). Once the roux is nicely brown, set over medium heat and in onion/pepper/celery, along with the salt. Stir and cook veggies out for 5 minutes.  Add in garlic and jalapeno, cook for another minute, then add in tomatoes, stock, pepper, thyme, and bay. Bring to simmer and do so for 20 minutes.

3. As gumbo finishes, slice andouille into thin slices and brown in a large sauté pan over medium heat, ~5 minutes a side. Also, this may be a good time to put that white rice on.

4. Once gumbo has simmered for 20 minutes, add in raw shrimp. Bring back to a simmer and cook shrimp for

6–7 minutes or until pink. Remove from heat and stir in filé powder. Allow to thicken slightly, then serve over rice along with the sausage.

*Yep, you can do this in your multicooker on medium sauté.

Minestrone Soup

Prep Time: 10 minutes
Cook Time: 20 minutes

Minestrone soup is a classic for a very good reason; hearty, easy, and super filling. This tomato-focused version is no exception; good for any weeknight, it can go from pantry to pot to bowl in minutes. Pair it like I do with some roasted salmon, or keep it as is for a killer vegan main.

Ingredients
2 tablespoons olive oil
4 cups chicken or vegetable stock
1 cup diced zucchini
(about 1 small one)
15 ounces cannellini beans
1/2 cup diced carrot
(about 1 carrot)
2 cups crushed tomatoes
1 onion, diced
10 fresh basil leaves
3 cloves minced garlic
Parmesan cheese (optional)
1 bay leaf
Italian bread (for sopping)
Black pepper

Instructions

1. In a dutch oven over medium heat, add olive oil, then sweat onion/carrot for 6 minutes along with a heavy pinch of salt. Add in zucchini and garlic for another minute, then add in bay leaf, stock, drained beans, and tomatoes. Bring to a simmer.

2. Simmer the soup for 10 minutes, then served, garnished with the basil, cheese, bread, and grinds of black pepper. Yeah, it's really that easy.

Panzanella Salad

Prep Time: 5 minutes
Wait Time: 5 minutes

The name Panzenella is a portmanteau of the Italian words "pane" (bread) and "zanella" (gutter...or a wide serving bowl). This stale bread salad could not be easier to make, and it screams spring in a bowl. This specific recipe is based upon a favorite from a classic farm to table restaurant here in Michigan. Without further monologing, let's make gutter bread salad; Panzanella!

Ingredients

4 cups stale bread, torn into
1 shallot, thinly sliced
1-inch cubes
1 tablespoon mustard seeds
2 cups cherry tomatoes, halved
2 tablespoons capers, drained
1 roasted red bell pepper, sliced
1/3 cup red-wine vinegar
1 orange bell pepper, diced
1/3 cup extra-virgin olive oil

Instructions

1. Whisk together vinegar and oil.

2. Combine bread and veggies in a large bowl, toss with dressing, and let sit for 5 minutes. Serve over a bed of greens and finished with a pinch of salt.

Pappa Al Pomodoro Soup

Prep Time: 5 minutes
Cook Time: 15 minutes

I adore this recipe. I made a version of this in college all the time, and for (food) good reason; it's affordable, easy, and feeds a crowd. This base turned into my world-famous Pizza Soup, but sometimes simplicity is divine. Add in some ready-to-eat shrimp and take it to 11!

Ingredients
2 tablespoons olive oil (plus some for garnish)
½ cup fresh basil leaves, divided
1 quart vegetable broth
½ loaf day old bread, divided
1 onion, diced
(reserve a few tablespoons)
1 cup parmesan cheese
4 cloves garlic, minced
1 teaspoon salt
28 ounces crushed tomatoes
Black Pepper
28 ounces diced tomatoes

Instructions

1. In your large Dutch oven or soup pot, place over

medium heat. Add olive oil, most of the onion, and salt. Sweat for 5 minutes, then add in the garlic and cook for another 2 minutes.

2. In your favorite blender (countertop or stick), add in the stock and 1 cup of the stale bread, torn. Blend for one minute. Add bread stock, along with tomatoes and a few basil leaves to the soup, and bring to a simmer for 10 minutes.

3. As the soup simmers, tear the remaining bread into 1″ chunks (no need to be precise) and lightly salt the remaining onion. Once simmer time is through, serve.

4. Soup, garnished with the parmesan, basil, bread, reserved onion, and grinds of black pepper.

Salads

All of the salads in this section will start with 6 cups of spring mix unless otherwise noted.

This section also assumes you know how to toss a salad, so the final step of "toss the base ingredients, top with dressing, then garnish" is assumed and omitted.

Southwestern Salad

Base
1 avocado, sliced
1 cup corn (fresh, frozen, all deadly)
1 cup hominy, drained
1 tablespoon saute oil
1 cup black beans, drained
1 cup cherry tomato, halved
1/3 cup pickled jalapeno
1 bunch fresh cilantro

Dressing
2 limes, juiced
Tortilla chips
1/3 cup cotija cheese (yes, grated parmesan works in a pinch

Garnish:
In saute pan over medium heat, add oil and corn. Cook for 2–3 minutes or until just soft. Assemble salad.

Autumn Bounty Salad

Base
1 cup chickpeas
1 cup cheddar cheese crumbles
2 sliced apples
½ cup Roasted Pepitas (almonds work here too)

Dressing
splash of olive oil and balsamic vinaigrette

Garnish
Sweet Potato Chips

Asian Miso salad

Base
1 cup shelled edamame
1 cucumber, diced
1 cup snow pea
1 cup jicama sticks
1 cup shredded carrot

Dressing
1/2 cup miso paste
2 Tablespoons honey
1/4 cup water
3 tablespoons rice wine vinegar
2 teaspoons light soy sauce

Combine all in bowl, whisk until smooth

Garnish
Wasabi peas
Sesame Seeds.

Greek Salad

Base
One cup feta cheese
One cucumber, diced
1 cup Cherry Tomatoes
1/2 cup roasted red pepper, diced
1/2 cup kalamata olives
1/2 cup walnuts

Dressing
1/4 cup red-wine vinegar
1/4 cup extra-virgin olive oil
2 tablespoons Dijon mustard
Pinch of salt
1 teaspoon sugar
Combine all in a bowl, whisk until Smooth

Garnish
Fresh mint leaves, torn

Tortilla Soup

Prep Time: 10 minutes
Cook Time: 20 minutes

Everything but the bottomless margs and the baskets of chips and salsa.

Ingredients
1-quart low sodium chicken stock

1 teaspoon ground cumin

1 (28-ounce) can diced tomatoes

1 teaspoon dried thyme

1 cup frozen or fresh corn

1 chipotle, with 2 tablespoon of the adobo, chopped

2 cups white hominy

1 teaspoon salt

2 cups rotisserie chicken, pulled

½ teaspoo black pepper (great spot to use leftover chicken here)

3 tablespoons sauté oil

1 red bell pepper, diced

4 cups corn tortilla chips

1 onion, diced

3 tablespoons chopped cilantro

3 cloves garlic, minced

1 ripe avocado, diced

1 jalapeno, seeded and minced

Instructions

1. Add oil to Dutch oven over medium heat. Add onion, corn, and pepper to the pot, along with the salt, and sweat for 5 minutes. Add the garlic, jalapeno, cumin, chipotle, adobo, thyme, and black pepper, and cook for another 2 minutes. Then, add in stock, tomatoes, and hominy, and bring to a simmer. Simmer for 15 minutes.

2. Once the soup has simmered, add in pulled chicken and cook for another 5 minutes. Serve with crushed chips, avocado, and cilantro as garnish.

Chicken Tikka Masala

Indiana boy goes Indian. It's a solid versatile sauce; don't be afraid to skip the chicken for veggies or tofu! This Chicken Tikka Masala recipe is easy, can be made in the Instant Pot, and is beyond flavorful!

Ingredients

4 cloves garlic minced

1 inch fresh ginger peeled and minced

1 shallot minced

1 teaspoon salt

1/2 teaspoon pepper

1 tablespoon garam masala

3 cups fire-roasted tomatoes

1 cup coconut milk

2 pounds chicken thighs

3 cups cooked rice

Instructions

1. In a large saucepan, combine shallot, garlic, and ginger. Saute for 2 minutes, then add in all spices and salt/pepper. Cook for another minute.

2. Once spices are cooked out, add in tomato and coconut milk. Simmer for 20 minutes.

3. As sauce cooks, place large frying pan over high heat. Sear chicken thighs again with a bit of sauté oil for 5 minutes a side. Once cooked, nestle in with the sauce to finish cooking.

4. Once chicken is cooked and sauce simmered, serve hot over rice.

Egg Frittata

This egg frittata recipe is made for brunch after hosting (and cooking for) a mess of people. The best part is the versatility; take a protein, some veggies, and leftover cheese and turn it into a winner. This feeds 6–8 easily!

Ingredients

12 eggs

½ cup milk (cow or any unsweetened non-dairy)

3 tablespoons corn starch*

½ cup cheese

1 cup cooked fillings (here I used pepperoni, onions, mushrooms, and peppers)**

Instructions

Preheat oven to 375 degrees F.

Whisk together eggs in a large mixing bowl. Sprinkle cornstarch into milk to dissolve, then add to the eggs. Once combined, add in fillings, season with salt and pepper.

Spray 12″ cast iron pan liberally with non stick spray. Pour egg mixture pan and bake for 20–25 minutes, or until toothpick comes out clean (don't open the oven until 15 minutes, or else the frittata won't properly rise!)

*You know how bad, overcooked eggs are watery, yet dry? This is insurance for such a thing.

**If you don't precook your fillings, no amount of cornstarch will save you from a watery mess.

Eggplant Parmesan

Eggplant Parmesan is a newcomer into my arsenal, but is now a mainstay. Straightforward to make in either baked the oven or air fryer, ridiculously healthy, and darn tasty to boot, this healthy eggplant Parmesan recipe is a winner!

Ingredients
1 large eggplant
3 eggs
1/4 cup milk
3 cups flour
1 tablespoon garlic powder
2 teaspoons onion powder
1 teaspoon salt (plus some for the eggplant curing)
1/2 teaspoon black pepper

3 cups panko bread crumbs

1/2 cup Parmesan cheese

1 cup tomato sauce

1 cup fresh mozzarella

olive oil spray

Instructions

1. Peel your eggplant. Slice lengthways into 1/2″ slices; I usually get 5–6 per eggplant. Place on baking sheet lined with paper towels or draining rack. Literally salt both sides of the eggplant and let sit for 30 minutes.

2. Preheat oven or airfryer to 375 degrees F. In three dishes, combine:

    a. flour/garlic powder/onion powder/1 teaspoon of salt/black pepper

    b. eggs (beaten)/milk

    c. Panko/Parmesan

3. Rinse eggplant slices under water and dry with a clean towel. Bread into flour, then eggs, then panko.

4. Cook eggplant for ~8 minutes in the air fryer or 14 in the oven or until golden.

5. Once eggplant is crispy, remove from oven. Spray or drizzle some olive oil on top, followed by sauce, then cheese. Cook for another 3–4 minutes until cheese is melted. Serve. Enjoy!

Greek Chicken and Orzo

Orzo is vastly underrated. The size of rice, but the texture and flavor of pasta. This dish takes advantage of both of those features, paired with a subtle yet tangy Greek chicken and a dressing that ties the dish together. The mint finish brings a nice freshness to the party, and it can't be understated.

Ingredients
1 pound chicken (cubed)

1/2 teaspoon salt

1/2 teaspoon black pepper

1 tablespoon dried oregano

1 pound orzo

4 lemons

1 cup cherry tomatoes

1/2 cup chopped scallions

2 tablespoons dijon mustard

3 tablespoons olive oil

3 tablespoons toasted pine nuts

10 mint leaves torn

1 tablespoon honey

Instructions

1. Combine juice of the lemons, mustard, honey, and olive oil. Whisk together and set aside.

2. Prepare orzo per package directions in heavily salted water. Undercook the orzo by 1–2 minutes.

3. As orzo cooks, place large saute pan over high heat. Toss chicken in salt and pepper and brown, 6–7 minutes. Once cooked, finish with the oregano.

4. As everything else cooks, halve tomatoes and chop scallions.

5. As everything comes together, toss chicken, orzo, tomatoes, scallions, and dressing to combine. Finish with the torn mint and pine nuts and serve with a roasted veggie.

Weeknight Pad Thai

This Pad Thai is very special to me, as it is inspired by a recipe given to me by one of my friends years ago. I learned a ton about cooking from her, exposing me to wonderful ingredients like tamarind or Sriracha. This quick Pad Thai is a bit more approachable than a fully authentic Pad Thai, but is 100% delicious and perfect for any weeknight. Let's Make Pad Thai!

Ingredients

8 ounces rice noodles

3 tablespoons tamarind (or 2 tablespoons more of both lime juice and brown sugar)

1/2 cups soy sauce

4 tablespoons brown sugar

2 tablespoons Sriracha

2 limes (one for juice, one for wedges)

2 green onions

2 shallots

3 eggs

4 garlic cloves

1 cup bean sprouts

2 cups Chopped Broccoli

1/2 c roasted peanuts (coarsely chopped)

3 tablespoons cooking oil

Optional: 1 pound of cooked protein (shrimp, tofu, etc.)

Optional: Sriracha Mayo

Instructions

1. Bring a pot of water to boil and cook rice noodles according to package directions, shy just one minute. Drain and set aside.

2. In a separate bowl, combine tamarind, soy sauce, brown sugar, sriracha, and the juice of one lime together.

3. In a very large pan over medium heat, add one tablespoon of the oil. Add the eggs and scramble until just set, and set aside.

4. Slice the shallots and green onions thinly, and mince the garlic. In the same pan, add the remainder of the oil, still over medium heat. Add green onions, shallots, garlic and broccoli. Sauté until broccoli is cooked through, 4–5 minutes.

5. Add the noodles to the pan and pour on the sauce. Toss to coat all noodles. Add the eggs, bean sprout, and your cooked protein. Sprinkle peanuts on top, and serve along with a wedge of lime and Sriracha Mayo.

Mini Turkey Meatloaf

Okay, quick. Think of the classic "comfort food". Is it meatloaf? Of course it is, because nothing is more comforting than a big slab of meat, seated next to a pile of fluffy white carbs all covered with gravy. Alas, meatloaf is not without its flaws. Its time consuming for one, and it, sadly, isn't exactly the healthiest meal either.

So, let's give meatloaf the Jim Cooks Food Good treatment (half the time and calories, all of the flavor); may I present Mini Turkey Meatloaf:

Ingredients
2 Pounds Ground turkey

1 Onion

3 Cloves Garlic

1 Egg

1/2 Cup Breadcrumbs

1 Cup Ketchup Bonus points if you use gojuchang

1 Tablespoon Hot sauce Optional

1 Tablespoon Worcestershire Sauce

1/3 Cup Italian parsley

Instructions

1. Preheat oven to 400 degrees F. Dice onion and mince garlic. In a large saucepan over low heat, sweat with a heavy pinch of salt and pepper, 6–7 minutes. As the veggies sweat, chop parsley.

2. Add onion and garlic to very large bowl. Fold in turkey, egg, breadcrumbs, 1/3 cup ketchup, and parsley. Loosely mix to combine, and spoon into greased muffin tins (you'll yield around 12 loaves). Bake for ~15 minutes.

3. In separate bowl, combine hot sauce, Worcestershire Sauce, and remainder of ketchup. After the 15 minutes, glaze tops of loaves. Bake for another 10–15 minutes, or until an internal temperature of 165 degrees F. Serve along side a roasted veggie (like the shown Brussels Sprouts).

CPSIA information can be obtained
at www.ICGtesting.com
Printed in the USA
BVHW010845130323
660315BV00005B/55

Energy Healing

The Ultimate Guide To Avoiding The Negative Energies, Unlocking, And Balancing The Chakras by Reiki Exercises, and Heal Yourself And Increase Positive Energy by Yoga Positions

By

New Mindfulness Lab

Introduction

nergy healing—we might be asking ourselves what this is. Well, you picked the right book. We are going to discuss energy healing in detail as we progress in this book. Energy healing has been in everyone's discussion of late. Although it is something that has always been there, people have always just shrugged about it, and it is only until recently that it has been embraced. It has existed for centuries. It is that we are only beginning to embrace this is a way of healing now as westerners and easterners who thought it was uncivilized to practice such and backward to use energy healing instead of modern medicine. Energy healing has now been embarrassed by people all over the world, do not be left out as we are going to discuss everything about energy healing. Energy healing will change your life, with energy healing your body gets rejuvenated, and you get a sense of healing.

Energy healing might be ancient, but it still works magic to date. Ever wondered why people during the past used to have a long lifespan? Well, this is because they used to practice healthy ways of living. They would facilitate the well-being of the body through energy healing, bringing about a natural healing of the body and without much stress, they would live more years than we do nowadays because we always have stress from everything around us. We are surrounded by stressful situations, and just getting rid of them could be key to some more years, and energy healing is just the right thing to help in stress-relieving. Why don't you also try out this method of healing and also experience the magic of energy healing the good thing is its completely natural. The first step to this is reading through this to know more as we all know knowledge is power, and this book could be all the power you will need to know about energy healing. By the time you are done going through it, you will be for sure more knowledgeable and know exactly where to go to, what to expect, and the best method that could work well for you.

In this book, we are going to take you through energy healing discussing in detail, what energy healing is, the types of energy healing this will give you an insight of every type we will discuss the benefits of energy healing and more about energy healing that we have not always known. This book could be the beginning of your beautiful life ahead because with energy healing life is beautiful. Your first step to a healthy life is by learning the facts about energy healing before starting to join the millions of people who are now living a happy life due to energy healing. Get on board and read through this; you will not be disappointed.

Chapter 1

What Is Energy Healing

Energy healing, also known as energy medicine, is a method of restoring or balancing the energy zones of the body in order to improve health by delivering energy healing through the hands of doctors to the patient's body. Therapy of energy healing is used to cure several ailments. There are many techniques for an energy treatment, including the palm, arms, and distance healing, that the healer and the clients are not in the same locations. Fascinatingly, 57 percent of long-term treatment trials showed a positive treatment effect on each disease.

There are many schools of energy healing that use many names, such as healing biologically, healing spiritually, healing by contact, healing in the street healing, qido, sensory therapy, Reiki or qigong. Do not think of traditional religious beliefs as a condition of healing. Unlike faith, healing is done in the context of traditional religion. Previous reviews of the literature science behind healing energy are categorical furthermore recommend further research, but the latest analyses have established that there is zero proof of clinical efficiency. The hypothetical foundations of therapeutic are criticized as irrational, the studies and evaluations that underlie energy therapy are responsible for the content of methodological defects and dysfunctions, and a positive therapeutic result is determined by well-known psychological mechanisms. The alternative drug at the University of Exeter said: "Despite the lack of biological validity or convincing clinical data, treatment is still encouraged. These methods are enough to prove that they are therapeutic, not ." Some of these allegations are known as "energy medicine" device fraud, and judicial practice is being prosecuted in the United States.

History

History captures a recurring relationship or the use of scientific discoveries by those who claim that the newly learned science can aid people in recovering. Back in the 19th century, magnetism and also electricity and which were the "innovations" of science, and the shamanism of electricity grew. These concepts motivate authors in the New Age movement. At the beginning of the 20th era, claims about the health hazards of radioactive materials were life-threatening, and in recent years, the quantum method and also fusion concept have provided chances for marketable use on a large scale. Thousands of devices are used that claim to be cured of energy used or estimated worldwide. Many people sell with statements that are illegal or dangerous, false, or unproven. Some of these devices are prohibited. From the point of view of energetic and also spiritual healing, this is linked with severe injuries or deaths in case the patients stop or cancel a treatment.

Beliefs

Energy healing depends on the confidence of the patient and the doctor in the doctor's ability to direct healing energy in various ways to those who want help, for example, in hands, arms and remote (or absent) positions. Practitioners say that this "healing energy" sometimes seems warm to therapists. There are many types of energy healing, including biomedical energy healing, spiritual healing, contact healing, distance healing, qi-do, sensory therapy, Reiki, qigong, and much more. Spiritual healing is largely non-religious. Traditional religious beliefs are not considered a prerequisite for healing. On the contrary, healing of faith takes place in a religious context. Energy medicine experts often refer to ministries, but they are not a "cure or death" practice.

Healing energy methods, for instance, Touch of Therapeutics, has been recognized in nurse's work. In the years between 2005-2006, The North American Associations of Nurses has confirmed the diagnosis of "energy field disorder" in patients, reflecting a different approach called "postmodern" or "anti-scientific" treatment. This approach is very important. The followers of these techniques provide a mysterious quantum appeal to non-local ones to explain remote healing. They also suggest that the therapist acts as a channel for delivering biomagnetic waves similar to important pseudoscience, for instance, org or qi. Drew Leder, in his article in the Journal of Complementary and Alternative Medicine, notes which the idea is "an attempt to remotely understand, interpret, and study psi and healing." And "physical models are presented as implicit, not explanations." Beverly Rubik relies on his beliefs based on articles in the same journal with reference to biophysics, bioelectromagnetic systems, and chaos theory. James Oshman introduces the concept of healing electromagnetic fields with varying frequency. Oshman had faith that the "healing energy" comes from frequencies of electromagnetic created by therapeutic devices developed by electrons that act as healing hands or antioxidants. Physicists and skeptics criticize this explanation as pseudo physics. Indeed, even those who are passionate about healing energy say: "There is a very narrow theoretical basis on which [spiritual] healing is based."

Scientific Investigation

Detached Healing

An organized review of 23 remote curative studies put out in 2000 was not completed due to the methodological limitations of the study. The year 2001, brought writers of the study, Edward Ernst, wrote a guide to cancer treatment, stating that "approximately half of this research shows that this treatment is effective," "very controversial" and "methodological defects." I did this. "Spiritual healing must be truly risk-free until it is used as an effective alternative," he concluded. In a randomized clinical trial since 2001, no statistically significant difference in chronic pain was found in the same group between the removed therapist3waaaaaaaaq and the "simulated therapist." Ernst's 2003 review, which updated previous work, concluded that the weight of evidence changed to long-term treatment that could be damaged. "

Contact Healing

In a randomized clinical trial conducted in 2001 patients, in approximation, with prolonged pain, were randomly assigned to doctors or "simulated doctors," nevertheless they were unable to demonstrate the effectiveness of the treatment from a distance or face. A systematic review of 2008 showed that evidence of certain effects of mental healing on reducing neuropathy or neuralgia is not conclusive. In a 2008 manuscript, "Trick or Treat," Simon Singh and also Edward Ernst said: "Spiritual healing is biologically irrational, the effect of which depends on the placebo response and, at best, the comfort response. If you have a serious illness that requires first aid."

Evidence-Base

Edward Ernst, an alternative medicine researcher, said that the first review of long-term treatment trials before 1999 positively identified 57% of the study, but subsequent examinations of randomized medical trials were carried out between 2000 and 2002. "The most rigorous studies do not support the hypothesis that there is a specific therapeutic effect for distant treatment," he concluded. Ernst defines the proof base for soothing practices as "very negative." Many reviews also question the lack of data found, transparency, and errors. He concluded: "This is not biological meaning or strong clinical evidence, but spiritual healing continues to advance. This method is therapeutic and sufficient to prove that this is not so. " Quality of life, symptoms of depression, in the 2014 Energy Therapy Study for Colorectal Cancer Patients.

Explanation for Affirmative Feedback

There are many psychosomatic enlightenments for the affirmative information of energy healing, among them are the placebo effect, impulsive remissions, and reasoning dissonance. According to a 2009 analysis, the "small accomplishments" info for the two treatments proposed together as "energy psychology" (breakthrough acupressure and emotive choice techniques) could be caused by known cognitive factors and behavioral factors associated with manipulating energy. Biologists and researchers should carefully use such methods to try to educate the community more of the negative effects of therapy that can lead to unbelievable claims. "

There are twofold treatment accounts or anecdotal descriptions that need not be replaced with bizarre. To begin is initial hoc ergo propter hoc, which means that actual recovery or impulsive palliation can be a coincidence, regardless of the actions or words of the doctor or patient. These patients will recover if they do not do anything. To follow is the placebo outcome that allows one to feel real soreness and other forms of relief. In this case, the easy-going really helps the doctor. This is not mysterious or many functions, but the power of his belief that he will recover. In both cases, even if no miraculous or unexplained events occur, the patient might know-how a marked decrease in signs. In both cases, this is very limited by the body's natural abilities.

The positive results obtained in scientific research can be methodological defects, such as the results of the same psychological mechanism or the results of experimental biases, lack of blindness or bias in the publication. Positive reviews in the scientific literature may indicate bias. Because there are no important studies that do not correspond to the position of the author, in assessing a claim, all these factors must be considered.

Classification of Energy Healing

The word "energy medicine" has existed for the user since the creation of the non-profit international association for the study of excellent energy and energy medicine in the 1980s. This guide is available to practitioners, and other books are intended to provide the theoretical background and evidence for this practice. Energy medicine often shows that an imbalance in the body's "energy field" causes disease, and restoration of balance can restore the physique's liveliness arena to wellbeing. Some forms define healing by way of liberating the physique from undesirable energy or blocking the "heart." Diseases or episodes of the disease after treatment are called "ejection" or "contraction" in the mind. In general, doctors recommend additional treatment for complete treatment.

The "National Center for Complementary and Integrative Health (NCCIH)" distinguishes between medical services known as "true energy drugs" and medical methods called "energy" that is not physically detectable, including scientifically observable energy. You can check. He called it "Estimated Energy."

Forms of "veritable energy medicine" comprise light therapy, magnetic treatment, and color puncture. Medicinal technologies that practice electromagnetic emission (such as magnetic resonance imaging or radiation healing) stay not deliberated "energy products" in alternative medicine.

The type of "putative energy medicine" refers to therapeutic treatment using biological energy therapy, which states that the hand directs or regulates "energy" that is believed to affect the healing of the patient; Mental healing and mental healing, sensory therapy, sensory treatment, soft hand, esoteric healing, self-healing (the former term should not be confused with magnetic therapy), dental healing, Reiki, crystal healing, remote healing. Ideas for instance "Chi (Qi)," Prana," "congenital Intelligence," "Mana," "Pneuma," "Vital Fluid," "Odic Power" and "Orgone" are some of the expressions used to refer to this claimed energy field. This group does not apply to "acupuncture," Ayurvedic medicine, manual therapy, and more methods of manipulating the necessary energy with the help of physical manipulations.

The polar therapy, established by "Randolph Stone," is a form of energy source founded on the assumption that human wellbeing is exposed to affirmative and undesirable burdens of the electromagnetic field. The treatment of various human diseases, from muscle tension to cancer, has become popular. Though, conferring to "the American Cancer Society," existing scientific proof doesn't sustenance the claim that polar psychotherapy is operational in treating cancer or more diseases. "

Chapter 2

Types of Energy Healing

H ere exist various diverse types of energy healing. These forms of healing cover a lot of types—more than 100 types are known.

Sound Healing Therapy

Acoustic therapy uses aspects of music to improve health, physical, and emotional well-being. The attending person participates in the experience with a trained speech specialist. Sound healing includes listening to music for music, translating music into the rhythms of music, changing the performance of instruments, and much more. There are several types of acoustics, including vibration therapy, which uses special sounds that create vibrational thoughts to increase brain waves.

It is believed that sound therapy began in ancient Greece when music was used to treat mental disorders. Historically, music was used to enhance the morale of the army, allowed people to work faster and more productively, and protected evil spirits with songs. Recent studies have linked music to a variety of health benefits, from improved immune function, reduced stress levels, and improved health in premature babies.

Types of Sound Therapy

There are several types of acoustic therapy, each of which has different effects, but not all have been proven.

Vibroacoustic Therapy

Vibrations are thought to affect body functions such as blood pressure and respiration. Acoustic vibration therapy uses sound vibrations to improve health and reduce stress. This type of acoustic therapy involves transferring music and sound directly to the body using the built-in speakers, mattresses, and special mats. There are several signs that show the ability to increase relaxation and relieve pain and symptoms in cancer patients and patients who recover from surgery.

Guided Meditation

Guided intervention is a kind of voice healing to meditate with voice guidance during a session, lesson, video, or application. Meditation may include invoking or invoking mantras or prayers. Studies show that meditation offers various health benefits, including reducing stress, anxiety, and depression, increasing memory, lowering blood pressure, reducing pain, lowering cholesterol and lowering the risk of heart disease and stroke.

Bonny Method

Bonnie's Way Helen L. Bonnie uses classical music and imagery to explore personal growth, awareness, and change. According to a 2017 study, there is promising evidence that a series of sessions can improve the mental and physiological health of adults with medical and mental needs.

Nordoff-Robbins

This sound restoration method is provided by a qualified musician who holds a two-year master's degree at Nordoff-Robbins. Use music that is familiar with the subject, create new music together, or perform. This approach is used to treat children with developmental disabilities and parents, mental health, learning disabilities and autism, dementia, and other disorders.

Singing Bowl Therapy

Klangbechertherapie was built in the 12th century and is used in Tibetan culture for meditation and rituals. The metal bowl creates a deep, clear sound, which is used to relax and restore the mind. A 2016 study shows that meditation in a bowl reduces stress, anger, depression, and fatigue. All this, as you know, affects physical health and increases the risk of illness.

Neurologic Music Therapy

Music therapy can reduce stress and increase relaxation. It has been proven that it is more effective than prescription drugs in reducing preoperative anxiety. A study published in 2017 found that a 30-minute session of music therapy relieves pain through traditional spinal surgery. Music therapy is performed by a provider who is authorized to assess human needs. This procedure includes making music, listening, singing, or moving. It is used to treat physical rehabilitation, pain, and brain damage.

Brainwave Entertainment

This method, also known as binaural beats, stimulates the brain under certain conditions. Pulsating tones are used to increase the level of rhythm and align brain waves. It helps improve focus, entry, rest, or sleep. Further research is needed, but there are some signs. A reliable source of brainwashing, which relieves anxiety, pain, and symptoms of premenstrual syndrome and enhances behavioral problems in children.

Turning Fork Therapy

In tuning fork therapy, calibrated metal forks are used to apply specific vibrations to various parts of the body. This can help reduce stress and energy and improve emotional balance. It works like acupuncture and uses sound frequencies for point stimulation rather than needles. There are several studies showing that fork therapy can relieve muscle and bone pain.

How Sound Healing Works

Voice control uses various aspects of sound to improve emotional and physical well-being. How it works depends on the acoustics used. Most wellness sessions are conducted independently by specially trained doctors. This session may include sitting or lying down, listening to music or sound from a speaker or instrument, or using special tools such as fork settings. Depending on the method, you may be silent, not singing, not moving, not using an instrument, and not moving to make a sound.

Benefits of Sound Healing

Good care is used to treat the symptoms of various disorders, such as depression, post-traumatic stress, anxiety disorder, autism, dementia, and behavioral disorders, as well as mental disorders with learning disabilities.

Instruments Used in Sound Healing

In addition to the sound, there are several instruments used to heal the sound: Cane-Forkspan drum flute song. This includes the use different instruments at once in many ways, including a guitar, piano or other instruments.

Touch therapy

In some energy therapies, the user uses a soft touch or the patient's hands to send energy to the body or balance the energy of the body. Proponents say the benefits of this therapy come from increased vitality or balance. Others suggest that the benefits are due to survival factors such as: For example, the biological effects of contact and the psychological effects of experience with health.

Reiki

This is used as a form of alternative therapy—Reiki—which usually called energy therapy. It appeared in Japan at the end of the 19th century is also alleged to include the transmission of collective energy to a patient beginning at the hands of a specialist. Some arguments relate to Reiki since this one is difficult to verify its success scientifically. But a lot of individuals who get Reiki confess that it functions and is growing in reputation. A 2007 study found that 1.2 million adults in the United States attempted Reiki or related treatments at a minimum of once last year. It is estimated that over 60 hospitals provide Reiki services for patients.

About Reiki

The term "Reiki," meaning "mystical atmosphere, a magical sign." This originates after the Japanese words, "rei" (worldwide) plus "Ki" (life energy). Reiki exists as a kind of energy treatment. Healing energy is directed to the drive arenas nearby the physique. Conferring to specialists, physical trauma, or emotional pain can lead to stagnation of energy in the body. Over time, this energy blockage can bring about disease.

This energy treatment purposes of maintaining energy stream besides eliminating blockages like acupuncture or acupressure. Practitioners said that increasing the stream of liveliness throughout the physique may provide easing, ache relief, quick curing, and additional signs of the disease. Reiki has remained everywhere for many thousand years. This method was initially established in 1922 via Japanese Buddhism under the named Mikao Usui. This practice spread in the 1940s through Hawaii to the United States and further in the 1980s to Europe. This is usually called hand care, otherwise direct care.

Techniques Used in Reiki

Related technologies have the following names: Focus on scattering while pumping, rotating and tilting, extracting dangerous energy extraction. Aura Some Reiki practitioners use it when a healing crystal or chakra can provide healing or protection.

A session can go from fifteen to ninety minutes. The amount of periods depends on whatever the patient wants to do. Other patients choose one session, while others prefer a series of sessions to solve specific problems.

Happenings in Reiki Sessions

Reiki is great kept in comfortable conditions, but then again can happen in anyplace. The client sits in a relaxed seat, otherwise puts a full dress on the table. Depending on the preferences of the patient, there may or may not be music. Practitioners use different forms of hands for two to five minutes to gently place their hands on certain areas of the head, limbs, and chest. The arm may be placed on 20 diverse parts of the physique. If you have specific damage (for example—you can hold your hand directly above the wound when you are burned. Energy transfer occurs when the practitioner gently grabs your hand above or above your body. Keep respective arm locations till the specialist insinuates that liveliness no longer flows in. A practitioner can raise his hand and place it in another area of the body when he feels that the heat or energy in his hand is asleep.

Health Benefits

Practitioners say that the healing effect is mediated by the delivery of widespread liveliness, well-known as "qi." In India, it is well-known as "Prana." This exists as liveliness associated with "tai chi" exercises. This exists as vital liveliness which other people trust atmospheres us completely. This liveliness must penetrate the physique. Reiki specialists note that liveliness is not measured using new technology, but many people who prepared it can feel it. It is believed that Reiki improves relaxation, supports the natural process of healing the body, supports emotive, intellectual, and mystical welfare. It's furthermore alleged that it provides profound easing, helps individuals overcome complications, release emotive tension, and progress general well-being. Those that take Reiki call this one "very convenient."

Situations which Reiki has existed to support treatment are:

- Malignance
- Heart disease
- Nervousness

- Hopelessness
- Prolonged ache
- Barrenness
- Neurodegenerative ailments
- "Autism"
- Crohn's illness
- Exhaustion disorders

Malignance patients that underwent Reiki said they felt improved later. This can be for the reason that it aids in ease. Additional cause, conferring to malignance study in the UK. Perhaps the therapist can spend a stint together and touch them. It possesses some calming effect on patients who may be affected by invasive treatment, anxiety, besides tension. People claim diverse experiences. Others said that practitioners' arms became hotter, some saw cold hands, and some experienced trembling waves. The most common report is stress reduction and deep relaxation.

Evidence of Reiki's Healing Power

As Reiki becomes popular, the answer remains. Reiki allows you to relax, relieve pain, heal quickly, and some symptoms, but some studies say that it supports certain health benefits. He was charged with claiming to have cured the disease without scientific evidence. Some describe his claim as a fraud. Critics say they fly earlier than our current understanding of natural law. Advocates say the profits of well-being besides tension reduction is actual, but they are difficult to a degree through systematic research. Researchers have found that there is no qualitative study of the effect. According to him, there are no studies showing that it's further operative than a "placebo."

Analysis of the literature available in 2008 showed there wasn't adequate proof in backing Reiki as an operative healing for the disease besides that its worth has not been proven. In 2015, a study was published on the treatment of Cochrane anxiety and depression. Researchers conclude that "there is not enough evidence that Reiki is suitable for people 16 years of age or older with anxiety, depression, or both." Utmost few researches performed were of meager value, small sample size, and without expert judgment or a control group.

Studies published by BMC Nephrology, on the other hand, show that it may be beneficial to provide a "therapeutic effect" to patients on dialysis, especially if it is provided free of charge by a volunteer. Pain relief may be weak, but not traumatic and not dangerous, and the patient feels "working" to relieve pain.

"Annie Harrington" recently voiced to "MNT" that the "Reiki Federation of the United States" currently has a large document, "to facilitate a lot of research." These results, which are being studied by the Federal Council on Supplemental Health and Natural Health (CNHC), are likely to help bring Reiki to the mainstream.

Safety of Reiki

"The US National Center for Complementary and Integrated Health (NCCIH)" says Reiki "has not proven its health benefits." But no side effects appeared. The main health problem is that people with serious health problems can choose Reiki and other additional methods of treatment, rather than strictly testing modern medicines. But this cannot be combined with other dangerous treatments. In fact, touching the "universal energy," it seems to have several advantages: from building confidence to improving overall well-being. Kosovo suggests that the costly existing treatments available today frequently have graveside paraphernalia besides could or could not be effective. Therefore, several individuals want to freely choose an alternative.

Where to Get Reiki

Reiki is becoming increasingly popular. A sense of well-being and less danger of injury. Equally an outcome, Reiki is currently accessible in other large clinics. For example, other health care workers, including hospitals, could provide you uncharged services as a portion of calmative maintenance. Secluded Reiki sessions range as of 30$ to 100$ which usually doesn't have a cover. Anybody looking for a trained and skilled Reiki specialist ought to pay attention to this because there are very few rules in this area. It will be helpful to ask practitioners about his education, together with professionalism. Reiki isn't a substitute medicine for curative problems, nonetheless an additional medicine that helps to heal and improve your health. It is best to consult with alternative doctors first.

How to be a Reiki Practitioner and Regulations

No teaching, tutoring, or practice is required to participate in Reiki preparation or tablets. In this method called "strong spiritual experience," the teacher delivers liveliness and curing to the scholar. Reiki teaching is different; a lot of students will study on energy throughout the physique, working with energy healing, and working with clients. To prepare for strengthening, you need to fast for two to three days, meditate, concentrate on the environment, and cause undesirable reactions. There exist three championship stages. Individuals who have reached the chief stage can learn from other individuals and receive distance treatment in the form of degrees.

Regulators at times request Reiki sites to transform their facts in accordance with authorized ethics. Locations vending Reiki merchandise could be held liable by maintaining that such a product is not a medicinal means and shouldn't be used to diagnose, treat, cure, or prevent any disease. The British Advertising Standards Organization (ASA) rejected the claim that Reiki can cure several diseases in many cases. Judy Kosovich presented a "new perspective" on the regulation of energy medicine in a study published by Physics Practical. Recognizing that there are governing forms to guard the community, he claims that additional action is needed as a means that is not understood or explained by scientific research.

Therapeutical Touch

Therapeutic Touch (usually abbreviated as "TT"), well-known as "Non-Contact Therapeutic Touch (NCTT)," is a "pseudoscientific" liveliness healing that helps physicians promote soothing, reduce ache together with unease. "Touch Therapy" is a listed symbol in Canada aimed at "practical and homogenous treatment practices executed by specialists who are sensitive to the area of liveliness received around the body. No contact required." Sensory physicians show that the patient's energy field can be recognized and manipulated by placing the patient's hand next to or near the patient. According to a broadly named research printed by the "Journal of the American Medical Association" in 1998, when Emily Rose was nine years old, sensory doctors could identify the existence of an arm a little edges overhead revelation. She stayed disconnected. "Simon Singh and Edward Ernst," inside their manuscript "Trick or Treat," concluded that "the field of energy is just an invention of a healing imagination." The "American Cancer Society" identified that "the available scientific evidence does not support the claim that TT can treat cancer or other diseases." The 2014 Cochrane Report established no convincing proof to support wound healing.

Dora Kunz, a theologian and former chairman of the Theosophical Society of America (1975-1987) and "Dolores Krieger," now a lecturer of nursing at "New York University," established healing contacts during 1970. According to Krieger, sensory therapy is not associated with religion or healing beliefs but is based on ancient healing practices, such as ordination. "A doctor (client) is the one who ultimately heals himself, so the doctor or therapist acts as a system for supporting human energy until the therapeutic immune system itself is sufficiently absorbed," Krieger said.

The validity of TT is carried out in the field of the science of modern man, associated with the mystical interpretation of Martha E. Rogers and quantum mechanics, especially the last of Fritiof Capra. The 2002 review did not find any of the two reasons to refute. Rogers 'theory turned out to be incompatible with the principles of TT, and the duplicate term was caused by a lack of accuracy in Rogers' work, which was very important for him. The reason for the interpretation of physics is that the "global interconnection" of the universe allows for remote healing. Followers of TT will be involved in interpreting "Bell's theory," together with the likelihood of substantial dysfunction. The understanding isn't reinforced with investigational data.

A 2002 research resolved that "TT theory is inexplicable" and that "evidence supporting the current situation with physical energy should be considered as evidence for TT theory." A procedure named "electron resonance transfer," that "physicist Alan Sokal" calls "nonsense."

Researched Evidence

During the years, numerous researches have been conducted to verify the effectiveness of TT, and one or more systematic reviews have been conducted with various meta-analyzes and various outcomes then deductions. "O'Matuna et al." When deliberating this researches, highlight issues that include the tendency to publish additional medical journals that cannot rule out the wrong research methodology and "outperform studies with positive results." They approve that taking in consideration contextual methodical information, the predecessor acceptability of TT is adequately low that any procedural mistake in research could constantly offer a further conceivable account for some optimistic discoveries.

"— O'Mathúna et al."

"Emily Rose," a nine-year-old, developed as well as conducted research of sensory therapy. Using the assistance of "Stephen Barrett of Quack watch and RN's mother Linda Rose," Emily became the youngest naturopath research group to take documents from the American Medical Association (JAMA) and participate in therapeutic touch research. Twenty-one therapists participated in the study and tried to find their aura. Specialists set up right across the wooden umbrella, and Emily set upright at the other end. Then the specialists put their arms in the hovels on the wood. Emily threw a coinage, helping to decide the hand the doctor would close (of course, without touching). Then, practitioners should indicate whether they can sense the biofield and where their hands are. All participants stated that they could do it, but the real consequences do not confirm the requirements they needed. Conducting recurring attempts, specialists can find their hands at a level that is not significantly different from a match. JAMA Editor George D. Lundberg, MD, advises casualties together with cover corporations to refrain from waging for healing, or first ask if the payment is accepted or not until an honest experiment works.

There isn't an existing medicinal proof for the efficiency of sensory therapy. "Cochrane's systematic review of this is not conclusive evidence that TT contributes to acute wound healing, and the American Cancer Society does not support claims that TT can cure cancer or other diseases."

How TT Works

Researchers remain not sure in what way sensory therapy helps, although there are two notions. The first notion suggests that the patient's cells have pain associated with painful physical or emotional experiences, such as infections, injuries, or complex relationships. The ache kept in those cells is destructive, thus stops other cells from functioning well with some cells in the physique. Thus leads to illness. Specialists trust that tonic contact improves wellbeing by reinstating intercellular communiqué. Another notion is grounded on the principle of substantial physical science. When iron lifeblood flows in the body, an electromagnetic arena is created. Conferring to the notion, we can altogether effortlessly recognize the area named the "aura," but currently simply definite individuals, for example, those with calming contacts, get this capability.

In general, the relaxing effect is founded on the impression that well-being needs a sensible stream of living loveliness. Therapists feel the energy with their own hands and send healthy energy. In treatment, ordinary people experience warmness, easing, and ache liberation. A specialist says that your liveliness is burning or icy, energetic or inactive, clogged or loose. There exist eight main areas where the energy of the physique, head, neck, heart, abdomen, lower abdomen, sacral, knees, and feet are felt. But a person who receives therapeutic contact is a doctor. A doctor provokes only the healing mechanisms of the body itself. The role of practitioners is to support this process.

Happenings in TT Session

Before starting the session, the therapist asks you to sit down or lie down. You do not need to take off your clothes. A session can be divided into four stages: the center. The therapist "centers" using breathing, visualization and meditation to achieve a change in the state of consciousness about himself.

Assessment

The therapist holds two to four edges as of the physique when touching commencing at the head to the toes. The purpose of doing this is to estimate the liveliness arena around the body. Counselors regularly define heat, cold, congestion, and tingling in an "overloaded" or "blocked" energy field.

Intervention

When the therapist discovers a blockage or blockage, he moves his hands in rhythm, starting from the top of the blockade and dropping from the body. This action, called fragmentation, is recurrent until the specialist does not feel constipated or at ease. The therapist also visualizes and transfers vital liveliness to precise parts of the physique to precise imbalance.

Assessment/conclusion

After a few minutes of rest, you ask the therapist the feeling you are having. The specialist can recheck the liveliness arena to see if there are blockages.

Health Benefits of TT

Most studies show that sensory therapy can relieve tension headaches and relieve pain. Blisters, osteoarthritis, or pain after surgical procedure. It could as well accelerate injury curing besides advance purpose in patients with inflammation of the legs. As a matter of fact, research indicates that healing contact arouses cell development. The healing touch similarly enhances easing. Patients with heart disease, cancer, besides burns report that therapeutic contact significantly reduces anxiety. As a rule, unfathomable easing linked to healing contact lessens tension, depresses blood stress, and recovers inhalation. Relaxation can likewise lessen fat and progress immunity and lower abdomen function. Only one treatment can reduce the difficulty of pregnancy.

Therapeutic contact may be useful in many other conditions besides treatment, including:

- Fibromyalgia
- Slumber apnea
- Fidgety limb disorder, an ailment that sources sleeplessness
- Antipathies
- Bronchitis
- Dependences
- Lupus
- Alzheimer's ailment, probably, some methods of dementia
- Prolonged ache

Other individuals said they felt emotive and mystical alterations when getting a healing contact. Such as better confidence, self-control, and self-esteem. The question of whether the healing power of touch is connected with "on-hand" remains a moot point. Critics argue that the healing observed after a therapeutic touch is associated with relaxation features that come with the treatment, besides the transmission of energy amid the specialist's arms together with the human physique.

Safety of TT

You can safely use sensory therapy as part of your care. There are no studies are showing that therapeutic contact is effective in all types of diseases. However, some health experts believe this can help with stress and anxiety. Those who come for treatment say that they have a fresh heart; they heal faster and feel better. Talk with your doctor about attempts or other additional medical practices that you already use. If your doctor knows all your medical recommendations, they will help you manage your health.

How to Become a TT Practitioner

Sensory therapy skills are taught not only in health contact schools but also in colleges, medical schools, nursing programs, and massage schools. During the session, the client fully dresses on the massage table. Doctors then use soft or physical contact (not in direct contact) to manipulate and balance the client's energy field, often feeling deep relaxation and calm. A session usually takes 40-60 minutes. Therapeutic sensory massage is used to treat stress and pain, recover from surgery, treat cancer, and treat other acute and chronic diseases.

Sensory healing programs are generally intended for practitioners in specific areas, such as healthcare or physical activity. At Touch Healing School, you will learn the relationship between the body's energy system and health, as well as special skills for treating touch. More advanced courses focus on work ethics and practice. Some programs may include instructions for related forms, such as Reiki Healing Touch. Certification for Therapeutic Sensory Therapy is provided by specialized organizations such as the Touch Treatment Program, a training program accredited as the Touch Therapy Practitioner (HTP). Healing across Borders, a non-profit organization that provides Touch Healing Practitioner (CHTP) certified certification. These two accreditation programs have been approved by the American Association of Holistic Nurses and the National Certification Council for Massage and Body Therapy.

ETF

EFT is a form of modern, rapidly developing expansion together individual healing which has been a technique used for a wide range of issues in the arena of liveliness psychology. Getting the roots from psychology, acupuncture, and kinesiology. It exists as an extremely operational and tender way to adapt to the sensation you want to change, to the energy system of your body. EFT is used to improve and develop people. Develop attitude and behavior, solve individual complications, fears, and reduce stress. EFT is very operational once it is used in all kinds of top metrics (e.g., sporting, civic talking, transactions, performing, etc.)

With EFT, certain "acupressure" parts of the physique are touched using tips of the fingers, while the problem is central. The procedure could be recurrent to reduce the force until the equilibrium is reinstated. This all happens normally in a chair. With the right EFT implementation, more than 80 percent of customers achieve a real improvement or complete problem-solving. Sessions can be held directly on the phone or Skype; all you have to do is get in contact with a specialist.

Advantages of ETF

He often works elsewhere. Usually, it is fast, durable, and soft and easy to learn. You can install it yourself. There are no side effects. There is no surgical intervention. Without pushing or stretching the body, there is no equipment, needles, pills, or chemicals.

Significant improvement or complete cure in many case studies;

- Undesirable Feelings
- Diet Desires
- Decreasing or Removing Ache, Ache Controlling
- Cig Dependence and Drug dependence, Liquor misuse
- Aversions and Fears
- Unease and Terror Spasms
- Forces and Preoccupations
- Misery and Sorrow, Anguish and Forfeiture
- Guiltiness and Mistrustfulness, Fury and Fright
- Sleeplessness and Bad dream
- Undesirable Recollections
- PTSD and Disturbing Commemorations
- Erotic Mishandling Concerns
- Self-perception and Coyness
- Dyslexia
- Top Presentation
- enhancing Attentiveness and Concentration
- Fulfilling Affirmative Objectives
- Civic Communication
- doing Examinations and Interviews

Acupuncture

"Acupuncture" is a method of substitute medication and the main constituent of "traditional Chinese medicine (TCM)," where skinny prickles are introduced to the physique. Acupuncture is "pseudoscience," for the reason that the theory, together with the practice of TCM, is not based scientifically and are called shamans.

There are various acupuncture options that have arisen from different philosophies, and the technology depends on the country in which they are performed. It is recommended by acupuncture for various other disorders but is most often used to relieve ache. It is commonly used in amalgamation with additional methods of healing.

Various acupuncture studies and systematic reviews do not match, indicating a lack of effect. A Cochrane review found that acupuncture is ineffective under various conditions. Systematic reviews by doctors in the "University of Exeter and Plymouth" have revealed slight proof of the effects of acupuncture on pain. Overall, data show that short-term acupuncture treatments do not have lasting aids. Other studies have shown that acupuncture can relieve some form of ache, but most studies have shown that the effects of acupuncture may not be brought about by the healing itself. An organized assessment showed that the palliative result brought by acupuncture seems to have no medical significance, which is indistinguishable from distortion. An analysis shows that acupuncture for prolonged lower vertebral ache is economical in addition to ordinary treatments, and a detached organized assessment does not provide sufficient evidence of the cost-effectiveness of acupuncture for treating chronic lower vertebral ache.

Acupuncture is mostly harmless if trained by a skilled user by means of hygienic needles and a disposable needle. With proper delivery, the percentage of the smallest side effects is small. However, there are accidents and infections associated with neglect of a doctor, especially when using sterilization methods. A 2013 survey shows that the intelligence of conduction has improved considerably over the past period. The utmost common side effects are pneumothorax and infection. As serious side effects continue to be reported, appropriate training is recommended to minimize the danger for acupuncturists.

Systematic studies haven't been able to find any physiological or histological proof found in customary Chinese conceptions which include "qi, meridians and acupuncture points," and numerous current practices do not have the main component of the early belief system: vital energy (qi) or meridian. It does not support existence. Acupuncture is supposed to be about "100 BC." China was created when classic medicine of Emperor Yuangdi Neking was published, but some experts suspect that this drug was indeed used in advance. As time went by, contradictory statements and faith methods concerning the influence of the circulation of the moon, sky, earth, yin and yang and the "rhythm" of the body appeared in the effectiveness of treatment. The popularity of acupuncture in China has ceased owing to modifications in national civil governance together with the preferences of western medication or rationalism. In the 6th century, AD acupuncture first extended to Korea, through to Japan via health campaigners and from France then to Europe. When spreading to the western countries together with the United States in the 20th century, mystical components of acupuncture, contrary to Western notions, were sometimes left to simply attach acupuncture points.

Clinical Research

Acupuncture is an alternative treatment. It is also used to treat various symptoms but is most often used to relieve ache. Acupuncture is commonly cast-off in amalgamation with some procedures of cure. For instance, the "American Society of Anesthesiologists" claims that healing for non-inflammatory and non-specific lower vertebral ache can solely be considered in combination with existing treatments.

In acupuncture, needles are inserted in the skin. Conferring to the "Medical Education and Research Foundation (Mayo Clinic)," the general period is interrupted when 5 to 20 needles are inserted. In most circumstances, the needle can remain in position for ten to twenty minutes. This may be due to the use of high temperature, stress, or laser radiation. In general, it is grounded in intuition and philosophy, not even an individual and systematic study. In Japan, there exists a non-invasive treatment established during the early years of the 20th century by the use of a series of complex prickles to treat children (Shonychin or Shawnee Hari).

Clinical practice varies from country to country. Evaluation of the regular amount of clients cured each hour shows substantial variances amongst the United States (1.2) and China (10). Chinese herbal medicine is regularly in use. There are different approaches to acupuncture that relate to different philosophies. Various acupuncture practices have developed, but methods that are cast-off in "traditional Chinese medicine (TCM)" are the utmost common in the United States. Customary acupuncture includes a syringe, cauterization, and cup healing, which could be complemented by some techniques, which include heart rate together with some physique and language recognition tests. Customary acupuncture suggests that "qi" flows throughout the physique along the meridian. The key techniques that the UK uses are BMT together with Western healing acupuncture. The word "Western Medical Acupuncture" refers to the alteration of acupuncture grounded on BMT with a smaller amount of emphasis on BMT. "Western medical acupuncture" approaches include the use of acupuncture after a medical diagnosis. A normal for limited acupuncture points do not exist since the contrasting acupuncture systems used in different countries are compared to identify different acupuncture points.

In traditional acupuncture, acupuncturists determine the treatment that should be treated by observing and asking patients in accordance with tradition. TCM uses four diagnostic methods: examination, stethoscope, and odor, examination, and palpation. On examination, much focus is given to the facade and especially the patois, such as examination of the tension, color, shape, size, and range of the tongue, as well as the presence of plaque around the edges. Auscultation and smell include listening to certain noises, which include wheeziness, and attention to physique scent. The study focused on the "seven surveys": colds and illness; Sweating Hungriness, dehydration and palate; Excretion and urine; Ache; Slumber; menstruation, and a white stream. Soft press focuses on the sensation of the physique of thin points "a-shea" and sensations of the pounding.

Needles

The utmost communal method for stimulating acupuncture is the use of penetration into the skin through skinny metallic prickles, that are controlled by hand, or using electrically stimulated devices (electroacupuncture), the needle can be further stimulated. Acupuncture prickles are usually prepared by "stainless steel," which is malleable and prevents rust or damage. Prickles are frequently thrown away afterward to avoid infection. Recyclable prickles must be sanitized after using them on a patient. The length of the needle is 13

45

to 130 mm (0.51 to 5.12 inches), with short prickles close to the facade together with the eyes and long prickles in thick matters. The diameter of the needle is from 0.16 to 0.46 mm. Thick needles are used for healthy patients. Thin needles can be flexible and require the insertion of a tube. Although blunt needles cause more pain, the top of the prickle must not be very piercing to avert damage.

In addition to thread-shaped needles, other types of needles comprise three-blade prickles and nine old prickles. Japanese acupuncture specialists consider very skinny prickles on the surface; other times, it does not penetrate the skin and is surrounded by well-known tubes(17th-century inventions adopted in the west and china). Acupuncture in Korea's copper needles are used and focuses more on weapons.

Needle Techniques

Insertion

Sterilization is done on the skin, and the needle is injected into the flexible directing pipe. The needle can be handled in many methods, such as rotating, blinking, or moving the skin up and down. Most of the ache is sensed in the epidermal layer of the membrane, so it is better to place the needle quickly. Often the needle is stimulated by the hand, causing a gray, confined, painful feeling known as "De Qi," and the tingling experienced by the specialist, and the perfunctory relations amid the prickle and membrane. Sore Acupuncture techniques can affect pain, and an experienced doctor can use the needle minus producing ache.

De-qi

"De-qi" "(Chinese: 得气; pinyin: dé qì; "arrival of qi")." De-qi indicates tingling, swelling, or electric tingling, which is transmitted to the needle position. If this sensation is not observed, inaccurate sharp positions, incorrect depth of penetration of the needle, incorrect physical handling is to blame. If "De-Qi" isn't observed instantly

46

during the injection of the needle, several physical influence methods are frequently used to facilitate the insertion of the needle (e.g., "pooling," "shaking" or "shaking").

After observing the solution, the technique can be used to "influence" the solution. For example, they say that a certain lethal dish is repelled from the body by means of certain manipulations. Other technologies are aimed at "improvement" "(Chinese: 补; pinyin: bǔ)" or "sedating" "(Chinese: 泄; pinyin: xiè) qi." The first method is used for the deficit model and the second for the increase model. De Qi is extra essential for Chinese acupuncture, but Japanese and western patients cannot be considered an important part of treatment.

Related Searches

Acupuncture is often accompanied by swelling, burns of moxa (dry moss) on or close to the membrane, but frequently not close or not at the acupuncture part. Acupuncture is traditional treatment for acute illnesses, and cauterization is used for chronic diseases. Cauterization can be applied directly to the skin of cauterization, either directly (a cone can be applied directly to the skin and burn the skin with the formation of blisters and scars), or indirect (or cauterization of garlic, ginger or chopped vegetables or cylinders).

Cupping is an ancient Chinese alternative medicine that causes topical inhalation of the skin. Practitioners believe that this mobilizes a cycle to endorse curing.

"Tui na" is a "TCM" method that uses many empty-handed techniques in which needles are not used to stimulate qi flow.

Electro-acupuncture is a method of acupuncture in that acupuncture prickles are put into a ruse that causes a constant electric shock (the so-called "stimulation of a transdermal electric nerve mask called acupuncture [TENS]").

"Fire needle acupuncture," also called fire aggravating, is a procedure for swiftly placing a hot prickle on parts of the physique.

Menopause is an incentive for the physique, such as acupuncture, which uses sound instead of needles. This can be done using a sensor that directs narrow ultrasonic light from 6-8 centimeters to the acupuncture point of the meridian in the body. Alternatively, you can use a tuning fork or other sound output devices.

Acupuncture injections are injections of various substances (e.g., medicines, herbal extracts or vitamins) to acupuncture. This method associates old-fashioned acupuncture with effective doses of injections of frequently approved drugs, making an argument that it can be additionally operative than a particular cure, specifically for treating several types of chronic pain. However, according to a review in 2016, most of the tests published for this technology are of little value due to methodological problems and will require more extensive tests to draw useful conclusions.

Ear artery therapy, identified as ear acupuncture, or acupuncture of the ear, is thought to have originated in earliest China. A needle is placed to stimulate the point of the external ear. A current method is established in France in the initial 1950s. Systematic proof that it could treat the disease is not available. There is little proof of helpfulness.

The acupuncture of the scalp established in Japan is grounded on reflex logical contemplations that belong to the scalp.

"Korean hand acupuncture" focuses on reflex zones. Medical acupuncture is trying to incorporate reflexology concepts, initiating part patterns, together with concepts of anatomy (which include the spreading of skin diseases) to acupuncture, emphasizing an extra formal method to localizing acupuncture points.

"Cosmetic acupuncture" This is using acupuncture to lessen facial creases.

Animal acupuncture is using acupuncture in pets. As for veterinary drugs, there is no detailed data on additional or alternative technologies, but the data is growing.

Efficiency

Acupuncture has been extensively studied. In 2013, about 1,500 randomized controlled acupuncture trials called PubMed were conducted. But the results of reviews of acupuncture effects are not decisive.

The development of rigorous research on acupuncture is complex, but not impossible. Acupuncture Due to the nature of acupuncture, the top main problems in efficiency studies is the development of a suitable placebo regulator. A research was made if acupuncture has a particular effect on the patient, the doctor, and blind analysis appear to be the most appropriate approach for "ruthless" forms of acupuncture. Artificial acupuncture uses needles or non-invasive needles at points other than acupuncture, for example, place the needle in a meridian that is not associated with the test condition, or in a position that is not connected with the meridian. This may be due to a completely unspecified effect or may indicate that improper treatment is not inactive or that a systematic protocol provides inadequate treatment.

According to a 2014 Nature Reviews Cancer report: "Unlike mechanisms that presumably divert the flow of qi through the meridian, researchers generally believe that the place where the needle is inserted as often as possible does not matter. (That is, there is no sleep-effect effect.) Even though the prickle is injected, that is, "acupuncture," "placebo," or "placebo" as a rule, has a similar effect as the "real" acupuncture, in other better circumstances acupuncture is effective for pain: the position in which the needle is placed, the amount of prickles in use, the user's familiarity or skill or condition during session (compared to false). The same analysis showed that the amount of prickles and periods is paramount. This is the result of an improvement in saliva compared to the control group without saliva due to the large number. There are several systematic studies in which the constituents of an acupuncture period could be vital for the healing consequence, comprising the location and deepness of saliva, the form, and strength of the stimulus, and the amount of prickles used. Studies show that needles should not stimulate or penetrate marked traditional acupuncture points to achieve the expected effect (e.g., psychosocial factors).

The "shy" acupuncture reaction to osteoarthritis can be used in older people, but placebo is generally considered fraud and therefore unethical. However, some doctors and ethics experts may suggest a placebo use state, which can be a hypothetical benefit of cheap cure minus side effects or drug or some drug interactions. Proof for utmost substitute medications, which include acupuncture, which is distant from convincing, so using substitute medication in conventional well-being can be a moral issue.

The application of proof-based medical principles to acupuncture study is still debatable having various implications. Some studies have shown that acupuncture can relieve pain, but most studies have shown that the effects of acupuncture are mainly caused by placebo. There is evidence that the profit of acupuncture is old. There is inadequate proof for the usage of acupuncture likened to mass therapy. Acupuncture isn't superior to a long basic cure. The usage of acupuncture has remained disapproved for the lack of scientific evidence about the effect or clear mechanism for its effectiveness in diseases other than placebo. Acupuncture is known as "Placebo Theater," and "David Gorsky" claims that while acupuncture advocates seek a "placebo effect" or develop a "meaningful placebo," they basically admit that it is more than just a drug.

Publication Bias

Publication bias was mentioned in a review of randomized control acupuncture studies (RCTs). An acupuncture study conducted in 1998 showed that tests from Japan, Hong Kong, Taiwan, and China were as useful as acupuncture, up to 10 out of 11 studies conducted in Russia. TCM quality assessment, including acupuncture in 2011, TCM resolved that the operational worth of utmost of these studies (such as methodology, investigational monitoring, and blindness) was normally low, especially in studies printed in the Chinese periodical. (I know that the worth of acupuncture tests is better than TCM testing tools). The study also showed that the quality of tests published in non-Chinese journals was higher. Chinese writers use more Chinese research, which turned out to be equally positive. According to an 88 systematic acupuncture trials review published in 2012, in Chinese periodicals, half or more of these appraisals stated prejudice tests, and most of them were printed in periodicals that had no effect. A study conducted in 2015, which compared records of previously registered acupuncture studies with published results, showed that participation in the study before the test was not uncommon. The study also showed that reports on sampled results and measurements modified to produce statistically significant results are often found in these writings.

Researcher and press officer "Steven Salzberg" usually refers to acupuncture and eastern medication as "fake medical journals," including meridian research and acupuncture in acupuncture and medicine.

Specific Conditions

Pain

Many studies and many systematic acupuncture tests are often inadequate. A systematic review of a 2011 systematic review showed that true acupuncture is not better than false acupuncture to treat pain, and some tests have concluded that acupuncture does not provide conclusive proof that this is an operational ache reliever. An identical study instituted that collar ache is one of 4 kinds of ache that are known to have a positive effect, but the main study used warned that there was a risk of serious displacement. A 2009 Cochrane review found that acupuncture is not effective for various conditions.

According to a systematic review conducted in 2014, the effectiveness of nocebo acupuncture is clinically significant and shows the extent to which side effects could make a measure of the "nocebo effect." "A meta-analysis" by the Collaboration of Acupuncture Trials in 2012 shows that "compared to herbal remedies" in treating four kinds of prolonged ache (urination and collar ache, lap arthritis, prolonged headache) and backache. I found a relatively simple acupuncture effectiveness. We settled for the fact that it was "more than a placebo" aside from being a sensible choice for the goal. Edward Ernst and David Kolhun mentioned a meta-analysis of minor clinical relevance. "I'm worried that I was able to get rid of this distortion," says Edward Ernst. The same researchers teamed up in 2017 to update its prior meta-analysis and once more established that acupuncture for certain musculoskeletal pains, arthritis, chronic pain in the head and shoulders is better than fake acupuncture. In addition, after a year, the effect of acupuncture decreased by about 15%.

According to a systematic review conducted in 2010, acupuncture is considered other than a "placebo-widespread" prolonged ache condition. However, the writers acknowledge it's not yet known whether the overall benefits are clinically significant or cost-effective. According to a review in 2010, real acupuncture and fake acupuncture have brought related progress which could be used only as proof of the effectiveness of acupuncture. A similar appraisal shows inadequate proof that actual and fake acupuncture yields biotic variances in spite of the same properties. A methodical appraisal and meta-analysis in 2009 showed acupuncture has a low palliative result, has no clinical significance, and is indistinguishable from prejudice. In the same study, it was not clear whether acupuncture eliminates pain, regardless of the psychological effects of conscious syringes. A 2017 methodical appraisal and meta-analysis showed that acupuncture of the ear could help reduce ache in a span of 48 hours after using; otherwise, the average variance concerning control and acupuncture was low.

Lower Back Pain

Acupuncture can be operative for non-specific subordinate backache, according to a 2013 appraisal. However, the writers pointed out that this study has the following limitations: In many studies, the heterogeneity of research characteristics and the low quality of the methodology. A 2012 methodical appraisal provided proof that acupuncture is further operative than the absence of non-specific chronic back pain. The evidence is contradictory and compared with other treatments. According to a systematic review of a 2011 systematic study, "For chronic lower back pain, personalized acupuncture is a toothpick that does not penetrate the skin and does not improve the symptoms of fake acupuncture or acupuncture." According to a 2010 review, champagne acupuncture was just as effective in treating chronic back pain as true acupuncture. Although the specific therapeutic effect of acupuncture is low, its benefits are clinically significant, mainly due to circumstances and psychosocial situations. Studies of brain tomography show that traditional and artificial acupuncture have different effects on the limbic system and have a similar analgesic effect. A Cochrane study in 2005 showed that for acute pain in the lower back, there was insufficient evidence of acupuncture or dry needles. The same study shows faint signs of pain relief and improvement in the short term immediately after treatment compared to lack of treatment or lower back pain. In a similar appraisal, we established that acupuncture is no longer operative than conservative and some substitute cures. According to a methodological appraisal and meta-analysis in 2017, collar ache can be compared to conventional acupuncture, while electro acupuncture reduces pain more effectively than regular acupuncture. The same review notes that "the included studies are difficult to complete because of the high risk of bias and inaccuracies." In the year 2015, a review of organized studies of various vaginas indicated that acupuncture could help patients with a chronic lower vertebral ache for a petite period. The appraisal showed this to be true when acupuncture is isolated or used in addition to existing treatments. A systematic review of the Clinical Practice Guide of the American College of Physicians for 2017 showed that there was slight proof of acupuncture being operative for chronic lower backache, or limited data on acute lower back pain. Strong evidence of two conditions in the same review. Back in 2017, clinical practice guidelines published by Danish health authorities recently recommended acupuncture for low back and lower back pain.

Headaches and Migraine

Two reviews of cocaine in 2016 showed that acupuncture could help prevent tension headaches and episodes of migraine. The 2016 Cochrane Acupuncture Assessment Study for Preventing Temporary Migraines concluded that true acupuncture has little effect on shamanic acupuncture. According to a 2012 review, acupuncture can help treat headaches, but safety needs to be documented in more detail to provide compelling recommendations in support of its use.

Some more uses included:

- Elevated and truncated blood stress
- Chemotherapy-influenced sickness and spewing
- Other digestive illnesses, comprising peptic sore
- Hurting periods
- Dysentery
- Hypersensitive rhinitis
- Faceache
- Dawn illness
- Rheumatoid inflammation
- Restoration
- Element, tobacco and liquor reliance
- Backbone ache Strains
- Tennis shove
- Lumbago
- Toothache
- Decreasing the threat of stroke
- Prompting labor

Other situations are as follows:

- Fibromyalgia
- Neuralgia
- Post-operative
- Tourette pattern
- Rigid collar
- Vascular dementia
- Hooting cough, or pertussis

Benefits of Acupuncture

Acupuncture can help. However, there could be a few lateral properties. It could be efficiently shared with some cures. This could regulate several kinds of ache. Painkillers can aid the sick who are not suitable. NCCIH recommends that acupuncture never visit an existing doctor.

Expectations in Session

According to the theory of traditional Chinese medicine, acupuncture parts are situated on the meridian, where vibrant liveliness flows. This liveliness is called "qi" or qi. A specialist examines a client, assesses the patient's condition, uses one or even more than one thin, antiseptic prickles, and provides guidance on personal maintenance and some additional treatment methods, which include: B. Chinese herbal medicine. The client should lie on his back, front, or side, depending on the location of the needle. Acupuncturists should use sterile disposable needles. The insertion of each needle can cause the patient a very short tingling or numbness. After insertion of the needle, a feeling of dullness sometimes appears on the underside of the needle and disappears. Acupuncture is normally fairly aching less. Other times, after insertion, needles heats up or is electrically roused. The needle lasts from five to thirty minutes.

The amount of treatment required depends solely on the person. An individual with a prolonged disease could be needing treatment one to two times a week for several months. Acute problems usually improve after eight to twelve meetings.

Risks

Nearly all treatments come with threats and advantages.

Potential Acupuncture Threats: This is harmful if the patient has abnormal blood clotting or is taking blood solvents. Blood loss, hurting, and tenderness could happen at the placement. Non-sterilized prickles can contaminate a client. In very intermittent circumstances, the prickle can damage and ruin inner organs. There is a risk of lung collapse in the chest or back. This though happens rarely. "The U.S. Food and Drug Administration" regulates acupuncture prickles as therapeutic expedients. Production and labeling require some principles to be met. The prickles are disinfected, non-toxic and should only be labeled for single use by a certified physician. Same as corresponding treatments, it's recommended that you use them with existing treatments for chronic or serious illnesses.

How to Find a Practitioner

To find a licensed physician, visit the National Council for Acupuncture and Herbal Certification (NCCAOM). In most states, this agency requires a license from practitioners. Individuals are encouraged to enquire from specialists concerning their practice and education. "NCCIH" points out that other cover plans currently cater to acupuncture, but first, it's prudent to inquire if expenses are covered. The cost is from 75 to 95 dollars and a regular visit from 50 to 70 dollars.

Crystal Healing

Crystal treatment is a substitute medical procedure that uses semiprecious "crystals" such as quartz, amethyst, or opal. Proponents of the technology claim that there is no scientific basis for this statement, but it has healing power. On the one hand, the practitioner makes decisions in other parts of the body, often in the chakras. On the contrary, the practitioner makes decisions all over the body to build an energy network that surrounds clients with healing energy. However, studies show that the assertion that chakras or energy tissues do exist has not been confirmed, and there is no evidence that crystalline therapy has a bigger consequence on the physique than supplementary placebo. For this reason, it's deliberated pseudoscience.

Gemstones are considered an object that can help to heal in various cultures. Arizona Hopi Native Americans use quartz crystals for fortune-telling, which also localizes pain or causes illness in the body. Hopi traditionally uses crystals for other types of fortune-tellers, such as prisms, for crystals that direct sunlight to medical pallets, as well as for other forms of consciousness, such as controlling the strength and intensity of crystals. Gemstones are considered an object that can help to heal in various cultures. Arizona Hopi Native Americans use quartz crystals for fortune-telling, which also localizes pain or causes illness in the body. Hopi traditionally uses crystals for other types of fortune-tellers, such as prisms, for crystals that direct sunlight to medical pallets, as well as for other forms of consciousness, such as controlling the strength and intensity of crystals.

In the English-speaking world, crystal healing is associated with new conscious ritual movements, such as the "bourgeois healing activity of the New Era of Perfection." Unlike other forms of complementary and alternative medicine (CAM), participants in crystal therapy see this practice as "individual." I. H. depends on extreme personalization and creative expression. When you start the healing crystal, certain physical characteristics, such as shape, color, and marking, determine the location that can be treated with stones. The list of links is published in plain text. Ironically, practitioners claim that "the solution has no essential characteristics, but the quality is different between the two participants." After choosing stones in accordance with their color or metaphysical characteristics, they are placed on the body.

Scientific Evidence

There is no scientific evidence that decision processing works. This is considered fake science. The success of decision processing is due to the placebo effect. In addition, there is no scientific basis for "blocking" the concept of "chakra," that is, the energy network or a similar term that needs to be justified. It is well known that these are just terms that followers use to convey their practice. The methodical word, energy, is a precise, clearly explained notion that can be easily measured and resembles the concept of esoteric energy used by proponents of fertilization therapy.

 Williams, a French researcher, shepherded research to examine the strength of crystals comparing it to placebo in 1999. Eighty unpaid workers were requested to deliberate on placebo or quartz stones, which are vague from quartz. Numerous partakers said that they felt a characteristic "crystal effect." But whether this decision is genuine or placebo. In 2001, Christopher French, director of the "Department of Anomalistic Psychology Research at the University of London" and a member of Goldsmiths College, discussed a crucial study that went beyond the placebo effect at the annual meeting of the British Psychological Association. "

The healing effect of the decision can also be associated with cognitive distortions (what happens when a believer really wants to practice and sees only those who support this desire). Other veterinary institutions, including the "British Veterinary Association," warn that this method has not been methodically confirmed and that individuals ought to look for veterinary guidance beforehand in exhausting substitute methods, but fertilization treatments are also used on animals.

Qigong

Qigong (/ˈtʃiːˈɡɒŋ/), [1] "qi gong," "chi Kung," or "chi gung" (shortened Chinese: 气功; customary Chinese: 氣功; "pinyin: qìgōng; Wade–Giles: ch'i Kung;" plainly: "life-energy cultivation") is a general method of harmonious pose and drive, inhalation and reflection, used to train well-being, religiousness, and fighting arts. Rooted in Chinese medication, thinking, and fighting arts, qigong is considered the practice of cultivating and balancing qi (pronounced "qi"), traditionally translated as "vital energy" in China and Asia.

Qigong exercises usually include meditation movements, coordination of slow movements, deep rhythmic breathing, and calm mind meditation. In China and around the world, qigong is practiced for relaxation, bodybuilding, preventative drugs, self-medication, substitute medication, reflection, self-development, and martial arts exercise. Scientists inspected pores in terms of various diseases (including high blood pressure, pain, and cancer) and quality of life.

Chi (or qi) is often translated as vital energy and represents the energy that circulates throughout the physique. A further universal meaning is a general liveliness, comprising electromagnetic liveliness, heat, and light; Descriptions frequently include the relationship between gas, matter, breath or air, spirit, and energy. Qi is the most important opinion in customary Chinese medication and fighting arts. "Gong (or

Kung Fu)" is regularly explained as self-development or development of labor, and meanings comprise exercise, skills, abilities, achievements, services, results or achievements and are usually performed in gong Fu (Kung Fu) in the logic of traditionally good achievements. These two words are combined to describe a system that processes and balances vital liveliness, specifically for good shape.

The word "pores," used today, has remained popularized to refer to various Chinese self-improvement movements and to emphasize healing and scientific approaches from the late 1940s to the 1950s. Focusing on spiritual practice, mysticism and elite perfection.

Benefits of Qigong

The pores are managed by "TCM," "CAM," "integrative medication," and some medical professionals. It is considered a "standard medical technique," pores are usually prescribed to treat various conditions, in China. Clinical uses include diabetes, menopause syndrome, chronic liver disease, peptic ulcer disease, hypertension, coronary heart disease, cancer, tumors, myopia, back and leg pain, obesity, insomnia, and cervical spondylosis. External parts of China, qigong can be used as an adjunct to medicines or as an adjunct to traditional methods of treatment, including relaxation, health, restoration, and healing of certain illnesses. Nonetheless, at hand, no qualitative indication that pores are truly operative in this condition. A systematic review of clinical trials suggests that, at the current level of evidence, it is not possible to determine the effectiveness of pores in certain diseases.

Safety and Cost

Porosity is generally considered safe. In clinical trials, side effects were not observed; the pores were considered safe for use in other groups. Minimum costs for self-management and high costs for managing the group. In general, the warnings associated with the stoma are similar to the risk of muscle deformities or strains, sprains to prevent injuries, general safety when used with existing medical procedures, and physical activity in consultation with a doctor. In combination with traditional medicine.

Intuitive Healing

Intuitive Energy Healing is a holistic healing approach that provides practitioners with access to their deep meditation conditions and altered awareness through alpha-theta and delta brainwaves that provide intuitive information about health or life. Practicing clients work with God to help change and change the emotions, beliefs, and energies that contribute to the imbalance. Intuitive energy healing can be used to create physical, emotional, spiritual, or mental healing.

How It Works

Intuitive energy therapists conduct self-meditation for several seconds in a state of delay (a change in the state of perception). In this state of meditation, practitioners may relate to superconscious or sacred thoughts about God, divine sources, etc. This full and complete communication with God allows practitioners to access and provide clients with intuitive or extrasensory reading. By reading this book, you can intuitively accept the physical, mental, emotional, or spiritual factors associated with your client's current problems.

Your faith is the matrix on which all reality is based. Faith is the energy that is the basis for creating your mind, your thoughts generate your emotions, and your emotions cause your actions and actions. Many intuitive approaches to energy healing with only that matrix - "secrets" that instantly change beliefs, can change your life! That is why I call it a "secret" secret.

The Secret Behind

The Secret movie teaches ancient wisdom that satisfies our thoughts and feelings create in our reality. This is true, but there are no elements in this image. I call this element "a secret hidden behind a secret." The answer lies in the material changes that create our thoughts and feelings in the matrix of trust. Your faith supports everything that you think, feel, and do, so the most effective way to start here is to change your behavior or lifestyle. Therefore, persuasion is a way to integrate and coordinate your thoughts and feelings. Intuitive healing is a special tool that can immediately change our faith. Only when we believe in work will we begin to change the source of reality from the source of creation.

Muscle testing and energy testing – Your intuitive doctor uses energy or muscle tests to test limited beliefs. Muscle testing is a simple technique used to effectively test a client's subconscious mind to determine if limited beliefs exist.

Download feelings and programs – Another important part of the intuitive treatment method is downloading certain emotions and programs from the creators. By downloading emotions and programs, you can teach your customers that they have such beliefs and fully accept them. For example, a practitioner may ask God or a source to impose on a client the belief that "I am rich," but if the client does not know what it means to be rich, it is unlikely that faith will last long. This may not work fully. Thus, the client can immediately feel at the cellular level what he is feeling. This will make it easier for customers to accept "new" beliefs at an unconscious level.

The Role of an Intuitive Healing Practitioner— Witnessing

What I like about this technique is that God / Source / Space is the main engine. The practitioner's role is to present the requested or proposed vocation or prayer and then witness the change. Witnessing is an integral part of the realization of healing, but it is God who does the real work. This differs from many other forms, which are highly dependent on the intention to move and manipulate energy as the healer wants. In intuitive treatment, the doctor can approach the highest vibration, unconditional love or god, the universe, the origin of God, etc.

The Seven Elevations of Consciousness

A metaphysical understanding of the structure of reality is seven spheres or seven consciousnesses. In fact, all levels are a manifestation of the same reality, but the concept of seven cats is useful for understanding how intuitive healing works, why it is different from others, and sometimes from others.

12 Strand DNA and DNA Activation

For decades, scientists have believed that only two strands of DNA are useful to us. They could not determine the function or purpose of ten additional strands, so they made the remaining ten strands of unwanted DNA. Now science confirms that this direction can have many goals. For spiritual healers, this junk DNA has a purpose! When 12 strands of DNA are activated, the body is ready for the next stage of evolution on Earth. DNA activation enhances our innate intuitive and mental abilities and helps our body get rid of the many poisons that we face today. Activated DNA can slow down the aging process by activating the so-called chromosomes and vitality. The chromosomes of youth and vitality are real "young glands" found somewhere other than our own DNA.

Clear Negative Energy

Intuitive treatments are effective in removing negative energy and effects on the body and inanimate objects such as houses and buildings. Souls, mental rings, wires, structures, and other energy effects can cause problems in everyday life. Worse, you may not even be aware that these "invisible" energies affect us. Radiation and other environmental islands can be removed from the body in a similar way. The doctor cleans all this by scanning the energy fields. Body Healing and Internal Observation: Medically Intuitive

You can also create physical healing using intuitive energy healing. Doctors observe changes in the body using the same connections as the gods, available through changing conditions of perception. Looking inside the body and communicating with various organ systems, doctors can get an idea and information about what can happen to the physical health of the patient. The term "medically intuitive" is that term. In general, trust comes from physical healing so that our clients are confident that they can accept and maintain a healthy state.

Manifesting Abundance

If you are looking for more abundance in your life, intuitive energy healing is also an amazing tool. The skills of self-expression and abundance in healing theta are very strong, such as financial abundance, finding a spouse, doing the best job. The work of faith and feelings is usually integrated into rich techniques that are easy to learn and apply.

Guardian Angels, Spirit Guides and the Deceased

Intuitive energy healing methods allow you to communicate with your guardian angel, spiritual guide, or a deceased relative. Sometimes, when God sends them as an important part of healing, these creatures automatically appear during the healing session. In spiritual healing, we can always come close to the energy of unconditional love (God, the Holy Spirit, source, etc.) before connecting with the mind of the keeper.

One Path Many Ways to Apply

In general, practitioners intuitively manage what should happen during the session. In general, many clone combinations are used for each session. Each session is completely intuitive, so each session is different. Intuitive energy healing works directly with this creative force, which we understand as creative forces such as God/Universe/Source, so our customers always get the best and best at the moment.

Spiritual Healing

Curing is frequently a combination of intermediations such as bodily, non-medicinal, violent surgery, and cerebral surgery. As soon as we change the source of the illness or overcome and overawed the difficult, we focus on curing. Curing is a full bundle. If you study just 1 component of the disease, then there will be very little recovery. In divine curing, the history of medication is created that consists of healing processes and places of healing. Spiritual recipes for the physique, mind, and soul and begin the path of healing, is created.

The Journey of Spiritual Healing

The path of spiritual healing refers to spiritual, mental, emotional, and physical poisons. Now this tactic, we remove the poison that pollutes the humanity. Then and there it provokes movement from someone and from oneself. You can do both. Soul healing is a combination of healing stages for the physique, mind, and soul. Several of us contemplate an act and then execute other acts. For instance, we contemplate we need to inscribe the present and actually go to the seashore. Otherwise, we have serious requirements, and we are moving physically in different directions. This happens to most of us every day.

Do Your Body Right

Consume Well. "What Does It Mean For Us Now? Is it possible to eat less sugar? Are we still eating fast food? Do you drink enough water?" Discover a little way to mend your eating behaviors. Consume extra root vegetables. Consume extra organic and local foodstuffs.

Practice finding fun, easy-to-integrate exercises in our day-to-day lives is one of the principal encounters that have various facades. Do what you want to dance, walk, surf, jump, swim, do yoga, and do whatever you want!

Take care of your body. Massage or spend your health with friends. Go to your chiropractor or physiotherapist. Find a healing circle that heals the body and responds to complaints that may be active.

Sleep

" Are you getting enough sleep? Do we feel rested?" Get enough rest switch off the television. Yield it overnight and wet the candle.

If our bodies are well taken care of, it usually restores our hearts and minds! Over time, you need to start and build your workouts so that they are easy to maintain and scale. We can always do something for the body!

Purify Your Relationship

"What does it mean to cleanse our hearts, relationships, and personal energy fields? Do you give and receive intimate relationships? Or are you doing your best? Or did you just get this?"

64

Practice love without judgment. When it is right and wrong to compare and judge others constantly, the heart cannot be pure. Find a trainer or help desk consultant to help you make the decision.

Growth Consciousness about, Building and Maintaining your Liveliness. We get exposure to lethal liveliness at workplaces, in interactions, and also from the Internet and television. First of all, reduce the negative liveliness that you get day in day out, now find some good activities that aid in maintaining and building liveliness. Acupuncture, qigong, and light visuals are only a few practices.

Use the Mind for Creative Freedom

"How do we free our hearts and use them to grow and create the life we love?" Exercise reflection. Here are various special ways to meditate in order to keep the mind clean. Here are many types of reflection. Attempt some of them and exercise what attracts your body, mind, and mind the most!

Follow the development of intellectual tasks. Find ways to read, take courses, graduate, and build your mind.

I tell a story. I am my own story. Write and tell your stories. Test your thoughts.

Liberate Your Soul from Ego

"How can we free the soul?" The soul is connected with the body, mind, and mind. They do not fight alone. Therefore, if you find your favorite movement for the body, mind, mind, the soul will be liberated. You will experience more moments when your thoughts are in harmony with the physical feelings and movements of your body.

Where to wake up. Be prepared to strengthen your mystical depth hence that you enclose biting bulk without discomfort, liveliness to attain your dreams and a clear intelligence for decision-making without interruption without hesitation. This will allow your soul to make the life you love!

Daily audits and practices. Make sure your practice is still relevant to your thoughts. "Are you starting to feel like zombies as a result of

65

exercise?" perhaps its stage to crack fresh exercises or expand your training!

Commence the Spiritual Trip

When you practice to keep your body healthy and happy, balance your emotions and energies, and keep your mind clean and clear, sometimes spiritual aspects of illness, anxiety, and disharmony arise. Our powers can benefit from spiritual intervention.

Charge the battery. In shamanistic culture, it must be powerful. Power gives us the opportunity to be the author of our lives (and not the instructions of other individuals). One feature to recondition the authorization of a family, person, or the public is to fix up the way of animal detach.

Remove the improperly installed power source. Near is no competent or regretful liveliness. This is not the place where energy should be, but it should not move. The liveliness rehearses that your request will aid nevertheless if it cannot be ready to lend a hand to access a shaman so that he can carry the energy entering the body.

Remove parts for lost souls. When we experience injuries in life, we leave the country to protect ourselves from injuries. This is called the death of people in the shamanistic culture. Soul extraction is a shamanic way to recover lost souls so that we can recover.

Reunite with your ancestors. Know the mountain. It is important that we stand on the shoulders of others and are rooted in it. Otherwise, we risk being cruel. Relations with our family, friends, and ancestors those who love us are very important in every medical history. Previous ancestral treatment over the past 100 years often helps solve physical problems that they cannot solve.

Bright spiritual healing with light is an intercultural technique of spiritual healing that helps to change the negative and poison around us and around us. If your body, mind, and mind can become more balanced and harmonized over time and remove stones laid in light groups, you will find that you can keep your core strong and energetic.

Walk the life of light, shine brightly, and inspire others to dive deeper into their light.

Often, more than one intervention is required to treat and improve everyday life. This is a fatal way to make a big story for our loved ones and us and lives a consistent and meaningful life.

Magnetic Field Therapy

Magnetic therapy supports overall health by using various types of magnets throughout the body. It may also help in the treatment of certain diseases. At hand are a number of types, counting

Static Magnetic Field Therapy

This way, you affect the membrane with a magnet. You can friction a captivating armlet or other alluring jewelry. This bottle can be a magnetic dressing or the use of a magnet as the sole for shoes. Besides, have a siesta on a unique mattress with a lure.

Electrically Charged Magnetic Therapy (Electromagnetic Therapy)

The magnet used here is electrically charged. Treatment with electromagnetic therapy is usually done with electrical stimulation.

Its Workings

Your physique obviously has an alluring handle and an exciting field. Each molecule contains a minor quality of captivating loveliness. The crucial model of compelling therapy is that sure harms arise due to an imbalance of magnetic fields. It is assumed that if you bring the magnetic field closer to your body, everything will return to square one. Ions, such as potassium and calcium, aids cell mails signals. In the course of the tests, researchers aphorism how magnets convert the exert yourself of ions. But accordingly significantly at hand is no sign that the magnet has the same effect on the cell when it is in the cell.

Uses

Most magnetic therapy is an option for treating various types of pain, including:

- Inflammation ache
- Twisting curing
- Sleeplessness
- Head pains
- Fibromyalgia ache

It's harmless for many individuals to put on a low-intensity motionless magnet, but magnetic therapy is not good at the time of the following:

- Are using a pacer
- Possess an insulin thrust
- Are expectant

All magnets must be removed before an MRI or x-rays. Other individuals receiving self-medication have the following side effects:

- Ache
- Queasiness
- Faintness

These effects are infrequent.

Workability

There is not a lot of self-healing researches. Created people do not have enough data to make a reasonable conclusion. Although some clinical studies have revealed the possibility of self-healing, such as treatment for lower back pain, there is no clear evidence that any disease can be treated.

Polarity Therapy

Polarity Therapy is a comprehensive liveliness-based structure that comprises recommendations for your body, nutrition, exercise, and lifestyle to restore and maintain the body's proper energy flow. The basic conception of polar therapy is that completely the liveliness of the individual amount is based on electromagnetic liveliness and the illness is the result of improper use of energy.

An Australian-American chiropractor, osteoporosis therapist, and alternative physician, Randolph Stone (1888-1981), developed polar therapy integrating East-West principles and treatments. During his stay in India, he learned the olden ideologies of "Ayurvedic philosophy." In search of the basics of individual vitality, he premeditated reflexology and herbal medication. He studied reflexology and herbal medicine.

Stone is dedicated to the principles of Ayurvedic medicine, interpreted in connection with scientific and medical discoveries for the definition of polar therapy. According to an Ayurvedic philosophy based on fixed ideologies known as The Trident, the liveliness of the mortal physique focuses on five organs or areas (large intestines, lungs, small intestines, diaphragm, heart region, and brain). One of the five forms of air or liveliness controls each area: "prana" of the mind, veins of the lungs and heart, diaphragm, small Adana of the small intestine, and pain in the colon. Five rays regulate the movement of all directions of the body; each air indicates its movement. Stone also discovered that cerebral prana ultimately regulates the combined forces of the body. Violations or restrictions of pranic blood flow, thus, affect the well-being of the whole organism. The power of "prana" is facilitated by the stream of air and food into the physique, interaction with additional breathing creatures, and the absorption of the five senses.

He spent a lot of time on detailed and detailed causal relationships between human anatomy and disease, based on the flow of vital energy. He also connected electromagnetic energy to an energy source. The medical symbol is used as a medicine symbol to determine the nature of the flow on the diagram of the human body and to describe in detail the movement of energy. Polar therapy is based on a graphical flow of energy. The basic energy model is determined by the spiral movements that occur in the navel and determines the initial energy flow of the uterus.

Benefits of Polarity Healing

Polarity healing releases and replenishes the stream of vital liveliness and eliminates the disease, restoring the balance of unbalanced energy. The patient learns to relieve stress by controlling stressors and acting accordingly.

This treatment can improve the health and healing of all those who seek a decent lifestyle. It has been reported that polar healing is operative for anybody exposed/unprotected from toxic poison. Similarly, HIV-infected patients may feel comfortable in polar therapy. It is also suitable for:

- Releasing overall tension
- Vertebral ache
- Stomach pains
- Other repeated illnesses and disorders

How It Works

After defining the precise cause of the client's liveliness inequity, the specialist commences running the first session of a sequence of physical work periods aimed at training and relieving the client of incorrect guidance. Therapy, such as massage, is based on energy pressure and includes blood circulation. During treatment, the therapist draws thoughtfulness to the force exerted on every point, even if limb pressure is applied to the anatomical points of each patient. Combining the central scheme or focus of polar therapy, this technique is very soft and unique to polar therapy. To stimulate the energy of the body, it captures subtle strains and skulls. Despite the intense and deep pressure used with massage techniques, polar therapists never come in contact with them.

To help the body, the therapist often prescribes a diet for the disposal and disposal of food waste from patients. The rules of polar healing take into account certain connections amid diverse foodstuffs and mortal liveliness arenas. In the same way, a series of exercises is often determined. This exercise, called Yogin polarity, includes squats, stretching, periodic actions, profound inhalation, and voice manifestation. They could irritate plus soothe. On request, counseling can be provided as part of a very personalized treatment plan to improve stability.

Before starting treatment, each patient has a complete medical history. Such preliminary oral examinations often monopolize the first treatment session. In some situations, the therapist may need to evaluate your body stability over scrutiny and bodily inspection.

Safety

Polar healing is harmless for almost everyone because of the inherent gentleness of massage therapy, including the elderly and the weak.

This therapy involves the release of very emotional liveliness (tears, laughter, or both combined).

Research and Acceptance

It is an adjunctive therapy for holistic spiritual therapy that can be used with a medicinal method. Polar healing is adept globally, but most specialists are located around the US. Present-day researchers use notions related to the simple theory of stone reality to define quantum void (QV) as the basis of all reality. But in 2000, this holistic system did not yet reach the widespread recognition that Stone expected in 1981 before he died.

This is an adjunctive therapy for complex spiritual therapy that can be used with medical approaches. Polar healing is exercised globally, but most specialists are located in the United States. Present-day researchers use notions related to the elementary theory of mountain reality to define quantum leakage (QV) as the basis of all reality. But in 2000, this holistic system was not widely recognized as what Stone hoped for in 1981.

Practitioner

"The American Association for Polarity Therapy (APTA)" permits two stages of education. "Associate Polarity Specialist (APP)" is an initial step grounded on the least stage of knowledge. Registered polar practices (RPPs) are assigned to graduates in a recognized curriculum. Graduate and special education is offered in various fields, and APTA provides certification to practitioners.

Chakra

Chakra translates as "Rad." The seven chakras of the body are other energy centers that begin in the upper part of the head and end in the spine. They regulate every part of the system and affect everything from emotional processing to disease resistance.

In general, the seven chakra meditation techniques focus on opening and aligning the chakra. If they are blocked or not synchronized, they can affect their physical and mental health.

After adjusting the position of the chakra, you can open the chakra and develop an intuition about a blockage. This will help you identify and solve problems that arise before they lead to serious consequences. You can also do what you need to find and remove old wounds. In short, healing can occur through proper knowledge of the chakras.

The chakra system began in India between 1500 and 500 BC. The oldest text of the Veda says: "Reiki's healer and yoga teacher Fern Olivia. The Vedas are the earliest Sanskrit literary record and the oldest Hindu scriptures. What is the purpose of the seven chakras? "Affects the emotional, mental, emotional and spiritual life and all areas of your life," Olivia said. "This chakra contains either prana or the best pure healing energy around us. The study of the location of the chakras (meditation, reiki or yoga) is based on the belief that our energy flows freely and prana can pass through it when the chakra is open and parallel. "

Root Chakra

What It Is

Imagine the root chakra (the first aka chakra) as the base of the house, separate from the body. It maintains and protects everything while it is solid, stable, and working properly. According to Olivia, this is due to the spine, the first three vertebrae, and the pelvic floor and is in charge of the logic of safety and human existence. Consequently, this applies to everything that you use on earth, including basic requirements comprising of security, water, food, and shelter, together with several emotive desires, comprising of a sense of anxiety and security. As we all have knowledge that, you do not need to worry too much when these requirements are met.

When It Is Blocked

Fans say that various diseases can be caused by various reasons, comprising of anxiety conditions, worries, or bad dreams. Bodily, the first chakra is allied with complications of the legs or feet, colon, excretion or vertebral, bladder.

The Sacral Chakra

What Is It

Think of the second chakra as the funniest of the seven. Olivia is said to be above the belly and under the navel and is responsible for our sexual and creative energy. Most convenient if the sacred chakras are aligned with elements of orange and water. It is friendly, vibrant, and successful, and at the same time evokes a feeling of well-being, satiety, pleasure, and pleasure. (Fun!) Keep moving the energy wheel, changing your body, and creatively expressing yourself.

When It Is Blocked

If you are inspired by creativity or experiencing emotional instability, the sacred chakra may not have been adjusted. In addition, this may be due to physical, sexual dysfunction, possibly dread of transformation, misery, or behavioral addiction.

The Solar Plexus Chakra

What Is It

Its name means "shining stone" in Sanskrit. The third chakra (now it should not be confused with the sixth chakra, the "third eye") should be a source of individual power over self-esteem. Or, as Olivia said: "A chakra based on behavior and balance that focuses on individual will, personal strength, and dedication." It is believed that from the navel to the chest, it solves all the problems of metabolism, digestion, and stomach health.

When It Is Blocked

You may be worse. It is difficult for you to make decisions, to have problems with anger or control. Olivia not only feels bad, but also indicates that she can express outward apathy, doubt, or easily be beneficial. Similarly, several types of abdominal pain can occur: Like digestive problems or gas. (UV).

The Heart Chakra

What It Is

The same applies to Chopra, since the mid chakra, this is the number four chakra in the middle of the rib cage, is the site of physical and mental encounters. The body should include the thymus (that plays an important part in the lymphatic and endocrine systems), chest, lungs, and heart. And as the name implies, everything is connected with love. "This is spiritual awareness, forgiveness, and the awakening of service," Olivia said. In terms of green and pink (yes, millennial types of rose quartz), when the heart chakra is balanced and stable, I think affection and love stream easily. "Good vibration is almost contagious," Olivia said.

When It Is Blocked

A closed chakra can give way to unhappiness, fury, possessiveness, a dread of treachery and hatred of oneself and other people, particularly fear of someone or somebody. Causing pain has negative emotions that lead you away from the possibility of love.

Throat Chakra

What It Is

How do you feel? The fifth chakra, which tells the inner truth or allows you to convey the inner truth correctly, can be balanced. The throat chakra controls all communications and, according to Olivia, is the first of three spiritual chakras (in contrast to the appearance of the bottom). Anatomically, the pharynx of the chakra is connected to the parathyroid gland, thyroid gland, mouth, jaw, tongue, larynx, and neck. If there is a positivity in this chakra, you can clearly hear, speak, and express yourself.

When It Is Blocked

Although it's easy to tell the truth, it's hard to pay attention to others, focus on others, or be afraid of punishing other people. Actually, this obstruction could be evident as thyroid problems, aching throat, stiffness in the neck and shoulders, or tension headaches.

The Third Eye Chakra

What Is It

Do not confuse the name. The third eye chakra is actually the number six chakra and is actually positioned amid the eyebrows. Body parts, including the eyes, lower brain, head and pituitary should be controlled by the third eye. And it must be able to control intuition, recognize and use it. In addition, the third eye should be responsible for everything between you and the outside world, acting as a bridge between two images so that you can carve fantasies and dramas to see clear images.

When It Is Blocked

It may be difficult for you to approach intuition, believe in that inward opinion, remember vital particulars, or learn fresh abilities. And when the lower chakras (sacrum, sacrum, solar plexus and AKA heart chakra) go out of balance, this may be the third eye, which looks more condemned, disgusting and closed. Third eye blocking is connected to a variety of problems, comprising of misery, unease, and more judgment. However, he claims to physically cause headaches, dizziness, and various other head condition problems.

The Crown Chakra

What Is It

According to the Chopra Center, this place, known in Sanskrit as the Sahasvara chakra or the Thousand Petals chakra, is the center of our higher self, others, and, finally, with God, enlightenment and spiritual connection. Just like the title proposes, it is the chakra number seven and is positioned on the peak of the head. Transformations that occur internally during synchronization are called pure recognition, recognition, non-separation, and extension lines. Mostly more than you and part of the universe.

When It Is Blocked

Blocking the crown chakra allows you to feel isolation or emotional pain—the main feeling that everything and everyone excludes. Or you feel like a normal self, but you are spiritually connected, and not in a state of sublime enlightenment. This is very nice and ordinary. Contrary to the other chakras, it usually completely opens with specific yoga exercises, meditation exercises, or a specific time. This is not a specific method that can be applied at any time. However, through daily practice, you can taste it through meditation, prayer, moments of silence and thanksgiving, and even spiritual relationships.

How to Unlock Chakra

There are several methods you can use to learn how to unlock chakras. Your energy path is not only clean, but your balance and harmony are restored. It also offers all the benefits of an open and flowing vitality.

Mantra

Short repetitions of mantras are often used as the beginning and end of yoga practice. Mantras are also practiced in various prayer ceremonies in monasteries and individual religious practices. The sounds of spells vibrate in the chest, lower abdomen, or neck in the form of healing sounds, creating an energy model that turns the energy field back into health.

According to the Chopra Center, if you use Mala, there are usually several repetitions of your order if you need to repeat the order. Hold the hammer in one hand to calculate how many times the spell is repeated.

Select a Mantra

Select the order or series of orders that you want to sing. Using mantras during meditation can draw attention to random thoughts. In the Vedic tradition, practitioners use bija mantras to cleanse and balance the chakras. Each mantra is a separate syllable corresponding to a particular chakra. When you sing, open each syllable and focus on the erased chakra and feel the mantra that the chakra sings.

Root - LAM (pronounced lahm)

Sacral - VAM (pronounced vahm)

Solar Plexus - RAM (pronounced rahm)

Heart - YAM (pronounced yahm)

Throat - HAM (pronounced hahm)

Third eye - OM (pronounced ohm or Aum)

Crown - silence

You can also use vocals to erase the chakras. Expand each vocal to make it a song.

"Root chakra" - "Uh" like duh

"Sacral chakra" - "Oo" like you

"Solar plexus chakra" - "Oh" like go

"Heart chakra" - "Ah" like craw

"Throat chakra" - "Eye" like cry

"Third eye chakra" - "Ay" like say

"Crown chakra" - "Eee" like bee

How to Use Mantra When Meditating

Choose a quiet place to the side. Choose a warm place where the rhythm of the body slows down, and body temperature can drop. Sit on the floor or cross your legs to meditate. Take three deep breaths to relax. Keep calm and talk about your intention to meditate, for example, step on the chakra or keep it in balance. Keep your hands on your hips or extended. If you use a rosary, hold each hand and repeat each ball to count each ball. Repeat your order in 9 groups. Breathe naturally, but be careful with breathing. Focus on vocals and visualize chakra of repeated spells. Finish your meditation by repeating scabies or other favorite songs.

Tapping

Eavesdropping or Emotional Freedom Technique (EFT) technology is best described by Nick and Jessica Ortner, one of the founders of the Tapping Solution Foundation. A prerequisite is the repeated touch of the fingertip at a certain point on the meridian. When you listen, repeat the words of gratitude and accept the emotions associated with the memory. Such feelings can affect the chakras and energy systems throughout the body.

Tapping Chakra Points

Amy B. Sher, one of the most important psychic, physical, and spiritual healers, explains that EFT can be used to open chakras. Time (see Chakra Image above for chakra points). Launch the crown chakra and continue to touch it nine times to the roots. Combine the bit with the order above if desired.

Reiki

Reiki Master works with symbolic and manual positions to deliver Reiki energy. After the necessary preparation and attention of the Reiki Master, the doctor may order reiki to open the blocked center of the chakra and release a stream of energy. You can also take advantage of Reiki processing using remote Reiki processing technology. If you are familiar with reiki, try activating the chakra by touching each energy center for three to five minutes. Or visit a Reiki specialist and ask him to focus on cleansing the chakra.

How Reiki Unlocks

Reiki energy is literally like a burst of high energy that moves and is removed through the chakra. According to the Reiki International Education Center, the introduction of reiki, a positive energy field, raises and removes negative blocking vibrations. This negative energy cannot support negative vibration levels and degrades performance.

Yoga

Yoga can open the chakra, stimulating this energy center, manipulating the several portions of the physique associated with the chakra, through the movement of the yoga pose. For example, there are five yoga chakra poses that you can practice to unlock a locked energy center.

Blocked Chakra

A blocked chakra does not stop spinning. It can also be burned like flesh. The chakra can restore natural torque instead of turning it off.

None of these answers are healthy or desirable. Each of these conditions negatively affects you, because the chakra is the door to the vital energy flowing through your body.

Learning How to Unblock A Chakra

There are many methods that you can use to unlock the chakras. Try a few methods to discover the technology that does it well in you, and practice it regularly to keep your energy center open and increase your energy flow.

Chapter 3

More About Energy Healing

Benefits of Energy Healing

One of the most common remuneration of liveliness curing is relaxation and stress cut; this triggers the physiques effortless remedial abilities and maintains and improves well-being. Liveliness curing is a native therapy that balances the physiques life-force gently and bring as well-being and health to the recipient.

The remedial of the liveliness coldness is conceded out manually the surge of liveliness to the client is possible by an energy healer. This is a very strong, but gentle energy sent intentionally. When the life stream stops, weakens, or is blocked, emotional or health problems can occur. In many situations, such as emotional or physical trauma, trauma, anxiety, anxiety, suspicion, anger, anxiety, negative self-talk, addiction, malnutrition, emotional or physical trauma, including a devastating lifestyle, trauma, negative thoughts and feelings. And the lack of relationships, neglect and love of other individuals and yourself because of sentiments that are not articulated in a fit method.

Healing liveliness can sound somewhat depressing. Sometimes people ask: "But what can cause healing with energy?" The benefits of healing energy can be at some stage: physical, spiritual, mental, emotional or vital. It could be theatrical, but regularly refined. They could occur instantly, but come in the future when a curing period is going.

Regularly, "results" arise at a stage that provides the greatest benefit. The main advantage of a healing session (or healing session) can be, for example, an understanding or change in attitude that leads to behavioral changes that continuously improve emotional health, physical health and / or value of lifetime.

Thanks to the personal experience of donors and recipients of energy, healing energy can benefit from:

Better Stress Management

What if you tend not only to cope well with stressful situations, but also to wear them? Stress does not arise in such a situation, but in how it is dealt with. And the way you deal with situations often depends more on the unresolved feelings that they aroused in the past. Past situations where someone feels useless, helpless, shy or unloved can destroy cellular memory. All trauma is not inherent to you, but to those who color the entire future experience. Energy therapy can dissolve cellular memory to increase your ability to think clearly and find solutions that no longer experience past situations. Stephanie solves this problem through a series of Reiki sessions. When they first met, he was so excited that he asked until his lips were growing. But after many sessions, he played without chewing his lips.

It's better not to take full advantage of this situation, because it releases old energy. Remember that you attract only external experiences that correspond to your inner self.

Better Self-care

The more energy you get, the more you take care of it. As the best energy flows through you, you will feel better. Andronicus experienced this on himself. The Reiki phase focused on it also provides for other practitioners (note: it is important for therapists to continue to receive support). Diet. Finally, he decided to get rid of refined sugar and as a result lost 40 kilograms.

Better Relationships

Regardless of whether we know it or not, our interpretation of what others say or do is based on the past. In general, an experience for one of my favorite childhood years. For example, as we know, my boss is very similar to the mother of my client, so I have a client who cannot compare with my boss. Each time my boss speaks critically, my client returns to feelings of child abuse from an unstable mother. The only way to improve my boss's relationship with my client is to solve my mother's old trauma.

Better Creativity and Productivity

True creation does not come from our mind. Our mind is a tool for influencing divine inspiration, interpretation and understanding. To be creative, you must believe that you deserve to be connected with God. You must believe that you are capable. You should not be attached to what other people think of you. You should think that you have all the support and resources needed to complete the production. Even if others are looking for time and attention to their goals, you should think of it as important enough to devote time and attention to them.

Emotional memories that cannot judge or judge your creation can interfere with all these needs. Disabling this cellular memory will allow renewing this channel for energy treatment, making it more creative and successfully completing the project.

Better Intuition

The same channel that stimulates creativity also contributes to intuition. If you want to speak with an angel, an ascended teacher, a deceased relative, or the source of God, you must believe that you are worthy and capable. No matter what you do, in the eyes of God or in "affirmation," you also must not limit your faith. Everything that causes healing energy provides creativity and intuition.

Better Ease and Happiness

These benefits combine, but happiness is the norm. Laugh more and laugh more. Your views and expectations are more positive. They expect something to happen to you easily. The betrayal of the universe is the betrayal of the universe. Because I understand and believe how the universe works, and I feel happy and calm when the universe does it.

If you exceed this threshold, you no longer have to worry about returning to your old ways. And it doesn't take long to get there! It took several years, but since energy flows faster, I realized that my clients who have been in therapy older than 6 months are a lot happier and at ease. And I also learned to support those who are not yet in this state.

Better Real Life Magic and Manifestation

The law of attraction is written beyond the threshold of happiness without this confusion; it reacts with happier things. Impulse develops and experiences more and more motivation. You better know it and use it. Your life begins to feel magic.

This is how life can be for you. Perhaps the short-term benefits of steps 1-6 will feel busy right now, but it won't take long to start seeing the eight signs of miracles in life until you reach standard seven of new happiness. If you continue to use it, this result is guaranteed because it is the desired result, simple, synchronous and truly magical.

- Natural relief or reduction of pain (or especially chronic pain relief, pain-related changes)
- It's easier to deal with stressful situations.
- It improves the health of the immune system - it is more resistant to diseases and recovers faster than from diseases and injuries.
- Healing energy also provides the extra energy needed to recover from illness.
- Bigger brains of emotional wellness absorbed feel of serenity and calm
- Emotional let loose and curative
- Enhanced mental clarity free of blocked energy Chakra healing, balancing, and payment
- Balancing of energy
- relief of deep, persistent muscle tension
- relief of nervousness
- relief from and better resistance to frequent mild depression education

- enhanced creativity, creative production, and badly behaved solving enhanced
- public insight accelerated personality increase and/or spiritual evolution
- emotional make public and curing enhanced mental clarity

Energy Remedial

Since energy therapy is indeed an additional cure, it could also be cast-off as an additional treatment. This supplements and improves the upkeep that patients receive in hospitals or some medical facilities.

Healing energy supplements western and eastern medication, and everyone could advantage. It's good for the well-being of females (including expectant women), males and kids, it is good for faunas (horses, dogs, and cats), water, plants, etc.

Healing Energy is an instrument that helps you relieve stress, relieve pain and quickly receive energy anytime, anywhere.

If we are calm and not stressed, we can restore natural healing abilities. If a person is healthy, regular treatment of hernias increases the body's defenses. This is manifested in harmony with external trust when working with everyday events. Man shows a positive attitude towards life.

Facts That Can Get Rid of Confusion and Misunderstanding Regarding Healing Energy

Healing Energy is Grounded on Scientific Philosophies

In high school we learnt physics, and everyone learns that matter comprises of particles. Some solid objects, including lumps, always vibrate. As humans, we also vibrate. When someone says that they have "good vibrations," they are speaking about the energy vibration of that person, that is, a happy person who shakes at higher frequencies. You can feel the spirit! There is also vibration in the seat. When you enter the room you just met, you can feel a strong energy and leave immediately. On the beach, light is through salty (an ordinary energy purifier) and poignant air. Beach air vibrates at higher frequencies.

Cultures Have Premeditated the Physique's Energy Hubs For Decades

Reiki is a custom of curing Japanese energy that began at the beginning of the 20th century. The Chakra, the center of the s7 energy transfers of the physique, is depicted in olden Hindu manuscripts. The body's liveliness path, the Meridian, is a roadmap for practitioners of traditional Chinese medicine to create acupuncture. In other ancient cultures, various forms were used to stimulate the body's natural healing abilities, but everyone regarded interior liveliness as a good energy.

You Don't Partake of to be Spiritual to Profit from Energy Remedial

Right like you don't hardship to realize the bylaw of gravity before falling, you don't basic to altogether appreciate the perception of full of life curative before being absorbed. For maximum benefit, it is advisable to enter with an open mind. It is always a bright idea to go to a liveliness therapist. If you've got stress, anxiety, or physical fatigue, healing energy sessions could aid you to be at ease and have an impression of stability. If you have a good feeling already, you can at all times get a bit improved! It should be noted that healing energy is an additional method that should not exclude affordable Western medicines.

Healing Energy Is Absolutely Available

Many are types of liveliness therapy devices that you could get anywhere. There are Reiki specialists in the globe, and the attractiveness of caring for Reiki is that they could give and receive, regardless of if they are in the similar room or not. Why? The supremacy of intent permits energy to stream to where desirable.

Acupuncture is easily available, but the client should be in front of the needle. This form arouses the stream of qi to balance the physique.

Another way to stimulate the meridian is through reflexology, tissues and structures through the parts of the legs, arms and ear, release blocked energy and promote healing.

Even massage is a method of energy healing, because it can relieve muscle tension, increase lymph flow and relax deeply.

If you are not familiar with this practice, contact a well-known specialist. Ask your yoga studio or friend for alternative medicine. Start a short 30-minute Reiki session and you will feel how powerful the healing energy is.

Your Energetic Health Can Be Maintained at Home

Like you take a bath every day and get your teeth brushed, cleaning energy should work every day. After visiting an energy therapist, if you begin to feel that your weight is returning back to your body, take a bath for 20 minutes with Epsom salt or pink Himalayan salt to allow vibration to flow. Staining or burning the sage's surrounding car will also remove any negative energy. High-quality crystal has its particular curative possessions and could enhance the liveliness arena. To start your energy healing journey all you require is inquisitiveness and a desire to study. How do you can break!

Reasons to Try Energy Healing

This reminds you that you are programmed to develop in any country where you grew up in divorce, harassment or insecurity. But first you need to erase all the "dirty" energy accumulated in your body. Every thought, action or action that you take is printed on the field of energy or aura. You blush and squeeze negative thinking, making this energy closer to your body. This thinking creates nerve trails in the head. This is also manifested by emotional, mental or physical pain.

What then if you can get rid of network problems? What if you could focus on more positive thoughts and reveal who you are? Energy therapy can remove "dirt" from the energy field. You can develop anyone before you! Here are 5 ways to use healing energy.

It dispels tension and strain to permit profound easing.

Stress is felt not only in the head, but throughout the body. EFT (Emotional Freedom) or printing technology is an effective way of persuading. By stimulating the meridian of a chiropractor, we say that the brain is safe to rest.

It reliefs liveliness obstructions so that you have an impression of energetic lightness and happiness.

The entirety universe, containing humans, is trembling. We vibrate beams of vigor. A liveliness therapist will aid you get stationary and stagnant liveliness. Make your life wider and happier in just one session. In most cases, you may not be aware that you are carrying less energy until it is gone.

The ability of the body to naturally heal is accelerated and escalates vigor.

Healing energy is in addition to customary medicinal practice shouldn't be used to exclude homeopathic medicines. Unilateral energy therapy can help with universal energy tubes. The energy therapist opens in such a way that energizes the client's body. It is believed that this energy activates your own healing system.

Clears mental thought and negative emotional patterns.

Unsaid feelings could enter the physique matter. Experiencing what occurred during the past and worrying about the forthcoming makes the yogi call "chitta vrit" or speak monkeys in the mind. If this conversation doesn't take a lot of time to ruminate or quiet your thoughts, then blockages arise. Like this lump with a small dam on a vibrant river. When energy cannot efficiently stream over this zone, you usually have an impression that you're stuck and wonder if you can completely eliminate such thoughts and feelings.

Helps with prolonged health problems, ache relieving and acute injuries.

The normal form of the body is well-being and vitality. He identifies the cure automatically. This extraordinary mind works regardless of your mind. The light of the body often shows what we must do, and still must learn. When energy gets to the point of attention, it's a prevailing strength. Healing energy stimulates and activates the physique's normal healing powers. Vertebral ache could be a bodily expression of anxiety associated with endurance problems. Dissipating the chakras and kidneys from this block could be very helpful over time.

How It Works

Traditional energy healing falls into the category of cycle / intuitive magic. This is one of the simplest forms of magic training, and we all do it instinctively.

Black Magic

The word "black" means that black objects absorb energy and produce energy in the same way. The word "white" means that energy is released just as the sun emits light. To heal, give and receive someone technically always working together is black and white.

Magic can be used to steal human energy, but this is not a tool flaw, as you can use a knife to cut vegetables or threaten people. Since the sword itself is bad, man has no intention of having it. Black magic can be used to protect people undergoing surgery from attacks, etc., as described in previous articles on martial magic.

For further healing, you will need black magic (man) on the dark side to trigger a higher energy field to get rid of parasites and implants, which will be explained later in this article. This is enough for other forms of magic. The rest of this article will focus on healing energy.

Basics of Energy Healing

To cure energy, do this with appropriate symbolic measures. This is a fantastic way to say that you need to do something, touch someone or think about your intentions. Symbolic actions cannot be anything else, they can run away with the intention of healing someone, but they can distract. Therefore, a symbolic action must be something that can maintain focus while maintaining focus. You tried too much. It should flow naturally.

The standard for good doctors is what really matters to them. If this is really important to you, and you can feel the love of strangers, then you are a good doctor. If not, then only care about close friends and family. You can be a good doctor if you want. There is no problem. Not everyone needs to be a healer. Each has its own role. It will be a boring world where everyone is the same. Positive / beloved thoughts / warnings will give the person healing energy. That is why we are all regularly treated. But with more direct intentions and concentration, he becomes stronger.

Attunement/Initiation

It should not be cured or started in any way. However, there may be advantages and disadvantages. All treatments are effective and heal all energy. The difference is in technique or frame. A wireframe is a set of beliefs, structures, and skills.

The study of certain treatment methods has the advantage of providing access to the beliefs, structures and fundamentals of this method. For example, in Reiki, you will believe that you will be treated simultaneously with the character (we will look at the character later) and the recipient. It gives you a head. But the disadvantage is that it also limits the scope. It's like a martial arts study. All are good, but mixed martial arts are better because they have more choices. And over time, everyone develops a style that suits them.

In particular, relationships and initiations are a kind of energy transfer in which the teacher unknowingly shares his healing skills with you. These skills are inherent in the goal of completing consciousness. Honestly, whatever the consciousness itself, actual actions and part of consciousness symbolize the transfer and receipt of technologies invested in common energy. But you do not need it, you can practice and come.

How It Works

Any action is a ritual. The action symbolizes the amount of energy (time is energy, movement is energy, emotion is energy) that you are putting into the intention. It also symbolizes/proves that you actually mean it — if you say that you're healing someone but you don't dare to put your hands close to them then you obviously don't dare to enter their energy field, so it's not going work. For example, it's easy for most people to say "I love you," but to buy flowers you need to go out and bring flowers. The action symbolizes the amount of energy that you give to others.

Hand signals also have a value that already exists. Both exist materially and immaterially, like words. The word "table" has a real meaning that already exists, but you can agree to use the new word with your friends, and it works if everyone agrees. You can also decide with your friends that the word "table" now means "chair" and works if everyone agrees. The laying on of hands may mean, for example, "stop." Hand digging carelessly. Culturally, we agree. It functions perfectly as a ritual, because it miraculously shakes hands and knows what it means, as if committing something similar to a secret and a secret.

The longer and harder the mind, the better. However, this applies only to the moment when the amount of physical time and energy invested in the consciousness coincides with the amount of energy, according to the intention of people that the continuation of consciousness is ineffective, which makes people feel uncomfortable. People are worried that people are beginning to suspect that they are doing more than you say.

Physical Presence and Remote Healing

To treat someone, you need some kind of connection. A physical being is a relationship similar to a relationship with this person. This means that you can treat someone you don't know when you are physically, only someone who is far away from you. To relate to someone you need to find spiritually, you need to think about whether you know what WhatsApp is (the Internet is basically a copy of the spiritual world, so the same rules apply). With them, wherever they are (if any). To get WhatsApp for this person, you need to interact with him to share something like a conversation. Therefore, you should not randomly treat people whom you have never touched. However, you can treat any people who have just made Skype calls within 5 minutes.

Some people can find people spiritually and can communicate with the people they hear without speaking directly. You can do this the same way you can search for someone on the Internet or request a number without actually meeting. But this is not the most useful technique. Because, if you have the best intentions, there is no reason for this - you are advised to obtain their permission. Put your hands on your hands when treating someone who is present in the body. Energy comes mainly from the hands. This is because energy helps flow directly to them. You may feel more energy flowing, but in reality, you feel resistance. The feeling of energy flow is resistance. If there is no resistance, it simply flows, without actually feeling how the energy flows. Therefore, do not try to feel the energy, believe in the flow.

Remote treatment is less effective than hand treatment. Sometimes this is better, because, according to the subconscious and your instructions, you do not choose where the energy flows, but leave it where it is most needed. But hand care can be more fun because it is more realistic! Both work similarly to each other.

They Need a Pickup

The other person has to accept your healing. Unless the person is unusually (and probably dangerously) open, you won't be able to remotely heal them unless they know and have accepted that you are doing it right now. You can also do it forwards or backwards in time, but again they need to have agreed to it, and it's confusing to arrange to heal someone at a different time.

This is a one-way street. You cannot consciously or unconsciously relate to a person who does not want to be treated or work (for example, contrary to reflective beliefs). This means that you can do this if you want to be very strong and aggressive, but never more useful. As long as you seek revenge and revenge for your attempts to attack your own energy, you are likely to have a mental struggle with a person. The fact that someone lets you touch to heal a physical being is at least accepted. But you can still take care of parts of the body, especially the wound that needs the most treatment. Therefore, trust is very important. If someone does not trust you, it is a waste of time and time. Typically, a stream of soft energy is used to treat non-invasive energy. When the wall is up, nothing flows.

Where Does the Energy Come From?

This is the most misunderstood part of energy healing. There are other comments. Some people think that energy comes from outer space and is sent by doctors (Reiki teaches this), while others believe that doctors use their own energy. Both are true. That's right, you use energy, but practically you can produce an infinite amount of energy. They are similar to factories that produce energy and are very efficient, so production costs are low. You can do this as soon as possible, which makes it virtually unlimited for practical purposes. The energy of each person is different, so each doctor has his own energy.

This only applies to the extent that you want to give what you have. Unfortunately, many people who have no experience of healing with energy try to provide the energy that they value most, but they have no energy! They do this automatically because they automatically accept that they need the same energy as others, and they don't like their language or they're used to smelling their own energy, which they don't feel. Therefore, you need to think that you really do not feel and have your infinite power - you feel it, just get used to it. And when you start to get tired, you may feel lost or dead! This is enough to feel healthy.

You do not have much energy that you do not have! You must! People who try to supply energy very quickly lose energy after treatment (give what they do not need) and feel weak. I believe that this interpretation of truth is closer than at least the transfer or use of your energy beliefs. Because he seems to have a unique energy, but in limited cases all the soloists are not so unique and true. You have infinitely large amounts, people who follow my advice and do not try to give away the energy that they value most, can no longer tolerate it.

To do this, you think that you have energy and want to give yourself what you have. This works if you make this intention only once, and then take a break from treatment with or without an attempt. If you set this goal in several sessions in a row, it is set unknowingly, so you don't need to think about it anymore. It is also very useful for this. Provide what you already have as a general rule of life.

How Does the Healing Really Work?

Your energy is your story. You are here (because you were born in accordance with these instructions), where you are now, including how your ancestors came. There have been millions of years of problem solving and adaptive growth. Therefore, energy includes solutions to all the problems that you overcome. If sick, the immune system disappears. After the fight, you now have disease resistance or immunity. Why? Because the immune system has learned a strategy to defeat the disease. The word "strategy" sounds very formal and courageous, but a real strategy is not a set of rules.

To get to the beach from my villa, go left, right, right, right (this is the rule). I did this, but I had to avoid the dog sitting on the road and waiting for traffic jams, etc. The whole story goes from A to B and contains the rules and events that need to be adjusted. If you close your eyes and try to follow Google Maps, you won't have to go there if you overcome obstacles in all directions. This metaphor is exactly how energy healing works. Your energy tells the story of how you deal with the same problem. They teach how to unconsciously overcome their problems.

Of course, this only works if you have solved the problem yourself. Everyone has their own experience, so everyone has something to offer, but it really works if the trustee solves the problem. This is why other therapists are attracted to other people. Sometimes your energy has a big impact on one person and another. They just give you energy for everything your body wants. Sometimes this person needs it because he has found a way to solve the problem. They have no energy to do this. But if they do not understand and do not understand, this will only help temporarily. It will not last long. You feel better for a short time and then return to normal after using the excess energy you just received. In other words, you do not need to search and spend the way to solve the problem with the help of energy.

Therefore, the doctor can greatly help. If you are looking for a cure, it is best to visit many different therapists, as everyone can offer different pieces of the puzzle. More precisely, your energy is not only your energy, but also your story, but you can ignore it. Use it as a story and energy. They melt it and turn it into their own energy if they want. Love food.

Healing Hurts

The pain is painless, healing, pain. If you get injured, pain behind the wound. You are drunk, not sick. I know that something is missing, not theft, and now I need to solve it. Therefore, people avoid healing because healing is painful.

If you are a doctor, some people will be brought to you. These are people who need your energy and who want to be healthy. Some people do not have an opinion in any case, they are people with problems, and you cannot help. Good. You can still be friends. And some people are actively hostile for no apparent reason. These are people who can be treated, but they cannot resist pain. When they are near you, they feel pain and blame you for what you can avoid. I have no idea to help them.)

95

What You Get in Exchange

When you relate to someone, you also receive energy, especially energy from them. This is good because they have their own infinite energy. This is a one-way street. Maybe their energy is very useful for you or not needed. Do not try to stop their energy from reaching you. Otherwise, your energy will stop them at the same time.

Therefore, Reiki says that he will heal the person he healed. Reiki says that you are healed because energy passes through you. I think that there is an element in the sense of resuming supplies by accumulating energy reserves and getting fresh energy from the surrounding energy. But in most cases, it is believed that the energy received comes from others. This is because mood changes after treating others.

Receiving Negative Energy from Others

I heard that some people get negative energy from those who are trying to cure. This did not happen to me, and this is because I could not believe what was said, that I did not accept it.

You should not be ready to accept negative energy from others. But if you are afraid not to get negative energy, you need to open it yourself. Fear of something is a strange masochistic way of encouraging desire, or at least that. They usually understand what you are afraid of, or rather understand what you are focusing on (positive or negative). I think the best advice is the best advice when you think you are devouring negative energy from someone or not treat her, or face this fear. If you are afraid of it, it will happen, face it or avoid it.

Some people perform a cleansing ritual after healing to "eliminate" negative energy after healing. This is good, but the idea of not using this energy seems to work well.

Symbols

The symbol is clear. The use of symbols in Reiki is less common under other conditions. In essence, a symbol is similar to a word, a form that is associated with a more complex intention / meaning, so you can only suggest or draw a predetermined symbol for this purpose so that you can offer all the intentions. Display. In the same way, I can say "table" and you will understand what I mean without explaining how it looks. Words contain meaning.

You do not need symbols, but they can be very useful. This is a matter of personal preference. The advantage of getting a predefined character in your form is that you get it with your natural intentions. You intend to accept the intent associated with the symbol and act as you think when you use the symbol. Here's how it works. Once again, this is another starter suitable for beginners. But there is no reason to create your own symbol with the intentions that you have set, or to follow the flow and express intuitive intentions that the energy will do everything possible for the healed person. Different approaches work best for different personalities, so it's up to you.

Intermediate Level

Now get your intermediate care first. Experience in improving treatment has shown the following:

Breath work

Deep, regular breathing is real. This allows most of the energy to come from breathing, which allows you to produce energy faster and more efficiently. Breathing is an area in which this technique has a certain effect that is actually useful for its purpose. Breathing improves healing. Never seen an episode that didn't help.

Grounding

Grounding, that is, breathing is especially good when the feet touch the ground. Feel how the energy rises through the earth, inhale, and flow from you into the fire.

Attention to Energy Flow

Passive attention to the flow of energy and / or the energy field works well. When you say that it is a passive intention, you do not need to try it or try to feel it, but knowing that you feel it, it will become smoother when the feeling becomes more realistic than you. This passive, convenient and pleasant attention is the key to a good flow of energy. Secondly, the best way to wander around the mind. Gives worse energy

You can practice self-healing simply by feeling the energy of your fingers, hands, or other parts of the body (or everything else). Passive attention to this part of the body becomes more sensitive and delicate, allowing more energy to flow into this area. After a little practice, you can fill every part of your body with energy.

Love and Intuition

If you evoke a feeling of love or another feeling suitable for this person, the healing effect will increase. Do not force it anymore. Do not worry if this does not come to you naturally. You will already be on the right track. The feelings that people call love are not the same for everyone. This is a comprehensive term that means that although most people do not change their lives, this person considers it important. With a little practice and empathy, you can intuitively see what this person usually needs. Do not leave it alone.

Looping Through the Rainbow

I read it in a book and tried it, and it actually works well. Tracking rainbow colors and representing each color seems to improve the healing effect. Since all colors are associated with energy, and all colors are associated with different chakras, I think you should consider everything that you want to get the full energy spectrum. I usually have bright red, bright orange, bright yellow, herbal green, sky blue, navy blue, purple, dark purple, honey, silver, gold and white.

Structures, Clouds, Bandages

You can do your best. Follow people and try to create a slow energy cloud. They are trying to end medical associations and more. Everything seems to work, and sometimes it's fun to end the session with one or more of these things, giving people extra healing. Of course, not everyone likes structure, so make sure you feel that you fit your style. Technically, he entered into a spell. Design, but based on structural magic (man), non-intuitive magic (woman), but good.

Masculine and Feminine Energies

When recovering, use a combination of gender and gender, like all of us. But in general, men have a lot of masculine energy, women have a lot of feminine energy, and in general there is more energy than a small difference. In fact, you need both for a better treatment session. For example, male energy is much more aggressive. Like a knife or needle that removes problematic energy that leads directly to the wound and causes clogging. The energy of a woman is much more healing, including contributing to the growth and healing of energy wounds.

Too much masculine energy can solve the problem, and then an open wound can damage the aura. This will only cause other problems and prevent the rooting of negative energy. Using too much female energy often helps transfer and restore the body's energy for healing, as it often fails to reach the root of the problem and usually requires the body to do this on its own. It is an absolute miracle that men and women treat the same person at the same time. But by practicing and experiencing, you can develop more different free energies. I found that the left hand facilitates the supply of energy to women, and the right - to men. Who knows! Has the meaning.

Advanced

We are entering this area now. Everything that I have said so far works on the first level of each aura, and even if it bleeds on a different level, it can directly affect other levels. Our bodies are based on the first level and form. It is a physical and tangible form. The next step is a general energy-based atmosphere, such as a cloud of soft energy in which you usually work. But the level continues, switching between form and energy aura. The next level is another level, based on the form, where you can visually (with your inner vision) see the structure or model that the body is trying to match. At this level, you can see the blocks, parasites and implants that cause the aura to interfere with the body. These objects actually exist physically at this energy level.

Cleaning the energy field is often temporary, because at the level of aura 2 there are blocks, parasites or implants. However, without

99

eliminating the cause, it eliminates and heals the effect of Level 1 aura. Now I know that the belief is widespread that all the underlying causes are based on feelings or beliefs. But emotions and beliefs are physical structures in a higher level mood! They actually exist in the form of higher frequencies. This is the same as the idea that it really exists as reality in this world, but at a higher level. If you know at this level that you can work through intentions and practices, you can do this level yourself.

Implants, Bids and Gags

Implants are metal-like structures. I. They are tough and do not move. I think they were posted by my other people or ghosts, but usually by others. Implants are usually in the form of rolls, needles or chips. I saw a cage full of heads and full belts. In fact, everything that you can think of at the physical level can be passionately introduced into the level 2 aura. Because both levels and some follow the same physical laws.

There are also fabric or leather covers that others can wear. For example, there are contraindications to limbs, such as giraffes in the mouth or throat, so that no one can say anything. The victim is often unable to speak due to such a mistake. These things are determined by the evil intentions of others. As a healing, you don't need to know what you are doing, but you are still doing a certain thing ... to deliver it to people, they don't need to know what they are doing, you are unconscious. This does not mean that you did not do this on purpose. This happens intentionally and unconsciously when something in your subconscious mind is unconsciously more honest with your true intentions (good and bad) than with your conscious / famous self.

This sturdy construction is easy to remove because it does not fight. They just work. To delete, if you are at this physical level, you must delete it in the same way. The second level of aura, in one form, is more sensitive to imagination than this physical level. People use these implants with their imagination, so you can imagine how to get rid of them here. For example, you can imagine and cut yourself with a saw blade. But be careful not to offend anyone. Sometimes they can be reduced only by reduction. Sometimes screws and screws hurt a person, which allows him to rotate sensitively. You should be able to see how to install it, and you can download it in the same way

When you imagine that you are interacting with a second-level aura, you do not need to exaggerate your imagination, imagining that what you do does not bring success. This should actually work. This is another way to present something. This is close to imagination, but you cannot imagine it. When you hit something, it's not just an imagination that it moves, it must move by itself. Another word is required to interact with Level 2 Aura. In the end you will practice. Caution - you are in a strange body! The needle is easily removed, cut into small pieces and carefully removed. Rolls are quite complex, and sometimes they need to be cut into small pieces to remove them without damaging the human body. Apparently, they later recovered and connected.

A chip is fun because it is like a sophisticated technical implant. In fact, I did not believe in it until I saw it myself, and then I didn't understand that another doctor saw it. But relatively easy to remove. They seem to emit unhealthy frequencies that interfere with the mind and body of people.

Parasites

Evil! This evil. They exist as a group of animals at this level, and parasites also exist at this level. They usually sit in energy centers, chakras, consume this energy or sit along the spine. They often find the necessary chips and parasites. I think this is because the parasitic frequency of the chip can attract the parasite or weaken the surrounding body, causing the parasite to take root. What I see is a millipede, very small spiky legs, similar to a head with teeth. In addition, people grow everywhere with paths such as octopus or tree roots.

What I see is a millipede, very small spiky legs, similar to a head with teeth. In addition, people grow everywhere with paths such as octopus or tree roots. If you have sharp legs, you cannot easily remove them. It is easier if you can work with others. When you remove a parasite, you can instruct it to remove the parasite, and when you pull the meat around you, you can imagine how slippery it is to cut. You can also cut and delete files a little, but you run the risk of leaving them behind. If you do not raise your head, it can grow. Exchange is usually possible, but it is a process that requires patience and patience. As I said, it is much easier if you can interact with healing and work together.

Parasites will also share love if they do not receive the negative energy that they eat. Therefore, you can get rid of it by changing your faith and behavior and healing the first steps of the aura with those who support negative thoughts or negative beliefs. But this is a kind of chicken or egg, because parasites cause negative behavior and way of thinking. Therefore, if you ask him to change his faith, you must ask him to reject the parasite. Remove it, cure the first stage of mood and change your negative beliefs, actions and thinking.

The Mind Is the Body and The Body Is the Mind

Everything in your body and in your body, the aura, affects your mind. Their opinion is not only your opinion, but also your opinion about everything. Your faith is not only your faith, but also faith in everything in you. When the parasite dies, the owner feels pain. Technically, this is part of it. When the parasite becomes hungry, the owner wants to feed him. It is the same. Those who have been partially treated are also parasites! If you do not want to get rid of parasites, then the host is at least partially identical. Therefore, you need to learn to distinguish the feelings of other creatures that have their own feelings and feelings. The general trick is that powerful and demanding voices are not real people, but calm and confident voices that they know tell the truth. It's true

The same as the chip affects the mind of the host. They make programs and do things that they don't need. That is why it is so difficult to change beliefs. Negative behavior is actually good for parts of the body (such as parasites) and not for parts that must exist. In addition, parasites and French fries can be useful in certain periods of life, in times of despair. People often invite them in difficult times of life, because the energy provided by the parasites helps them to strengthen, not feel, ignore the truth and act more actively. No one has the energy to do this. He refused to leave, helping them in a desperate situation when there was no one to turn to them. Or he seduces the owner, tells them that they can help, says that they can do it for a while, and then stops doing it when they depend on him. Sometimes people want parasites. Even if it causes all kinds of problems, it depends on energy. For example, they do not want to find something in their life, their parasitic energy calms. In this case, no one can delete it. They will secretly upset attempts to remove it.

Maybe someone invited the parasite a few years ago and said: "Thank you for what you did for me. That might work. Once a parasite grows with people, it can exist at a young age and in a strange way, like a couple. I have a stubborn parasite that refuses to make every effort to eradicate it, but in the end, I apologize. Broken love!

For all these reasons, a person must actually change his beliefs and act accordingly. This often means acting against your feelings (parasitic feelings, not others). Then you need to suffer from dying parasites. Because it hurts, because it is in him. You must choose and act with your harsh feelings so that a soft and subtle voice whispers the truth. For this reason, energy operations are very useful for quickly redirecting this process. In addition, this parasite is the same as an evil spirit. But on the second level, their aura: On the first level, they are more like ghosts.

Super Complex Stuff

A year ago, I conducted a test in which 20 experienced meditators were recruited to meditate on a symbol to add healing energy to the pond, consuming energy in the pool. Each person treats other people at the same time and can be contacted at any time. All of these are based on symbols programmed with complex spells/complex intentions, including many conditions, including temporary contact, only positive energy can be shared—in this context, proverbs are contracts, computer programs.)

After some trial and error, I managed to fix the spell! The group reviews were very positive. Many people say how their lives have improved, and they can feel the energy when I participate. I learned a lot from this. Especially when I was looking for a group, I learned a lot about what worked and what did not work for the healing distance of time and distance. Unfortunately, if I did not pay people, they stopped doing it. I am very disappointed because I think that they will continue, but everyone is returning to normal life without money and incentives for this. There is a lesson about how most people really do not want to heal. They want to live their life, as they already do. No problem protecting him! (But I admit that I was disappointed with the experience.)

I present this example as an example of the longest and most likely opportunity for healing, working with energy and magic. But there is another lesson learned from this experience. We are in spiritual law. This was slightly improved before the spell worked. This should be determined in accordance with certain rules. They just can't do anything. In particular, you need to know how this works when creating an existing framework for creating something new and creating something new. If this is intuitive, use methods and structures created by others. This is good, but if you want to do something that has not been done before, or to solve an unsolved problem, create a new structure from the existing structure in the same way—existing or new homemade of the existing stone.

Conclusion

L ife phenomena have two constituents. The first is energy, and the second is biochemical. Energy strengthens and penetrates into matter. Removal from the physique means medical decease. If the ECG and EEG are not recognizable, scientific demise leads to the destruction of the physique into tiny biochemical elements. We're consistent with two modules: energy and biochemical substances. The vigor that refreshes the body of animals and humans is called life energy. This strength environs each cell with a mini-cable provides a plan for the physique and acts as an intermediate for the stream of data all through the physique. Bioenergy goes beyond the body and generates low-frequency electromagnetic fields (and other sly energy fields, not thus for renowned by science). In a bigger content, bioenergy is a central quality of widespread liveliness.

Bioenergy specialists give information in these areas, as great as the liveliness end through the physique. All that happens in the lions share is reflected in the course of liveliness and secondary versa. After these rivers and fields take back to normal, bioenergy practitioners are supposed to be intelligent to bring back the poise between bioenergy and biochemical mechanism in order to improve their health.

We all know that stories describing abnormal healing reach people. They are passed down from cohort to cohort, in every culture and continentally. When medical research begins, students learn that medicine comes from Greece and that Greece is the main source of medical knowledge. It is no secret that the first medical punishment began in thousands of years in honor of the victories of India, Ancient Egypt, Peru, Mesopotamia, Babylon, India, Mexico, Assyria, and China. It's untrue that we don't have evidence about the initial medication. European archeology, anthropology, and maritime history, as well as reports on traders, missionaries and first adoptive parents, provided valuable information on the complex medicinal processes that were effectively done many years ago. Nowadays new and other medicinal volumes are being interpreted into tongues

Bodily welfare is closely linked to mental well-being, emotive stability, and mystical ethics, and there has always been a common understanding that well-being reflects a person's environment. Most olden and modern medicinal performs base on unaccustomed ideas about death and life are very hard to comprehend because we cast-off priorities, despite documentation and other proof that individuals have done comparable performs all through the past. Affirmative outcomes that indicate mental, physical, and emotive health is understood otherwise dependent on the stage of understanding, conviction systems, and the level of understanding of the essence of the universe. As these performs are incompatible with our worldview, it cannot be explained, based on whatever you studied in school and college, so you decide on the simplest method. These phenomena are very common among those who call themselves "scientists," but their neglect contradicts the norm of methodical methods. Among the early performs known as surrender or, most often, healing through energy transfer.

In the past, ordinary people often severely restricted or prohibited ordination. If you look closely at the culture, you will see that the more structured the societies, the more restrictions there are in this matter, and in many cases, the hands of the community are limited to special groups. For example, in ancient Egypt, only the highest priest and the god of one person or another priest of his choice could heal. Interesting information on how to put your hands on pain relief can be found in Ebers-Papyrus from 1550 BC. In Mesopotamia and Babylon, healing occurred in the provinces of kings and the high priesthood. In ancient Greece, doctors, mathematicians, philosophers, and fortunetellers lived in the 6th century BC. He considered treatment his most distinguished mission. He described "pneumatics" or the energy associated with this process as the energy of light that appears around the body. After a hundred years, the famous Dr. Hippocrates insisted that the feeling of heat and sensations associated with the placing of arms and the transfer of energy lead to loss of pain. He tells the doctor to use energy, so we can assume that the doctors of ancient Greece have information about this practice.

In some European countries, the "touch of God" is intended only for the king, while in other countries monks can perform such healing methods. Later, many of these monks became innocent. In medieval Europe, there was a time when healing called "middle ground," which healed the disease and acted as the vehicle of god, was healed. Some people are considered "untouchables" because they act as a mediator or passage of God's energy. The Bible contains many explanations for the miraculous healing of the placing of arms. The healers of Christ and his disciples have experienced this conversion many times. Agreeing with those that follow traditions that are not Christian, such as "Taoism (China), Buddhism (Tibet), Hinduism (India)," the healing procedure is determined by the conviction in the supremacy of the all-powerful essence of the world that pervades the entire creation. Each of us is a person with this mental element. More than this mystical component could aid other people to have a higher level of awareness.

In "Taoism" in the Far East, the use of qi (energy) for martial arts and healing is known. At first, only the "monks" in the monastery were acquainted with the notion of qi. Their time is full of prayer, meditation, and other diplomatic and modest events. Since they believe that including a background will aid uphold their flag and will enable communication with the essence of the omnipotent world. Neighboring hosts give food and pay for prayers. When thieves began to attack villages and temples, some monks decided to take active protective measures to sacrifice their monastic lifestyle and protect themselves from unwanted intrusions. During the battle, these monks use their ability to focus energy on their opponents, making it difficult to defeat them. This discovery led to the emergence of a martial arts school with a focus on defense, which eventually learned to use intense liveliness for attack drives. Another routine of liveliness is the curing of injured fighters. Often, it hurts in battle. To hasten the curing procedure, a fresh cluster of individuals has been designed, the supposed main pores, which can heal wounds with energy. The ability of this legendary qigong master to heal physical and mental pain has made them known for centuries. Today, China's new official name is people with special features. The energy released by the hand is used not only at the level of the body but also at all levels to restore proper energy balance and restore its integrity.

Legend has it that the defensive skills of the Shaolin monastery were considered a harbinger and developed after visiting the Bodhidharma, an Indian monk who paid attention to the poor health of the monks when they arrived at the temple. To advance his well-being, Bodhidharma educated him a sequence of liveliness maneuvers. As time went by, as the holy place grows and becomes more visible to attract thieves, an energy-based movement turns into a defensive training, turning into an offensive skill.

Handshakes have long been held by local shamans from the two zones. They will treat patients with the contact of hands and potions. This healing occurs only during the moon, when the moon grows, minimizing all healing actions when the moon decreases. (On all ancient continents, plants were harvested only during camouflage.) As part of healing rituals, local and African shamans dance almost unconsciously and bring their hands to sore spots on the body. Ancestors help to heal. In the two beliefs, melodic gadgets were used to generate definite pulsations and speed up the healing process. The indigenous people also draw dots and lines on the body that reflect the meridian (the passage through which energy moves), which the Chinese use for acupuncture!

For millennia, people of different cultures and beliefs have created a halo and mood round the skulls and statistics of people with "special powers," including healing supremacies. They go with Mary, Jesus's mother, and other essential Christian facts in the many ancient portraits, but people seem to be mistaken because they appear only around adult Christians. Christ as a doctor is usually showed not just with an aura and halo, similarly with light that originated in his arms. The Old Testament often remarks about the existence of brightness around other figures. In India and Tibet, you can see shining auras in the images of yogis, Buddhist monks, and all gods and goddesses. The Buddha is depicted not only by the energy around the body but by all the attributes in which the fully developed energy is depicted, that is, all the chakras (energy centers).

The head of the artistically crowned priest, warrior, and the leader of India represent a halo. Tibetans and Hindu mystics will demand this a completely established crown chakra or a thousand petal chakras.

Unluckily, these images of mortal liveliness fields have misplaced their principal significance over the centuries. John White shows 96 different cultures in his book Future Science. Despite the differences, each explanation shows signs of bright light or rays. Hello, their aura and all imitations symbolize originality and divinity and distinguish between those who have it and those who don't. But here is a fundamental variance amid the halo and other procedures of the crown. This circle is used to represent human virtue and good deeds and is a sure sign of spiritual development in all cultures. For crowns and other hats, the problem is often very different. Initially, the crown shows love, kindness, forgiveness, wisdom, and emotions, accompanied by high mystical growth.

In most of the olden customs, the primary connotation of the term "energy" is the original lifetime strength or liveliness of life. This liveliness seals and environs everyone and the environs. Rendering to this opinion of the world, the power of lifetime strengthens substance and generates natural life. In other arguments, natural life happens once liveliness enters nonliving substances. This natural life strength was famous as pneumonia in ancient Greece. "Paracelsus" called him a whale. In Sanskrit, in India, the term prana and mine, Prana means global liveliness, and mine is an individual procedure that streams over people and is distributed to schools of Bindu and Nibu. It is supposed that Prana can change the level of vibration and turn it into waves. In Tibet, this liveliness is known as Tikle, lungs, and Ca. In olden Egypt, it was known as "Ka." Chinese, the named Ki or Chi depending on the section of the republic. This last word comes from "tai chi" and qigong, the practice of meditative exercises based on the flow of energy. As mentioned earlier, anyone who can regulate and regulate the flow of energy is called a pore master.

Japanese, vital liveliness is known as "Ki." Its flow is used by "Aikido," schools offering martial arts and an active school of karate martial arts. In the United States, Japan's most famous energy tradition is Reiki.

The Hebrew text describes this authority as a lie. People should reflect four levels, three features of the Neshamah, Ruach, and soul-Nefesh. In Hawaii, this liveliness is known as "Mana and Ka," as in India, a human-level space vehicle is transformed into one or more aspects: what energy, what, that's it. "Mana or Ka" is cast-off for curing and self-regulation. The rulers of Hawaiian liveliness were known as kahuns. In Latin American nations, healers work with liveliness. The healer originates from the term "shams," meaning "sun" in olden Egypt, in Arabic and Hebrew. The solar is a source of energy on Earth and is worshiped in many ancient cultures.

Modern designations for this important liveliness consist of: "Odil (Karl von Reichenbach), Org (Wilhelm Reich) and Bioenergy (Professor Zdenek Reidak from Charles University in Prague, Czech Republic)." Since Kirlian began photographic experiments, many scientists who studied this subject were still engaged in this matter; another term was created in the former Soviet Union—bioplasma.

Today, it is becoming increasingly popular, as is Dr. Paul's approach to medical practice. Med. The sacred works of Randolph Stone and the skeleton of the Therapeutical Touch Technique, a liveliness management arrangement established by "Professor Dolores Krieger and Quantum-Touch Bob Rasmusson," are widespread with caregivers in the United States and several other nations. Bio vigor, by now is well recognized in Europe, extends to the United States. Far Eastern martial arts (exercises and vigor), these include "Aikido, Tai Chi, Kung Fu, and Karate," are recognized worldwide. Due to the point energy pressure of the body, acupressure and shiatsu massage have gained popularity in spas and beauty salons. Qi Gong is located outside of China and is currently developing in the East and West. Should I consider this approach a medical act? Agreeing with the current description of the medicinal exercise, the response is no. Is there a relaxing effect? When I saw the results, they made it clear. Slowly found something missing in orthodox medicine.

A universal and energetic medication of the upcoming will certainly help from our experience in applying such procedures. Faced with fresh innovations, they will accept new interpretations that, unlike the past, do not put them in the category of magic or superstition. For clarity, the term "energy cure" is used in connection with functional outcomes obtained in electromagnetic, electrostatic, sperm or aural arenas, such as those cast-off for electrocardiography, electroencephalography, ultrasound, tomography and magnetic resonance imaging. This does not apply to the medical field X and more. The point that we expedition this device just endorses the presence of this field.

Many modern scientists conquer that in the universe, there is just one elementary system of vigor. At least from the point of view of the relativity of the magnetic field, this point of view is completely consistent with the point of view of occult energy. We believe that the universe in which we reside in, from spheres to stars, the sun, the astral system, and the galaxy, constantly vibrates, but most scientists do not even want to discuss spiritual energy. In addition, the Earth and all living things are in the same vibrational state as the cellular level. This vibration shows the vitality of the world. Conferring to this understanding, all flesh, comprising of human beings, is also liveliness beings. Most of our olden evolutions have known this for an extended time. This methodical information has been handed over from cohort to cohort in the Far East, India, Tibet, and China. As an invaluable fragment of the custom, this information is cast-off and used nowadays, and is also growing in popularity in other regions. There is no doubt that in recent years, part of this expansion is owing to the swift growth of studies that show and confirm the electromagnetic properties of a lifetime in the world.

Recent studies of the brain receptors, human, and brain waves, restrained at various levels of awareness, demonstrate the unbelievable possibility of self-regulation methods, as well as self-curing. Gradually, we began to understand the bigger fact that was removed in the period of reductionism. In utmost circumstances, a true cure for the disease requires more than just surgery or medication. You learn to give handy consideration to the entire physique, even if the delinquent happens just partially. We find that we feel better when we move the body, walk, breathe better, and spend more time in nature. We also know that what we eat and how to eat strongly affects our overall health. We take vitamins through a balanced diet and weight loss program, sometimes experimenting with fasting minerals.

Using this recent tactic, it was found that the whole physique is recovering, not the whole body or some organs. We are finally beginning to recognize the simple fact that organs and functions are not separated from other parts of the body. If it does not contain invisible components, such as our emotional, mental, and spiritual levels, the body should be considered and considered as a whole and incomplete system. There is no doubt that our feelings can kill or heal us and have a big impact on our health. In addition, we have no doubt that another inseparable reality, that is, our thoughts, dominates in our feelings. And our opinions and intents appear in a cerebral environ. The intention is the connection amid our cerebral and mystical levels. Our capacity of awareness decides the value of our intents, while our intentions and next steps represent our level of awareness.

The previously immeasurable self-healing potential that cannot be scientifically explained is clearly associated with our advanced levels of non-physical functions. In our desire to look good and survive extends or saves our lives, with the exception of many medical statistics and predictions from doctors. Representatives of homeopathic medicines often witness "voluntary relief" or "unexpected treatment." In many circumstances, these people will mask on a "diagnosis," and not admit that a miracle happened with the fact that the medicine they made cannot explain. Our ability to treat is rarely mentioned, and the ability to be treated by doctors is still mocked by the utmost customary doctors. The notion of remote treatment is deliberated very stupidly. This is completely incompatible with the paradigms of the past, but this skepticism is now seriously questioned by science itself.

What do you do with research based on scientific criteria (for example, double-blind) and showing affirmative variations in the focus's well-being when there is a doctor? More and more of these studies give very provocative results. For example, in the West Gulf of Medicine, Volume 169, Number 5, a study is published in which healers send energy prayers to Yatld to remote those sick with AIDS in "the San

Francisco Bay area." The doctor and this patient not once saw each other or even talked to one another phone. But everybody must acknowledge that the variance amid the specimen cluster and other groups is very surprising.

Those that support the customary Western tactic to edification will only explain this as an occurrence showing that this result is an inexplicable event. This is not in line with the paradigm. Representatives of the culture of the Far East, on the other hand, will not be surprised at this result. They will understand that the energy in the form of prayer has been transferred to the spiritual level from afar. In the backgrounds, the precise flow of liveliness outside and inside our body is deliberated as an integral attribute of emotional, physical, spiritual, and mystical health. For those fascinated by this topic, see Ying Daniel Benor. Convincing evidence has been published on this subject, and many studies have been conducted on the country in which the study was conducted.

At the West, the conception of general liveliness medication or emerging vibrational medication is grounded on the supposition that people and the surroundings are made up of numerous systems of similar density. In a broader context, bioenergy is very compatible with this new drug model. This is such a procedure of skill as a medication of that period, which considers every person as a person and concerns the whole person, and not a specific service situation. Like creativity, bioenergy is based on vision, intuition, and art. There are definite instructions, but they should be free. It takes years of training and practice to be recognized as an artist or a doctor.

In a Chinese energy management system called qigong, internal and external energy flows can be slow, blocked, and weak or blocked due to damaged skeletons, broken or injured joints, damaged or broken nerves, meager movement, etc. Products that are too acidic or too basic (for example, too much yin or even in Chinese terminology), such as damaged skin or dirty, can cause an energy imbalance. We also get pretentious by demanding circumstances, when the nerve structure is not able to cope with tension correctly, and the electrical indicators in the head interfere with the stream of liveliness.

It processes the wrong flow of information when the flow of energy in the body is blocked, weak, or overloaded. As we are acquainted with, neurotransmitters regularly transmit data from the head to every cell and send data back as of each cell to the head. These "conversations," which take place in the form of information exchange in our bodies, occur beneath the surface of consciousness and are naturally biochemical and electrical. The mistake of "water supply" always bothers others. If this condition persists lengthier, the whole data structure in the problem zone is at risk. Cells misplace their capability to converse with one another and settle in the brain. Disorders that affect the stream of data through the physique has a similar consequence as the violation of data in new tissue systems. This will cause confusion and cause the system to crash. Now this incident, confusion repeatedly reveals itself as a disease. Thus, the disease could be initiated by a violation of the stream of liveliness in the physique.

The physique matrix could be considered to be a liquid or crystalline arrangement. There are many small tubes in this matrix that flow through the body. This tubule is commonly called the cytoskeleton. In fact, these are microfilaments observed at the subcellular environs, which are a fragment of a new-fangled vision that arises from the functions of the physique in "molecular biology." The dimension of the microfilament is four to six nanometers (imagine the regular granite and pay attention to the size: the marble faces the Earth at a speed of 1 nanometer per meter). This microfilament is present in every cell: it transfers proteins to specific targets, regularly moves organelles through cells, and even transfers RNA fragments beginning at the center to a precise conversion region. It is customarily believed that this microfilament or cytoskeletal collection plays a minor character in upholding cytoplasmic flow, cell integrity, and cell division. However, researchers recently recognized that the cytoskeleton is convoluted in signal transmission, molecular, and metabolism transportation of cells.

The base is the supposition that every breathing thing, including a human being, is bordered by general liveliness. We continue to receive energy from this sea, but each living creature has its own energy plan. Each relation amid breathing creatures involves an altercation of

114

liveliness if we like it or we do not, whether we recognize it or not. Since we know the whole process better, we can learn more about ourselves.

Healing is an art that helps change the flow of energy to restore physical, emotional, mental, and spiritual health. Health-giving is a non-invading technique that can be used for all diseases, anxiety, or hurt. This is a medicine that has no recognized lateral properties and is equipped with every other treatment methods. People can learn liveliness exercise skills to bring back the fitness and well-being of their own and that of other individuals.

Balance Chakras

The Ultimate Complete Beginners Guide
To Unblock and Balance Your Chakras,
Radiate Positive Energy, Healing Yourself
Body and Mind With Yoga Meditation.

By

New Mindfulness Lab

Introduction

Welcome to "Chakra Balance: A Beginner's Guide to Unblocking and Balancing Chakras". In this book, you will find a complete guide to chakras and how to balance them in order to achieve health, wellbeing and overall feeling better about yourself and your life.

In the following pages, you will have a full guide that will explain every aspect of this topic in great detail. So, whether you have plenty of experience with this topic or brand-new to it, you will find a great deal of useful information.

Chakra balance is something that many people often wonder about, but most people do not understand this topic in depth. Balance Chakra is a complex topic but a very helpful one. We often hear from spiritual people telling us that our chakras are not balanced, or unbalanced chakras is the reason for some undesirable situations. This book will cover the basics of having a balanced chakra and the benefits that come with it. Achieving balanced chakras could bring back your health and positivity in your and can revive your glory days. So, what are you waiting for? Participate in the journey of learning about chakra balance today, and you won't regret it.

Have you ever been told that you have negative energy or even positive energy? This is because of certain things that you do can make people believe you have either positive or negative energy. In this book, we take a deeper dive into the different energies that people radiate regardless of it being either be positive or negative. However, we will take a more in-depth look on positive energy because that is the energy type that most people strive for. We will teach you the process of gaining positive energy and getting rid of negative energy in your life. We will also learn about yoga as it is a popular topic nowadays. You probably know at least two people in your life that consistently practice yoga or talk about it. If you are interested in different chakra energies, you may also be interested in trying out yoga well.

In this book, we will teach you more about yoga and why practicing yoga is necessary. You don't have to worry about having questions that will be unanswered. Simply grab a seat and have this book at hand, and all your questions are going to be answered. As you make your way through this book, I wish that you enjoy the process and learn a lot of helpful topics.

Chapter 1
Fundamentals of Chakra Balance

D o you feel "turned off" these days? Are you making silly mistakes at work? Are you sick for the third week in a row? Many things can explain these problematic situations, but the main indicator here is the imbalance of your chakra system.

First of all, what is a chakra? What are the signs of a damaged chakra?

Chakras are the energy center of the whole body.

There are hundreds of different chakras, but there are seven main chakras that are commonly focused on. This colorful energy wheel displays Shushumna Nadi, the central channel of the body. The Chakra along Shushumna Nadi is the center of power where the right channel (Pingala Nadi) and the left channel (Ida nadi) intersect. These energy channels and mental health centers form the so-called "subtle bodies." The subtle body is in a different space from the body and psyche and it has a powerful effect on the body, mind, and the whole system. Any disorder or illness of the body, mind, or soul can cause blockage and imbalance. The goal here is to find harmony. For the people who don't think this is something they can possibly achieve, simply pay attention to the chakras to see what is happening within and find a balance.

If you have lost your balance, consider the food you consumed (experiences, ideas, drinks), current living conditions (big chances, travel,) and the current season (heat, cold, wind, rain, wind, etc.) Each of these factors can have a significant impact on the whole sensitive human system. In the philosophy of yoga and Ayurveda; the chakras play an essential role in understanding the social network, "similar" and "opposite balances" increase. This means that you already have an excessive temperature in your body in the form of anger or an upset stomach and adding more heat to this such as hot weather or spicy foods will allow you to experience excessive heat and excitement. Therefore, when you wake up in the morning, add the opposite temperature such as taking a cold shower or eating fresh fruit in order to feel a balanced mood.

In general, there are five warning signs of damaged chakras. Searching for too much or too little energy in each chakra creates an imbalance. Remember, the goal is harmony. It takes effort to balance the chakras. Here are the general warning signs:

- Everything feels 'out of place'
- You are constantly sick
- You find yourself making stupid or silly mistakes
- Everything feels and looks 'messy'

Each of these common imbalances manifests in a particular physical, mental, emotional, and spiritual imbalances in each chakra. Let's take a closer look at how imbalances in each chakra can cause a sense of disharmony in all body systems. As such, we will dedicate an individual to each of the chakras located throughout the body.

Chapter 2
The Root Chakra

The Root Chakra or otherwise known as Muladhara is the most critical and fundamental energy center of our body. It is situated at the base of the spinal column or groin. The Root chakra regulates energy related to our instinct, survival, and security. When the root chakra is out of balance with trauma, mental problems such as chronic anxiety, psychosomatic oppression, suppression, the flow of life is disrupted. Often our blocked energy centers cause problems in our lasting and personal relationships.

The root chakra is one of the most closed off and limited energy fields in our body. Everyone struggles with the deficiency of the root chakra at a certain point in their lives. If you grew up in an unhealthy environment such as having divorced parents, living in poverty, or exposed to any type of physical or emotional abuse, you may have broken root chakra.

Mending the root chakra requires the act of opening, refining, purging, keeping up, and reinforcing the root chakra in our body. Recuperating the Root Chakra includes the use of specific affirmations like food, yoga practices, sounds, healing crystals, smells, and other holistic medicines in order to restore harmony in the mind-body.

Symptoms of an Unhealthy Root Chakra
The most ideal approach to find out if you need to heal your Root Chakra is to focus on your contemplations, emotions, activities, and physical sensations in the body. Here are a few instructions that must be considered.

For instance, you may be someone that is obsessed with money. You worry that you don't have enough; you have thoughts of disaster around the poor and homeless, and you are too worried to focus on overcoming your financial problems. They are triggered every time someone in your family spends too much or if they have full control over their family's financial situation. Here are some indications that you are exhibiting unfortunate chakras:

- You have mistrust towards others (trust issues)
- You believe that the only person you can rely on is yourself and you avoid asking others for help
- You are a workaholic
- You have a problematic relationship with your family
- You are afraid of losing control
- You are aware of threats towards you from other people or your environment
- You feel dizzy, anxious, roomy, and unfounded almost all-day
- You find it hard and scary to be authentic to yourself
- You feel disconnected from others and nature
- You stop eating when you become depressed or anxious
- You have problems with your feet and legs, such as swelling, infections, cramps, circulation disorders
- You tend to gain weight around the lower body

Root Chakra Blockage

When people mostly talk about unhealthy root chakra, what they mean is that the chakra is "blocked" or is suffering from a deficiency that limits the flow of energy. However, did you know that your chakra can both too active or inactive? So, what is the difference between a deficient and overactive root chakra? The wrong root chakras can be defined as a passive root chakra and overgrown is defined as aggressive.

Deficient root chakra indicates that you are lifeless, lethargic, passive, clogged, and inward.

Overactive root chakra indicates that you are lively, energetic, reactive, aggressive, outgoing.

If a person has a harmed root chakra, they are progressively powerless to issues. For example, they will feel emotions of tension, doubt, and withdrawal. On the other hand, if you have unnecessary root chakra, you tend to experience emotions of anger, workaholic, greed, and accumulation. The question is, which do you have? It is also possible to fall somewhere in the middle.

What is it like to have a healthy and balanced root chakra? If you have a transparent, secure, and agreeable root chakra, you will initially feel grounded and quiet. You will never again have to deal with the dread of being losing control and you will believe in the intelligence of the divine life. Not only will you trust yourself more, but you will also feel more connected to others and nature. If your root chakra is healthy, it will be easy for you to become be your true self and find the inner peace that was always there. You will be able to connect with it more easily. They will yield to the need to fight, defend, and defend rather than adapt to spills and the flow of life.

How To Heal The Root Chakra
Here are some of the best ways to cure a person's root chakra:

- Listen to ethnic music. I recommend the sounds of thunder, Mongolian throat, and didgeridoos (Australian aboriginal instrument).
- Set a "LAM" for yourself. This sound corresponds the vibration of the root chakra. Take a stab at drawing letters with sounds "llllllaaaaaammmmm." You might also want to listen to binaural beats (a type of music mending treatment) that will actuate and eradicate all chakra by intruding on the sound waves.
- Take a walk within nature regularly. Pay attention to the relationship between your feet and the ground.
- Introduce yoga into your life; stretch your body with comfortable yoga postures such as; baby poses, forward flexion, mountain poses, squats, and fighters.

125

- Eat root vegetables such as sweet potatoes, carrots, turnips, and other root vegetables.
- Practice mindfulness every day for at least 30 minutes at a time. Make it a habit to stop every day and watch your own breath. This simple exercise will help you build more mindfulness.
- Use and Meditate with Crystals that utilize the Root Chakra Crystals such as Jasper, Hematite, Smoky Quartz, and Cornelia. My favorite chakra root crystal is black tourmaline.
- Peel the root chakra with aromatherapy fragrance. Use oils such as vetiver, patchouli, cloves, sandalwood, black pepper, ginger, and cloves.
- Practice grounding exercise; grounding is an act of walking on grass or on the ground barefoot in order to replenish the human energy field.
- Wear a totem or a piece of runway jewelry. Wear items related to the awakening of the root chakra.
- Sit still and imagine a red ball of light pulsing on your root chakra (groin). Imagine all the turbid energy dissolving when touching a red lightbulb.
- Take time every day to sit outside and connect with nature. Watch what happens. Watch the birds, clouds, wind, light, and you feel your connection to it.
- Use Affirmations or Mantras. Use spells or affirmations to reprogram your subconscious mind. Examples of affirmations and mantras are: "I am grounded", "I am centered and holistic", "I believe in the wisdom of life", "I have everything I need", "I am confident and safe", "I surrender", "I am strong, stable and peaceful."
- Drink herbal tea. Drink powdered tea with chakra roots, herbs like ashwagandha and cloves.
- Bathing with soothing water is a powerful method for removing clogged and clogged energy. Or, you can use a bath with mineral salt such as Himalayan rose rock salt.
- Check the cause of your fear. Fear arises from your unresolved pain, inner beliefs, and dissatisfaction. Take the

126

time to reflect on the roots of your worries in a diary or with a trusted friend, partner, or therapist.

- Train catharsis every day at purification to actively dissolve the blocked root chakra energy. You might want to explore dynamic meditation or actions like jumping, kicking, punching, screaming, or dancing to release your tension.

Chapter 3
The Sacral Chakra

The Sacral or Swadhistan Chakra is the center of our emotional, creative, and sexual energy. The sacral chakra is located three inches below the stomach and above our genitals. It is associated with an orange color. It regulates energy related to desire, sensuality, and pleasure. When the sacral chakra becomes unbalanced due to traumatic experiences in early and old life, many physical, emotional, psychological, and interpersonal problems begin to arise.

When was the last time you felt sexually desirable, passionate about life, feelings of love or creativity? The vitality that you want to achieve is possible when your sacred chakra is in perfect harmony. People with balanced sacred chakras radiate warmth, joy, and good mood. Unfortunately, many life experiences can cause a blocked sacral chakra. If you have experienced authoritarian education, sexual harassment, toxic relationships, religious teachings, or critical forms of social conditioning that have restricted your flow of vitality, you may have damaged sacral chakra.

Healing the sacral chakra is the act of opening, filtering, purging, supporting and fortifying the sacral chakra in our body. Recuperating the sacral chakra includes the use of several holistic solutions, such as sports therapy, aromatherapy, crystal, and sound, crystal, to restore harmony in the body-mind.

Symptoms of an Unhealthy Sacral Chakra

- You are dependent on anything that gives pleasure, such as food, sex, gambling, drugs, work, forced shopping, alcohol, etc.

- You feel emotionally numb or cold, and it is difficult for you to feel any emotion
- You are sexually frigid and have a weak libido that does not exist, or they are too sexually impulsive
- You are neurotic and cannot handle spontaneity or insecurity
- You have reproductive problems such as infertility, impotence or menstrual problems
- You are always tired and don't have much energy
- You feel disabled and depressed because you express your true feelings and desires, or you are very emotionally reactive
- You are emotionally over sensitive or overly insensitive
- You have diseases related to your lower back, kidneys or stomach

Sacral Chakra Blockage

Did you know that there are two kinds of chakra that have irregular characteristics? What's more is that Yoga is a great method to conquer a person's body an unblock their vitality. The following are the details of the differences between the two:

When you have a deficiency, you are lifeless, passive, listless, and/or sluggish.

When you have an overactive chakra, you are aggressive, lively, reactive, and friendly.

If the sacral chakra is not active enough, you are more vulnerable to problems such as overly emotional, sexually uninterested, and even feel physical discomfort during sexual activity. Overactive sacral chakras, on the other hand, are susceptible to addiction, sexual addicts, and emotional outbursts.

What are the shapes of a healthy and balanced sacral chakra? If you have transparent, secure, and harmonious sacral chakras, your skin will actually feel better at first. You will no longer fight against guilt or sexual pleasure but respect and enjoy your sacred sexuality in a

129

balanced way. Not only will you enjoy the pleasures of life, but you will also be open to experiencing life even further and increase your desire for it. You will be open emotionally and feel more connected with firm boundaries. You will also get your creative flow back and enjoy the spontaneity of life.

Healing Sacral Chakra
The best way to treat the sacral chakra is:

- Open the "frozen" energy channels inside you by perfecting your emotions through catharsis. Try to shout, jump, cry, or other physical forms of purification that trigger emotions.
- Check your creative self-expression. This is most suitable for the blockage of your sacral chakra. Choose activities that interest you, such as jewelry making, sculpture, cooking, painting, quilting, and photography! Remember that art requires practice, commitment, and time. Think about what you want to express mentally or emotionally and begin to build, paint, tie, or describe your inner desires.
- Check for sexual disorders. Sacred closure without chakras. What beliefs, ideals, and prejudices did you learn in childhood? You can record this by talking talk with a good friend. After identifying your blockages, they can be improved further.
- Meditate and use the most suitable crystals for overactive chakra and blocked chakra. Use sacral chakra crystals such as; moonstone, jasper, calcite orange, and carnelian moonstone. My favorite holy chakra crystal is yellow.
- Pay attention to your emotional triggers. Emotional triggers can be improved by better adapting to them. For example, when you are angry, slowly relax and take a deep breath. If the blood temperature rises during a specific topic, ask yourself why, and begin to manage your feelings.

- Increase your consumption of ginger. Ginger is a warm and irritating herb, ideal for sacral chakras. Use ginger oil, cook more with ginger, or drink more ginger tea.
- Explore the sources of addiction. Often, substance abuse is a way to cope with reality and fill the void in your life. Ask your diary or friend or therapist why you rely on something. Ask questions like "Where am I when I'm addicted?" "What do you think of this addiction?" I think you are suffering from a severe addiction. Book with an addiction specialist.
- Practice personal care for your body. Accept all body types and other physical discoveries using materials such as meditations and books, and seminars, and reflections. Do not apologize for your appearance but begin to feel your body and its unique needs. Find out which diet plan works best for you and stop eating processed foods. Try to eat foods such as; sweet potatoes, coconuts, apricots, oranges, papaya, almonds, carrots, and mangoes.
- Use color therapy to block overactive sacral chakra. The color of the sacral chakra is orange, so add the color of orange through consuming peaches and apricots. You can also put on orange clothes, wrap yourself in orange items, and express yourself with creative oranges.
- Imagine a 3-inch neon orange light beating or spinning under your stomach. Feel how the orange energy of the ball dissolves all your blockages or the flow of aggressive energy.
- Break out of your comfort zone! For example, go see a movie that you have never thought you'd see or go to a place you could not imagine
- Explore other creative forms of sexuality with a partner. Explore various forms of creative pleasure in solitude. Ask yourself if you feel any blockages, such as guilt or shame.
- Clean the sacral chakra with aromatic oil. Suitable for the absence and obstruction of the overactive sacral chakra. Use oils such as bergamot, ginger, neroli, orange, jasmine, and rosewood.
- Eliminate clogging with yoga. Yoga is a phenomenal method to conquer your body's blocked vitality barrier.

- Speak positively to yourself every day, this will cause reduce the overactive blockage of the sacral chakra. Say words like; "Accept my inner desires," "Respect and respect my body", "I abandoned my creative inner feelings."

Chapter 4
The Solar plexus

The sunlight-based chakra is the focal point of our will, confidence, and energy. The solar plexus chakra is located about 5 inches above the center of the diaphragm and is associated with yellow and fiery elements. This chakra regulates the energy associated with vitality, intentions, behavior, and personality. The solar plexus chakra shines as bright as the balanced sun, which is why it is known as the energy center of the "brilliant stone." Have you ever experienced confidence, independence, and internal motivation in your life? This is easily achievable when the sun powered plexus chakra works in congruity with our inner selves under optimal conditions.

However, life is full of traumatic experiences and thoughts that can cause blockage, suppression, or stagnation of the solar plexus chakra. If you experienced a strict upbringing, bullying or have been subjected to sexual, mental, physical and emotional abuse as a child you may need to focus on your solar plexus.

Healing the sun-oriented plexus chakra requires you to open and sanitize the sunlight-based plexus chakra in our body. The treatment of the solar plexus chakra involves restoring the harmony of the body and mind with a range of solutions such as; emotional therapy, aromatherapy, exercise, sound, and exercise.

Symptoms of an Unhealthy Solar Plexus

The best way to determine if your solar plexus chakra needs to be treated is to focus on the physical feelings of your body. Here are a few things to look out for:

- You generally feel worn out and apathetic
- You have problems with overeating

133

- You tend to be easily manipulated by others for their own gain
- You tend to harass or be aggressive to others
- You have a lack of trust in society
- You seek validation from other people
- You have low self-esteem
- Your body temperature is either freezing or really hot
- You tend to easily get addicted to things
- You struggle with setting boundaries with people
- You have stomach related issue, for example; diabetes, IBS, hypoglycemia, or ulcers
- You often suffer from gas, abdominal pain, or constipation.
- You are overweight around the abdomen

Solar Plexus Blockage

Solar plexus chakra can either be at deficient levels or overactive levels. When a person has an inadequate solar plexus, they feel sluggish, aloof, and low energy. When a person has overactive levels, they are aggressive, lively, reactive, and agitated.

Therefore, inadequate solar plexus chakras are more vulnerable to problems such as fatigue, inferiority. Then again, if you have a chakra with a deficiency of sun-oriented plexus, you will express traits of selfishness and anger.

Healing the Solar Plexus

At this point in the book, we have learned several types of transcendent sunlight that is based plexus chakra therapeutic practices. By participating in it, you will maintain a distance that you set for yourself in order to get back in touch with your dynamic focus. Below are a set of instructions to follow in order to heal your chakra:

- Get out of your comfort zone and start exploring the world around you.
- Remove people from your live that do not encourage you. During this time of healing, you will need the help of

people who can encourage you and not the involvement of unsupportive people who will drag you through the mud. This is entirely dependent upon you to figure out who get to stay in your life and who need to go.

- Identify the biggest obstacles in your life. What is something that you are continually battling against? Are you anxious about? Could you repeat that? Frequently, people with blocked sunlight-based plexus chakras keep a close eye on contributing to more battles and obstacles.

- Eat more nourishing foods. Incorporate whole grains such as oats and rye which are very effective for healing. Make an effort to include supplementary vegetables in your eating routine such as lentils, chickpeas, and beans. Make sure to incorporate flavors like turmeric, ginger, cumin, and cinnamon as these flavors help warm the body. In addition, include foods that are grown from the ground like capsicums, lemons, pineapple, bananas, and corn.

- Spend more time out in the sun. The main solution to recovering your solar plexus chakra is to use the sun itself because the sun is an extremely restorative resource. When a person is suffering from Vitamin D deficiency, they will feel sadness and tiredness. Try talking a brisk morning walk in the daylight, or spend some time watching the sunset.

- Find ways to alleviate any annoyances that you feel. When you are able to relieve yourself of any annoyances you will be able to free your sunlight-based plexus altogether. You can relieve yourself of any annoyances and aggression through the use of actions such as working out, crying, punching, kickboxing, or singing.

- Utilize refinement herbs. Use herbs that have the ability to clear out the sun-oriented plexus. For example, chamomile, rosemary, lemongrass, marshmallow leaf, and ginger. The best way to consume these herbs is to make tea from it.

- Use the following assertions: "I can!", "I will!", "I can make my own choices!" and "I am splendid person!" The more you repeat these assertions to yourself the more they will become your reality. You will be able to reconstruct your personality into one that you deem most suitable.

- Develop a good sense of humor. Humor is a great way to make light of dark events in our lives. The darkest times of someone's life can be improved just by using a little bit of humor. Making jokes in light of dark events helps create more freedom in our emotions. The more serious you are, the more effect negative things will have on you.
- Make use of the following healing stones: yellow calcite, citrine, golden, tiger's eyes, and topaz.
- Be sure to practice your breathing and take a step back to see the bigger picture. In the event that you are struggling to effectively communicate with other individuals, learn to concentrate on your breathing. This will help your body relax and allow you to take a step back to be able to properly deal with the problem at hand. Concentrating on your breathing will help you calm down and be able to look at a situation from an objective perspective.
- Clear any obstructions within through the use of yoga. Yoga is a great way to reset your inner self. Try these yoga stances; downward dog, shivasana, and tree pose. Yoga can help you tame and balance all the different chakras and energies inside of you. It will help you be free of stress and be in tune with your physical body.
- Visualize the sun-oriented plexus. Start by envisioning a whirling circle of cheerfulness in your stomach. Imagine yourself stroking the globe of light and dissolve any blockages within yourself.
- Flush out any overactive chakras through the use of essential oils. Use oils such as dark pepper, cinnamon, rosemary, cypress, clove, and sandalwood. You can put these oils into diffuser or rub them all over your body.

Chapter 5
The Heart Chakra

The chakra of benevolence, or Anahata, is the center of love and balance. Heart chakra is found in the middle of a person's chest in the ribcage area. This chakra is associated with art and the finer aspects of life. This chakra is responsible for a person's self-esteem, self-acknowledgment, genuine love, empathy, and receptiveness of others.

The heart chakra over the last many years has been recognized as the energy of adoration, solidarity, and balance. Do you recall another other time where you felt open, liberal, responsive, tolerating, and excusing to other individuals? This should nearly be possible if your heart chakra was balanced and in good physical shape. However, if you are familiar with loneliness, isolation, resentment, fear or hatred, you are possibly inflicted with a blocked spirit chakra.

Compassion chakra responsible for clearing, opening, supporting, and purging the center point chakra in our bodies. Center chakra's medicinal qualities include a few producing life-powers into a person's body and brain. Here are the qualities for a person who is suffering from lack of heart and compassionate chakra:

- You feel separated from the network around you
- You judge others from a distance in order to avoid mingling with other individuals
- You feel deprived in human connections
- You are afraid of life
- You acquire your self-esteem through other people and not through yourself
- You continuously feel anger towards other individuals/life

- You always feel like there is social tension
- You frequently feel envious of other individuals
- You are consistently replaying or remembering feelings of hurt
- You always feel an overwhelming sense of dread
- You fight for other people to give you affection
- You are constantly suspicious and doubting of other individuals
- You have health issues with your heart, lungs or chest state, for example; asthma or high blood pressure

Symptoms of an Unhealthy Heart Chakra

Did you know that there are two types of chakra that are opposite in character? While an uneven personality chakra is characterized as "numb," an uneven soul chakra is characterized as forceful or hyper. Here is a breakdown of the differences between the two:

- Deficient: You are inert, drowsy, inactive, and hindered (not enough vitality is streaming in).
- Overactive: You are energetic, upset, responsive, and forceful (too much energy flows in).

Therefore, if you have an inadequate amount of soul and personality chakra, you will be subject to additional issues such as; social uneasiness, detachment, and self-basic considerations. On the other hand, if you have too much compassion chakra, you will be subject to tenacity and repressing feelings of love.

What you are able to balance your heart chakra, you will initially feel responsive. You feel as if you will never again battle with disengagement, dread, and harshness. However, you will showcase a large amount of kindness to other people. You will fight through your own weaknesses in order to acknowledge the love you have for yourself and others. Therefore, your friendships will grow, and you will prevent others from harm even if they have hurt you in the past.

How to Heal your Heart Chakra

As traditional form of balancing your center chakra, you will practice a technique called 'Woodland bathing'. 'Woodland bathing' is a technique that originated in Japan and was known as 'Shinrin Yoku'. It has numerous advantages that has been proven through many experiments. Here is how you can practice woodland bathing:

- If you don't live close to a forest or the woods, don't stress out about it. Simply take a trip to the nearest forest, national park, or any region with a lot of greenery. If you live in a big city that has very limited nature, visit your nearest park or simply surround your home with indoor plants and greenery.
- Begin to practice mindfulness and analyze your thoughts when surrounded by nature. If your benevolence chakra feels clogged, begin to reflect in oneself.
- Find a private area to sit and be mindful in. Begin to analyze the times in your life where you are allowing different people to affect you. Think of the times where you have said "yes" to requests when really what you wanted to say "no". Whom in your life requires a lot of time and effort from you? Prepare yourself to say "no" during the times where you want to say it.
- Treat yourself with herbs. Use herbs such as roses, bounces, astragalus, hawthorn, angelica, and blessed basil to clear the love chakra. One of the best ways to use herbs is to drink them in a tea. To heal your center point chakra, I suggest Buddha Teas' serene and the natural soul Chakra Tea.
- Sympathize with yourself and others by asking "How would I feel if I were in their shoes?" This technique is able to clear any blockages that is capable of having the mind make up rash judgments about other individuals. These judgments are often unforgiving, and cold. For example, if an unpleasant person is being impolite to you, ask yourself, "What has happened in their life to make them the way they are now?" Or you can dig even deeper and ask, "What happened in that person's childhood that shocked them so much that they don't have the ability to connect with others?"
- Connect with other people more. People are well-known animals that need socialization in order to maintain the

harmony within themselves. Acts of physical socialization like hugging or cuddling opens up a person's energy. Hang out with your friends and family more. In the situation where you are not close enough to an individual to hug or have physical contact with them, you may ask if they are comfortable in holding your hand in order to exchange energy.

- Show our feelings instead of hiding them. One of the worst types of savagery within human nature is the one where we avoid feeling our own feelings. Our feelings were not made to be controlled or locked away. Instead, they are the innate nature of mankind. Open up your heart and allow yourself to encounter your emotions.
- Grow our love for ourselves and others. We deny love for ourselves and other people as a form of protection. Not allowing ourselves to receive love means that we cannot lose it. Denying love or compliments is a way to unbalance your chakra, instead, test the love that you receive with your thoughts.
- Consider healing with the healing stones.
- Be grateful.
- Fix your shadow self. Once our essential chakras are shut down, we are in the act of putting away a part of our miserable vitality into our subliminal minds. Your shadow self is the combination of all aspects of your old and denied character. This includes all contemplations, emotions, propensities, and socially heinous self-image parts that are put away. When you begin to accept those dark parts of yourself, your soul opens a little more. Focus on accepting parts of yourself that you have tried to hide away and repress.
- Sanitize your inside chakra with the use of essential oils. Use oils such as; angelica, marjoram, ylang, neroli, lavender, and rose. You can put these oils into a diffuser, rub them on your wrist, or spray them on articles of clothing.
- Carry out an exculpation ritual. Write a loving communication to yourself by requesting absolution and carry out this ritual in a place where you deem it is safe. In the event that you are in an argument with another individual, try a self-structured

ritual that incorporates one of the four elements of the world; earth, fire, water, and air.

- Keep yourself well-nourished. Introduce the following leafy foods into your eating routine which will help recuperate your soul chakra; celery, kiwi, grapes, spinach, zucchini, kale, peppers, apples, cabbage, pears, chard, avocados, lettuce, peas, and broccoli.
- Clear out any chakra blockages through the use of yoga. Stretch out and activate your core chakra vitality with yoga postures. For example, camel, cobra, nose, feline, and falcon poses.
- Learn about breathing exercises. Since your center chakra is led by the flow of air, learning how to inhale and exhale is fundamental. You can utilize different breathing methods such as; nostril breathing, or organic breathing. Remember, breathing shallowly using your chest does not produce the results that you want. The deeper our breaths are, the more oxygen we present to our cells. The more oxygen that we have within us, the more it can enhance our digestion capacities. In the event that you are sick due to an overactive warmth chakra and begin to feel symptoms of nervousness, low breathing is a compelling practice.
- Use positive Affirmations. Affirmations are positive statements about yourself that remind you of the good parts of yourself and help you to feel positive inside. For example, "I am open," "I am who I am," "I love others" "I listen with my heart," "I pardon others and myself" "I care for my internal identity," "I am worthy of adoration," "I cherish myself" test opening every one morning with one of these insistences.
- Be sympathetic. Do this by reviewing how to let go of your ego
- Complete something consistently. Stick with things when they become difficult. Removing blockages
- Would you say you are a thoughtful individual? Gathering blocked point of convergence chakras allows you to act naturally and with sincerity. In classification to begin your heart, shot liability a little sympathetic all day and speak with others. For instance, your power to give a compliment to somebody or support somebody.

- Laugh! Laughing is great medicine and it works with the center chakra. Get back in touch with your inner child and laugh often. While you watch funny cat videos on YouTube.
- Yell "YAM!" This positive exclamation matches the fear of the consideration chakra. Try dragging out the letters into sounds, for example, "yyyyyyaaaaaammmmmmm." You can also prefer to tune in to binaural beats (a way of using music as therapy or treatment) which serves to actuate and clear each and every one of the chakras through sound waves.

Chapter 6
The Throat chakra

The throat chakra, or Vishuddha, is the foundation of vitality contained by our bodies. It is associated with truth, correspondence, and being accountable. Situated at the base of the neck, the throat chakra is related to the color indigo and the bit of ether. This chakra is responsible for the vitality and credibility, imagination, and comprehension.

As per the Hindu custom, the throat chakra is the vitality inside in our bodies in control of conveying our individual truth! When tune into the pink throat chakra we are inventive, legitimate, sure, decisive, and certain of communicating our reality to the world.

In any case, when we have a blocked throat chakra we battle with disasters, for example, dread of communicating our verbal forcefulness, musings, untrustworthiness, bashfulness, determination, social uneasiness, deceptive nature, dishonesty, and not have of imagination. In the event that you get a blocked throat chakra, it may have to do with your adolescence. Were you left out of a fortune by your folks or guardians? Did your family make fun of you? Were your considerations, thoughts, and sentiments ignored? On the off chance that you had an inclination that you couldn't transparently share your thoughts and emotions, you developed an unfortunate throat chakra. This handbook will help you start recuperating your blocked throat chakra. Throat chakra restoring involves opening, adjusting, and filtering the throat chakra in our bodies. By and large, throat chakra medicine uses a wide range of all-encompassing therapeutic solutions to align the body, brain, and soul. These cures involve the practices of, for example, recuperating, self-care, self-inquiry, yoga, aromatherapy, dye therapy and countless others.

Symptoms of an Unhealthy Throat Chakra

The technique to identify unhealthy throat chakra regardless of whether you need to unblock your throat chakra is to rediscover intrigue to your emotions, activities, and human environment in your body. Here are specific examples;

- You recover it thoroughly to express your feelings in a way
- You struggle to express your thoughts
- You think nobody cares about your sentiments, or ...
- You probably impulsively express your sentiments to others
- You battle karma because of miscommunications in your connections with others
- You always feel unnoticed or misunderstood by others
- You worry you won't be seen by others
- You are on edge in discussions
- You are timid around others
- You find it unacceptable to be your true self
- You are at risk of being stubborn, or ...
- You battle to share your own thoughts
- You have trouble being understood
- You repeatedly spend time with people that don't understand you or your feelings
- You find it difficult to be genuine with others
- Your actions don't match your words
- You are inflicted with swollen lymph nodes in your neck
- Your weight fluctuates or remains low
- You have hypo or hyperthyroidism
- You often have ear infections
- You often have sinus, throat or high respiratory infections

Throat Chakra Blockage

Did you know that close to each other are two different kinds of chakra? While a blocked throat chakra is manifested as uninvolved or effectively "numb," an unbalanced throat chakra is manifested as forceful or hyper. Here's a breakdown of the difference between the two:

When you throat chakra is blocked, you are tired, drowsy, uninvolved, and hindered (no vitality in you).

When you have an unbalanced throat chakra, you are vivacious, disturbed, responsive, forceful, outwards (too much vitality in you). In this manner, on the off chance that you have a lacking throat chakra, you will not show the following; modesty, vulnerability and mystery. Then again, on the off chance that you get an unbalanced throat chakra you will be obstinate, unfriendly, and have the tendency to be socially oppressive.

What does a nourished and balanced throat chakra look like?

When you have a solid and wonderful throat chakra, you will be self-assured in your aptitude to state your opinions and sentiments confidently. You will be open, familiar, and bold to express how you truly feel. Authenticity will be apparent in your connections with others, and you will show your trustworthiness. With a healthy throat chakra, you will have lucidity, trust, euphoria, and bluntness as a final product of a mind that is happy to talk with certainty.

Healing of the Throat Chakra

At this time are the best throat chakra relieving practices which will benefit you if you have a blocked throat chakra;

1. Advantage from having a mantra
   Useful for: Blockages

Mantras are comprised of repeated phrasing or on the other hand sounds that help you to remember things and bring them to your awareness. Within reach are heaps of ancient mantras, for example, "Om," "Ham-Sa," "Om Mani Padme Hum," "I am," and so on. Some choose mantras related to their preferred spirit or divinity for example, "Shiva," "Kali," "Hecate," "Osiris," "Neptune," and so on. You can also come up with up your very own mantra.

2. Mantra Example "HAM"
Useful For: Stronger blockages

This ideal mantra matches the throb of the throat chakra. Hear what you feel into sounds, for example, "hhhhhaaaaaammmmmmm." You can also use binaural beats (a professional form of music treatment) which actuates and clears all of the chakras through unpredictable music sound waves.

3. Helpful foods
Useful for: lacking and unbalanced blockages of throat chakra

Introduce the following leafy foods into your eating routine for the throat chakra: blueberries, blackberries, cerulean grapes, currants, kiwifruit, apples, grapefruit, lemons, pears, plums, peaches, figs, and apricots.

4. Firm mending
Useful for: insufficient and undue blockages

Sound healing treatment is useful for decontaminating the throat chakra. Instruments, for example, singing dishes, gongs, and tuning forks because of the selective sentiments they transmit. As well as other sound therapeutic treatments.

5. Start journaling your thoughts
Useful for: lacking blockages

On the off chance that you are battling with verbalizing your thoughts and emotions, try different things like expressing them in a private diary. Designate time each day to write down how you feel, and don't worry about grammar, for example, language structure or discipline structure. Permit your emotions and sentiments to course energetically through your hand and onto the page.

6. Inhale into your stomach
Useful for: lacking and outrageous blockages

Talking unnecessarily quickly and rashly, or on the other hand not in any manner, are like a secret language that your throat chakra is aware of and it can thus become imbalanced. Inhale seriously into your stomach therefore that it extends delicately. Concentrate on this sensation and allow it to center your vitality.

7. Control the following herbs
Useful for: inadequate and undue blockages

Use herbs, for example, elm tree leaves, peppermint, fennel, elderberry, Echinacea, clove, spearmint and cinnamon. One of the top propensities to buy herbs is to lift me-up them as tea. For the throat chakra, I propose Buddha Teas' soothing and 100 percent natural Throat Chakra Tea. This tea is injected with the substance of sea green/blue.

8. Grade treatment
Useful for: inadequate and undue blockages

Blue is the color of the throat chakra. Try gazing at the night sky, covered with blue, or encompassed with cobalt and comment on the distinction. One of my favorite types of treatment is painting. On the off chance that you are good at art, building your throat chakra by painting with dark colors as the main shading.

9. Show appreciation for life by saying "thank you"
Useful for: lacking and pointless blockages

Now and again our throat chakras are blocked for the reason that our minds are full of suspicions and let this "thank you" bubble up within you.

10.   Consider with the following,
Useful for: insufficient and strong blockages

Use gems as totems that will support you while you heal your throat chakra vitality. Try using, for example, "lapis lazuli, blue kyanite, azurite, larimar, tanzanite, and sea green/blue."

147

11. Listen carefully
Useful for: unreasonable blockages

If your throat chakra is increasing in levels of vitality, you may battle with overwhelming discussions and overlooking other individuals. This affection may advance you into getting irritated with your companions, relatives, accomplices or associates. To combat this, practice breathing into your mid-region and listening steadily to what the other individual is saying. Survey their group language – now and then an individual's demeanors don't mix with their words. To tell them that you're listening, nod.

12. Laughter and fun used for clearance
Useful for: lacking and an excess of blockages

Purging is a vitality discharging technique which will help you get rid of impurities in your throat chakra. show your disappointment through giggling or shouting. For instance, on the off chance that you have an extraordinary throat chakra blockage, shout into your pillow.

13. Clear obstructions with yoga
Useful for: lacking and unbalanced blockages

Fix your throat chakra by doing yoga stretches, for example, the fish, lion, and dog. You may also prefer to add in words of one syllable while moving your body around tenderly to activate the blood stream.

14. Sing to yourself
Useful for: insufficient and undue blockages

Singing is an appealing sense to delicately begin the throat chakra. On the off chance that you think unsure, sing to by hand gently absent from other people. You force similar like to pay attention to music or keep an eye on a motion picture that causes you to search for to sing.

15. Flush out the throat chakra with significant oils
Useful for: inadequate and outrageous blockages

Use oils, for example, rosemary, frankincense, myrrh, ylang-ylang, clove, neroli, and eucalyptus. From the canister put these oils into a grease up diffuser, rub them on your wrist (in a watered-down mixture), or clothing them in a diffusing pendant.

16. Drink pure water
Useful for: lacking and an overactive amount of blockages

Pure and/or distilled water is critical for your throat chakra wellbeing. In the event that you accept that your stream is debased with contaminants, for example, fluoride and chlorine, purposeful putting resources into a load up with tears channel.

17. Renew your throat chakra representation
Useful for: lacking and extraordinary blockages

Envision an agonizing or whirling circle of splendid naval force diverting in your throat chakra region. Think about the circle of sad vitality dissolving out and out blockages or forceful progressions of vitality in you.

18. Enjoy your downtime
Useful for: lacking and extraordinary blockages

As strange as it might appear, use time your downtime to drown out that incessant voice in your head. By enabling your center impact to rise, you will fortify your throat chakra. Yogis constantly lead pledges of quietness to loan a hand them interconnect included wholeheartedly with senior awareness.

19. Using massages and rubs
Useful for: insufficient and superfluous blockages

Neck back rubs are hence quieting and comforting as they improve to reallocate the vitality captured in your neck. Get out a polo neck rub from a rehearsed masseuse, or then again reason an oversee massager, (for example, this one) to manipulate your neck. I guidance warming up a warm pack and applying it to your segment of land before you rub by hand as this will cheer your muscles to unwind.

20. Learn to say "no"
Useful for: lacking blockages

Learning to say "no" can be one of the most effective things that you can do to improve your throat chakra. Often, we feel compelled to do everything that your friends and family want us to do. However, there is a limit in which we cannot be any more productive. At this point, it is important to say "no". While that may cause some displeasure in your interlocutor, it is important to ser clear boundaries both at home and work.

Chapter 7
Third eye chakra

The third separation chakra, or Ajna, is the vitality center point contained by our bodies that is in control for instinct, creative mind, thought, and mindfulness. Situated in the point of convergence of the temples directly above the eyes, the third judgment chakra is combined with the color sky blue and the pineal organ contained by the cerebrum. This chakra orders the vitality connected with knowledge and intelligence. The third eyeball chakra is the vitality hub in our mass faithful for instinct, reality, thought, recognition, and showing. As per yogic way of thinking, the third eye is identified with duality which is a catch of recognition that contradicts truth and is designed only by the brain.

On one event the third eye chakra is in agreement with the have a rest of the chakras, it is asserted that a passage towards profound illumination is opened. At the point when our third segregation chakra is vacuum and adjusted, we set up energy with clearness and have furious passionate balance, understanding, instinct and mindfulness.

Then again, when our third eye chakra is blocked or imbalanced, we watch out for to battle with tribulations, for example, distrustfulness, shut mindedness, uneasiness, pessimism, sorrow, and arranged other psychological instabilities and state of mind clutters. In the event that you meditate you power experience a blocked third look at chakra, accept help to your youth. Is it true that you were brought up in a shut disapproved of family? Was illuminated positive about your adolescence, or were you molded to "comply without addressing"? Was your underlying energy condition genuinely steady? Did you guardians or overseers review your bits of knowledge and points of view? If not, you perhaps battle with third gaze at chakra issues as a

151

finish of your youth molding. Try not to stress, this escort will help you start your private single technique for third acumen chakra recuperating. Third judgment chakra medicinal is the experience of purging, opening, and adjusting the third eyeball chakra in our bodies.

Thirdly, take a gander at how chakra therapeutic utilizes a broad range of comprehensive relieving solutions for pass arrangement to the body, brain, and soul. These cures hold onto practices, for example, contemplation, care, paint treatment, reverberation mending, yoga, self-request, fragrant healing, and a great deal of others.

Symptoms of an Unhealthy Third Eye Chakra

The most important signs to consider whether your neediness to experience third eye chakra therapy is to relinquish fixation to your contemplations, activities, sentiments, and crude emotions inside your body. Here are a few secret signs to be on the lookout for:

- You are not often surprised or engaged by the things around you
- You get rid of tuning into your instincts
- You are excessively energetic or enthusiastic
- You are consumed by the thought of following a "master plan" that will guide the way that you expect things to be done
- You are over and over again preoccupied with your thoughts
- You routinely drift into inattention to pass up on reality
- You are unusually fixated on extraordinary "powers" (ability to interpret dreams, clairvoyance, predicting the future and so on.)
- You are sincerely receptive and deal with chaos effectively
- You're dependent on material assets which you acknowledge as necessary to accomplish your goals

(shopping, connections, status, sustenance, cash, sex, and so on.)

- You are overly fixated on attaining social status and economic wellbeing
- You don't seem to be too concerned with connecting with your higher self
- Your communications with other people are shallow or impersonal
- You have trouble relating to people at a personal level
- You don't concern yourself with environmental issues or think about the importance of nature
- You are obstinate or set in your ways
- You seem to be overly liberal
- You may choose to flaunt material wealth or social status
- You are seen as egotistical and conceited
- You may experience headaches and other physical discomfort on a regular basis
- You seem to "tune out" at times
- You're far more concerned about getting the results you want
- You need center and definitiveness
- You might suffer from blurry vision and sinus infections
- You experience daydreams or drifting away

Third Eye Chakra Blockage

Third eye chakra blockage generally makes you feel as if you are "out of tune" with yourself and the world around you. It is like you are aware of everything that is going around you, but you can't really make heads or tails of what's happening. For example, you are in a meeting, you hear what everyone is saying, you actually understand every word that is uttered, yet you can't really make sense of what the meeting is about. By the end, you don't have a sense of what actually happened. All you know is that you were at that meeting and that various issues were discussed.

Another sign that is illustrates blockage of this chakra is your inability to focus and concentrate especially for longer periods of time. Often, it can be difficult to really sit down and focus on something which you are doing. For instance, you might be watching television but may feel compelled to be on your phone or checking your messages every couple of minutes. If you are reading or attempting to do any type of cognitive tasks, you may find it virtually impossible to actually center your attention for a period exceeding a couple of minutes.

Other folks experience issues with sleep and rest. When this occurs, you may feel tired and very sleepy. However, you may not be able to actually fall asleep once you are in bed. The main culprit behind this inability to sleep is a sense of restlessness and inability to relax. Now, it might the result of anxiety over something in your life. However, a third eye chakra blockage might make it hard for you to just relax and get a good night's sleep.

Lastly, blockages of this chakra are also associated with the inability to establish a good relationship with the circumstances surrounding you. For instance, you might feel that everyone is out to get you at your job. You feel that everyone's got something they want from you or you feel that they are out to get you. The reason for this is that you don't feel entirely comfortable with yourself and the situation you are in. Often, your suspicions and feelings have nothing to do with actually hatred. However, your inability to find a sense of ease may lead you to feel this way. As a result, you won't feel comfortable with yourself and the circumstances you find yourself in.

So, it is important to pay attention to these signs that are being transmitted by your third eye chakra. When you are able to free the blockage, it will be like lifting the veil from your eyes thereby enabling you to see things are clearly as you possibly can. This would certainly be a great way to make your life a lot more interesting and rewarding.

Healing the Third Eye Chakra

This section is dedicated to a collection of practices which are intended to help heal the third eye chakra thereby restoring its functionality and returning the vitality back to your body and life. Here are the practices in no particular order:

1. Open your mind to other points of view and perspectives.
   Useful for: unreasonable blockages

One of the biggest issues that affect most people with third eye blockages is being unreasonable and even intransigent. This means they are close-minded and have a hard time accepting the viewpoints of others. So, make an effort at being more open-minded and accepting what others have to say and the things they have to offer. It could be that something or someone you dismissed may end up providing you with a wealth of knowledge and guidance.

2. Decalcify your pineal gland
   Useful for: physical blockages

Your pineal gland is a minor pea-shaped gland that is located at the top of your head, but deep inside your brain. It is commonly associated with third eye chakra blockages. The pineal gland is in charge of a number of regulatory functions including sleep and mood. Countless ancient societies such as the Tibetan, Egyptian, and Chinese had the idea that the pineal organ is the center for otherworldly awareness. To decalcify your pineal organ, a reduction in fluoride is recommended. This can be done by drinking purified spring water that is free of this chemical.

3. Incorporate mindfulness into your life
   Useful for: deficient blockages

Mindfulness is that state of being constantly aware of your surroundings at all times. This can provide you with a great sense of joy and pleasure as you being to see how wonderful the world around you really is. So, don't concern yourself too much with what's bring you down. Rather, take the time to enjoy what's going on around you.

4. Venture out into the daylight
   Useful for: inadequate and lopsided

Exposure to sunlight in one of the best ways in which you can stimulate the pineal gland. Sunlight activates the functions of the pineal gland in such a way that you won't have to concern yourself with doing any additional exercises. If you spend a great deal of time indoors under artificial lighting, make a point of spending a few minutes outside every day. This will help recharge your body of valuable sunlight.

5. Increase consumption of herbs
Useful for: deficient and extraordinary blockages

Herbs such as lotus, mugwort, rosemary, star anise, passionflower, saffron, jasmine, basil, and lavender are all great at helping develop your third eye. Many of these herbs can be consumed in the form of herbal tea. This is perhaps the easiest way to do so. Other ways in which you can achieve the desired effect on your body is through incense and essential oils. Scented candles work very well, too.

6. Find out what is limiting your convictions
Useful for: unreasonable blockages

Since being unreasonable is one of the main issues with a third eye blockage, it is important for you to figure out what is causing you to become overly unreasonable. Of course, the blockage itself is spurring you to act in this manner. But could there be something else that is also affecting the way you react? For example, could it be that you are somehow afraid of something? Is there a person, or situation, which is causing you a great deal of stress and anxiety? Finding these sources can go a long way into determining what is actually blocking you.

7. Making use of the mantra "OM"

Useful for: inadequate blockages

The mantra "OM" is a staple of meditation practice. It is used to help focus the mind on the present and clear up consciousness of the incessant amount of information that comes and goes. Through this practice, the mantra is able to help harmonize the mind and the body in such a way that all chakras (not just the third eye) can begin to open up. This leads the body to open up its natural energetic pathways. It is perhaps the single-most effective meditative practice that you can engage in.

8. Improve overall quality of nutrition in order to free up blockages
Useful for: physical blockages

One of the most common elements that promote blockages is a poor nutrition. Now, it should be said that it is not the nutrition itself that produces the blockages. Rather, it is the intoxication that occurs in the body as a result of a poor nutrition. A diet based on high amounts of sugar, carbs, alcohol and even toxic substances such as narcotics and nicotine can lead to a significant intoxication of the body. This is why reducing the consumption of all of these elements can promoted the body's detoxification. In addition, the consumption of fruits, vegetables, fresh water and tea can help promote the physical liberation of cellular process that, in turn, promote the growth and opening of all chakra centers and not just the third eye.

9.   Seek spiritual guidance
Useful for: inadequate and spiritual blockages

Seeking spiritual guidance is a great way of clearing up blockages. If you are connected with your faith, then leaning on it will certainly help you improve your chakras' energy processing. If you are not overly religious, it is a good idea to seek a connection with your spiritual self in the manner that you feel most comfortable.

11. Engage in self-reflection and analysis
Useful for: lacking and a lot of blockages

Self-reflection is a great habit to build as it enhances your mindfulness. Self-reflection essentially consists in asking yourself questions about what you do, what you feel and what you plan to do. You can take on a greater understanding of these ideas by journaling. You can write as much or as little as you want. By having a written record of your ideas, you can get an idea of the progression of your thoughts.

12. Try out stargazing
    Useful for: unreasonable blockages

Looking up at the night sky can be a wonderful and exciting task. By staring into the vast expanse of the universe, you can gain a better perspective of the place you occupy in the universe. While this isn't intended to help you feel small, it is intended to help you concentrate your energy on the here and now.

13. Aromatherapy through the use of essential oils
    Useful for: blockages resulting from overactivity

The use of essentially oils is a great way to help you relax and calm your nerves especially when you are overactive. My using essential oils, you can help unblock your chakra's energy pathways. Oils such as lavender are ideal to do this. Burning incense is also a great idea.

14. Contemplate yourself as a "third person"
    Useful for: insufficient and undue blockages

When attempting Vipassana contemplation, you are embarking on a type of reflection exercise in which you literally see yourself as a third person. This means that you try your best to visualize yourself from the perspective of an outside spectator. The main objective of this is to observe your actions, behaviors and attitudes in such a way that you are not actively involving your feelings. This will help you gain an additional perspective which you may not have at this moment.

15. Visualize your third eye in action
    Useful for: mental and emotional blockages

In this exercise, you will close your eyes and literally visualize a glowing disk in between your eyes. This exercise will help you focus on opening the third eye in such a way that you can bust through whatever blockages there may be. Generally speaking, it is not easy to make this exercise work at first. Over time, you will find that it is not hard, and you can sustain this image for a long time usually lasting several minutes.

16. Visualize the outcomes you wish to achieve
Useful for: inadequate and extraordinary blockages

Visualization is one of the most powerful tools you can use in meditation. It helps to liberate blockages by allowing the power of the mind to open the chakras in such a way that you can harmonize your energy's pathways. When there is a blockage, your energy gets stuck and subsequently stagnates. That is why visualizing the outcomes that you wish to achieve, for any type of situation, helps your mind direct the energy that you seek to channel through the various energy points in the body. For example, if you have an upcoming job interview, you can take the time to visualize the situation playing the outcome in your mind. When you do this, the creative energy of the third eye manifests itself in such a way that you are able to literally create your own reality.

17. Exercises using crystals
Useful for: insufficient and unbalanced blockages

The use of crystals and gems is a common practice in this area. Ideally, you would find a pure stone which you can place in a well-lit area. The sunlight that passes through it will radiate a light which you can absorb by watching it. Examples of these gems and stones include amethyst, shungite, labradorite, sapphire, kyanite, lapis lazuli.

18. Practice a good dose of self-love
Useful for: insufficient and undue blockages

A great way of practicing self-love is through the use of loving affirmations. These affirmations can range from anything such as "I am one with love" or "I am connected to the loving energy of the Earth". Any of these affirmations will help you embrace the loving feeling that comes to you from all corners of the Earth.

19. Regularize your vitality with yoga
Useful for: physical and emotional blockages

Practicing yoga has long been considered to be one of the best exercises to balance out both physical and emotional blockages. You can engage in this practice as much as you like but keeping in mind that you can get the most out of it by practicing it on a regular basis.

20. Staring at fire
Useful for: inadequate and an excess of blockages

Staring at a fire is known as Trataka in Hatha Yoga. This technique is intended to help you visualize the matter that is contained within fire. As such, you will be able to imbibe the healing energy of light and warmth. Also, fire's sacred qualities are useful at stimulating all of the body's chakra energy centers and not just one or two individual ones. Best of all, you can carry out this exercise with a scented candle or in front of a roaring fire in a peaceful and serene area.

Chapter 8
The Crown chakra

The crown chakra, or sahasrara, is the vitality center contained within our bodies. It is liable for mindfulness, thought, shrewdness, and our bond to the Divine. Situated at the top part of the head, the crown chakra is linked with the influence purple light and the pituitary gland inside the brain. This chakra helps to transform the energy of consciousness. The Crown Chakra, also commonly known as Sahasrara in Sanskrit. This energy center is considered to be the "thousand-petaled" blooms at the excellence of our control and is emblematically depicted as a lotus flower.

This sacred energy core is the seat of cosmic consciousness that all and every one of us carries. As the seat of divine awareness, the crown chakra connects us to the eternal. In Tantric philosophy, the crown chakra, when in balance gives and receives the energy of consciousness. In other words, it is the connection that we have, as humans, between the restricted and infinite. What does our crown chakra express? How can you be aware of what it's like when it is healthy and open? As soon as our crown chakra is balanced, we can become aware of the various signs that indicate we are at one with our Higher Self. That means that we are in touch with the more sensitive aspects of our being. On the contrary, symptoms of a blocked crown chakra include depression, a feel of disaffection or fleeing from life, and need of empathy.

A blocked crown chakra tends to be the outcome of living in highly stressful environments, fast-paced lifestyles, and dealing with trauma such as those experience from early childhood. But overall, having a blocked crown chakra is the result of neglecting our spiritual self. While this doesn't necessarily mean embracing an austere and religious lifestyle, it does imply that we do not pay the same attention that we would normally to our spiritual needs.

The crown chakra is the gateway to the soul. As such, we need to be aware of the manifestations that our soul has on us. These manifestations can some in a number of ways. Mainly, our sensitivities to the world become more prominent. For instance, you might become more empathetic to the needs or others or feel compelled to take part in charitable actions which can lead to alleviate the suffering of others.

Symptoms of Unhealthy of the Crown Chakra

As we with other chakras, there are telltale signs that indicate a blocked chakra. While there are general manifestations across the board, the fact of the matter is that some symptoms become more pronounced as compared to others. So, here is a list of symptoms to watch out for when it comes to a blocked crown chakra.

- Apathy
- Lack of sensitivity and compassion towards others
- Excessive selfishness
- Insomnia
- Nightmares / night terrors
- Boredom with life
- Feeling of disaffection from others
- Narrow-mindedness / dogmatism
- Existential depression
- Spiritual disconnection
- Rigid and close-minded self-identity
- Greed and materialism
- Lack of purpose and direction
- Mental fog / confusion
- Loneliness
- Chronic fatigue
- Headaches / migraines
- Light sensitivity
- Mental illnesses that include delusions (e.g. Schizophrenia)

While there is no conclusive literature, there have been some links to neurological diseases that suggest that a blocked crown chakra can exacerbate mental illness. As such, it is an often-overlook cause.

A deficient or overactive Crown Chakra

An overactive chakra generally tends to lead the individual to have attitudes that seem exaggerated when compared to the "normal" behavior or regular folks. This behavior can be identified as people who tend to overthink everything, that is, they cannot seem to stop thinking about the problems and situations that may be hidden in everything. They are also overly concerned that everyone around them has a hidden agenda. As a result, they are constantly looking over their shoulder waiting to see when the next attack will come.

Overactivity isn't nearly as common as a blockage, though overactivity is a type of blockage. Nevertheless, when a person has an overactive chakra, it can be rather difficult for them to make the most of their cognitive abilities. This can be seen in people who have trouble concentrating or may display signs of hyperactivity. These folks may not be able to concentrate on a single action or activity while attempting to carry out multiple actions at the same time. This is attitude is hardly conducive to a productive lifestyle.

People who manifest an overactive crown chakra may also have an active imagination. However, this imagination can go overboard at times and even lead to delusions. If this were to be the case, it could be the sign for the onset of some type of mental illness. This is the reason why delusions and hallucinations may be associated with an overactive crown chakra. When this occurs, meditation is the best way in which the individual can harness the power of their "visions" in such a way that they don't torment themselves, but rather, they can find a creative outlet for such feelings.

Healing the Crown Chakra

1. Meditate, meditate, and meditate

Meditation is the best way to restore crown chakra functioning. In short, this meditation ought to be focused at connecting the crown chakra with the violet light that comes from the center of the universe.

163

This light feeds the chakra and allows it to blossom. As a result, the chakra begins to open thereby allowing the individual to connect with their higher being. Also, visualization is useful to connect the chakra with the outcomes that the person wishes to achieve. Again, connect to the light while imagining positive outcomes enables the Higher Self to emerge and connect with waking consciousness.

2. Conscious shift in mindset

The old philosophical truism that we are what we think rings very true. As a result, it is important to begin replacing negative and unproductive thoughts with positive and creative ones. To do this, all you need to do is tell yourself that you are whatever you want to be. For instance, if you are looking to lose weight, you must begin by replacing thoughts of "I look fat" to thoughts "I am slimming down". If you are looking to be successful in your chosen profession, then you need to begin by telling yourself that you will achieve your goals and dreams. If you constantly tell yourself that you have bad luck and that nothing does right for you, then these negative thoughts permeate your consciousness. Consequently, the crown chakra gets clogged up with negative thoughts. When you shift mindset, you allow the positive energy to flow through your unconscious mind and eventually break through to your conscious mind.

3. Working with your energy

Energy management is crucial. This includes all types of exercises which can help the free flow of energy throughout the various centers of your body. This many include both mental and physical exercise. Of course, it should be noted that physical exercise is always a great idea to help you get the most out of the physical energy that your body is able to produce. Examples of activities which you can do to improve your energy as qigong, massage, gong, yoga, reiki, acupressure, acupuncture, among others.

4. Educate yourself

The pursuit of intellectual endeavors is algo a good way of helping the crown chakra get into high gear. Intellectual abilities are important because they help the mind develop its abilities in such a way that the individual is able to further their understanding of the world around them. In such cases, reading about any number of topics, watching educational videos, or even taking a class are great ways in which the mind can open up to new information and new challenges. Since the mind acts like any other muscle in the body, the more that it is exercises the stronger it will get. As the crown chakra opens up, you will find that you become "more intelligent" though that intelligence that you have uncovered is mostly the product of a clear chakra as opposed to increased cognitive abilities.

5. "Cleanliness is next to Godliness"
Simplify your surroundings. While this doesn't mean becoming a minimalist overnight, it does mean that reducing clutter around you will help you improve the overall amount of disorder in your life. When you are able to do this, you will find that your mind becomes free to explore the world around it. Perhaps having a tidier workspace will enable you to focus better on your tasks. As a result, you will become more productive and more adept at getting work down under various situations.

6.   Use the "OM" mantra.
The "OM" mantra is a powerful too. This channel matches the pulsation of the crown chakra. The effect of "OM" on the brain is similar to that of binaural beats. The effect it has on brainwave patterns is rather similar. So, it can be inferred that the vibration produced by this sound will enable the individual to get the same benefits without having to resort to the equipment and sounds needed to produce the effects of binaural beats.

7.   Explore the benefits of herbal medicine
When you suffer from physical ailments (so long as they are not serious diseases) it is best to explore plant-based medicine as an alternative. The reasoning behind this is that natural or herbal medicine helps the body process vitamins and minerals that are needed in order to help the body produce the elements it needs to repair itself. In this way, you can also achieve a healthy mind-body balance derived from your ability to make the most of your ability to choose healthy ingredients to feed your body. So, do take the time to explore the power to herbs when you are suffering from ailments such as a cold, flu, fatigue, or any other type of condition that doesn't require a major medical intervention.

165

8.   Firmly commit to your personal spiritual practice

A personal spiritual practice can differ from person to person. The fact of the matter is that there is no right or wrong way to go about it. We all have different types of activities in which we engage. Some of us a more dedicated to following the guidelines that are established by a specific religion while others are more dedicated to the teachings of a given school of philosophical thought. The truth is that it doesn't matter what type of approach you take. The main point is to ensure that you are aware of what you need to do in order to help you achieve a direct connection with your Higher Self.

That is where meditation and contemplation help connect your conscious mind with your Higher Self. At first, you may simply try to communicate without much of a noticeable difference. Over time, you will notice that your perception of the world around you will begin to change. So, make the time to dedicate your attention to your spiritual practice. It will definitely help you clear any blockages in your crown chakra.

9.   Acknowledge the power of prayer

Prayer doesn't have to be religious. You can pray to the higher power in which you believe in, whether that be your Spirit Guides, Ancestors, God/Goddess, Universe, Life, Spirit, or Soul. Prayer is about connecting to the more subtle nature of the universe. The power of prayer is undeniable as it provides a great deal of health benefits. It can also help you to focus on your more subtle energies that flow from yourself to the expanse of the universe.

10.   The power of crystals and gems

In earlier sections, we have talked about the importance of gems and crystals. They can help to hone energies into a single spot. The most effective way is to surround yourself with them much in the same manner you would with essential oils and flowers. At the end of the day, this combination will help you focus your energies and concentration on the tasks you need to accomplish

.

11.   Be approachable to guidance

By being approachable to guidance you are not submitting your will to the teachings and direction of others. What you are going is opening your mind so that you are willing to become more receptive to the teachings and guidance that others, basically any person, can offer you. As a result, you will become more open-minded in such a way that you can take advantage of the various ways in which knowledge can come to you.

When you are approachable, you won't dismiss other perspectives and new ideas simply because they are not the same as yours. You will learn to take everything with a grain of salt while also making the most of your own ideas. When you are able to mesh new ideas with your own, you will begin to grow as a person in such a way that you can achieve a greater understanding of the world around.

12.   Positive affirmations

Positive affirmations are related with the universal concept pertaining to the power of word. When you make a declaration, you are letting it be known to the universe that something will happen. For example, when you declare that you are free of all mental bondage, you open up your mind to become liberated of all negative conditioning. Likewise, when you make the most of your understanding of the world around you, you can begin to make sense of how powerful you really are. That is why you need to be careful with the way you express yourself since negative affirmations can work just as well as positive ones.

13.   Perform a crown chakra visualization

For this exercise, visualizing your charka as a spinning disk sitting atop your head works very well. This exercise allows you to literally open your mind. As you gain more proficiency with this exercise, you will be able to make the most of your talents by giving your chakra the exercise it needs.

14.   Beneficial herbs

Use herbs such a lavender, holy basil, gotu kola, and lotus. As we have discussed earlier, you can consume these herbs by means of an infusion tea, essential oils or even incense. The scent of these herbs stimulates the chakra while allowing your consciousness to become clearer and unimpeded. Also, consuming these herbs in a tea helps your body to absorb the nutrients in a natural and healthy manner.

15.   Wear the color violet
The color that is associated with the crown chakra is violet. So, wearing clothing or accessories that contain this color can be helpful in aiding your chakra absorb the energy that is emitted from the center of the universe. In a manner of speaking, it is a way in which you can become more receptive to this type of movement.

Chapter 9
Benefits of Chakra Balance

O nce you have put into practice the guidelines which we have outlined in this book, you can look forward to achieving balance among your entire chakra system. As you begin to achieve this balance you will find that it is much easier to reap the benefits of a healthy flow of energy throughout your body.

As, here are the most important signs which you can identify as you begin to feel healthier, more in balance and in tune with your entire chakra system:

1.   Chakra balance renews overall physical health and wellbeing Barring any serious physical diseases, most ailments tend to go away when the chakra system falls back into line. The benefits range from a number of minor ailments such as headaches, physical discomfort and digestive distress. A vast majority of folks indicate that many chronic conditions such as fatigue and even weight gain reduce as a result of chakra balancing. Also, conditions such as diabetes, thyroid and hormonal imbalances are noticeably more manageable. So, the physical health benefits are definitely evident when the entire chakra system enters into a state of balance.

2.   Chakra balance promotes spiritual and emotional wellness Balanced chakras tend to complete rejuvenate a person's spiritual wellbeing. Much of this is due to the release of blockages that may be the result of trauma stemming from childhood incidents or the accumulation of stress that occurs over a large period of time. In reality, achieving emotional and spiritual wellness is not nearly as hard as might be considered. Through meditation, visualization and

the use of the various techniques highlighted throughout this book, you can ensure that your chakras will slowly, but surely, all fall back into line. So, in addition to physical wellbeing, emotional conditions such as anxiety and depression all have a noticeable improvement over the long run.

3. Chakra balance promotes the release of negative energy stored in the body

The clearing of blockages leads to two things in the individual. The first, is the release of negative energy that is stuck in one, or various, chakra centers. This energy can come from any number of sources but may not find a natural release point. When the chakra system is balanced, the negative energy that enters the body flows through the various centers and exits accordingly. However, when there are blockages, the negative energy has nowhere to go. This is what leads to the overall accumulation of negative energy. In the end, the person feels drained, mentally distraught and emotionally frayed. The second thing that happens when balance is achieved is the flow of positive energy. As such, there is a balance as positive energy cancels out the negative kind. This promotes health, wellbeing and an overall sensation of wellness throughout the body. Mentally, this leads to sharper faculties and better performance in various aspects of life.

4. Chakra balance leads to a greater feeling of happiness

Given the fact that happiness is a relative term, we are referring to a feeling of fulfillment and joy in your life. Happiness is seen as the ability to achieve whatever it is that you wish to accomplish while enabling yourself to enjoy the fruits of your labor. In this manner, you are able to make the most of your time and efforts by leading yourself down a path in which you are surrounded by satisfaction as you transit from one productive stage to another. As you begin to accumulate success and make progress in life, you can then feel a sense of relief and enjoyment at the circumstances in your life. Eventually, you can trade negative feelings pertaining to the situation that you find yourself for a more positive outlook on life. This is especially true when you find yourself in a negatively charged environment such as a bad job or relationship.

5. Chakra balance allows you to connect with your Higher Self

The Higher Self is your soul, essence, spirit, or whatever you may call it. This essence is your connection to the vital core of the universe. Also, it is the way in which you are able to link with the vast expanse of the universe in a type of collective consciousness that most religions refer to as "God". This relationship is fostered regardless of faith as all faiths seek the same close relationship to the divine deity that it worships. As a result of chakra balance, you are able to achieve this closeness insofar as you are able to communicate appropriately, be it through prayer, sacrifice or any other means that you feel adequate such as meditation. In this regard, connecting to your Higher Self is the byproduct of raising your conscious awareness of yourself through practices such as mindfulness.

6. Chakra balance is beneficial in transforming your weaknesses into strengths

Considering that chakra balance involves emotional health and equilibrium, you are then able to tackle some of the bigger issues that may be surrounding you. For instance, you may be dealing with emotional conditions such as anxiety or depression. In this case, you have the opportunity to take a weakness (e.g. anxiety) and transform into a strength. This occurs when you are able to acknowledge the source of such feelings and then transform them into a context in which you are able to process the source of your feelings. In this event, you can now be proud of having defeated the condition which had you down on your knees. While it is true that some of these conditions never fully go away, that is, you may still feel the onset symptoms from time to time, you will be able to manage them in such as way that you will no longer be prey to a debilitating condition. Moreover, you may be able to help others who are going through the same circumstances as you once did.

7. Chakra balance can help you get a grip on your finances and material wellbeing

Healthy chakra balance may also influence your financial life in a positive manner. This is due to the fact that your emotional wellbeing can be translated into a renewed lease on life focused on the positive. For example, if your previous state was one of fatigue and negativity which was negatively impacting your performance at work, your newfound energy and drive can lead you to find a practical sense of efficiency in your day to day tasks. This will lead you to become more effective at work to the extent that you will now be more productive. This, in turn, may represent a financial gain which may have seemed like nothing more than a dream some time ago. A good example of this can be seen in a promotion at work, or the attainment of your targets. As a result, you will be able to make the most of your time and efforts by focusing on what really matters. All of that negative energy which was dragging you down will now be nothing more than a forgotten memory. So, it certainly pays to work on developing your emotional health through chakra balance as it will definitely have a positive impact on your personal finances.

8.   Chakra balance can help you turn your dreams into a reality
A simple example of this is procrastination. When you become a chronic procrastinator, you are falling prey to the cocktail of negative energy that is swirling around your being. As the negative energy vanishes, you can then set out to accomplish what you really want out of life. Ultimately, this may represent going back to school, improving your job skills, learning a language or starting a family. Whatever your plans may be, you will now have the motivation to set out and get it done. This is something which you might not have thought possible just a short while ago.

9.   Chakra balances improves your intuition
Intuition is often seen as some type of superpower in which a person is able to "feel" the truth or reality about something. The fact of the matter is that intuition is a byproduct of that connection with your Higher Self. Your Higher Self is nothing more than that pure essence which is connected to the overall hierarchy of the universe. As your consciousness links up directly with the universal consciousness, you are then able to intuit things that are about to happen, may be happening, or happened without your knowledge. In this regard, you'll be able to "predict" things that will happen, or at the very least, avoid potentially difficult situations. A common example of this can be seen in the way mothers protect their children by intuiting that danger lurks at some point. This is not a superpower, but rather, it is a connect that a concern mother develops with the universe out of the

concern for the safety of her child. This is a skill that anyone can develop so long as they achieve chakra balance.

10. Chakra balances helps promote healthy emotional management

Emotional instability is general a consequence of pent up negative energy that has nowhere to go in the body. At first, this energy is processed by the body through a series of symptoms such as headaches, physical discomfort (aches and pains) and other conditions such as a weakened immune system. When balance is restored, the body enters a phase in which negative energy can flow out of the body while positive energy transits in the same manner. This gives the impression of emotional balance. However, it is not that there is a presence of balance; the fact is that the overwhelming accumulation of negative energy is gone thereby giving the body the opportunity to process all of these negative conditions.

11. Chakra balances involves full mind-body balance

Perhaps the biggest benefit can be seen in the full mind-body balance that can be achieved through concerted effort in developing chakra balance. In this scenario, the mind and the body synch up in such a way that the body feels what the mind is feeling, and the mind can be used to heal the body.

It is really that simple. The body is able to perform up to the level that it was meant to be while the mind serves as the main processing control unit for the entire being.

12. Improved sense of empowerment

When chakra balance is achieved, a sense of empowerment is built up in the body. What this means is that the body is able to feel in good health while the mind is focused on what is currently at hand. As a result, the sense of empowerment emerges. This sense of empowerment is essentially the feeling of control that you have over your mind and your body. One of the most common symptoms of chakra imbalance is a sense of powerlessness over the circumstances surrounding the individual. With full chakra balance, it feels as if the individual is now in total control of not only themselves, but the entire universe around them. If you feel that this is nothing more than gobbledygook, then you will surely think twice when you see that empowerment is entirely possible. You will develop a sense of being the master of your destiny even when it seems like you are not.

Chapter 10
Radiate Positive Energy

E very moment of our lives is an opportunity to immerse ourselves in positive energy. Even when we sleep, we are putting ourselves into a position to receive positive energy from some corner of the universe. Believe it or not, positive energy travels through the universe just as negative energy does. In this manner, we, as humans, absorb energy on a constant basis.

As we pointed out earlier, when you achieve chakra balance, you are able to take both positive and negative energy and let it flow through its natural causeway. In the end, you are able to balance out your feelings and emotions to a degree in which they will no longer hinder the body. Moreover, this free flow of energy will enable you to feel more at ease with yourself and the universe around you.

Still, for all the negative energy that we receive on a daily basis, we are perfectly capable of becoming a source of positive energy for all of those around us. When you become a center for positive energy, everything around you begins to morph into a more positive environment. This can lead you to achieve your goals while helping others to achieve a better emotional, physical and spiritual condition. Ultimately, the only thing you are left with is a sense of happiness and fulfillment as you have been able to help others around you feel better.

As such, there are 50 ways in which you can become an agent for change and a source of positive energy.

50 Ways to radiate positive energy

1. Blast out a smile!

Studies have demonstrated that smiling is the only gesture that is universal across all cultures. This means that a smile is a smile in any part of the world. Moreover, it is contagious. A smile will almost always be meet with another smile. So, blast out a smile as often as you can. That way, you can get off on the right foot every time you meet someone.

2. A phone call can go a long way

Phone calls may be a thing of the past... well, maybe not so much. Still, phone calls aren't as common as they used to be. So, a well-placed phone call such as on a birthday, anniversary, or any other special occasion can lead to a pleasant reaction in someone special.

3. FORGIVE!

Forgiveness is one of the most overlooked reactions we can have. When you forgive, not only does your body actually let go of negative energy, but you are releasing positive energy to the source of your frustration. If you blame yourself for something which happened, then maybe it's time you forgave yourself.

4. Get into the habit of complimenting

Complimenting for the sake of complimenting is not the idea here. The main idea is to give well-placed compliments when they are earned. For example, when someone is looking their best especially after going through a tough spell is a good idea.

5. Be civil on the road

All too often we find ourselves duking it out in traffic on a regular basis. There are careless, inconsiderate and rude drivers. And yes, we tend to lose our cool and fight back when need be. However, try your best to be courteous. Give someone a chance to cut in when they are attempting to make a lane change and say thank you when someone gives you a chance. It could certainly make a difference in someone's day.

6. Give small tokens of appreciation

There are times when you can't do much to express your gratitude when someone does you a favor. Sure, you can always say "thank you", but that's often not enough. So, small tokens of appreciation can go a long way to ensuring that your helpful friends and colleagues feel that you truly appreciate what they have done for you.

7. Give encouragement

This is one of the most powerful things that you can do. If you see someone who needs a word of encouragement, do it! It doesn't matter if they are a stranger. They will surely pay it forward later.

8. Positive notes

Leaving positive notes lying around is a great way to help you stay on the right side of the ball. Motivational phrases that have a special connection to you work best. Also, inspirational pictures and paintings will help you get through long days.

9. Tip it!

Tipping for service isn't a custom in all parts of the world. Yet, a server will appreciate it if you leave them a tip for their kind attention. Often, they will appreciate the gesture and can brighten up their day.

10. Spread the wealth

By this we mean sharing your good fortune with others. No, this doesn't mean splattering your social media accounts with pictures of your good fortunes. It means that you can take the time to share your good fortunes with those who are needy. For example, you can give to charity or support causes you believe in.

11. Be mindful of the environment

What could be more positive than helping the environment? You can do your bit to help Mother Earth recover from pollution cause by humans. Recycling is a great place to start while ensuring that you do your part by conserving energy, water and trees. Plant a tree if you can. You can watch it grow over time.

12. Keep in touch

Social relationships are a great way of spreading positive energy. Often, all you need is to say hello in order to make someone's day. By being kind and sociable, those around you will feel that you care about them. This is a great way to boost their overall feelings of positivity.

13. Compliment a stranger

When you give kind words to random people such as saying nice things about their dog or thanking them for holding the door, you help spread good will and positive energy. Even something as small as saying "good morning" or "have a nice day" can go a long way.

14. Set goals for yourself

When you set goals for yourself, you are making declarations and statements of what you plan to achieve. As a result, you are not thinking with a limited mindset. Rather, you are thinking with an expanded mindset that is intended to help you make the most of your ideas and aims.

15. Use positive affirmations

Rephrasing everything in life, even problems, in positive language can go a long way toward helping you make the most of your situations. For example, if you are short on cash, replace "I don't have any money" for "where can I get more money?" In essence, you are shifting from a limited mindset to a growth mindset.

16. Donate to a good cause

Often, you don't need to become a billionaire philanthropist to help those in need. You can start by donating unwanted items that are cluttering up your home. You may not need them, but there are others who do.

17. Have dinner as a family

Sitting down and enjoying a meal together as a family, without any phones at the table, can really help foster a positive relationship among everyone. When you are keen on making this a custom in your home, your family will automatically become closer.

18. Pray for someone

This is a powerful way to help someone who needs it. If you find that someone needs positive vibes, then the power of prayer is not to be neglected. So, spare a moment and send those positive vibes along.

19. Look after children

Parents do this all the time. But beyond that, you can help causes that aim to help and support kids in need. Often, all a child needs is someone who believes in them.

20. Love thy enemy

This is more literal than metaphorical. By this, we advocate letting go of ill and bitter feelings toward those who have harmed you at one point or another. Letting go is often the best thing you can do.

21. Be kind to the elderly

Just like children, the elderly often need someone to show they care about them. So, donate your time or your resources toward helping those older folks who need kindness and attention.

22. Everyone deserves a second chance

Even when someone lets you down, you ought to make a point of giving them a second shot. After all, we all deserve another chance to prove that we have learned from our mistakes and moved on.

23. Get into books

Books are a great way of spreading cheer and joy. This can be in the way of donating books, reading them and sharing the knowledge they contain. You never know who needs a hand in learning.

24. Become a teacher

No, we don't mean changing professions (unless you're already a teacher). We mean sharing your knowledge and experience with others. There is surely something that you can teach others that will improve their lives.

25. Become an inspiration

Yes, you can become an inspiration by sharing your life story. You can share your hardships and how you overcame them. We all have something that we can share with others.

26. Be mindful of others' space

We generally invade others' space without noticing it. This is not only distressing, but it can be downright annoying. So, make sure that you respect others' space as much as you would like them to respect yours.

27. Hold the door

Pretty straightforward. It is a simple thing you can do show your appreciation for others.

28. Think twice before you speak

If you get into the habit of thinking before speaking, you won't have to apologize as much.

29. Apologize

And when you do make a faux pas, don't hesitate to apologize. By apologizing, you can quickly diffuse a situation. This can enable the relationship to emerge unscathed from a simple mistake.

30. Make amends

However, there are times when your mistakes cannot be correct with a simple apology. There are times when we need to make amends in one way or another. So, set out to do what you need to do in order to rectify the situation which you have caused. Often, it is not nearly as tough as you think.

31. Show your appreciation for your loved ones

When we get caught up in the day to day grind, we may not take the time to show our appreciation for our loved ones. So, make a point of telling them what you feel. They may already know it, but it is always nice to hear it especially when they are going through a rough patch.

32. Respect others' time

Time is such a valuable commodity. Once it's gone, it's not coming back. So, make the most of showing your respect for others' time by being punctual and sticking to the point. When you do this, you will show that you are both respectful and mindful of others' needs.

33. Create a positive environment for those around you

When you make a concerted effort to becoming a positive influence, you can help create a positive environment for others. This means being more cheerful than not while provide positive vibes. This is especially important in the workplace since we tend to spend a great deal of time surrounded by colleagues.

34. Verbalize your power to the universe

It's one thing to have positive thoughts and it's another completely different thing to say them out loud. When you declare, in your own voice, the positive things you wish to accomplish, both in your life and the life of others, you will attract the positive and creative energy of the universe. This will lead you to become more powerful than you could have ever imagined.

35. Discover what's inside those around you

How can you "read" people's minds? Ask them! Sit down and talk to those around you. Ask them about their lives and how they feel. Then, make a point of being present when they tell you about themselves. When you listen actively, you create a sense of appreciation in your friends that is unrivaled to anything else you can imagine.

36. Keep an open mind

When you go about your day with an open mind, you won't be thinking about the limiting feelings that come with being close-minded and set in your ways. The end result is a feeling in which you are committed to making sure that others feel you are truly engaged in their needs. So, when someone talks to you about their feelings and ideas, you'll be ready to really listen to them.

37. Live in the moment

When talking about mindfulness, we discussed the importance of living in the here and the now. So, when you do this, you are able to ensure that you are not distracted by things that don't really exist. This allows you to enjoy every second that you spend with your loved ones. Plus, it can help you to let go of those things which may be causing you pain and sorrow.

38. Tend to others in need

Often, we are faced with sick and infirm friends and relatives. In such situations, we can show our appreciation and concern by being in constant touch. This means frequent visits and constant phone calls. You don't necessarily need to be at their bedside 24 hours a day. But by being able to show that you are genuinely concerned for their wellbeing, you can help your loved ones in their recovery from illness.

39. Honor your promises

There is nothing more powerful than a person who is able to honor their word. When you make a promise, you need to make every reasonable effort to keep your word. When you do, you not only boost your personal sense of satisfaction and empowerment, but you are also creating a sense of security and confidence in those who have placed their trust in you. When you build your reputation as a trustworthy person, all of those around you will feel better just by knowing you are around.

40. Sing a song

Yes, singing a song can create a positive environment. It seems a bit childish, but it's true. You don't need to be the next great pop star to sing a song. Still, you can foster a positive environment for those around you when you are able to communicate good vibes through some good tunes. After all, what do you have to lose? Everyone loves to hear a good tune now and then.

41. Set healthy boundaries

It's important to set healthy boundaries around you. Sometimes, it can be challenging to deal with everyone around you especially if the invade your personal space or don't respect your position in life. This is why you need to set your boundaries in a healthy manner. This means that there is a limit to which people cannot cross without making you feel uncomfortable. At that point, you can then make sure that they know they ought to step back.

42. Laugh as much as possible

When you laugh on a regular basis, you release a great deal of positive emotional energy. In this case, you are able to help your body process good emotions while disregarding negative ones. Also, laughter is a sign that you are in a good mood, or at least in a positive one at that moment. Research has also shown that laughter is good at boosting the immune system and helps keep the mind fresh.

43. Wear bright colors

Colors a definitely power tools. If you were dark, somber tones, they will reflect your overall mood. This includes colors such as black, dark brown and dark blue along with all shares of gray. However, if you choose to wear bright colors, you are automatically signaling that you are in a more positive mood. So, these colors reflect your overall mood. As a result, you won't have to worry about becoming overwhelmed with negative emotion. The colors you wear will help you take a step in the right direction.

44. Disconnect from electronic devices

Recent research suggests that electronic devices have been a good source of stress and anxiety among people of all ages. In this case, it is a good idea to disconnect from these devices for a while. When you do this, you are able to break free from the constant attention that such devices receive. This is important because freeing yourself from the incessant chirping or messages and notifications can help stabilize your mood and get you to spread the wealth, that is, sharing with others while being in a good mood.

45. Start off your morning with positive affirmations and gratefulness

There is nothing worse than starting out your day in a bad mood. After all, don't we all dread Mondays? Indeed, there is nothing worse than getting out of bed only to dread the day that lies ahead. When you are able to transform your attitude from "it's Monday again..." to "thankfully, I have a job", your positive outlook will help offset any pessimistic feelings you may have about the world. Gratefulness is all about focusing on the positive things you have in life and foregoing thoughts that are focused solely on what you do not have. Start off your day in this manner and you will soon find that it is not hard to make a positive change overnight.

46. Focus your energy

One of the worst things that we go as humans is spend our energy on tasks and activities which aren't overly productive. Now, there is nothing wrong with watching TV and surfing the internet. However, these activities become unproductive when you engage in them for the sake of doing so. So, instead of spending your time on activities which you can use to facilitate the achievement of your goals, all you are doing is mindlessly going through the motions of life. Try making a concerted effort to focus your energy and you will find that being ultra-productive is very straightforward.

47. Get the low-down on your friends and family

As we have mentioned earlier, listening closely while others are talking is a great sign of respect and affection. However, remembering what they said is even more powerful. For instance, people tend to drop hints around their birthday or when they are keen on something in particular. It's up to you to pick up on those signs and acknowledge their feelings. When your friends and loved ones see that you are truly paying attention to their needs and wants, they will feel loved, and in turn, give that positive vibe back to you.

48. Effective body language

For all of the positive language which you can use, you can easily derail that by using body language which contradicts everything you have attempted to do. In that case, it's important to make sure that you have coordinated your words with your body language. For example, if you constantly keep your arms crossed and standing in a defensive position, you will instinctively signal to others that you are not exactly in a friendly disposition. When you smile, open your arms and use a welcoming tone of voice, you will find that you won't have trouble relating to others on a personal level.

49. Stop and smell the roses

This is not in the literal sense, but rather, take the time to appreciate the world around you. There are wonders at every turn. You can appreciate the marvels of nature or the incredible diversity in people. You will be amazed at how many wonderful people there are in the world. By the same token, you can take the time to make sense of the bad things around you. That way, you can avoid such circumstances, or make an effort to help those in need.

50. Take care of yourself

The last reflection in this chapter is about yourself. You must make taking care of yourself a priority. This includes a healthy diet, getting enough sleep and doing regular exercise. When you are able to make the most of your efforts to take care of yourself, you are already setting yourself up for wellness. Also, make a point of dealing with stress and negative emotion in a productive manner. At the end of the day, this will help you process your feelings and emotions in a constructive manner.

Chapter 11
Benefits Of Having Positive Energy

P ositive energy can have almost immediate impacts on your life and your wellbeing. When you become positively charged, it's easy to make yourself become more attuned to the wellness of your mind and body.

In general, positive energy immediately boosts mood and attitude. In this manner, you can see how easy it is to let go of a bad attitude. This can be achieved through a pleasant experience or perhaps having a good time with friends and family.

This is why positive energy is so important in our lives. Yet, there are several valid reasons as to why positive energy is important for your development and the improvement of your health and wellness.

The following is a list of ways in which you can observe the benefits of positive energy.

1. Stress Reduction
Positive feelings offset the pessimistic effects of stress. For example, you will find a sense of relief even when things aren't going exactly as you'd like them to.

2. Better interpersonal relationships
This seems like a given. When you are in a better mood, that is, feeling better about yourself, you can almost immediately see the changes in the way you get along with others.

3. Love and romance

From the perspective of marriage, you will find that positive energy will improve the quality of your relationship with your spouse. From a dating standpoint, your chances of meeting new people will increase significantly. This is a clear boost for your chances at find the right person for you.

4. Performance at work

A generally happy person will be more productive at work. This means that you will be able to do your job more efficiently thereby opening the door for better professional opportunities.

5. Life expectancy

In general terms, people who have a more positive disposition tend to live longer, and better, than those who do not. This means positively charged people tend to be a lot more prone to having a better quality of life. Now, this has nothing to do with money. It's a question of your attitude and your outlook on life.

6. Better stress management

When you are feeling better about life in general, it's a lot easier to deal with problems. So, when you are faced with a difficult situation, the likelihood of you losing your mind is far less. However, if you are filled with negative emotions, it can be very easy for you to go over the edge and lose your cool. The end result will be far less tolerance to stress and emotional management.

7. Improved health

Research has shown that patients who are in a better mood show a much better recovery from illness as compared to those who are more negatively charged. This effect is known to help boost the immune system. As a result, you can find that being a positive person will help you become healthier, but it can also have an effect on those around you. That's why one happy patient in a hospital can create a positive effect on those around them. While it may not make others' suffering go away, it will at least alleviate the burden they carry while helping them improve their chances at making a full recovery.

8. Better success with money

In many ways, being more optimistic will help you with your finances. Partly, this is due to the fact that a more optimistic person will see opportunity in places where more pessimistic folks won't. Generally speaking, optimistic folks find ways to make money especially under dire circumstances. This is why you will find that people who have a better outlook on life will find it easier to make money and become materially wealthy as compared to those who only find trouble and strife in their daily lives.

9. Count your blessings

When you are optimistic, it's easy to see the goodness in life. This means that you won't focus on what you lack, but rather, you will focus on everything that you do have. This means that it will be easier for you to count your blessings as opposed to complaining about the things that aren't working for you in life. As a result, your overall attitude can lead you to bigger and better things in life. One very interesting effect of this attitude is that being grateful about the things you have in life tends to open the door to more blessings. While outside observers may think that it's nothing more than just good luck, the fact of the matter is that it is your good will and nature that attracts positive things around you.

10. The world becomes a better place to live

While we can't ignore the obvious problems with the world today such as pollution and violence, we can see the world as a better place to live thanks to a more optimistic disposition. This is due to the fact that happier and more optimistic people tend to see the good things in bad situations. Pessimistic people will always find the bad things in a good situation. What this means is that they will never be satisfied no matter how good things can be.

So, what does this mean for you?

Your disposition and your outlook on life essentially depend on your attitude and the way you wish to go about your life. Of course, this doesn't necessarily mean that everything will come up roses. The challenges along the way will certainly test your mettle. However, your positive attitude will allow positive energy to radiate through your being thus enabling the positive effects which we have discussed throughout this chapter.

Perhaps the single-most important thing you can do at this point is to make a conscious choice to make your life better than it currently is. This begins my making the choice to embrace positive energy and make the most of the life you have around you. In the end, the only thing you have to lose is the fear that comes with constantly being negatively charged. Plus, when you really commit to making the opportunity that the universe has given you, you won't struggle to commit to being an optimist; it will come naturally to you.

So, don't be afraid to embrace positivity. You will find that it's much easier than you could have ever possibly imagined!

Chapter 12
Importance Of Positive Energy

There is no question that positive energy is vital in our lives. While it is possible to live without it, it is not the ideal way to live. In fact, living without positive energy leads to an overall decline in health, wellness and poor mood. So, there is no doubt that positive energy helps improve all of these areas.

However, positive energy goes beyond just smiling and feeling happy. Positive energy is all about making the most of your life and the experience that you are living. As a result, your entire environment will begin to shift from your current reality into a more positive one in which everyone around you will have the opportunity to perform at a better level.

Now, it should be noted that negative energy is not necessarily *bad*. The thing about negative energy is that it does not allow you to progress in achieving your goal as it consumes so much of your vitality.

Think about it this way:

What consumes more energy, love or hate?

Sure, you might say that loving someone is hard work. Indeed, it is not easy to love someone day and day out. This is especially true when the object of your affection isn't going through a good time in their life. Nevertheless, hatred consumes people from within. It requires a great deal of energy to hold on to hatred. People who succumb to resentment tend to age faster. This is the result of the vast amounts of energy that are required to hold on to grudges.

As you can see, it is a lot easier to make sense of love in your life as opposed to hate. This is why allowing positive energy to flow through your being is a lot easier than letting negative energy take hold of you.

So, let's explore the ways in which positive energy becomes highly important in your life and the lives of others.

In the workplace

1. Start with yourself!
Often, it is easy to pin the blame on others, that is, it's easy to say that negative energy is the consequence of others' bad habits, moods and attitudes. But the fact of the matter is that you also play a role in allowing negative energy to find a foothold in the environment around you. So, it's important that you begin with yourself. Make sure that you have the right mindset that will allow you to grow within your environment. When you have a growth mindset, it's easy to spread that to others in such a way that you become a catalyst for positive change.

2. Conserve you viality
Mindfulness is a fantastic promoter for development. That is why you ought to try your best to conserve your energy and focus so that your vitality doesn't dissipate into unproductive endeavors. For example, if you find yourself with a toxic colleague, don't fall prey to their game. Let them fight their fight. Unless you have no choice but to confront them, make the best of your energies and allow yourself to live in the here and the now. That way, you can let the negative energy flow through you while allowing your positive energy to radiate.

In personal relationships

3.   Managing antagonism

Quite often, we are faced with having to deal with antagonism in our personal relationships, that is, differences of opinion or disagreements. This is a natural part of life. If anything, you should be suspicious if there are no disagreements in your personal relationships. The fact of the matter is that differences create negative energy. When you let these differences get a hold of you, you nurture that negative energy to the degree in which it gnaws at you, it creates an infection, and then that infection festers until the relationship is no longer salvageable. So, handling antagonism is of the utmost importance. If you let your positive energy radiate, a difference of opinion can be solved by way of dialogue and understanding. Ultimately, you won't have to concern yourself with negative emotions. You'll find the right way to solve your differences.

4.   Handling your desires

Your desires should not take precedent over the needs of others. By this, we mean that your needs and desires are just as important as those of others. So, there is no reason why you should obtain what you wish for at the expense of others. In fact, it is perfectly reasonable to find a middle ground in which everyone can get what they want to a greater or lesser extent. The fact of the matter is that your ability to situate your desires in their proper place will go a long way toward generating positive outcomes for everyone.

In your community

5.   Empower your group

To empower your group, all you need do is make sure that everyone has a voice that is heard. There is no need to have one individual dominate the group over the rest. Everyone is perfectly capable of leading at one point or another. So, when you empower your group, you are providing them the opportunity to take charge of those areas in which they are truly competent.

Chapter 13
Dealing With Negative Energy

T hus far, we have talked about positive energy and how wonderful it is to be charged with it. But we are yet to focus on the effects of negative energy in your life beyond the obvious effects. When you allow negative energy to take hold of your life, chakra blockages are just the beginning. In fact, negative energy can be so difficult to deal with that the physical symptoms alone can be enough to drive anyone mad.

That is why we are going to dedicate this chapter to discussing the reasons why negative energy is so detrimental to your overall health and wellbeing. In addition, it makes a great deal of sense to hone in on the reasons why negative energy can make your life an utter nightmare once it grabs a hold of you.

Negative energy is nothing to be afraid of nor dread. As a matter of fact, we need a dose of negative energy in order to balance out our chakras. The truth is that our world runs on a duality of energies. So, there is a definite place for negative energy. It's essentially the way electricity works. However, if you let yourself get too consumed by negative forces, then the following signs and symptoms will make their appearance in your life.

Signs

Denial is contagious

Think of a time in which you visited a colleague who was having a difficult time. Chances are that they had a hard time accepting the fact that they were going through a hard time. If anything, they will tell you they are perfectly fine though their behavior indicated otherwise.

Negativity is contagious

Over time, being around toxic people in a negative environment will lead you to feel a series of physical and emotional symptoms. These symptoms are not the kind that are clearly apparent at first. However, they will become evident as you deal with them. By the time you actually begin to notice them, they may have a strong hold on you. Consequently, it may be hard to get rid of them. Here are some examples:

- Headache and migraine
- Digestive distress
- Unease or despair
- Unexpected mood swings
- Impatience
- Constant anxiety

Among many others...

It is also true that these symptoms can emerge as a result of pent up energy, that is, feelings that have lingered inside of you for a certain period of time. These feelings may not be easy to let you. So, instead of tossing them to the side, you are carrying around them like a lump of bricks. When this happens, these feelings fester inside of you until they cause serious damage to your spirit and body.

What can you do about it?

Well, let's take a look at the various ways in which you can deal with negative energy.

How to know you have negative energy

1. It is very hard to socialize with friends and family
Negative energy has a way of zapping your vitality. This is evident in chronic fatigue. Often chronic fatigue is the result of prolonged periods of stress. When this occurs, you may find that sleep is insufficient leaving your exhausted all the time. As a result, you may have trouble working up the energy to go out and have fun with your friends and family. Even something as simple as a family dinner may be tough to work up the nerve to go to.

2. You have trouble making friends
This one is fairly straightforward. It is hard to make friends when you are unable to socialize. Moreover, nurturing existing relationships can be tough if you don't have the energy to go out and spend time with loved ones. Even something as simple as picking up the phone and calling a friend can be tough. So, if you find yourself having trouble relating to people you meet, then you might be in the grips of negative energy.

3. You are always in the middle of an argument
This is another sign that needs no introduction. When you are negatively charged, you will find that it is very easy to be engaged in constant bickering with everyone around you. You don't have to work very hard to pick a fight. In fact, your negative energy will predispose those around you to bicker with you. The end result is a number of issues that can lead you to become bitter and isolated as others around you simply try to avoid you as much as possible.

4. Acquaintances are continually "busy"
This point ties into the previous one. When you are negatively charged, and your relationships go down the drain, you will find that

everyone around you is busy. So, when you work up the courage to ask someone out to lunch or try to set up a social gathering, everyone around you is busy, has to work or simply can't make it. This should be no surprise as your foul mood can rub people the wrong way. The same goes for business associates who suddenly don't want to do business with you. Perhaps this might ring a bell...

5.   Others avoid any type of contact with you

When we mean "any type of contact", we mean "all types". This includes having to talk to you even if their job depends on it. Think about it this way, have you ever had to work under a mean boss? All staff in the department try their best to avoid having to talk to the boss. And when they do, it's usually a very brief interaction. There are situations in which employees will try to get someone else to talk to the boss since they fear the boss will lash out at them.

6.   You are prone to using foul language and profanity on a consistent basis

Cussing is nothing to be ashamed about... well, unless you say something that's completely inappropriate at the wrong time. This can be a serious issue... but barring a monstrous faux pas, you can get away with saying bad words here and there. However, people who are negatively charged tend to find themselves filling up the swear jar rather quickly. This is nothing more than an expression of their inner feelings and emotions. So, do pay close attention to this aspect of your life should you find yourself cussing more than you ought to.

7.   Constantly dwelling on the past

It's perfectly fine to reflect on past events. In fact, it is healthy to dissect things that have gone wrong in the past in order to extract valuable lessons and insights. There is such a thing as constructive criticism. However, when you dwell too much on the things that have happened in your life, especially negative experiences, you may find it hard to close that chapter and turn the page. By reliving a bad experience, you are literally producing the same stress and anxiety as you did the moment you went through it in the first place. So, definitely make a point of cleaning up past experiences and putting them behind you.

8. Playing the blame game

This is one of the most common things you need to look out for. When you are negatively charged, it is quite easy to find a culprit for the way you feel. If you happen to find someone who fits the bill, then you will have someone to pin the blame on your downward attitude. For instance, you may blame your parents for you lot in life, or your professional missteps are your boss' fault. You might even blame your spouse for holding you back. If you happen to catch yourself playing the blame game more often than not, then you need to take inventory of those things which are bringing you down in a negative manner.

9. Your acquaintances don't show up when you need them

There comes a point when others simply stay away at all costs. This implies bailing on you when you need them. While they may be perfectly happy to help you when you need it, they will think twice about being there for you. This is especially true if you didn't help them when they needed you. Sadly, highly negative people tend to find themselves forgotten and lonely during their most crucial time of need.

10. Animals have a propensity to shy away

Have you ever noticed how dogs almost automatically bark and snarl at certain people? By the same token, have you ever noticed how dogs are magnetically drawn to certain folks? This is a clear indication of the end of the spectrum you find yourself in. When you are negatively charged, animals tend to perceive it. As a result, they will stay away out of fear or threat.

11. You may experience a breakdown

In this regard, a "breakdown" can be an emotional collapse, that is, a moment when you can't go on anymore and your body gives out on you. This could be manifest in an aggressive cold that keeps you in bed for days. In the worst of cases, it can lead to a heart attack. This is a clear sign that your body can no longer tolerate such high amounts of stress and negativity. As a result, your body begins to breakdown and show signs of physical illness. While doctors may not be able to pick up on a specific physiological cause, a trained therapist may quickly figure out when the problem lies.

12. Your attention span is shot

Folks who are dealing with large amounts of negative energy find that their attention spans are completely shot. By "shot", we mean that they cannot focus on anything or concentrate on their tasks. They may experience what is known as "brain fog", that is, a condition in which the person feels dazed and confused at various points throughout the day. Consequently, they may be unable to concentrate on their tasks leading them to be unproductive and unable to successfully get ahead. This may also be the result of poor sleep as a consequence of the ill effects of negative energy.

13. Promotions are passing you by

This point refers to your professional life. If you find yourself missing out on important employment opportunities or getting passed up for promotions, then you might very well be in the grips of chronic stress and fatigue. This creates an even larger feedback loop that fuels the negative energy to the degree in which you cannot function properly. There are times when a change of scenery is beneficial. However, there are other times when a person needs to stop and take a break. We don't mean a vacation but rather, time away from the life that is causing them to feel this way in the first place.

14. Your skin is acting out

Your skin is a highly sensitive organ. It lashes out in an attempt to filter out the negative energy that is within you. It is often common to see rashes, red spots, acne and other dermatological conditions when a person is overly stressed or negative charge. If you happen to see your skin breaking out in unsightly conditions, then you may very well take that as a warning sign.

15. Your romantic relationships suffer greatly

This point is quite clear. Negative energy can do a number on your romantic relationships. In fact, it can be so bad that you it can lead to a breakup. Divorces usually stem from a lack of understanding between spouses. While this isn't the only cause, it is certainly a valid reason for the detriment of a relationship.

16. Intimacy goes out the window

Intimacy doesn't refer just to sexual relations. In fact, intimacy is one of those situations that arises when a couple is perfectly comfortable with each other. In that regard, they are able to share wonderful moments of closeness. Negative energy acts as an invisible barrier which keeps partners from being intimate especially when one isn't negatively charged. As a result, relationships can break down very easily and lead to the end.

17. Constant gossip and complaining

Negative energy can lead to engaging in constant gossip. In fact, gossip is one of those situations in which you are looking to spread negativity about others. Unless you are somehow able to find a good use for gossip, it will only cause others to feel the detrimental effects of this attitude. As for complaining, negatively charged people are consistent complainers. They are never happy about anything. As a result, they will find it impossible to be satisfied with anything. These are the people who own fortunes and still find something to be upset about. These are the folks who have a perfect life, yet consistently come up with ways to get mad about something.

18. You are overly impatient

It is said that patience is a virtue. Indeed, it is when you think about the need for keeping your head on your shoulders at all times, especially when you are desperately seeking answers to your problems. Yet, impatience can grab a hold of you so fast it can make your head spin. You become intolerant to the needs of others especially if waiting on them somehow affects your perception of your wellbeing. Think about it this way, you're waiting in line at the bank. And, the person in front of you is taking a long time to make a deposit. They need that money just as much as you do. However, your impatience is such that you don't care about their needs; all you're concerned about is going first and that's it.

19. Your conversations degrade into arguments

It's hard to have a good conversation when you are constantly on the edge. In fact, it's easy to simply fall into an argument in which you are bent on having your way. If you don't get your way, then the conversation can quickly escalate into a shouting match. Think about all of those boardroom meetings that end up in yelling. That's when everyone wants to be heard but could care less about listening.

20. Your lover shuts down

This is perhaps the toughest situation you may have to deal with. When intimacy is gone, your love may still stay with you, but may shut down completely. They may want to stay away from you in such a way that they are not connected to you any longer. This attitude can lead to infidelities or simple a breakup. The end result may be an unhappy relationship that simply leads nowhere despite a semblance of normalcy and agreeableness on the surface. However, beneath the surface lies a broken relationship that may not be leading anywhere.

Chapter 14
How To Get Rid Of Negative Energy

At this point, it is vitally important to discuss how to get rid of negative energy in an effective manner, that is, how to rid yourself of this situation in a simple manner that you can do at home or your place of work. In fact, you will find that ridding yourself of negative energy is far easier than you could have ever imagined.

1.   Get rid of toxic people and toxic environments
Earlier, we made a point about how a change of scenery could be beneficial to your overall wellbeing. Indeed, a change of scenery can help when you find yourself surrounded by negative people in a toxic environment. By this, we mean that you are in a situation in which everyone around you has nothing nice to say or do, and the place you are in is not conducive to your overall emotional health. A good example of this is the workplace. There are jobs in which your co-workers are all aggressive and unfriendly. In addition, your boss isn't very helpful while the overall scheme of the job is stressful and hinders your growth. Sure, you might be concerned about putting food on the table. But there comes a point in which you need to decide between making money and your mental and emotional health. At this point, you may have no choice but to go job hunting. If you happen to find yourself in a job with a toxic environment, then you must make this change a priority. The same goes for the community you live in. If you find it too hard to live peacefully in this area, then it might be time to move to a better location.

2. Clear Your Aura

Clearing, or cleansing, your atmosphere is ideal to clearing your aura. You can achieve this through a number of ways. For instance, you can use incense to cast out negative vibes. Floral scents are great at achieving this. Also, essential oils work very well in setting a more positive mood. Beyond that, meditation is a great way of clearing your aura. Picture yourself placing your negative emotions in a balloon and watching it drift off into space. All you are doing is watching it leave you slowly but surely. Also, staring into a fire can help clear your aura. You can literally watch the flames burn your negative energy as it dissipates into the air. You can visualize as it goes up in smoke. This is a great way of making sure that it will never come back again.

3. Using visualization as a means of cleansing your mind

Through the use of visualization, you can create a force field around you that will protect you from negative energy. This force field is really effective in keeping negative thoughts and vibes at bay. One great exercise is to imagine yourself being wrapped up in a bubble. This bubble can be any color you wish. But it must be a distinguishable color. That way, you can actually picture yourself becoming enveloped by this force around you. As you are totally covered up, you can then picture attacks of negative energy bouncing off of your force field. This is a shield that you can carry around everywhere you go. While it may seem a bit childish to picture your safety blanket covering, the fact of the matter is that you are setting up an emotional barrier between you and unwanted energy. This type of exercise is great at keeping you away from others who may not have your best interest in mind.

4. Reiki to purge negative energy

Reiki is a practice which you can engage in if you so choose. It has been known to produce significant effects as far as clearing the aura and helping individuals make the transition from negatively charged environments into positive ones. Overall, Reiki can be practiced individually or as part of a larger group. Do give it a look if you are looking for a viable alternative to your emotional health.

5. Listening to sounds of nature

Listening to nature sounds such as the rain, birds chirping, or other types of natural sounds can help you find a deep state of relaxation.

This can be part of a meditation practice, or it can be done as part of your background music as you work or study. By listening to these types of sounds, you can help your mind connect with nature and the planet. If you can combine this during your mindfulness sessions, you can be sure that you will get a great deal of benefits from such sessions. In addition, making the most of your time during concentration can help you rid yourself of the ill effects that come with negative emotions and other unpleasant side effects.

6.   The power of prayer or mantra

Depending on your particular religious or spiritual beliefs, you can rely on the power of prayer to help you navigate the negative energies that swirl around you. Whenever you feel overcome or overwhelmed by negative energies, you can say a short prayer to help you deal with the onset of such energies. In some cases, you can use a prayer that is part of your religious beliefs. Alternatively, you can use a mantra. A mantra can be any phrase which you find that resonates with you. In this case, you can pick a message that makes sense to you and allows you to focus on your needs at that moment. For instance, something like "I am safe" is a very short, but meaningful mantra. In other cases, a mantra such as "I am one with the universe" can help you fall in line with the world around you. A mantra can be an inspirational quote or even just one word. The main point is to find words that can give you solace especially when things are getting really rough. You will find that implementing this practice into your life, but especially when you are not at your best, will help you find the drive you need to deal with negative energies. While this isn't about bottling up feelings, it's about helping you let negative energy flow away from you and allowing it to following its natural course. As a result, you can feel more confident when it comes to facing negative emotions of those around you.

7.   Breaking patterns

Often, we have triggers that bring about the onset of negative energy. Triggers can be anything around you. There are folks who lose their mind in traffic. These are the folks you see displaying road rage at the slightest provocation. In such cases, you need to identify patterns that trigger negative emotions inside of you. Once you detect when the onset of such energies is coming on, you can use any of the techniques we have outlined in this book to help you deal with those feelings.

Consequently, you'll be able to nip those feelings in the bud leaving you with a much clearer mind and conscience.

8. Defending yourself from attacks from negative people

It is said that a good offense is the best defense. In this case, the best defense is a proactive approach in which you guard against attacks from negative people who only wish to cause harm. Now, it should be noted that most of the time, these people don't really intend to harm you, that is, it isn't a personal thing against you. All the seek is to discharge their negative energies on the closest person possible. As a result, you may find yourself caught in the crossfire. So, a great way to guard yourself against attacks from negative people is to recognize when they are about to happen. If you notice that your boss is in a foul mood, you can proactively get away from them before they look to pick a fight. By the same token, you can avoid a confrontation before allowing the other party to engage you. Often, not falling into their trap is the easiest way to avoid the oncoming rush of negative energies. This is a great way of taking a proactive stance.

9. Stay true to your values

This point plays into the previous one. When you stick to your values, it can be nearly impossible for an ill-intended person to get you to deviate from them. For instance, if you are committed to avoiding violence at all costs, then it won't be very easy to draw you into a physical confrontation or a shouting match. You'll be prone to walk away before an incident escalates. By the same token, your ability to make the most of your own values will keep negative emotions and energies at bay. The fact of the matter is that by making the most of your abilities, you can be true to your values while staying in touch with the world around you. So, if you are keen on avoiding confrontation, then you can be sure that you will be able avoid needless aggravation and pain when you run into negatively charged people. At the end of the day, you are in control of the situations you are in.

10. Attracting energy from the universe around you

The universe is an incredible network of energy. Every being in existence radiates energy, whatever the kind may be. As such, you will find that it isn't hard to draw energy from the universe around you. In fact, you can draw energy from it in your times of need. When you are feeling down and even in despair over the circumstances in your life, you can draw on that energy to help you deal with whatever you are going through. Best of all, you won't have to concern yourself with ever running out. There is an inexhaustible source of energy in the universe. Take the sun, for instance. The sun is an interminable source of energy that radiates positive vibes every single day. So, take advantage of sunny days and spend some time outside. You will find that sunlight is a great way to help you feel much better about yourself and your overall circumstances. By literally charging yourself with the energy from the sun, you won't have to struggle with keeping up your levels of positive energies.

11. Wash away negative energy

Yes, you can literally wash away negative energy. This can be achieved through the power of baths. The first and most common is the shower we all take on a regular basis. After all, haven't you found it relaxing to take a shower at the end of a long and tiring day? Of course! But you can take that a step further. Taking a bath with scented bath salts can provide you with an incredible release. Taking 20 to 30 minutes in a warm bath can be enough to let you get rid of those negative instances of pain and discomfort. In addition, a hot steam bath, such as a sauna can literally get you to sweat away the negative energy contained within you. The reasoning behind this is that a hot steam bath forces toxins out of your body through your skin. As a result, you will find that your skins releases such toxins away. Then, taking a warm bath will allow you to wash away these toxins. The end result is a much more comfortable and relaxing state of mind. Lastly, f you have the chance, visiting natural springs can be a great way for you to find a relaxing and charming spot. When you visit these springs, the pure water coming from the mountains can be a great spot to take a dip. These waters are so positively charged that you will automatically feel the difference in yourself!

12. Harnessing the power of nature

Being around nature is a great way of helping your discharge negative energies. If you have a green thumb, then this should be quite easy for you. If you don't, or if you have not tried your hand at gardening, then do so. Being in contact with plants and soil is a great way in which you can dissipate negative energy. This functions like an electrical circuit which grounds negative energy. As a result, you can let go of negative energy by letting it disperse in the ground. If you aren't keen on trying your hand at gardening, you can always take a hike, or just sit in the middle of a forest or park. The idea is to surround yourself in nature so that your negative energies can be released back into the ground.

13. Burning candles and incense

We have mentioned scented candles and incense at various points throughout this book. The fact of the matter is that this is one of the most effective techniques you can find since it really helps to trigger positive emotions in the brain. Whenever you find yourself breathing in pleasant aromas, your brain automatically begins to react in a positive manner by altering its chemistry. In this regard, you can expect to have your brain chemicals react in such a manner that you are filled with pleasant feelings leading to pleasant thoughts. Indeed, the best way in which you can continue to maintain a positive mindset is to surround yourself with pleasant aromas. You can also achieve the same effect by wearing your favorite perfume or cologne. This will always draw positive feelings.

14. Get away from toxic people

Earlier, we talked about how you may need a change of scenery. This might include getting a new job and so on. But then, there are cases in which you can avoid certain places altogether. For example, highly sensitive people find it particular distressing to be in the midst of large crowds. For instance, large sporting events or concerts can be particularly draining. So, if you are aware that certain settings may lead to a concentration of negative energy, then it might be best to avoid such situations. In doing so, you can improve the chances of freeing yourself from the accumulation of gratuitous negative energies.

15. Purge yourself of emotional baggage

This sounds easier said than done. After all, how can you purge yourself of emotional baggage? Often, there are times when you just need to let go of particularly damaging experiences that have affected you from the past. Unless they are serious traumatic experiences in which it is nearly impossible to just forget about them, there are experiences which you can strive to just put them behind you. In those cases, it is best to forgive and forget if possible. If this means forgiving yourself, then my all means let go and start of ver. If you find it hard to do so, then perhaps some professional help may be required.

16. Burn ginger And Lemon Peels

Burning lemon peels or ginger can have an incredible effect on your mood. The smell of both of these plants is conducive to stimulating positive brain chemistry in addition to providing you with a boost to your mood. In general, making the most of your changes in mood is ideal when looking to avoid negative energy. Plus, you will find that lemon scent is always a great a idea when it comes to creating an overall pleasant environment.

17. Laughter following a complicated event

Whenever you find yourself coming out of a negative situation, laughter is really the best medicine. Sure, there are serious and somber events such as a funeral in which it would be completely inappropriate to laugh. However, you can make time following such events to have fun. You can watch a funny movie even if you are not really in the mood for a laugh. The main point is to lighten the mood in such a way that you can let go of the negative energies and allow yourself space to forget about what is affecting you. Best of all, laughter has an analgesic effect on the body. This mean that a good laugh is a great way to alleviate both physical and emotional pain.

18. Using sea salt as a means of detoxing

Sea salt is great for both cooking and bathing. In cooking, sea salt is great as a means of helping you let go of the negative ingredients that may be contained in good. Regular table salt may be too high in sodium along with other impurities. Sea salt is great as it is generally lower in doses of sodium while also allowing your body to better digest food. As for bathing, sea salt is great become it can provide you with detoxing properties. Just like a steam bath, a hot bat with sea salt can help you purge impurities from your body through your skin. So definitely make a point of incorporating sea salt into your life.

19. Release your inner child

Often, we repress many of our emotions out of concern, and even fear, of being judged as immature. This means that if you don't take the time to let go of the emotions which are trapped inside, you may find them building up to a point in which there is nothing left but bitterness and resentment. So, letting your inner child out your core being means engaging in activities which truly fulfill you. These activities may include games, sports and even watching cartoons. Yes, there are those who will judge you, but ultimately, what do they know? They may be bitter individuals who don't want anything else than to make others feel as miserable as they do.

20. The power of applause

Something as simple as applauding can attract positive energy to your life and help dissipate negative energy. Think about that for a moment. Why do we clap when we like something? Look at athletes, they generally clap their hands together when they are looking to boost their mood and energy levels in the middle of a sporting event. You too can harness this power when you find yourself in need of a boost. Your hands are the most powerful parts of your body as they can both build and destroy. As a result, using your hands is a powerful way to transform negative energy into powerful positive emissions of light. So, don't hold back when you feel the urge to put your hands together.

21. Dancing your troubles away

For those folks who enjoy dancing, this is a great way to do away with negative energies. Now, the fact of the matter is that dancing is a form of physical exercise which can help you improve your overall mood. So, the fact that you are moving around is what makes dancing such a powerful emotion. By the same token, moving to music that you like is also a great way to get your energies flowing in the right direction. As such, if you enjoy dancing, then make a point of going about it in a constructive and meaningful way.

22. Stretching can be a lifesaver

When we spend too much time in a single position, such as sitting or standing, your muscles tend to get stiff. This is a natural response to the lack of movement. That is why stretching often can help you dissipate negative energy. The reason why this works is that the energy that is built up in your muscles due to inaction can be released. This concept illustrates the reason why yoga and pilates are very helpful in shaping your body and molding your overall physical condition. As a result, don't hold back when you wish to get your muscles loose. You will be better off for it.

23. Get your blood pumping

Much like stiff muscles due to inactivity, blood can stagnate in a certain spot, for example, in your legs. That's why it's important to get your blood moving. This can be achieved by any type of physical activity regardless of what it is. Also, some yoga positions look to promote blood circulating back to the head. The reason for this is that when blood gets stuck in the legs, the legs can become uncomfortable while the brain doesn't receive the supply of blood it needs to keep working at optimal levels. One great exercise is to relax with your legs elevate. This will help keep the blood from accumulating in your legs and flowing back to the rest of your body.

24. Cry, if you must

Whenever we become overloaded with negative emotions, sometimes it might be enough to just have a good cry. When we try to hold back tears, we may be creating the opposite effect by accumulating negative energy that doesn't have anywhere to go. This can lead to a psychosomatic effect in which the body simply finds an outlet to that negative energy by means of physical illness. So, cry, if you must. But make sure that you find a positive outlet for your emotions, too.

25. Don't forget that you hold the power

Above all, you are in control. That's right, you are in control of your life and your emotions. While there may be circumstances in which there isn't much you can do about the things which are happening, you are in control of your emotions. This means that even if you can't stop something from happening, you can stope it from ruining your life. As a result, you have the power to control the way the world affects you and those around you.

Chapter 15
Yoga

Yoga (/ˈjoʊɡə/; Sanskrit: योग; elocution) is a gathering of physical, mental and profound practices or trains which began in antiquated India. Yoga is one of the six orthodox schools of Hindu philosophical conventions. There is a broad assortment of yoga practices, objectives and schools, in Hinduism, Jainism and Buddhism.

The residency "yoga" in the Western society constantly indicates an overarching produce of Hatha yoga, yoga as exercise, comprising essentially of the stances called asanas. The inceptions of yoga orchestrate been theorized to arrangement wager on to pre-Vedic Indian customs; it is referenced in the Rigveda, yet for the most part likely urban around the 6th and fifth centuries BCE, in outdated India's plain and śramaṇa developments.

The sequence of most crude writings relating yoga-rehearses is vague, varyingly licensed to Upanishads. The Yoga Sutras of Patanjali date from the main incompletely of the first thousand years CE and picked up reputation in the West in the twentieth century. Hatha yoga writings rose once in a while between the ninth and eleventh century with sources in Tantra. Yoga masters from India a short time later acquainted yoga with the West, after the impression of Swami Vivekananda in the dear left nineteenth and untimely twentieth century with his adjustment of yoga custom, excluding asanas. Outside India, it has transformed into a mechanical stance based physical wellness, stress-alleviation and relief system. Yoga, in Indian customs, nonetheless, is extra than target work out; it has a contemplating and profound center. One of the six key universal schools of Hinduism is besides called Yoga, which has its individual epistemology and transcendentalism, and is carefully united to Hindu

Samkhya theory. The impact of postural yoga on animal and psychological wellness has been a topic of precise investigations, with sign that reliable yoga routine yields repayment for desolate put a wager on irritation and stress.

Kinds of yoga

Hatha yoga

The Sanskrit stretch "hatha"is an umbrella call for each and every one rudestances of yoga. In the West, hatha yoga effectively alludes to each the other styles of yoga (Ashtanga, Iyengar, and so forth.) that are stranded in a crude practice.

In any case, in participation are different branches of yoga, for example, raja, and kriya which are individual from the physical-based yoga practice. The physical-based yoga is a decent number stylish also, has a few styles. Hatha yoga educational programs are superlative for learners since they are for the most part paced more slowly than other yoga styles. Hatha educational program in our day are an exemplary loom to breathing and activities. On the off chance that you are fresh out of the box new to yoga, hatha yoga is a courageous access sense to the training. Iyengar yoga Iyengar yoga was established by B.K.S. Iyengar and spotlights on arrangement as all directly as careful and severe developments.

In an Iyengar class, understudies organize an arrangement of stances as determined by their breathing. By and large, students are in guardianship for a longer period of time, and at the same time, alter the intricate details of the posture. Iyengar depends extraordinarily on props to help understudies flawless their come to fruition and endeavor further into postures in an anodyne way. Indeed, despite the fact that you won't jolt around, you will unquestionably turn into a workout and stroke extraordinarily start and loose after an Iyengar class. This solace is in truth mind blowing for locals with wounds who neediness to perform a little bit at a time and efficiently.

211

Kundalini yoga

Kundalini yoga practice is both otherworldly and physical. This plan is each and every one about releasing the kundalini energy in your lion's share supposed to be caught, or snaked, in the lesser spine. These courses genuinely impact your fundamental and breathing with quick moving, invigorating stances and breath works out. These courses are alluring extraordinary and have the option to require reciting, mantra, and reflection.

Ashatanga yoga

In Sanskrit Ashtanga is interpreted as "Eight Appendage Path." Ashtanga yoga includes a particularly physically demanding game plan of stances, along these lines this state of yoga is decidedly not for the fledgling. It takes a proficient yogi to completely be pulled into it.

Ashtanga begins with five sun affirmation so and five sun signal B's and right then and there moves into a cycle of presence and flummox stances. In Mysore, India, fill gathering to set up this appearance of yoga as one at their yield pace—on the off chance that you foresee Mysore-drove Ashtanga, it's foreseen of you to live through the arrangement.

Vinyasa yoga

Originates from Ashtanga as the streaming energy between breaths to development. Vinyasa is a term used to depict, "To position in a remarkable manner" what's more, in this claim yoga stances. Vinyasa is the great number incredible yoga style. Vinyasa was adjusted from Ashtanga yoga during the 1980s.

In Vinyasa classes, the advancement is in time with your breath and weight gathering to current starting with one posture then onto the next. Incalculable sorts of yoga holder furthermore be cautious Vinyasa streams, for example, Ashtanga, strength yoga, and prana.

Vinyasa styles canister differ contingent upon the instructor, and here protect be a ton of atypical kinds of stances in assorted groupings. I for I mentor an arrangement based adjust of Vinyasa and plan new streams without fail, however I excessively like to sew in chose of the represents a bit longer in the wake of heating up.

Birkam

If you are looking to sweat in yoga, this is the type for you. Yoga On the off chance that you are hoping to sweat in yoga, this is the sort for you. Bikram yoga is named after Birkam Choudhury and facial appearance a cycle of prearranged presents in a sauna-like room— commonly park to 105 degrees and 40 percent moistness. The course of action incorporates a movement of 26 simple stances, with each one performed twice. Yin yoga Yin yoga is a moderate paced adjust of yoga with situated stances that are in care for longer timeframes. Yin is a pivotal division for tenderfoots, as stances realize that how generally will be seized from 45 seconds to two minutes. Yin bottle moreover be a scrutinizing yoga endeavor that encourages you accomplish interior harmony. The modules are loose, as you're made to execute challenging poses in a variety of contexts.

Therapeutic yoga

Recuperating yoga centers around slowing down following a broad day and loosening up your brain. At its center, this elegance centers on dead body unwinding. You devour included time in littler sum poses all through the class. Scores of the postures are specially designed to be simpler and included unwinding.

Like Iyengar, heaps of props are old and are sited totally revise, for example, covers, supports, and segregation pads. All aspects of the props are within reach to improve you sink further into unwinding. Relieving yoga besides cleans and free your brain. Pre-birth yoga is reasonably adjusted for "moms to be" and is custom-made to ladies in each one trimesters. various hold held that pre-birth is one of the most brilliant kinds of errand for trusting mothers as of the pelvic confound work, center around breathing, and bonding with the on the expansion infant; pre-birth yoga other than enables moms to prepare for buckle down and conveyance.

I also capable my surrender come to fruition of pre-birth yoga during similarly of my pregnancies.

Anusara yoga

Anusara is a cutting-edge sort of hatha yoga, a huge sum comparable to Vinyasa in that it that spotlights on arrangement yet with included center the mind-body-heart connection and various verbiage. Anusara centers around spirals and how both principle part isolate must move. Anusara is plus celebrated for its weight on inclination opening. Attempt to constantly dwindle in talk and pick around a student as the educator separates a posture.

Jivamukti yoga

Jivamukti was established in 1984 by Sharon Ganon and David Life. Jivamuktiis the most part Vinyasa stream style educational plan imbued with Hindu otherworldly lessons. A movement of serenades usually opened the establishment of gathering of understudies followed up by a series of represents that line up with the five group of Jivamukti yoga and theory.

At its center, this mode underlines relationship to globe as a breathing being, as a result nearly everyone Jivamukti devotees go after their vegetarian viewpoint. As such, it is highly beneficial.

Benefits of yoga

1. Increases your flexibility
Physical pain is one of the most common symptoms that accompanies stiffness is joints and muscles. This is especially true when you don't

get a lot of exercise or you spend a great deal of time in a single position. As a result, you can begin to suffer from the ill effects of stiffness. This is where yoga can help you improve your flexibility thereby alleviating the pain that you may feel when related to muscle stiffness and sore joints.

2. Shapes muscles

Yoga is a great exercise that helps is molding your physique. While you shouldn't expect huge, bulging muscles, you should expect to slowly improve your overall shape by reducing flabby muscles and toning your body. This will help you look better even when you don't necessarily think that it's going to make a big difference. Yoga is also great in tandem with any other type of physical exercise such as weightlifting or aerobics.

3. Improves your posture

Back pain is generally associated to bad posture. Bad posture can occur as a result of sitting too much, standing too long or simply not paying attention to proper physical symmetry. Also, bad posture can be the result of weak back muscles. So, yoga is a great way to strengthen not only back muscles, but core muscles as well. So, this will help you to improve your overall posture and cut back on back pain. Ultimately, you will feel much stronger while alleviating potential agonizing pain.

4. Helps prevent joint damage

Yoga is great at strengthening ligaments and tendons as a result of the various stretches and positions it requires you to do. Consequently, you will find that your joints suddenly become stronger while pain reduces significantly. Since your tendons and ligaments get stronger, your joints also reap the rewards. As a result, it will be harder for them to break down. This is a great aid when looking to protect knees, ankles and hips. Moreover, it helps with flexibility and mobility especially when getting older.

5. Helps protect the spine

One of the great things about yoga is that it helps place your spine back into its proper place. Much like posture, improper spinal placement can lead to painful conditions. As such, having proper spinal alignment can go a long way toward promoting a pain-free life while strengthening your back. Over time, this will help keep degenerative diseases at bay while affording you the ability of better movement and improved quality of life in your later years.

6. Improves bone health

Bone health tends to decline as we age. Most people seem to think that it's inevitable and therefore feel condemned to low bone density and the issues that come with it. However, you will notice that yoga is a great way to help prevent bone health. Since yoga helps strengthen joints, it does a fantastic job in alleviating the pressure that bones have to deal with. As a result, bones don't take on nearly as much stress and they generally do. This allows bones to grow strong well into old age.

7. Boosts blood circulation

Earlier, we talked about poor blood circulation and how that can deprive the brain of oxygen-rich blood. The fact of the matter is that poor blood circulation is due in part to a lack of physical activity. While you will hear a host of experts talk about the importance of vigorous physical activity, the fact of the matter is that all you need is any type of physical activity to get your blood pumping, literally. So, it begs the question, how does yoga boost blood circulation? This occurs due to the demand that yoga poses have on the muscles. If you have ever tried some of the classic poses, you will realize that holding such a pose for any length of time can be challenging. As a result, there is a considerable need for both blood and oxygen. Consequently, doing yoga on a regular basis is a great way to promote healthy blood circulation.

8. Enhancements immunity

While the link may not be quite as clear as it is with blood circulation, doing yoga regularly helps boost immunity by allowing the body to release pent up energy. This, in turn, reduces stress and the production of hormones such as cortisol. The end result is a condition in which stress goes down and immunity goes up.

9. Increases tolerance for stress

For all of the wonders that yoga does to help reduce stress, it actually helps boost tolerance to stress, that is, you are able to deal with

216

stressful situations in a better way thereby reducing the amount of negative side effects. For instance, is you are prone to stress headaches, practicing yoga will help you develop a greater sense of tolerance for stress. Therefore, you will find that headaches won't be quite as frequent even if you go through a tough day at the office. This is certainly a considerable benefit particularly when you consider the fact that being able to tolerate higher levels of stress is certainly useful in today's fast-paced environment.

10. Reduces your blood pressure

High blood pressure can be the result of any number of factors. Most notably, stress, anxiety and lack of exercise all check boxes when it comes to causing hypertension. Consequently, the effect that yoga has on reducing hypertension can certainly alleviate many of the symptoms and potential risks that are associated to this condition. So, it is definitely worth making the most of yoga in order to give your body a chance to boost its overall blood pressure levels.

11. Adjusts your adrenal glands

The adrenals are tiny glands that sit atop the kidneys. They are responsible for the production of hormones related to stress. And, they can be wiped out due to prolonged exposure to stress. When this occurs, a condition known as "adrenal fatigue" might become manifest. The result of this condition is chronic fatigue, poor mood, anxiety and even depression, among many other symptoms. The end result is the sufferer going through a series of unpleasant stages that may lead to more serious physical conditions such as diabetes. While that isn't the only factor that is derived from chronic adrenal fatigue, it can certainly contribute. Yoga helps to reduce the negative effects of adrenal burnout by promoting the release of healthy emotions which, in turn, help heal conditions such as chronic fatigue. So, if you are looking to recover from a period of prolonged stress, practicing yoga is definitely the way to go.

12. Yoga can boost your mood

Research suggests that any type of physical activity can help boost positive moods while developing a better sense of self-esteem. In the case of yoga, these assumptions seem to ring true as the development of positive habits can lead to creating an overall positive environment for growth and development. In fact, you can chalk up your psychological wellbeing to the fact that you can see improvements in your shape and health. These are factors which can certainly contribute you boosting your mood and self-esteem.

13. Helps you get away from counting calories
When you are looking to lose weight, it is common to "count calories", that is, very extremely mindful of the amount of calories you consume through the foods your eat. However, yoga is a great way to get away from counting calories as it stimulates the reduction of the hormone known as "cortisol". Cortisol is almost exclusively associated to stress. Therefore, if you reduce the amount of stress in your life, you will reduce the production of cortisol. Given the fact that cortisol is known to hinder calorie consumption, by practicing yoga on a regular basis, you won't have to concern yourself with having to count calories. All you will need is to be consistent in you day to day routine and eat a balanced diet.

14. Helps process glucose
Since yoga can help you reduce the amount of cortisol in your body, you can also process glucose in a more effective manner. As a result, you won't have to concern yourself too much with the amounts of things you eat versus the quality of the things you eat. Consequently, the main thing to keep in mind is that when you are able to help your body process glucose more efficiently through the reduction of cortisol, you will not only lose weight, but also reduce the likelihood of developing diseases such as diabetes. So, yoga can definitely aid you in your efforts to get your glucose levels in check.

15. Helps with concentration and focus
Perhaps the biggest known effect of yoga is the improvement that concentration and focus present. In most individuals, concentration and focus is rather limited due to the constant bombardment from TV, social media and other forms of communication. The end result is a very low attention span that makes it hard to concentrate on most tasks. In fact, the average adult has an attention span of less than 30 seconds. This means that anything that takes longer then 30 seconds will almost invariably be meet with some kind of resistance from the individual. This resistance is evident in the fact that most folks need

to turn away or do something else before they can resume focus. As such, yoga can help boost cognitive abilities which, in turn, helps boost concentration, focus and overall cognitive performance. So, if you are looking to get a mental benefit in addition to physical ones, then yoga is definitely worth taking up.

So, there you have it. These are the benefits that you can expect from yoga. The most important thing to keep in mind is that over time, you will find it easier and easier to reap these benefits as you won't have to struggle to get into a healthy routine. At the end of the day, you will be able to make the most of your time and efforts in developing yourself, your skills and your abilities to become a better and healthier person.

You already have everything you need. So, it's just a question of time and effort!

Conclusion

Thank you very much for reading this book. By now, you have seen how important it is to find ways of dealing with negative energy through achieving chakra balance. Most importantly, the ways and techniques which we have described in this book will help you get the most out of your efforts to improve your overall quality of life.

So, what's next?

In case you haven't already begun working on implementing the practices we have outlined in this book, it is definitely time to begin looking into it. You see, when you make a conscious decision to take up habits such as yoga, healthy eating and managing negative energy, you will begin to make the most of your ability to balance your overall chakra system. When this happens, you will almost immediately begin to see the benefits that a healthy chakra system has on your mind and body.

Best of all, you will find that many emotional and physical ailments begin to subside if not disappear altogether. If you think that's not possible, then it's time to think again. Not only is it possible, but it also rather simple to do. The hard part is getting into the habit of taking on these new customs into practice.

So, what are you waiting for?

The longer you wait to get started with these practices, the harder it will be for you to become the best version of yourself. After all, you are surely looking to find the best way to become a better person, improve your performance at work and simply feel better about yourself. Perhaps the biggest benefit that you will find is the increased sense of self-satisfaction that you can derive from making a concerted effort to be the best that you can possibly be.

So, thanks again for taking the time to read this book. We wish you all the best in your efforts to become that perfect version of yourself. See you again soon!

Chakra Awakening

The Step by Step Guide to Open Your Chakras and the Third Eye; Activate the Pineal Gland to Achieve Greater Awareness and Increase Mind Power with Kundalini Yoga

By

New Mindfulness Lab

Introduction

Although all the chakras of the body are important, the health of the third eye, or the Ajna chakra, is especially important. One of the main goals of the chakras is to provide an uninterrupted connection between the mind and the surrounding world, and the Ajna chakra is the place where the flow of energy meets your consciousness.

The third eye is considered the so-called invisible organ that every person has. An increasing number of people successfully activate it, thereby gaining new opportunities.

Esoterics, yogis, and followers of oriental culture assure that every person has a third eye. The phenomenon is compared with the sensory organ, gives a different perception of reality, allows you to see the energetic component of the world, and reveals many opportunities inherent in psychics.

There is an opinion in the literature that people are born with an open third eye, but the human subconscious mind blocks an additional sense organ. People stop using it and do not believe that it exists. In most, the third eye is blocked, and there is no paranormal ability. Agreeably, public opinion oftentimes replaces one's own view of the world.

People with an open third eye become clairvoyant because they really know more than those who chose not to believe in the existence of chakras or paranormal abilities. Ready for an additional sensory organ?

Let's go!

Chapter 1

Chakras : Their Meaning and Significance

What Are Chakras?

Chakras are subtle energy centers located in places of nerve plexuses. Chakra in Sanskrit means "wheel." In our subtle body, there are seven main chakras, each of which corresponds to a stage of evolution. Each chakra is responsible for the embodiment of a person of certain spiritual qualities that most people are in an unmanifest state.

Chakras are the most well-known elements of the theory of the subtle body since many authors interested in yoga, Tibetan Buddhism, Theosophy, and parapsychological research have provided various descriptions of the chakras and comments on them. Although the seven stages of samadhi are already mentioned in classical yogic sutras, the development of the concept of chakras probably began only with the advent of tantric practices.

Often trembling, twitching, twisting, or vibration occurring in the areas of the chakras in people during a massage session or during emotional or physical stress. It seems that in these places, there is a block that does not allow energy to move uniformly throughout the body. It is possible that blocks are created by unresolved issues or mental problems associated with chakras. This is associated with

227

physical disorders in the functioning of the organs of the human body since most of the chakras control the work of certain organs.

Another phenomenon that can be correlated with the action of the energy of the chakras is the spontaneous occurrence of special images, sounds, and symbols, which in tantric cosmology are considered to be inherent in all chakras. Their appearance during crisis conditions can give information related to those issues that need to be resolved, or indicate the area of the body, focusing on which will bring the greatest effect. For these reasons, it is useful to have an idea of the chakra system, which is outlined here - in general terms.

Chakras are called such objects as neurohormonal mechanisms of controlling zones of the body; multidimensional passages through which creative forces flow between three bodies; centers of the body's energy system; energy funnels; intermediaries that transfer energy from one dimension to another; "interdimensional transforming systems that can be controlled by thought and which turn matter into energy" (Joy); centers of subtle forces, cosmic consciousness and prana generation.

According to Goswami, the Bindu of the chakras in the sphere of pranic energy play the same role as atoms in the material sphere. He said: "A moving or active pranic force concentrates and gathers to form petals of Bindu at various points in the body, which in yoga are called chakras, or lotuses. This formation begins with the Sahasrara chakra and continues with the lower chakras with how human consciousness is formed and his material body. All this is invisible to the naked eye. The chakras function on a supermaterial level. "

Usually, the chakras are considered the connecting link between all types of activities of the causal, subtle, and gross bodies. From them come the vritti (waves of thoughts), as well as other energies that are distributed throughout the body. Therefore, each of them is attributed to certain emotions and properties. If we take the chakras as the main converters and transmitters of energy between bodies, it will become clear that increasing the tension of consciousness and energy is a powerful additional load on the chakra system. Often, chakras are described as lotuses moving from bottom to top with energy rising through them.

The chakras contain all the untangled nodes and problems of a person's personal and emotional life, and during spiritual transformation, they can contribute to the integration of forms of consciousness that are more characteristic of a unifying function and which are less ego-oriented.

There are seven main chakras and 43 less important, which are attributed to many properties in different texts. It is believed that throughout the day, prana alternately dominates in different chakras according to a sixty-minute rhythm. Several types of symbols are associated with each of the main chakras. The latter include an animal personifying the subtle forces that control the chakra; God, which denotes one of the forces of divine manifestation; a goddess who indicates the type of energy placed at this point. Other symbols denote the dominant element and one of the five senses associated with this chakra. Meditation on each chakra awakens the energy of the goddess who is there, which will open up unique divine opportunities for man. Lotus petals represent various qualities, emotional tendencies, and possibilities.

The First Chakra - Muladhara Chakra

Located almost at the very end of the spine and touching the anus and testicles or cervix, this chakra is designated as the four-petalled lotus, whose petals represent ultimate happiness, innate bliss, the bliss of unity and bliss of courage and strength. She is considered a reflection of the crown chakra on the physical level, and therefore her petals are blissful. The nature of this chakra is identical to Brahman, the creative principle of the universe. We can assume that it preserves the material form of the body and that its underlying history and potentials of human evolution are hidden.

This is the foundation and support of the body, and its safety and self-preservation depend on its normal functioning. This chakra corresponds to the element earth, orange-red color, and sense of smell. An elephant with a black stripe around the neck is its symbol and represents earthly qualities: strength, firmness, stability and support, these qualities are represented by the yellow square inscribed in the circle of yantra or mandala depicting this chakra. It also has a triangle called Tripura and represents will, knowledge, and action.

Muladhara affects the rectum, kidneys, sperm accumulation, and the genitals, as well as bones, skin, muscles, nerves, and hair. It is associated with the occurrence of physiological disorders such as hemorrhoids, constipation, sciatica, and prostate diseases. It is associated with a sense of smell, and its vibration causes expansion or contraction of the lungs.

Mishra writes that through pratyahara (distraction of the senses), anger, lust, and greed are curbed on this chakra. Longing and depression are also considered symptoms of an imbalance in it.

Meditation on this chakra establishes control over attachments to luxury, lies, pride, envy, and narcissism. Pandit said that the Muladhara controls physical or subconscious movements or impulses. In the yantra (the symbolic image of the chakra), there is a blood-red triangle of fire that inflates the kandarpa vayu, the cause of sexual arousal, which is important for reproducing the human race. Motoyama wrote that when this chakra awakens, it releases suppressed emotions explosively, which can lead to the emergence of extreme irritability and psychological instability in a person, a violation of sleep patterns, excitability.

Meditation on the god of this chakra, Mahadeva, who sits with his face, turned back, cleanses from sins. Brahma, the god of absolute creative power, also gives this chakra the goddess Dakini Shakti, the energy of creation. If you repeat the mul mantra, while maintaining the serenity of the mind and devotion and focusing on this chakra, then you can awaken her goddess. In yoga cosmology, exactly under this chakra is the Kundalini energy, curled up in three and a half turns. Yogis believe that this is where the confluence of sushumna (nadi, carrying the stream of life), Vajra Nadi (nadi carrying the electric stream), and Brahma Nadi (sound stream or stream of spirit) merge.

The Second Chakra - Svadhishthana Chakra

Located slightly above the muladhara at the base of the penis, or in the center of the lower back, this chakra is associated with the conquest of water; its symbols are the crescent and the god Vishnu, nourishing the principle of the universe. Its color is usually considered red or scarlet and sometimes - white. Rakini Shakti, a dark blue goddess with three red eyes and four hands, from whose nose blood flows, carries the energy of this chakra. She holds in her hands a trident, a lotus, a drum, and a chisel. A light gray or green sea monster resembling a crocodile is an animal symbol of the chakra, it personifies dominance over the sea and indicates a connection with the unconscious. By meditating on this chakra, a person defeats the elements.

She has six petals, which represent the mental qualities of neglect, numbness, credulity, suspicion, desire for destruction and cruelty, and also represent six nerves associated with the colon, rectum, kidneys, bladder, genitals, and testicles. This chakra promotes the circulation of liquid substances in the body, their conservation, and nutrition; it is also considered a center of the heterosexual orientation of a person.

Mishra wrote that this chakra controls, controls, and nourishes the feet. By focusing on it, a person feels a magnetic pulsation, circulation, and vibration and can get rid of all the unpleasant sensations, pains, and illnesses in his legs. Other conditions associated with this chakra include sexual problems, diabetes, kidney and bladder diseases. By meditating on it, a person is freed from egoistic feelings, small impulses, and desires. The equanimity and serenity of the mind develop. The normal functioning of the Svadhishthana is associated with a sense of self-confidence and well-being, and with the frustrations in her work, disappointment, addiction, and anxiety. This chakra is also associated with a sense of taste and language. According to some tantras, in order to master it, a person must master the language.

The Third Chakra - Manipura Chakra

Located above Svadvishthana opposite the navel, Manipura is associated with Rudra, a god who distributes goods and creates fear, personifying the destructive principle of the universe (the world of the mind). The goddess Lakini Shakti, dressed in yellow clothes, is called the benefactress of the universe, and one of the texts describes that she loves animal meat, her chest is covered with blood, and fat is dripping from her lips. The animal symbol is a ram, an animal sacrificed, which personifies the need to sacrifice addictions, impulsive urges, and other strong emotions.

Concentration over manipura brings comprehension of feces or eternal time. Perhaps this level of openness can be associated with the return of memories of other lives or states that take people beyond the boundaries of consciousness created by time. This chakra is also associated with control of heat and directs the agni, the fiery principle, which is believed to control the creature's unbridled movements and digestive system. Manipura controls the internal organs of the abdomen, in particular, the functioning of the stomach, liver, and large intestine, and is associated with a section of the central nervous system located above the lumbar region. Some say that focusing on this center can cure diseases of the abdominal organs, especially if you meditate on the red color in it.

Ten petals that carry the qualities of shame, treachery, envy, desire, drowsiness, despondency, vainness, delusion, disgust, and fear make up this chakra. However, according to one of the tantric texts, when a yogi meditates on this chakra and pronounces a mul mantra, he is always in a good mood and illnesses cannot penetrate his / her body.

Such a yogi can enter into the bodies of others and see siddhas (saints and teachers of yoga), can, at a glance, determine the qualities of material objects and see objects underground. It is clear why this chakra is so often associated with gaining power and finding a good place in the world. It is also an area of hara that one focuses on during some Zen meditations. This concentration gives rise to a sense of stability and resilience in the being,

The opening of this chakra requires the participation of the eyes and such control over their movements so that they do not for a moment come off the center located between the eyebrows.

The Fourth Chakra - Anahata Chakra

The location of the heart chakra is usually indicated opposite the center line running between the nipples, but sometimes it is moved slightly to the right of the sternum, although not directly above the heart. It is associated with the conquest of the element of air, as well as with the heart and nada, the sound of cosmic consciousness. By meditating on this center, you can feel how the energy flows throughout the entire nervous system as if it is filled with magnetism. Many traditions of spiritual development emphasize the importance of the heart chakra as the chakra that needs to be awakened in the first place in order to experience a spiritual awakening since it is here that the energies of the lower and upper levels of consciousness merge, which symbolize two intersecting triangles. In addition, anahata, combining the energies of different chakras, also connects the left and right sides of the body, the qualities of yin and yang.

Isha is the god of this chakra; he sits on a black antelope or gazelle, which symbolizes the speed and ease of air. Isha is the supreme God, endowed with complete yogic power, omniscient, and omnipresent. It is white and symbolizes purity; it has three eyes; the third represents knowledge of samadhi. When its form arises during meditation, fears disappear, and concentration intensifies.

233

The yantra images of the heart chakra include intersecting triangles, inside which are a bright golden creature and Kakini Shakti, the lightning-colored goddess who radiates light and joy. Kakini is called the keeper of the doors of Anahata and meditating on it; a person learns to stabilize prana and remove obstacles on the way to Isha. When the goddess is red, it means that her power is used to control pranic energy; when she is white, she is Isha consciousness.

The twelve scarlet petals associated with Anahata represent waiting, excitement, diligence, affection, hypocrisy, weakness, selfishness, separation, greed, fraud, indecision, and regret. Meditation on this chakra brings possession of sound, and if you say the mul mantra during meditation, you are more prepared to understand God, as a person gains control over his feelings, in particular, reducing the sense of touch. Then, as they say, not a single desire will remain unfulfilled - then a person will forever plunge into a state of bliss.

If you look from a different point of view, we can assume that, freed from attachment to all "heart" desires (as evidenced by the qualities embodied in the petals), a person gains the ability to distract the senses from all worldly things and thus acquire a state of bliss first for short periods and then forever.

The qualities of compassion, acceptance, and unconditional love are signs of the balanced functioning of this chakra. Indifference, passivity, and sadness are signs of an imbalance — some authors associate arthritis and respiratory problems with cardiac chakra, as well as cardiovascular disease and hypertension.

The opening of this chakra is considered feasible with the help of the skin; that is, you need to surpass the sense of touch, which is done by achieving control over sensory perception through kumbhaka (breath-holding). A common way to discover the energy of anahata is a meditation on it with the simultaneous presentation of light or breathing in and breathing out air from it.

The Fifth Chakra - Vishuddha Chakra

Located in the throat is the vishuddhi lotus - gray or silver (and sometimes smoky purple) and has sixteen petals. They contain seven musical notes, poison and nectar, and seven "invocations," which are used to protect against demons, during sacrifices, to light sacred lights, to give determination, to bless and glorify. Here begin the priestly or occult powers associated with the forces of projection or expression. This chakra is also associated with the conquest of the etheric state of matter (space). This chakra is usually associated with creative activity and inspiration, as well as receiving moral instruction, especially when in contact with an inexhaustible source of "grace." A person begins to feel that the inner giver and taker are one and the same.

The god of this chakra is Shiva in a half male, half female form (Ardhanarishvara), he sits on a white elephant, and with him is the four-armed yellow Shakini Shakti (goddess). He owns a variety of knowledge. She rules in the kingdom of the moon over insignificant secrets.

Vishuddha controls both hands and is the center of pratyahara or distraction of the senses. When a person focuses attention here, he loses his hands sensitivity to heat, cold, pain, pressure, touch, and temperature. Tantras say that the instruments of this chakra are ears, they are used in such a way that the noise of the world does not distract, and only one sound is heard: either nada (the sound of Ohms is of less intensity) or the name of God. Meditation on this chakra leads one to the threshold of great liberation.

The Sixth Chakra - Ajna Chakra

Ajna is located above the nose between the eyebrows is the source of two nerve flows, one of which passes through the eyes, and the other through the midbrain. There are three main nadi (sushumna, ida, and pingala). The ability to create and achieve is generated by mental waves emanating from this point. This chakra controls the inner vision and dynamic activity of the will and knowledge. This "third eye" in many cultures is associated with light, inner knowledge, intuition, and mediumistic abilities. The discovery of these abilities involves the integration of both intellectual and emotional poles.

The goddess of ajna is the six-faced and six-armed Hakini Shakti; she personifies the five principles concentrated in the lower chakras and the gifts of the ajna chakra. When its color is described as red, then the knowledge of Kundalini is fully awakened; when she is white, she represents a state of rest; when it is dark blue, it is on the verge of transitioning into a shapeless state. When seen in a combination of white, red, and black colors, she shows a mixture of three gunas: sattva (harmonious consciousness), rajas (activity) and tamas (inertia).

Meditation on this center brings visions of the highest truth, yogic powers, liberation from all Sanskars, and ultimately wisdom, higher knowledge. This is the center of individual consciousness, which through pratyahara, can be expanded to universal. Ajna is often referred to as guiding all other chakras, and some yogis advise to concentrate only on it, or first of all, before awakening energies in other centers. Thus, the development of the qualities inherent in all previous chakras can be influenced, and so the student can achieve a state of nondual consciousness. It is believed that it is not possible to fully master the lower chakras before Ajna is awakened.

The Seventh Chakra - Sahasrara Chakra

According to some texts, sahasrara is located at the top of the head in the brain; others believe that it is above the physical body and is identical with Parabrahma, the supreme creator. Her lotus has a thousand petals, five of which represent all the letters of the Sanskrit alphabet. Samadhi, felt through this chakra, is a complete merger with existence, without the limits of ego-consciousness in the body. (Although there are yoga systems in which other levels of chakras are indicated, extending further beyond the physical body and to this first level of higher consciousness.)

Parabrahma governs this center, symbolized by the triangle of consciousness, which is called Vija - this is another name for the divine essence of sat-chit-ananda. It represents overcoming obstacles and merging with emptiness or the Upper Light outside the form, a state which, according to most yogic sacred books and the saying of the saints, a person cannot describe.

Meditating here, according to Bose and Haldor, a person crosses the boundaries of creation, preservation, and destruction and can taste the sweet nectar (amrita) flowing in a continuous stream from sahasrara. A person is freed, all Sanskars are destroyed, and then he is not subject to either birth or death. At this stage of awakening, individual identification disappears forever, and a person is identified with a higher consciousness. (It is important to remember that when yogis talk about the state of immortality, they usually do not mean that a person will literally never leave the body, but rather imply that conscious fusion with the infinite is achieved forever and will not be destroyed with the death of the body.)

Chapter 2

Chakra Awakening tutorial

What Does It Mean to Awaken the Chakras?

I agree that we are often overreacting to difficult life situations. No matter what we feel - anger, fear, or aggression, we feel completely unprotected at this moment. However, we do not even realize that we ourselves are the source of such sensations. External life only provokes us to manifest our inner imbalance.

The situation can be corrected by learning to distract from external problems and concentrate on internal energy - the energy of the chakras. After all, it is her imbalance that is the cause of the violation of our internal balance.

Harmonizing the energy flow of the chakras, we transfer consciousness to a qualitatively different level. And what is interesting: as soon as we begin to perceive life calmly and joyfully, external circumstances also develop more favorably.

How to Awaken the Chakras

Working with chakras requires mental balance. You must believe that equilibrium exists, and by believing it is imperative to achieve it.

However, there is one paradox: in order to understand whether the equilibrium is reached, you must know about a sense of balance. Otherwise, you simply will not have a starting point.

Learn to live, accepting mercy from nature, and you will see how harmonious your existence will be. Life will be much simpler and more meaningful. The balance will bring purification to your life. Your feelings will be elevated, and you can enjoy the most subtle sensations, easily satisfy any desire.

You must be aware of the balanced state of energy and be able to merge with it.

Exercises

Exercise 1. Self-healing in an unbalanced state of the first chakra

Go for a walk just to mingle with Nature. Take a closer look at the life boiling around you. Feel imbued with life force. Nature fills life with everything that exists - trees and grass, animals and birds, rivers, and mountains. Her power pervades you, feel it.

Realize that it is not you who live life, but life lives by you. Understand that there is a force that gives you life, makes your heartbeat, your lungs breathe, and blood runs through your veins. Recognize yourself as part of nature, and a sense of fear will leave you.

Exercise 2. Achieving a balanced level of consciousness of the first chakra

All your actions must be permeated with a bond with the earth. To improve this connection, imagine that your feet, like trees, sprout roots in the ground. Feel that strength, wisdom, and healing energy rise to these abdomen on these roots. Imagine all this during

239

meditation, on a walk, or at any time when you want to replenish your energy.

Sports help to develop the consciousness of the first chakra, especially those types that are risky, competitive, aggressive, for example, parachuting, soccer, or boxing. Generally useful are any activities that are breathtaking.

The first chakra expresses the deep, personal aspect of the inner "I." It can be called defensive, competing, and self-oriented chakra. Indeed, self-preservation is perhaps the most powerful instinct dictated not by faith, but by fear.

Thus, it turns out that this level of consciousness is far from spirituality and is built on the animal principle. And if you are at this level, then you are unlikely to be able to especially enjoy life: now you are faced with a question that concerns you much more - the question of survival.

Therefore, go to nature and give free rein to your animal beginning. Feel the joy of life; only then will manifestations of the second chakra become available to you.

You need to achieve balance in life - at home, in the family, at work. And for this, you must find resources sufficient to satisfy basic security needs.

The main thing is not to have dominant needs. You must be sure that all your needs are feasible and you are able to find resources to satisfy them. Only in this way can you achieve a state of equilibrium. Only balanced energy can naturally rise to the second chakra.

If your needs become insatiable, if you are missing something all the time, you will not be able to rise above the first chakra.

Exercise 3. Awakening the first chakra

We do many things in obedience to a sense of fear. If you feel uneasy, analyze the situation, and you will surely find any fears that dominate your consciousness. So your first chakra needs balance.

Even the natural need to feel safe indicates that you need to pay attention to the first chakra.

Take a "tree pose" (yoga) and try to achieve inner balance. It is best to go to nature and feel like a part of all life. Try to understand that your roots feed on the same vitality as the roots of the trees. Imagine the red color and feel how its strength fills you. If you have beautiful things, then put them on to achieve a greater effect. Wear pomegranate, ruby, or obsidian jewelry. You can even just put a pebble in your pocket and touch it from time to time to recharge it with its vitality.

Fear should fulfill the function of a signal, but not completely absorb your consciousness. By learning to activate and balance the first chakra, you will cope with a fear-based mentality. You will know that animal instincts are in control. Just imagine that they stand guard over your well-being; then you can concentrate on more pleasant things - those that form the basis of the second chakra.

Exercise 4. Self-healing in an unbalanced state of the second chakra

Remember the feeling of satisfaction that caused you to feel guilty. Restore the object of pleasure in your memory and try again to experience all the sensations, but this time fully aware of them. Describe your feelings. Did this experience bring you pleasure? In what place of your body are the experienced sensations concentrated? Realize them fully. Surely you will find that your ability to enjoy has become much wider. Now it's much easier for you to achieve it.

We give an example. Next time you eat a cake, focus on the pleasure you enjoy. Try to slow down the process of eating it to enhance the feeling of pleasure. Savor every bite. Revel in its aroma. Let each of your cells enjoy its fabulous taste. Let this feeling bring you to ecstasy. Do not cast pleasure in the past. See that you will be able to feel such complete satisfaction that there will be no need to eat up the last piece. You have already achieved the absolute fullness of the sensation.

Exercise 5. Achieving a balanced level of consciousness of the second chakra

If your passion for life is creative and controlled, then this means that your second chakra is balanced.

Show your enthusiasm for nature, art, music, literature, in a word, beauty in any of its manifestations, and then you will reach the balance of the second chakra.

Having risen to such a level of consciousness, you will feel a huge need for creative activity. It will be based on two components - a deep admiration for the beauty and a desire to make as much pleasure as possible in your life.

The second important sign of balance is self-confidence. A positive perception of oneself, a feeling of confidence in one's attractiveness is a right given to us by God. It has nothing to do with physical beauty. We are talking about an internal sense of attractiveness, which reflects external magnetism.

When you get pleasure (being in someone's arms, trying something tasty, listening to beautiful music or enjoying the magnificent scenery), close your eyes for a moment and concentrate on the feeling of satisfaction that you are experiencing at this moment. Feel how every cell of your body is enjoying this moment. Develop a sense of satisfaction. Soon you will find that you are able to feel the fullness and completeness of your sensations.

The search for new pleasures, balanced by the ability to experience pleasure in full, turns life into an endless series of pleasures.

Desire and the ability to value are the two sides of the second chakra. Desire makes you concentrate on what you want but don't have. In other words, you are in a state of insufficiency; you are constantly missing something. The satisfaction of desire, in this case, is not achieved when it is fulfilled since it is associated not with possession, but only with aspiration.

But the ability to value is the highest form of manifestation of the consciousness of the second chakra. Instead of concentrating on what you do not have, you learn to enjoy the affordable. You focus your consciousness on momentary sensations. You are able to appreciate them with every cell of your being. Only in this way can you saturate and balance the second chakra. When you learn to do this, you will live according to the laws of magnetism, that is, follow the energy without experiencing any anxiety. After all, you realize that life flows around you, and you will never find yourself in a void. Calmness caused by the feeling that you are always able to enjoy will give life extra dynamism. You will have new opportunities, and this is when you realize that life, with all its pleasures, is also at your disposal.

If you have awakened the second chakra, but still have not balanced the first, then the feeling of insecurity is projected onto the sensations of the second chakra. This leads to a feeling of jealousy and envy. We give an example. The second chakra makes us communicate with people, with its balance, the ability to enjoy this communication increases, and the envy of other people deprives us of this opportunity. Our task is to learn to perceive people as they are and not to demand more. Then any relationship will enrich us as a person.

The same can be said about sex life: if it meets our needs, then intimate relationships enrich us and are not a source of constant anxiety.

Exercise 6. Awakening of the second chakra

If you suddenly think that life has lost its meaning and there is no place for joy in it, try to consciously feel pleasure. Make yourself a warm bath with foam, light candles, turn on your favorite music.

243

Focus on enjoyment. Feel how each of your cells responds to the gentle touch of warm water. Relax, enjoy the sounds of the melody, and don't think about anything.

Open your eyes, look at the candle flame. Watch the light and shadow on the walls. Forget about business, drop the guilt, and enjoy the moment.

Exercise 7. Self-healing in an unbalanced state of the third chakra

The unbalanced state of the third chakra can manifest itself in two opposite ways - in the excessive use of one's own will and in its underestimation.

Excessive use of the will is easy to detect. After all, our life is a constant competition. The imbalance of the third chakra leads to distrust, fear of being overboard, inability to manage events. As a result, we are constantly on the alert, always ready for new challenges.

With the unbalanced third chakra, the need for self-affirmation is so great that energetic conflicts arise all around you. They cause an adrenaline rush, which gives a feeling of a surge of energy.

It is very easy to get into this adrenaline addiction, and then exploit the energy received. If this energy is not balanced, it conflicts with the outside world and leads to new conflicts.

A person who has fallen into adrenaline is constantly in a state of righteous anger. He believes that he has every right to do this, and implicitly creates situations for which, in his opinion, only anger can be the only just reaction to it.

Thus, in order for conflicts to disappear, we just need to realize our nature. You need to understand that our energy is primary, and events are secondary. It is energy that is the cause of events, and not vice versa. Therefore, until we balance the internal energy, the events of the external world will not change.

The main signs of instability of the third chakra are as follows: a guilty feeling that embraces us when someone refuses something, fawning over others, a constant sense of ourselves as a victim, a feeling of helplessness and an inability to fend for ourselves. The reason for this type of behavior is low self-esteem and lack of self-confidence, which leads to an imbalance.

A person's life with an unbalanced third chakra is governed by the desires of others, not his own.

The imbalance of the third chakra can be caused by the imbalance of the first two chakras. When we do not feel safe, do not know how to enjoy, someone inevitably appears in our life, whose point of view on the world we unconditionally accept, and oppose everything that at least partially contradicts it.

If minor energy conflicts constantly arise around us, we must, first of all, analyze whether our sense of security is satisfied and whether we are able to sincerely and fully enjoy life.

In the case of "failure" of one of these components, it is necessary to deal with its completion and then balance the third chakra.

This is the law: if the energy of the lower chakras is not balanced, it is impossible to achieve a balance of the higher.

Exercise 8. Achieving a balanced level of consciousness of the third chakra

When the third chakra is in a state of equilibrium, we can concentrate on achieving our goal and relaxing to enjoy the results. This is the effective use of will: it must always be applied in such a way as to achieve a result, but never use it more than necessary.

With a balanced third chakra, we are able to succeed without involving other people and without infringing on their interests. At the same time, we feel safe and enjoy the results of our actions. It is as if we are freeing ourselves from the influence of the outside world and are concentrating our attention on working with our own energy.

We do not radiate energy imbalance, which means that energy conflicts do not arise around us. We are becoming more flexible, looking for cooperation, not competition. We are confident that if the situation requires our intervention, we can make a decision.

In a usual, non-critical situation, we can allow ourselves to relax and enjoy harmony. "For our life to be calm and harmonious, we must abandon the need to be right" - this is the motto of a person with a balanced third chakra.

After awakening the third chakra, we will begin to attract people who also work on their own will. And only we ourselves decide whether to avoid unnecessary conflict or join the fight if the issue is really important to you. Once in a conflict situation, we can balance the third chakra by asking ourselves two very important questions:

1. Is something really threatening me? (Is my safety or even survival in jeopardy?)

2. Do I really care about the outcome? (If I win the fight, will it mean something to me?)

Answers to these questions will help to understand whether this conflict is important for us or not. If nothing threatens our security, if the result is not important to us, then this is not our business. If it comes to our honor, then we must fight to the "last drop of blood." The main thing is to have absolute confidence that the conflict we are entering into is of vital importance to us. Otherwise, those around us will have a great opportunity to test our strength on us, and we will indulge them, allowing us to engage ourselves in completely unnecessary conflicts.

With a positive answer to both questions, we must join the fight and strive for victory. We have to combine willpower and reason, analyze the situation, and think about what needs to be done.

The level of consciousness of the third chakra is the awareness of one's own strength and significance in the surrounding world. The main characteristic of this level of consciousness is the assertion of one's will. Often it comes after a number of negative examples related to the occurrence of energy conflicts. When the time comes for positive examples, that is, the correct use of the will, we are aware of our own strength and can stand up for our beliefs.

When we move to a balanced third level of consciousness, our life becomes clear. The ability to make a sound assessment of the situation and one's own strength minimizes accidents. We abandon our defensive attitude and understand that opposing points of view do not threaten us at all. We begin to interact effectively with the world without entering into conflicts.

Having achieved the balance of the third chakra, we do not stop thinking about energy and will; we begin to perceive intention as the energy of the third chakra; we analyze our own intentions, rather than trying to understand the motivation of others.

The best way is diplomatic. In this case, we can defend ourselves if necessary, but we will not be constantly in a defensive position. Since we do not expect a trick from others, conflicts cease to haunt us. Sensibly assessing reality, we understand the simple truth: "How many people, so many opinions." Now no one and nothing will prevent us from finding a business that we would like to do; others will seek to cooperate with you and not compete.

Exercise 9. Awakening of the third chakra

When we need to make a decision, we rely on the energy of the third chakra. What should be done to awaken her?

When in a difficult position, try to concentrate and balance the third chakra. Then, based on the sensations that arise within you, make a decision. And do not look back!

Often, we need only a small push, and here the third chakra is indispensable. It allows you to concentrate energy. When exercising, be mindful of the third chakra. It is she who will allow you to truly want to do your job. Then you will get a second wind.

Use the third chakra when resolving conflicts, during sports, during exams. She will help you when talking with the traffic police inspector, when he stops you for speeding, in a word, wherever you need to defend your positions. Breathe deeply and concentrate on yourself. Throw away all the reactions that distract you from the third chakra, and act.

Exercise 10. Self-healing in an unbalanced state of the fourth chakra

The main manifestation of the unbalanced fourth chakra is sentimentality. When our heart is broken, we are not able to separate our problems from those of others. That is why communication with other people becomes painful for us. As a result, we strive to do something for others in the hope of a good attitude on their part.

The imbalance of the fourth chakra is also manifested in an exaggerated immersion in love and dependence. Love becomes a need and loses its luster.

We say, "I love you," meaning by this: "I need you." This is how the needs of the lower chakras manifest at the level of the fourth chakra. The result is love, weighed down by many conventions. Yes, she awakens in the heart, but she is deprived of her freedom because she is overshadowed by the imbalance of the lower chakras.

If you are worried about an object of love, realize that the reason for your concern is not love, but the lack of a sense of security. Try to find the source of the problem. Analyze the state of the first chakra. Embark on nature, soak in the inexhaustible vitality that manifests itself in everything around. And only after you gain a sense of security in relation to yourself and to life, enter into a relationship with another person. Now you do not need to strive for security in relation to your partner. Just keep your sense of security from nature.

The awakened fourth chakra can give rise to another problem - an exaggerated desire to give. This approach becomes a source of false morality: "It is better to give than to receive." As a result, you refuse what other people are offering you: from their help, services, or gifts. People whom you push away in this way feel unappreciated.

Accept with gratitude what people want to give you. Let them feel the joy of doing a good deed.

There is another "pad" for awakening the fourth chakra - the so-called unconditional love. In testing it, we attribute to other qualities that they do not possess. We imagine a person as we would like to see him. This means that our heart becomes a source of distorted perception.

Restoring balance requires an honest attitude. How to check it? Ask yourself: "Do I love what the other person brings into my life by my own efforts, or do I love him for who he can become if he changes?" If the last statement is true, then you love not your own person, but your own idea of him. In this case, your life force constantly flows into a partner so that it matches your perception. But, when this perception does not coincide with his own self-image, a problem arises. You are constantly deprived of vital energy, and it cannot correspond to your ideas since this contradicts his will. He returns to the old image, and you feel that all your efforts were in vain.

The prospect of the fourth chakra is not only love and light. Such a spiritual quality as compassion also awakens a heightened sensitivity to other people's misfortunes. If this sensitivity is not balanced, then you can plunge into the abyss of grief.

People whose fourth chakra is not balanced are familiar with feelings such as guilt and shame. You cannot perceive the suffering of others as if it was your fault. This problem is rooted in the lower chakras. Not a single life can do without suffering, and we need to learn not to exaggerate them.

Passing through the heart the suffering of the world, we destroy ourselves, but this life experience, when it is already behind, paves the way for us to a new life.

Exercise 11. Achieving a balanced level of consciousness of the fourth chakra

Maintaining the fourth chakra in a balanced state requires full commitment. We are drawn to succumb to the call of the heart and plunge into the ocean of emotions. But we must emerge from this ocean in time and turn our attention to activity and awareness. Only in this way can we stay afloat.

When we begin to live through the fourth chakra, our life changes dramatically. We stop fighting with others; love and joy await us everywhere. Trials and difficulties are inherent in every life, but if your heart wakes up, even these events will be illuminated by the light of grace, since they are associated with the subtlest levels, and life goes on.

The balanced fourth chakra fills our life with the deepest meaning. Compassion for universal torment develops into action.

We do not just suffer for everyone but strive to do everything in our power to ease the pain of others.

Love consciousness is divided into three levels - personal, compassionate, and universal.

Personal love: At this level, we experience unimaginable enjoyment of love for loved ones. This is a true feeling that encourages us to share our joy with people close to us. Personal love is closely interconnected with the first three chakras, so on a personal level, there is a strong sense of affection. We are afraid of losing a loved one. But with the transition to compassionate love, this fear wanes. When we reach the level of universal love, it disappears altogether.

Compassionate love: Moving to this level, we completely move away from personal love. Compassion can be experienced not only for close people but also for complete strangers. This love is not based on possession, like personal love. She has nothing to do with our inner self. Compassion arises from the realization that the suffering of the world comes from the remoteness of people. The reason for this is the action of the three lower chakras.

One of the basic attributes that a heart has that has awakened to compassionate love is forgiveness. We are all not perfect, and sometimes we do not quite specious acts, and therefore, should not deprive ourselves and others of the right to make mistakes. Compassion is required to understand this.

However, the compassion generated by the fourth chakra can make us too immersed in the torment of others and lose interest in life. This is completely unnecessary and will not bring any benefit. The fourth chakra does not require sacrifices. So that compassionate love does not cause harm, our inner "I" must be healthy, and the first three chakras - absolutely balanced.

Recognize the simple truth: if you are completely plunged in compassion, then only increase the suffering of the world, and not reduce it. And compassionate love should not lead to additional suffering. Try to get rid of the pain caused by compassion. Having found support in your heart, you will find divine protection. You can alleviate the suffering of others by conveying to them the goodness that you are endowed with.

Universal love: Being on the third level, we are approaching the sensation of Heaven on Earth. This unbound love, not seeking possession, leads to a state that we call unconditional love.

Having balanced the consciousness of the heart chakra, we plunge into the ocean of love. Others strive for us, and we generously give them our energy. At the same time, we feel how universal energy permeates us.

This should not scare us - the source of our energy is inexhaustible, and those around us will never absorb our entire energy. Even weary, we do not feel exhausted.

If the feeling of complete powerlessness comes, then we are simply acting incorrectly. It is urgent to turn to the heart chakra and personal levels of consciousness. Having regained strength, we will again be able to share them with others.

With a balanced heart chakra, we realize the inexhaustibility of life; we no longer fear the lack of something. Universal love allows us to be grateful and generous. We are grateful for the countless gifts of life and generously share them with other people.

Exercise 12. Awakening of the fourth chakra

Open your heart, and your sensations will be inexpressible. Resisting anything, you deal a double blow to your energy field. Firstly, you do not feel the influx of energy that occurs when you get something, and secondly, you spend energy on resistance. Having removed protection, you will feel how forces come back to you.

During any conflict, focus on this chakra. Bless the attacker, go into a state of gratitude. All these feelings live in your heart. Feel compassion, because before you is a different soul. Focus on the cordial connection that exists between you. Never expel anyone from your heart.

Exercise 13. Self-healing in an unbalanced state of the fifth chakra

With the unbalanced fifth chakra, we realize our right to independent thinking, but we cannot put its manifestation in order. We are in a constant struggle for personal freedom and strive to contradict other points of view simply because "we have the right to do so." However, we are missing out on many new features. Indeed, with this approach, we do not express ourselves, but only prove the fallacy of the judgments of other people.

What do we achieve with this? Only the warlike reaction of others. And this is at the time when we need the approval of our actions!

Realizing this, we begin to constantly analyze our own and other people's thoughts. At the same time, our ability to share our thoughts and feelings with others is suppressed. It seems to us that our ideas are not interesting, and we refuse to participate in the discussion. And this does not mean that we become good listeners: we simply do not know how to express our own thoughts.

We are not able to use energy. The crowd's energy suppresses us: we feel it from the inside and try to suppress it, which, of course, does not work out for us.

What to do in such a situation? You must immediately stop analyzing your feelings; feel free to plunge into energy; merge with the group mind! Then we will begin to freely express such thoughts that we had not even guessed before.

Exercise 14. Achieving a balanced level of consciousness of the fifth chakra

By balancing the fifth chakra, we gain new knowledge due to the fact that we begin to look at life in a new way. We gain some insight: ordinary events and relationships suddenly become living and developing. A fresh look and a sense of reality help us make the most of any circumstance. We move away from the logical perception of life and allow ourselves to see abstract connections between completely unrelated, at first glance, events. Now we can calmly discuss our ideas with others, even if they do not agree with us.

What needs to be done to achieve equilibrium?

Concentrate on your breathing, as it is through it that energy comes to you. Focus on the depth of breathing; try to make it even deeper and slower. You will feel that your anxiety disappears. You are immersed in a state of peace and tranquility. You must be very well prepared for understanding the nature of universal energy. To do this, all previous chakras must be balanced in advance.

You will express your opinion, even if it contradicts the opinion of others. You should not worry at all whether your opinion coincides with the generally accepted or not.

Realize life as a set of opportunities. This philosophical outlook on life is the beginning of your career.

Exercise 15. Awakening of the fifth chakra

Do you know what creative blockade is? Her most common example is the fear of the scene. Recognize that the fear and joy of the scene are one and the same energy. The only difference is your reaction. Do not try to resist the energy of the situation. Renounce the separate "I" and allow energy to circulate freely within you.

The fifth chakra will help you deal with this. Imagine that your energy is blocked and you can't break this wall.

Inhale through the fifth chakra, and then give your creative freedom. And do not try to influence its manifestation.

Exercise 16. Self-healing in an unbalanced state of the sixth chakra

With the unbalanced sixth chakra, our imagination has nothing to do with everyday reality. Its action is negative: we run the risk of getting lost in unreal dimensions of the astral plane. The unbalanced sixth chakra allows fear to completely absorb our personality. But if we realize that we are in an unbalanced state, if we can look inside ourselves and find the source of this fear, then we are able to overcome it.

Having calculated our energy field, we will understand what state we are in - fear or faith, inspiration or illusion, creativity, or avoiding reality. The main thing is to learn to understand your own energy, its nature. A sense of balance lies within ourselves.

Another sign of imbalance in the sixth chakra is an overestimation of one's own achievements in spiritual development. A sense of superiority is inappropriate here since spiritual development is not a contest.

Feeling guilty is also one of the manifestations of the unbalanced sixth chakra. You feel your separation from God, and therefore you consider yourself unworthy. Another distorted idea arises when you feel like an "extra person" thrown overboard life.

The danger of the unbalanced sixth chakra is that a person can resort to alcohol and drugs to get away from a feeling of internal imbalance. In fact, it is better for people with such reactions to try to change their lifestyle and move to a cleaner energy field.

Exercise 17. Achieving a balanced level of consciousness of the sixth chakra

When your sixth chakra is balanced, you are in a state of complete harmony, which, combined with an elevated perception of everything around you, brings pleasure and relief to your life. Now you are able to feel the movement of energy before it manifests itself in reality.

Having realized the flow of reality, you can merge with it and develop your intuition. You easily adapt to situations beyond your control. Your main purpose is to merge together with the life force that exists outside the personality.

Being in balance at this level of consciousness, you begin to understand what cannot be expressed in words. Now you think in images, pictures, intuition. The highest voice guides you, and you inspire others to listen to the voice that sounds inside them. You have become higher than conflict because you have abandoned the polar view of life and thereby gained wisdom.

Exercise 18. Awakening of the sixth chakra

If you do not see the point in your existence, feel lost and superfluous in this world, concentrate on the sixth chakra and start looking for the meaning and significance of your life. Look for signs, ask for advice, interact with your higher self.

In other words, make your life more meaningful, look for meaning in all its manifestations. In any conflict situation, look for an opportunity to see a broader perspective, some of which are polar judgments. Realize that there is a path lying between two opposites. Make yourself find this way. Remember that your first step is to rise above the conflict. Do it, and the path will open for you.

Learn to breathe life into yourself, be able to understand the divine providence, realize that depression and depression are contrary to it, and you will successfully cope with them.

Exercise 19. Self-healing in an unbalanced state of the seventh chakra

The unbalanced seventh chakra is a dangerous business. There is a threat that we will begin to live in an independent reality that has nothing to do with the outside world.

Another imbalance at this level is called the "shopping list" mentality. Suppose we have an idea of how we would like to see our own life. For example, we have a list of requirements that we would like to satisfy when entering into a marriage or getting a new job. We compose it and meditate on it until our wishes are fulfilled. The method may be effective, but this list is compiled by our Ego. In other words, our Ego claims to know more about what we need than God. We do not surrender to the will of providence but try to independently direct the course of our lives. With this approach, equilibrium is impossible to achieve.

There is a simple mantra for this case: "Go and go to God." What does this mean? And the fact that you first need to find your true "I" by establishing control over your life and awareness of responsibility, and then surrender completely to the will of a higher life force. Only then can we feel the merging with God.

Exercise 20. Achieving a balanced level of consciousness of the seventh chakra

In order to balance the seventh chakra, completely surrender to the will of providence and submit to a higher power. You should no longer wonder about your path. You simply live, abide in this world, and your consciousness is on a divine level. At this level, we come to the realization that we will have to answer for our actions in the face of Eternity.

In general, the seventh chakra cannot be felt at will. Most often, this happens as a divine intervention that does not require our participation.

After you feel a surge of new strength, falling to the source of vital energy, everything around you will gain a new meaning. So far, you have tried by any means to achieve spirituality. But after merging with God, your whole life has turned into a spiritual path.

Exercise 21. Awakening of the seventh chakra

If it seemed to you that life "turned away" from you, try to determine the measure of your despair. Absolutely come to terms with this. Move forward and fully submit to what is happening, not just submit, but with the belief that you can gain a higher power that will enter into you. Your previous path turned out to be untenable, so why not make a new attempt? The moment of despair is a kind of needle eye through which you need to go through to achieve a higher level of consciousness.

If despair has not yet taken possession of you, there is no need to wait for its appearance. Try to achieve this level of consciousness without waiting for the driving force in the form of some negative circumstances. And then you will have brilliant opportunities!

Chapter 3

The Third Eye: What Is the Third Eye?

The third eye (sixth chakra) is located at the bottom of the forehead, centered above the bridge of the nose, between the eyebrows. It is oriented horizontally from front to back. The third eye is your source of extrasensory perception, the seat of psychic sight and wisdom. Spiritual intuition enters your system in this way, giving you a "global vision" of life, with all its levels of energy interaction. Here resides your clairvoyance, your intuition, and your personal awakening, your gateway to inner and higher knowledge. This chakra works in a unique way with all the others because it has a connection to the root chakra, sacred chakra, solar plexus, throat, and crown.

The third eye governs the eyes, ears, sinuses, nose, pituitary gland, and hypothalamus. When this sixth chakra works well, you communicate adequately with both the inner self and the higher self; from then on, you can accomplish more in terms of inner healing and spiritual growth. This chakra allows you to clearly see your energy problems and lessons, so you can take responsibility. Most therapist practitioners have a very strong, very sensitive third eye because they rely on it to establish their diagnosis in their holistic work. As for the harmonization of your physical body, the more you "exercise" your psychic senses, the more they are refined!

People whose third eye is clogged feel cut off from their intuition and deny the existence of higher levels. Some believe in nothing but what they have learned or experienced in the physical world. Their ability to cope with the ups and downs of life is severely diminished so that they often repeat the same lessons without understanding why or how they should exceed them. The fear here is that of the connection to the inner self and the obligation to face "spiritual" duties. This creates a ball of guilt, blame, and shame that prevents them from taking responsibility for what they have created. The intellectual and creative incapacity, thus envied can settle in these people, who do not progress while others advance. So, it is essential to purify the sixth chakra; otherwise, you will continue to obstruct you!

Emotional problems related to this part of the body are anxiety, paranoia, and psychotic behavior, including schizophrenia, depression, mental and emotional instability. Physical imbalances occur in the area of the eyes, ears, sinuses, nose: they also affect the functionally the pituitary and hypothalamus. The pituitary regulates the endocrine system (the glands that secrete hormones directly into the bloodstream) and, as a result, several bodily processes. The hypothalamus regulates the pituitary, body temperature, as well as your dietary and sexual needs, and your need for sleep. Migraines are lodged there; physically, they come from the organs located in this region or are due to hormonal problems that disequilibrate the other chakras. Conceptual or functional learning disabilities are also governed by the third eye, although they often originate from the crown, which regulates the brain and functions of the central nervous system.

Meaning: Knowing or order

Location: Middle forehead

Color: Indigo

Element: None

Symbol: Lotus 96 petals

Fundamental principle: Perception and conscious knowledge of the Essence

Function: Intuition

Sensory function: All the senses, also in the form of perception extrasensory.

Endocrine Gland: The pituitary gland has a secretory activity exerting a stimulating function on all other glands. By these stimulants, it harmonizes the glands.

Minerals: Lapis lazuli, indigo sapphire, azurite, Labradorite, silver, quartz crystal

Consciousness:

This chakra is located in the middle of the forehead just above the eyebrows. It is from him that intuition is transmitted to the lower chakras and the mind. This is why Ajna is called the third eye, the eye of intuition.

The third eye is the seat of all awareness processes. We can create new realities on the physical plane like dissolving old realities. In general, this process is automatic and occurs without our conscious intervention. Most of the thoughts that determine our existence are directed by our emotional archetypes blocked or programmed by our own judgments and prejudices, as well as those of others. Thus, the mind is not always the master, but rather the servant of our emotionally charged thoughts that we only partially dominate.

However, these thoughts are realized, literally in our life because what we perceive and live is a manifestation of our subjective reality.

Thanks to the evolution of our consciousness and the gradual opening of the third eye, we are ready to lead this process more and more. Essential knowledge comes to us in the form of intuition, clairvoyance, or any other extra-sensory perception. Thus, everything that we had can only be felt very vaguely becomes a clear and precise perception.

The sixth chakra is the link between our higher consciousness and the ego and between the higher cerebral faculties and the instinctive brain functions.

Linked to the mind, this chakra is represented with two petals that are connected to the right and left lobes of the pituitary and are also attached to the left and right hemispheres of the brain. The right hemisphere is the seat of the intuition; the left is the seat of intelligence. Here takes place the heavenly marriage of the sun and the moon, culminating in the opening of the third eye and the evolved sixth sense. The three main nadis, Ida, Pingala, and Sushumna, unite here before climbing to the crown chakra.

Note the importance of gradually opening this chakra. The complete mastery and balance of the lower chakras is an absolutely necessary condition. Without conscious control of the lower chakras when opening the Ajna chakra, various types of disorientation appear.

1) Harmonious functioning:

Bright spirit, faculty of mental abstraction, good visualization ability, intuitive understanding of many things, open to mystical truths, thoughts animated by idealism and imagination. The detachment of material possessions, fear of death disappears, the gift of telepathy, clear hearing, clairvoyance, access to past lives, and other dimensions.

2) Disharmonious functioning:

"Big head," proud, religiously dogmatic, manipulative and egotistical. Refusal of spiritual knowledge because not scientific and unreal. Try to influence others by the force of thought, to demonstrate power, or to satisfy personal needs.

3) Malfunction:

Dominated by material desires, physical needs, and unthinking emotions. Hypersensitive to the feelings of others, uninsured and unable to distinguish the ego from the higher self. In an extreme case, thoughts can be fuzzy and confused and totally dominated by repressed emotional structures.

Possible causes leading to dysfunction:

1) Physical level:

All that touches the brain, also we find everything that alters consciousness, drugs, alcohol, psychotropic, soothing medications, etc. Sounds too strong or too long, flashes (momentarily), too repetitive words (skull stuffing, indoctrination, hypnotism)

2) Psychoemotional:

Give others the right to think about his place (or let do), to base oneself in his reflection on principles without having understood them, to be delighted in the appearing or the illusions (the style, the conventions) without being aware of it, or preferring to pretend not to see them so as not to spoil their pleasure (for example), not wanting to see the negative of oneself (or that one expresses, etc.) to get over this and make yourself believe that you are "good" and that everything is fine, etc.

3) Spiritually:

Do not succeed in thinking for yourself: by religion or indoctrination, or by giving the authority of your choice to someone else blindly (the spouse, the family, the parents one or more friends, models references to which we do not appropriate the truth).

However, do not forget that it is named here direct influences, there are many indirect influences that may have led to dysfunction, sometimes in relation to the energy of other chakras or the physical, however, one will find the above-named interactions in interrelation.

How to Activate the Third Eye

How to open the third eye is of interest to people who dream of becoming psychics and perceive the world not only as usual with the basic sensory organs. Esotericists are convinced that everyone has inactive abilities. There are special exercises to develop superpowers.

Work with ajna chakra is available to everyone. Initially, the organ of the sixth sense is closed. There are ways to help activate the ajna chakra or third eye. They are used by yogis, esoterics almost regardless of the direction of practice, even among Tibetan monks (according to legends).

While there is a belief that working with an invisible organ threatens with treatment in a mental hospital, it should be noted that the development of abilities does not affect the psyche. The practitioner will gradually gain new opportunities. With the help of the ajna chakra, the world is perceived in a special, supernatural way.

Exercises will be the first steps towards a clairvoyant career. If you set the task of how to open the third eye quickly, you have to first forget about your previous knowledge of the extrasensory.

Working with ajna chakra is not a momentary matter. However, learning to open an additional sense organ is no easier than learning a foreign language. Another important point is the belief in success. Even if the results are not immediately noticeable, without faith in one's own strength, nothing will come of it. Abilities are easily blocked by distrust and thoughts about the impossibility of development.

Techniques for Awakening Your Third Eye

Opening the third eye with a candle

This exercise will take a candle. The method is used in the evening or at night, there is no mysticism, but darkness is required. It is advisable to turn off electrical appliances, especially those equipped with LEDs, which distract from the exercise with a candle.

Take a comfortable position, put a candle in front of you, and light it. You need to peer into the flame, focusing only on the fire. They try to blink as rarely as possible, without being too distracted, looking at all the colors in the flame. After a few minutes, unusual shades of fire appear - violet or green. After it was possible to consider all the colors of the flame, close the eyelids. The flame is imprinted on the retina, and it is visible. So you can understand how to open the third eye on your own without paid courses, in the usual home environment.

The blue ball method

This exercise to open the third eye is a form of meditation. Sit comfortably or lie down, achieve inner silence. You can turn on the appropriate mantras or chants that distract from extraneous thoughts and tune in the right way. Relax, breathe evenly, and calmly - your eyes should be closed.

Direct your inner gaze to the area between the eyebrows, where the ajna chakra is located. When you are ready, imagine a blue ball that rotates. The speed and direction of rotation are chosen intuitively, uneven indicators are allowed at different sessions of the task.

As you inhale, imagine how a blue ball draws pure blue energy from the environment into itself. The stream shines and does not raise doubts about the positive direction. There is no need to be afraid that in this way you can "pick up" the negative - problems are possible if the stream turned out to be dirty in appearance, dark and unpleasant.

As you exhale, imagine how the sparkling energy received from the outside world is absorbed by a ball, remains there, condensing the ball. Tension, pressure, and some pain in the area of the eyebrows are a normal reaction to exercises to open the third eye. The optimal time for doing meditation is about 10-15 minutes.

Exercises to open the third eye are necessary for people who want to gain spiritual integrity. There is no need to refuse what nature has granted to man because every person has abilities; just the majority prefers not to work with the Ajna Chakra due to a lack of confidence in mysticism. The development of abilities provides many opportunities that gradually, a person will learn to use.

Breathing technique to help in third eye activation

As noted, the third eye is your ability to see and understand the world beyond the lens of thought. A good way to increase your knowledge of the world and your self-knowledge is to observe your body and your breathing. This is not about studying anatomy in a book, but about focusing on your physical sensations. For this, you can practice physical relaxation, meditation, or sophrology, for example.

Here is a small breathing technique that teaches observation of the body:

- Release your body from top to bottom, from head to toe. Step by step, focus on the sensations of your body as it relaxes: Relax the muscles of the face, neck, shoulders and arms, chest, belly, glutes, and legs.

- Then adopt ventral breathing. When you inhale, the belly swells and welcomes the air. When you exhale, the belly deflates and accompanies the air towards the exit of a soft natural contraction. Breathe in this way over three to four breaths.

- Then take a moment to focus on your body sensations in calm and silence. Observe everything you feel in your body from head to toe.

- Stretch and open your eyes. The exercise is over.

How to Illuminate the Power of the Third Eye Chakra

By repeating this exercise, you will gain a broader awareness of your body, and your mind will learn to plunge into calm and silence.

Meditation - the way to keep your third eye active

Meditation on opening the third eye can be accompanied by pleasant meditative music or mantras. For example, the mantra of intuition, which is associated with the development of dormant opportunities, will do well. The right musical accompaniment for meditation will help you tune in the right mood.

Meditation should be comfortable. Take a comfortable position while lying or sitting. They try several options: sitting in Turkish pose, lying on your back, sitting on a chair in the usual pose. There is one condition - you should relax in the position chosen for meditation, but the back should remain straight.

Stop the internal dialogue. Try not to think about anything; do not talk mentally. Get complete inner silence and maximum concentration on the body or breath. Sometimes, refer to the ajna point. Try to feel pressure, vibration, or heat: sensations mean that everything is done correctly.

Regular meditation is a failsafe way to keep the third eye open.

The dangers of opening the third eye

Your third eye is not inactivated by default for no reason. We are not designed to see what cannot physically be seen. When you activate your third eye, you open your second vision. It means that you begin to perceive and feel the spiritual world. Do not think that from the moment you have activated your third eye, you will spend your days and evenings to see the angels, and you will be in a state of permanent ecstasy.

The spirits that will appear to your vision will be spirits of the astral bottom. The reason being that these are the spirits closest to our physical plane. The worry is that these lost souls will notice that you notice them and will, therefore, begin to come to you. They will appear at any time, no matter if you are driving (I let you imagine the danger), a job interview, in the street, at home, and so on.

These spirits of the lower astral are called "shadow people" within the Anglo-Saxon spiritual community. The "people of the shadows" because they often appear scary, dark, often as shadows.

I live in a house in the countryside. I can tell you that meeting in the middle of the night, walking in my hallway or going back to my room to sleep would be surprising, to say the least.

How to Deal With the Dangers of Opening the Third Eye

These low spirits are to be seen as insects attracted by the light when, in summer, you leave the window open. The activation of your third eye increases your spiritual light, and in doing so, it attracts these spirits as are the mosquitoes by a lamp.

You will be more inclined to perceive and interact with these low spirits that you will not have a spirituality high enough to preserve you. Most people who activate their third eye have only limited spiritual meaning if nonexistent. As a result, they attract to them beings that vibrate to their own vibrations.

It is also very likely that if you have not done work on you, your thoughts, your fears, you will see them appear in demonstrations. The world of the astral is the world of thought, everything that you think is manifested there. If you are a person filled with hatred and anxiety, you will be in contact with the latter, who has taken the form of these "shadow people." Finding yourself face to face with yourself and your own demons is an experience that can be a nightmare.

Many people worry about the dangers of opening the third eye. Well, perhaps not worth it. Just remember that each journey has its own problems and dangers. In every journey you make, problems and dangers will befall you. These dangers will make you stronger as you learn a lot from them. The dangers will make your trip even more interesting. Just be informed about the dangers that may arise and try to overcome them with all your strength and courage!

So, open the third eye or not?

The activation of the third eye should not be an end to itself, and energy work on its lower chakras is indispensable. This allows the circulation of energy in a fluid and safe way. Otherwise, there is a risk of energy imbalance that can not only create significant emotional and spiritual effects, but also physical effects.

A knowledge also of how to manage the activation of the third eye is essential in order to be able to put it in "on/off" mode at will and not to be haunted by day and night visions. Additionally, a knowledge of the spiritual world and its spirits, how to protect yourself and banish them is also essential.

Do not be fooled by the sweet song of the sirens that promise you wonders with the activation of the third eye and be aware of the shadow that also implies. Everyone speaks to you only on the good side but is careful not to warn you about the bad ones. The main reason is that most of these gurus themselves have not activated their third eye and do not know what they are talking about.

I am lucky to have people around me who have activated their third eye, so I have benefited from their experience and direct testimony.

Pay attention. As with everything about the Occult and the Spiritual World, it's not for mere entertainment. We are talking about forces about which most people have no knowledge or experience. Opening such a door can be catastrophic. Opening the third eye is not a hobby or a fad. It must be the result of an important spiritual and magical preparation, be done in a careful and knowledgeable way.

Chapter 4

The Pineal Gland: What Is the Pineal Gland and What Are Its Functions?

It is called pineal because it has the shape of a pineapple and is responsible for the production of serotonin, a substance that regulates our circadian rhythm and controls the life cycles of the human body.

The pineal gland controls the action of light in our body and is located below the cerebral cortex, where two hemispheres of the brain meet. This is the place where the brain regulates consciousness and interprets the sensory and motor functions of the body. Knowing how to activate the pineal gland, people are more open to feelings of ecstasy and unity. They may also have a feeling of understanding everything or a sudden understanding. In addition, when activated, people more easily develop the ability to travel to other dimensions, known as astral projection or side observation.

According to Theosophy, the pineal gland is a source of clairvoyance and intuition, as well as a kind of portal for higher dimensions, since the "third eye" gives us perception beyond the limits of general vision.

How to Activate the Pineal Gland

Activation can be achieved through yoga, meditation, and other more esoteric methods. Here is an exercise that you can perform without leaving your home.

- Sit comfortably and place the index finger of your right hand between the eyebrows, marking the point.

- Concentrate on feeling a finger touch your forehead. Try to feel the heat and throb at this point on your forehead.

- When you clearly feel the pulsation at this point on your forehead, remove your finger and begin to deepen this feeling in your head.

- Then begin to visualize the bright light coming from the top of the head directly to the pulsating point in the center of the eyebrows and inside the head.

- Concentrate on the sensation of pressure at the point on the forehead where light accumulates and enters. You may feel tinnitus and slight discomfort in the forehead, such as pressure.

With this exercise, you activate the third eye and begin to decalcify the pineal gland. This exercise should be repeated daily or several times a day, as you wish. Little by little, you can develop your clarity in dreams, intuition, and clairvoyance.

Why Is the Pineal Gland Blocked?

Researchers claim that the main element that is responsible for calcification of the pineal gland is fluoride in water. Also, chlorine, a low-nutrient diet, processed foods, electromagnetic fields (such as mobile phones), and environmental toxins are harmful to the pineal gland, which is ultimately calcined with substances consisting of calcium phosphate, calcium carbonate, phosphate magnesium, and ammonium phosphate.

Activities and exercises to decalcify the pineal gland

First of all, for this to work, it is imperative to avoid calcium supplements. Artificial calcium supplements are the main cause of calcification. Now, industrial food usually contains calcium in one form or another: calcium phosphate, calcium carbonate, or dicalcium phosphate. So do not eat "all done" anymore, and make smoothies! You will see why.

Raw cacao: Raw cacao contains many antioxidants, which makes it an excellent purifier. It is also good for stimulating the pineal gland, the "third eye" and intuition.

Citric Acid: Squeezed lemon juice is great for detoxifying your pineal gland.

You can mix this lemon juice with spring water; it is refreshing, and it is less bad for the teeth because of less acidity.

Garlic: A garlic cure is excellent for decalcification because garlic helps dissolve calcium and acts as an antibiotic. Garlic is also good for the immune system. During your cure, increase your dose gradually to a head of garlic a day! To avoid bad breath, squeeze the garlic and mix it with apple cider vinegar or fresh lemon juice.

Boron: Boron is excellent for detoxifying and cleansing of the pineal gland. It is also effective in removing fluoride. You can try adding 1/4 teaspoon of sodium borate (borax) to your green tea. A cheap source of boron is classic borax, which can be purchased in most supermarkets. Borax should be taken in very small quantities, in pure water, with no more than 1/32 to 1/4 teaspoon of borax per liter of water. The safe and effective way is to consume this mixture in small quantities throughout the day.

Chlorella: Did you know that chlorella has a phytochemical element that can effectively rebuild nerve damage in the brain and nervous system; in this way, chlorella is used to recover patients with Alzheimer's disease and Parkinson's disease. You can live literally just by eating micro-algae like Chlorella and Spirulina; they are superfoods from 2 to 8 microns, so the size of the blood cells.

The fact that chlorella is green comes from its chlorophyll content. It does not contain refined carbohydrates, contains a high level of digestive protein, contains fatty acids, not bad fat, contains chlorophyll. It is said that chlorella is a perfect whole. In addition to being a complete protein it contains all the vitamins; B, vitamin C, vitamin E, and the main minerals (such as iron zinc in amounts large enough to be considered complimentary), it has been found, that it improves the immune system, improves digestion and detoxification; accelerate healing, protect against radiation, it helps in the prevention of degenerative diseases, helps in the treatment of disease, and relieves arthritis pain, because of its nutritional value, and helps the success of many diets to lose weight.

Zeolite: Zeolite is a mineral found in the ancient seabed and derived from volcanic rocks. Its honeycomb-shaped molecules have the ability to capture large quantities of toxins of all types safely and expel them through the urinary tract. It can be considered +++ clay. It is delivered in very fine powder obtained by a special micronization process.

For excess calcium, we will also focus on vitamin K2, which acts as a regulator of calcium in the tissues, promoting on one side the fixation of calcium in the matrix of the bones and cleaning on the other all the deposits useless.

Avoid all foods that contain pesticides: To detoxify the pineal gland, the best is to make a cure composed largely of raw fruits and vegetables, but of course, without pesticides. The meat also contains pesticides, often when the animals eat cereals or grass having have been treated. Some people recommend vegetarian diets to detoxify the body or to protect the pineal gland against potentially harmful substances. Yet some meats are still recommended, so how to manage priorities?

If you cannot pronounce the chemical name of a product, it is probably bad for your health. Among these chemicals we find:

Artificial sweeteners such as aspartame (there are slightly more natural sweeteners like xylitol).

Refined white sugar (to be replaced by brown sugar, honey, molasses, agave syrup or maple syrup, cooked wine).

Deodorants and products against bad odors, industrially produced

Dental mouthwashes (replace with saltwater, enough!)

Chemical cleaning products.

Activate Melatonin Production

Melatonin: Although there is no really conclusive evidence, many people believe that melatonin helps eliminate fluoride by increasing the decalcification of the pineal gland, which helps to degrade existing calcification.

To produce melatonin, our body uses an essential amino acid, tryptophan, which is extracted from the food proteins we absorb. Tryptophan is then converted to serotonin, which will itself be converted by the pineal gland into melatonin, which the liver will then metabolize. Melatonin limits oxidation in all cellular compartments, it increases the activity of other antioxidant enzymes, so it has an anti-aging effect.

Tips to Naturally Maintain a Good Level of Melatonin

Melatonin is mostly synthesized at night, and its production is stimulated by the absence of light.

At night, expose yourself as little as possible to an excess of light, which could lower or even suppress the concentration of melatonin. Even try to avoid any light source (avoid sleeping with a night light, for example). The light disrupts the production of melatonin. If you need to have a light in the hallway or the bathroom, use a light that filters the blue spectrum. (Yellow light bulbs).

The day, if you expose yourself to the sunlight, the production of melatonin at night will be favored.

Eat foods that promote the production of melatonin: melatonin is synthesized from serotonin, and this is derived from tryptophan, an essential amino acid. It is, therefore, necessary to focus on foods containing tryptophan. What are they?

Parsley, pumpkin seeds, cheese, cod, parmesan, milk and soy, turkey, pineapple, eggs, dates, lettuce, bananas, plums, rice, corn, and oatmeal, walnuts and hazelnuts, tomatoes, potatoes, and red wine are rich in tryptophans. It is, therefore, necessary to consume these foods regularly, so as to obtain an optimal serotonin level. For example, nut consumption increases blood melatonin levels in rats by a factor of three.

The Miracles of the Nettle

The forgotten nettle is a real wealth of the wild world. Its particularity is to facilitate the decristallization of the pituitary and pineal gland.

Its leaf is particularly rich in calcium, iron, boron, beta-carotene or pro-vitamin A, α-tocopherol (vitamin E) and vitamin C. In 100 grams of fresh nettle leaves, has all the recommended daily contributions of calcium and iron, as well as 6 times the RDA of pro-vitamin A and 4 times that of vitamin C. Reason for which the nettle is to be consumed rather in the morning or at midday than in the evening.

Nettle leaf also contains a large quantity of 18 different amino acids (out of 20 existing), including the 8 essential amino acids (isoleucine, leucine, lysine, methionine, phenylalanine, threonine, tryptophan and valine) necessary for the development of an organism. By comparison, cereals are all deficient in lysine (some also tryptophan), while legumes are deficient in methionine. The nettle leaf contains the 8 essential amino acids in harmonious proportions, making it a complete food.

The nettle leaf still contains, among others, chlorophyll in large quantities, silica, flavonoids (quercitin), secretin (hormone stimulating the activity of the pancreas). Some are rare components, such as choline acetyl transferase, an enzyme that synthesizes acetylcholine, and nettle is the only known plant to possess this enzyme. If one was not yet convinced of it, it is proof that the nettle is not a plant like the others.

Other Basic Methods With Which You Can Start Work on the Activation of the Pineal Gland

1. Take the maximum from night and day

For the development of the pineal gland, it is very important that the schedule of sleep and wakefulness of a person does not go astray. The most useful sleep regimen for the pineal gland is early falling asleep (around 10 pm) and early rise (ideally, at dawn).

In addition to sleeping in the dark, it is also necessary to learn how to maximize the benefits in the daytime - more often to be in the sun (or at least sit by the window).

2. Electromagnetic fields are your enemies

Electromagnetic fields haunt us everywhere: we even carry them with us in our pockets (telephones), spend leisure time and working hours with them (computers). Of course, such an impact negatively affects the development of the pineal gland, so it is so important to use every opportunity to stay away not only from the bustle of the city but also from worldly goods.

3. Meditate whenever possible

Meditation is a powerful practice that can change a person's life. It is scientifically proven that it has a beneficial effect on the state of mind and the entire human body, helping to find harmony, to know oneself, and to be distracted from the bustle. during meditation, focus your attention precisely on the pineal gland, on the Third Eye.

275

Meditate regularly and chant mantras. Singing causes resonance in the nose, and this resonance makes the pineal gland work. The more often it is excited, the more hormones of youth are secreted into your body. The sound "OM" resonates with the fourth chakra, known as the center of the heart, or the place of Unconditional Love. The repetition of OM opens the path to universal and cosmic consciousness. You can repeat it for 5 minutes, 10 minutes, or any other amount of time.

4. Do yoga

Yoga pays considerable attention to the development of the pineal gland since the pineal gland is considered to be the very antenna with which our brain is able to perceive the most important information from the outside. The most useful posture for the development of the pineal gland is Shashankasana, i.e., hare pose, as it stimulates the pineal gland and upper chakra. Thanks to this asana, one can also improve memory and concentration.

5. Use such aids as crystals

Amethyst, laser quartz, moonstone, purple sapphire, tourmaline, rhodonite, sodalite. In general, any natural stone of blue, indigo or purple colors can be used to activate the pineal gland, as well as work on Ajna and Sahasrara.

Take the stone and place it between the eyebrows for 15 minutes. Try to look at it with your eyes closed. Maintain a maximum concentration of these 15 minutes. It is very good if you can do this under direct access to the sun - then its rays will pass through the stone into the pineal gland. Moreover, it will be easier to concentrate on the light.

6. Use aromatic oils to stimulate the pineal gland and alleviate the general mental state

They also help with meditations and various other practices. It is recommended to use lavender, sandalwood, frankincense, pine, lotus, wormwood. Oils can be inhaled, ignited in special lamps, sprayed, or added to the bathwater.

7. Use magnets for detoxification

Just put it between your eyebrows for several hours. They attract alkali and thus remove calcium crystals from the pineal gland.

8. Forget about alcohol, nicotine, and caffeine

These stimulants interfere with the established melatonin production system. The less you consume them, the better for you and for your sleep.

Some drugs also have the ability to disrupt the production of melatonin - do not forget to consult a doctor.

9. Clear your mind at the new moon.

The new moon is considered an excellent time not only for all kinds of undertakings but also for the development of the pineal gland. If you manage to clear your mind, you will feel how the pineal gland activates and brings calm, balance to your body and cleans it. That is why in yoga, the day of the new moon is of such great importance: yogis are fully committed to spiritual practices, not being distracted even by eating food and water.

10. Make it a habit to look at the sun for 15 minutes immediately after it rises and at sunset daily.

Chapter 5

Kundalini and the Power of the Chakras

Kundalini Introduction and Overview

K undalini is the Sanskrit word for spiritual power that resides in every person. This is the essence of the inner Self, which is also called the Holy Spirit, the Divine Light, the Divine Mother, and is known by many other names. This is the most subtle manifestation of an inexhaustible source of energy. All people, regardless of the historical era, religion, or culture, are filled with the highest energy of kundalini. The realization of her sacred presence is the goal of all spiritual efforts. Kundalini lives in a subtle body; in a dormant state, it supports the vital functions of a person and his consciousness; the awakened kundalini leads a person to spiritual heights and helps to achieve liberation. The awakening of kundalini imposes a great responsibility on a person; from this time, he begins a new stage in his internal development. The ascension of spiritual energy becomes a pleasant process leading to holiness and enlightenment. This is how the Divine Plan of Human Development is realized.

Kundalini means "coiled," like a snake. The image of a serpent coiled up in rings is associated with infinite power, hidden power, or unused potential that each person possesses to achieve a life that is best in all respects. Another image associated with kundalini is an ocean of creative energy that rises like a tornado along the spine. Kundalini should not be thought of as some kind of alien force hostile to man. It must be perceived as creative energy, transforming consciousness.

The concept of kundalini can also be considered in a purely psychological aspect. Here it is permissible to consider it an endless source of psychic energy or gates to the world of the superconscious.

The awakening of kundalini is the beginning of spiritual enlightenment, the main step towards self-realization and enlightenment. According to the authoritative researcher Swami Prajananda, the main purpose of awakening kundalini is to help a person achieve the Divine. The awakening of inner strength becomes the beginning of the process of spiritual transformation.

To work with kundalini, it is not necessary to devote yourself to yoga or to be a Hindu or a Tibetan. Anyone can use the wisdom of spiritual science. The doctrine of kundalini is intended not only for people engaged in Eastern methods of self-realization, such as yoga. Each spiritual tradition has its own way of transmitting transcendental wisdom, using its own terminology and symbols. A study of metaphysical traditions shows that even in orthodox religious schools, there are innumerable cases of conversion to the kundalini energy.

The scientific method of research is quite applicable to the idea of kundalini. Gopi Krishna says that kundalini is the evolutionary power of consciousness and that its full development ends with the formation of a spiritual person.

Kundalini is the key to unraveling the mysteries of psychological, mental, occult, and spiritual phenomena. Its importance to people is enormous, as it offers a clue to the very secrets of life and demonstrates the capabilities of the human person.

The science of kundalini is one of the most difficult branches of yogic knowledge. To understand the meaning of the term kundalini, Swami Rama points to the need to perceive it in the context of the concept of shakti. The concept of kundalini comes from the word kadala ("folded"). As indicated above, the idea of kundalini is traditionally conveyed in the form of a coiled snake. The word shakti comes from the root of shak ("to have power," "to be able"). Together, these two Sanskrit words can be translated as "resting power."

From physics, it is known that energy exists in two forms: (1) dynamic, or active, and (2) hidden potential. Any activity or power has a static phase. When consciousness manifests itself as a creative or dynamic principle (shakti), it, in turn, polarizes itself into these two forms. With the manifestation of the Universe, part of the shakti energy becomes involved in self-manifestation, while an even larger part remains unused. The dynamic aspect is shakti in a certain differentiated form. In the Indian tradition, the main force that remains after creation is symbolized by coiled energy in the form of a snake that supports the universe. Spiritual development is a natural, universal process characteristic of any culture, era, and spiritual tradition. Such a process is associated with the development of the nature of the spirit. World religious and metaphysical traditions use various symbols and metaphors to describe the process of spiritual growth. Symbolic representations of spiritual development and experience can be found in all religions. A common ancient symbol to denote the sacred process taking place inside a person is a maze.

Why Is It Important to Learn and Practice Kundalini

Studying kundalini is an understanding of spirituality. The science and practice of studying kundalini provide an understanding of how to properly maintain and manage spiritual growth. Kundalini is only a name, a name used to denote a special field of study and practice in the ancient spiritual tradition of India. Amazing in its breadth, technical accuracy, variety of methods, and applicability, the traditional science of kundalini is a comprehensive, universal system for understanding and improving spiritual life. Kundalini is a factor that is the key to all spiritual experiences.

Based on scriptures, oral tradition, individual leadership, sociological research, and direct spiritual experience, the science of kundalini is today a powerful tool for transforming and raising consciousness.

Awakening and Ascension of Kundalini

As long as Kundalini remains in Muladhara (root and basis of existence), man is completely attached to this transitory world. But when a person carries out a religious or yoga practice, the kundalini wakes up and (although, as already mentioned, she does not sleep) begins to send energy pulses to various parts of the body through ida, pingala, Lakshmi and Sarasvati-nadi. But kundalini can fully rise only through sushumnu-nadi.

Different people are prone to different methods and ways of raising the kundalini. That is, there are different ways of raising. There are several of them.

1. Mantra japa, "chanting mantras and prayers with love and devotion."

2. The blessing of the great saints.

3. Rituals, temple worship, and bhakti.

4. The joint chanting of the name and glory of God (sankirtan).

5. Asceticism and austerities.

6. Selfless activity for the benefit of people and service to God (karma yoga).

7. Jnana Yoga.

8. Pranayama.

9. Mudras, bandhas, asanas.

10. In-depth study of the subject.

11. Other ways.

Raising kundalini is not an easy task. This can take years of hard and inspiring work. But Mother Kundalini is very supportive of determined to students and constantly gives them spiritual joys that strengthen them and illuminate their path.

Now we will consider methods, ways that contribute to raising the kundalini.

Mantra Japa

The mantra japa is the repetition of the mantra. A mantra is a power, the carrier of which is sound, audible, or inaudible. According to Vedic tradition, a mantra is a manifestation of Shabd-Brahman. The name of God is a mahamantra, a great mantra. The name of God is not different from God himself. In the divine name, all the energies of God are embodied. The mind focused on the divine name in continuous meditation, becomes divine and pure as the Divine itself. The mind accepts the qualities of the object that contemplates. This principle is the basis of religious and yogic practice.

Each letter of the Sanskrit alphabet is considered a mantra, and fifty letters are imprinted on the fifty petals of six lotuses. Of course, they are present there in a subtle and causal form. Their subtle form is called the matrix.

Mantras in all forms are manifestations of the kundalini itself. And kundalini fills the mantra with power.

Due to the constant focus on the Divine, on the glory, power, and qualities of God, the constant chanting of His name, the mind becomes pure and powerful.

If the mantra is repeated regularly and correctly, then the body, heart, mind, and nadi are purified. This facilitates the rise of Kundalini to higher planes.

The Blessing of Saints and Teachers

Thanks to the grace of the guru, a person can instantly gain all perfection. A guru is a person who owns his mind, feelings, and motives, comprehends the truth, and abides in God. Such great souls, with the help of their powers, can make the kundalini rise. For this, one glance or touching the student's body is enough. Through diksa (initiation, initiation), the true guru gives impetus to kundalini. But so that the raising of kundalini is safe and does not cause negative consequences, the student is recommended to properly prepare. For a certain time, the student is obliged to observe restrictive principles, maintain celibacy, meditate, worship the Deities, chant mantras.

All these actions purify the mind, heart, body, and nadi.

Kirtan

When people loudly with devotion chant the names, deeds, glories of God, then this is called kirtan. At the highest point of kirtan, when all thoughts are concentrated on the Beloved Lord and feelings are pulled like strings, believers forget about music and at the same time, dissolve into the music of kirtan. They begin to dance in glee.

Often the raising of kundalini is accompanied by an unexpected appearance of emotions - then the worshiper cries, laughs, trembles, or falls unconscious.

Often after kirtan and dancing, neophytes can feel a strong sexual desire. This means that the raised currents of the Kundalini descended to the sexual center. If a person does not have a purity of mind and patience, he can commit an immoral act.

An abrupt lowering of the kundalini currents is very dangerous. Because of this, many sincere aspirations for the knowledge of God ended in immorality.

Aspiration alone is not enough; spiritual knowledge and purity are required.

283

An ignorant attempt to raise Kundalini is like a child playing with a sharp razor. The razor is useful only in the hands of an adult who knows how to handle it.

Asceticism and austerities

Asceticism means voluntary abstinence from sensual pleasures. Asceticism and penance help a person to form character, strengthen the will, maintain mental strength and purity. Of all the ascetic feats, celibacy (brahmacharya) is the highest. This refers to the celibacy of the body, mind, and speech. A lot of valuable energy and time is wasted on sex and sensual pleasures. The cleansing of the mind and nadi with austerities and abstinence makes it possible to raise the kundalini to higher planes.

Devotional service to God and selfless activity (karma yoga)

Attachment to the fruits of activity deprives the mind of peace and binds with the bonds of karma. If a person performs all the actions, devoting the results to the Almighty, then his mind quickly finds peace, purity, and focus on Paramatma, the Supreme Spirit. All this facilitates the raising of kundalini to the higher chakras.

Here it should be said once again that without bhakti, devotion, it is impossible to achieve success by any efforts and methods.

Jnana Yoga

Jnana has two meanings: pure consciousness (svarupa) and the intellectual process of recognition (kriya jnana).

This process consists in distinguishing between what is true and what is untrue, what is Brahman and what is non-Brahman. In the process, the yogi comes to understand his true essence, the true Self.

First, the yogi asks himself the question: "Who am I?"

Then he analyzes and discards everything that is not a true Self. "I am not a body, not feelings, not objects of feelings, not will, not mind, not prana, not intelligence. These substances change and disappear. This is not I. I am spiritual; I am eternal; I have no death and birth. "

But man is not only intelligence. He has feelings and a body. Therefore, so that they do not interfere with the practice of jnana yoga, they are occupied with worship or hatha yoga. Through various methods, control over the mind, feelings, and prana is exercised. And when chitta-vritti (modifications of the mind) are eliminated, then the Supreme Spirit, Paramatma, is revealed.

Hatha Yoga

This is body cleansing. Hatha yoga includes those forms of yogic practice that relate primarily to the gross physical body. Since the physical body is associated with the subtle body, control of the physical body leads to control of the subtle body, consisting of the mind, intellect, false ego (ahamkara), feelings, and, conversely, work with subtle bodies affects the gross body.

Hatha yoga is prescribed for special individuals who, in order to control the subtle body and mind, must first master the physical body. Hatha yoga is auxiliary to other, more refined processes. The word hatha has two roots: ha and tha, which mean, respectively, "Sun" and "Moon," that is, prana and apana vayu. Practical hatha yoga consists of seven steps:

a) purification (shodhana) through six processes (shatkarma);

b) gaining strength and endurance through asanas;

c) strength and endurance (sthirata) through mudras (special positions of the body);

d) peace of mind (dhayriya) through curbing the senses (pratyahara);

e) achieving ease through pranayama;

f) self-awareness (pratyaksha) through meditation (dhyana);

g) detachment (nirliptattva) through samadhi.

Body cleansing

Those whose body is slagged and suffers from ailments and diseases are recommended to practice six cleansing exercises (shatkarma), which cleanse the body and facilitate the practice of pranayama. Such purification of the body and nadi achieves perfect health, longevity, and endurance.

Shatkarma

Shata - six, karma - action) are very effective for cleansing the body and mind. They should be performed in a clean place under the guidance of an experienced mentor.

Dhauti

This is otherwise known as throat cleansing. For such cleansing, a thin cotton cloth (such as gauze) is used with a width equal to the length of the index finger and fifteen measures long (one measure is the distance between the end of the index finger and the wrist). The fabric is moistened in warm water and slowly swallowed and then gently, quietly pulled out. On the first day, they swallow one measure of length, increasing by one measure on each subsequent day.

Dhauti practice takes fifteen days. People with diseases like phlegms can continue this practice longer. Dhauti cleanses the digestive tract, cures diseases of the bronchi, asthma, skin diseases, spleen.

Vasti

This is bowel cleansing. A tube of young soft bamboo is inserted into the anus with a length equal to the length of the middle finger and half a finger thick. The tube is oiled. Then the performer squats in the water (in the pose of Utkatasana) and draws water into the anus and then pushes it out. Repeat many times.

Vasti increases appetite, kindles a fire in the stomach, and cures dropsy, metabolic disorders, diseases of the intestinal tract, gall bladder, hemorrhoids, removes toxins.

Neti

This is nasopharyngeal cleansing. To clean the nostrils, use a piece of cord, lubricated in ghee. The end of the cord is inserted into the nostril and pulled out through the mouth, or threaded through both nostrils. Neti can be made by passing water through the nose. This is jala neti. Netty cures sinusitis, chronic runny nose, stimulates the nervous system, improves vision, and grants subtle vision.

Trataka

This is eye cleansing. Carefully, without blinking, look at some object (most often they look at the flame of a candle and the image of the Divine) until tears appear in the eyes. When tears flow, close your eyes and visualize the image.

Trataka helps with eye disease, increases the strength of concentration, gives subtle vision.

Nauli

Sequential compression and twisting of the left and right and right abdominal muscles.

Nauli stimulates gastric fire, massages internal organs, improves skin color, stimulates the nervous system.

Kapalabhati

Exercise "blacksmith furs." Inhale and exhale sharply and noisily, like blacksmith bellows. Stop as soon as you feel the tension. This exercise destroys diseases caused by excess phlegm.

In addition, there are other ways to cleanse. Ayurveda, for example, prescribes fasting as the most effective method. Three-Day fasting in warm water cleanses the body of toxins and diseases without drugs. Sometimes oshadhi yoga, that is, herbal medicine is used to cleanse.

Bandha

Bandhas (castle) are physical methods of controlling prana. The three most important of them are uddiyana, mula, and jalandhara. Thanks to the first, activated prana enters sushumna. The second connects prana and apana and directs them together into sushumna.

Mula bandha is performed like this: you need to hold the anus with your left heel, place your right foot on your left thigh, inhale and hold your breath as much as possible, then slowly exhale. During air retention, one should focus on sushumna. The usual direction for apana is down, but through compression in the region of muladhara, it goes up, where it meets prana. In this case, the internal heat in the body increases sharply, and the kundalini, sensing this, awakens from its sleep. After that, she must be sent to Sushumna.

Jalandhara bandha is performed with a deep breath. The chin is held firmly to the base of the neck.

Mahamudra

Gently squeeze the anus with the left heel, stretch the right leg, grab the fingers, inhale slowly, and hold your breath. Press the chin on the chest, fixing the look between the eyebrows. Hold this pose as much as you can, then exhale slowly. Then do the same by changing your legs. This mudra cures hemorrhoids, tuberculosis, enlargement of the spleen, gastritis, leprosy, fever, and helps to raise the kundalini. Mudras and bandha should be done regularly in the morning, after dousing, on an empty stomach.

Pranayama

The word pranayama is often translated as "breath control." But we must take into account that the word prana means not only "rough air," but also "life force." Thus, pranayama is the science of the mysterious, invisible, all-pervasive power and its management.

Cosmic higher prana manifests itself in various forms. Prana Shakti is a synonym for Kundalini Shakti, the energy of God. Prana is the subtlest substance, and it is not perceived by the senses. Prana manifests itself as gravity, like an electromagnetic field, as a life force. Breathing is just one of the functions of prana. The grossest manifestation of prana in the body is breathing.

The mind, prana, and virya (seed) are closely related. The subjugation of the mind leads to the subjugation of prana and virya. By controlling breathing, one can control prana, and controlling prana leads to controlling the mind and virya. Virya (or sukra, seed) exists throughout the body in a subtle form, and as a result of sexual desire, it goes down and is embodied in a gross, dense form in the genitals. The true brahmachari must know how to use the help of pranayama to turn the gross seed into subtle and to prevent the formation of gross seed. The body of a man who is a true urdhvareta exudes a lotus scent. If a practitioner does not strictly observe celibacy, then his practice of pranayama can lead to a fall or madness.

To perform pranayama, sit facing east or north in any position convenient for you in which you can sit for a long time without tension (but best of padmasana). The spine should be straight. Pranayama is practiced on an empty stomach, at least three hours after eating. (During pranayama, imagine that kundalini rises in sushumna.)

The place for practice should not be too remote (for example, a dense forest) so that there is no feeling of anxiety. Not intended for pranayama and the city due to the bustle and polluted atmosphere. Food should be clean and vegetarian.

Fasting is not permitted during the practice of pranayama. The yogi should not be left without food for more than one pit (3 hours). Hard work and tedious exercises should be avoided.

There are various types of pranayama, but they all serve the main purpose: to prepare the nadi, body, and mind to raise the kundalini, introduce prana into sushumna and allow it to reach the sahasrara after the Devi Kundalini, accompanied by its surroundings, various forces and pranas, passes all the lotuses - chakras.

Here I describe one pranayama that can be performed without a teacher:

Sit straight, close the right nostril with the thumb of your right hand. Inhale very slowly without noise. Fill the lungs as much as possible through the left nostril and, closing the left nostril, with the index and middle fingers of the right hand, slowly exhale through the right nostril as quietly and silently as possible.

After exhaling through the right nostril, inhale through it and exhale through the left. That will be one cycle or one pranayama. Do four such cycles without interruption. Practice this pranayama four times a day: morning, noon, evening, and midnight.

If you perform this pranayama systematically for several months, it will purify the nadi. As you inhale, think carefully that breathing fills you with strength, love, goodness, holiness, and wisdom. When exhaling, imagine that all weaknesses, vices, diseases, and desecrations leave the body and mind. During this process, try mentally pronouncing your mantra or sacred syllable OM. It spiritualizes consciousness. Thanks to the practice of pranayama, your face will become calm, enlightened, rude, and harsh features will disappear, your mind will become persistent, your voice deep and pleasant.

But pranayama is a preliminary step in laya yoga or kundalini yoga. To raise the kundalini, daily practice is prescribed, which most often takes years of hard work, although in exceptional cases, success is achieved in a relatively short time. In the beginning, kundalini can be raised to the lower centers. The one who brought her to a center next time easily reaches this level. But, to go higher, further persistent efforts are required. Upon reaching each center, the practitioner experiences a special kind of bliss and acquires special powers. However, in the very early stages, Shakti has a tendency to return.

Constant practice eliminates the possibility of spontaneous return back. A perfect yogi is able to keep Shakti in sahasrara for as long as he wishes.

The Health Benefits of Kundalini

While there are several benefits of kundalini, I outline ten basic points for self-improvement, which are easily achieved with regular classes in this spiritual and physical practice.

1.) Benefits for all body systems

Kundalini helps to cope with migraines, problems in the functioning of food systems, headaches, and also puts in order the hormonal, genitourinary, endocrine, cardiovascular, and other body systems.

2.) Gives beauty

Despite the fact that practice belongs to the category of sedentary, it is quite possible to achieve a beautiful, developed and harmonious body with it. Due to the fact that kundalini charges from the inside, this inner radiance also affects the appearance. In addition, it normalizes hormonal processes, which in turn has a positive effect on the appearance and psyche.

291

3.) Charges with power

For some, the essence of strength lies in physical superiority, while some consider strengthing a character's resistance to stressful situations. Kundalini will provide you with both of them, and will also help you feel in harmony with your body, give peace of mind and peace of mind.

4.) The joy of life

It is very difficult for someone who does not know how to relax to see the positive aspects of life. The self-confidence, peace, and spiritual component that the kundalini gives will help you find gaps even in the most critical situations and enjoy every day.

5.) Promote emotional balance

Thanks to kundalini, you will cease to react sharply to trifles that are not worth your attention, you will be able to quickly make decisions and immediately migrate to actions, as well as be able to control your emotions and prevent their unreasonable splash.

6.) Heightened perception

Many things will be revealed to you on the other, true side. Kundalini yoga will allow you to more clearly feel what is happening around and give events a sober assessment.

7.) Reveals the sixth sense

Kundalini exercises affect the areas of the brain that are responsible for intuition. So, now you can easily make decisions in contentious issues, relying on the sixth sense.

8.) Helps to break a bad habit

Yoga itself becomes your main habit and carries the philosophy of cleansing the soul and body of things that can harm you.

9.) Unleashes creativity

Due to the increase in energy and activity, you will want to try yourself in new areas all the time, which implies that the use of kundalini is also in the disclosure of unknown talents.

10.) Spiritual development

You will begin to look at life differently, learn to make efforts to improve living conditions, and stop being upset over trifles.

Chapter 6

Kundalini : Practical Tips and Notes

When kundalini first enters sushumna, there will be great pain. Many are afraid of these pains, mistakenly believing that this is caused by some kind of disease. When kundalini fully enters sushumna, the activities of the major nadi freeze. Then prana and the emanations of kundalini pass only through sushumna. The passage of kundalini shakes the whole body like an unexpected shock from an earthquake.

The scriptures speak of various ways of promoting kundalini, depending on the element (tattva) prevailing in a person.

This is a movement similar to the movement of an ant — a movement like a frog jumping on lotuses. The movement of the kundalini is felt like the movement of a wriggling snake. The movement is similar to a bird flight. It is perceived in the region of the heart and is accompanied by a feeling of flight and lightness. Kundalini jumps from one center to another, flying two or three in a row. A movement like a monkey jumping from branch to branch. Shakti can "slip through" three or four chakras.

If the emanations of kundalini began to rise along Sarasvati or Lakshmi-nadi, they should be lowered through meditation to muladhara and sent to sushumna.

Clearing Out Negative Energy

Yoga teachers prescribe the following method for this. It should be performed on an empty stomach. Sit cross-legged. Inhale slowly through both nostrils. Pull the lower abdomen towards the spine and up. Squeeze the anus and slowly lead the kundalini up, presenting it as light, energy, or a luminous Goddess. Throughout the path of movement, mentally follow her ascent. When you lead it to the soma chakra, exhale, relax the stomach and muscles of the anus.

At first, imagination and suggestion are necessary, but after a long practice, you can really raise the kundalini to the higher centers.

Start with three minutes in the morning and evening, gradually increasing the time to half an hour.

Through systematic practice, one can easily eliminate negative energy, turning it into ojas (psychic energy), and strengthen meditation. After exercise, it is recommended to drink cow's milk.

Blockages That Prevent Kundalini From Rising Smoothly, and How to Clear These Blockages

All sorts of currents, impulses, emanations come from the kundalini; most of them exit through the anus and genital canal. In order to close these channels, ascetics and sannyasis wear a kaupin, a tight loincloth.

With the loss of seed during intercourse, a tremendous loss of energy is produced by the Kundalini Shakti. Strictly observe celibacy; otherwise, the practice of yoga will be useless to you and even dangerous. For a family man seeking spiritual perfection, sexual relations are permissible only for the purpose of conceiving children.

It is said that the energy spent during one sexual intercourse is equal to the energy spent on physical work within 24 hours. If energy is not wasted on sexual pleasures, then a person gains a strong memory, a strong will, a powerful mind, and moral purity. The scriptures say that loss of seed brings physical death closer. If a man often engages in sexual relations, then he becomes irritable, weak, painful, his memory and will weaken, his intellect becomes dulled. He becomes a toy in the hands of low passions.

You should completely abandon the use of alcohol, drugs, and tobacco. These substances pollute the nadis, make the mind restless, feelings, uncontrollable, and excite low passions. He who smokes and performs pranayama is a suicide. Even tea and coffee have a stimulating effect on the mind and therefore interfere with concentration.

Eat right. Avoid unclean, stale, indigestible, and poorly prepared foods. Eliminate meat, fish, and eggs from your diet. Do not take any food or drink from the hands of immoral, depraved people. Such food is contagious. As you take precautions when dealing with people with tuberculosis, cholera, or plague for your physical health, you should also take precautions for spiritual and mental health. If you do not pay serious attention to this, you will suffer, and your spiritual progress will be complicated. Mental emanations and karma are included in food, especially in legumes during cooking on a fire. That is why the yogis of India have established very strict rules regarding food. And this is not superstition. Try to cook for yourself and eat only consecrated food, so you will avoid many traps and dangers. After preparation, offer it to God by reading prayers, mantras. It will sanctify food.

Fill the stomach halfway with food, a quarter with water, leave a quarter empty.

Control your speech. Say only that which brings spiritual benefit to you and others. Speak calmly and softly, avoid rude and deceitful words. Be silent for one day, and you will see how much energy is saved.

Do not get carried away with healing with the help of prana (or a biofield, as many say). This is associated with a risk to life and spiritual practice.

When a person acquires a certain purity of body, nadi, and mind, he can easily heal, but the subsequent reaction will be dangerous. Often the healer takes on the disease of the person he cured. At first, he will successfully heal people, but after several successful cures, he will fail and begin to suffer from incurable diseases and life troubles. Many engaged in such healing, for vanity or for show, end up with mental and bodily diseases, unbelief, and apathy. To get rid of the negative effects of healing, you must have great spiritual strength and know how to neutralize unwanted reactions.

When the kundalini reaches anahata, the yogi can hear various sounds emanating from anahata that help to achieve a state of deep meditation: birds chirping, shell sound, guilt, mridanga, flute, pakhawaja (drum type), lion roar, cricket sounds, bell ringing, pipe sounds.

Visions depend on the student's inclinations and intensity. All this is given only for encouragement or verification, but no more. But some foolish people create a lot of noise around these phenomena. They are vain with their small achievements, advertise themselves, try to find students, but pride and vanity take away all the fruits. To keep followers around themselves, they go on deceit and fraud and unscrupulously use the trust of simple-minded people in order to enjoy power over souls. Because of these scammers, people lose faith in religion.

For meditation on the twelve-petalled Anahata lotus, it is recommended to repeat the twelve-syllable mantra OM NAMO BHAGAVATE VASUDEVAYA (Om. I worship the all-pervading Lord Vasudeva).

Lotus petals are numbered by the number of working energies in this chakra and by the number of nadis that are found there. These energies are controlled by different deities. (To work successfully with the chakras, one must read with the mantra and mentally worship all the deities.) By worshiping the Supreme God, Bhagavan, all demigods can be satisfied.

There are fifty mantra buckets in different parts of the body, and there are fifty different kinds of energy. There are fifty letters in the Sanskrit alphabet. The letters are imprinted on the lotus petals in a causal form, and when these sounds or letters are properly pronounced, they vibrate with the letters on the petals, causing the corresponding energies to act.

Be careful when working with kundalini currents and emanations. If they do not function properly, then this can cause illness. These currents can be controlled with the help of concentration of the mind, meditation, massage, exposure to acupuncture points, cleansing procedures, working with the sun and fire, special mantras, medicinal herbs, pranayama, proper nutrition. These methods are described in detail in Ayurveda, yogic medicine, Tibetan, and Chinese schools of working with subtle body energies, such as the qigong school.

Many practitioners of kundalini yoga and other types of yoga can manifest various ailments and disorders. Not understanding the reasons for their occurrence, they go to doctors and healers, who most often instead of treatment and relief, only complicate the situation.

There is simple pranayama available to everyone, regardless of gender and age. If it is performed in the morning and evening for a long time, it can regulate the work of currents and heal even chronic diseases. It must be performed on an empty stomach, in a clean, calm place. You can sit in any comfortable position, keeping your spine straight.

Inhale through both nostrils, squeeze the throat and force the air to collect in the upper part of the lungs, slightly pressing the stomach up and to the spine. Hold your breath as much as possible, then exhale slowly and carefully through the right nostril and inhale again through both nostrils and, holding your breath as before, exhale again through the right nostril. Exhale through the right nostril for 5 minutes, and then through the left 5 minutes. You can bring the cycle time of this pranayama to one hour. This pranayama drives out laziness, drowsiness, lack of will, passivity, fatigue, sublimation of sexual energy to the highest is achieved, the nadis are purified, the mind calms down.

Below the anahata chakra, there is an eight-petalled lotus in which Ishta Devata, the chosen Deity, is worshiped. For meditation on this lotus, the eight-syllable mantra OM NAMO NARAYANAYA is used. In this center, as stated in the Hamsa Upanishad, there is atma (individual soul) and Paramatma (Supreme Soul).

Sometimes the passage of the kundalini through various centers is considered a metaphor that reflects the path of the soul through different planes of being and consciousness. But the experience of yogis and scriptures shows that this is far from a complete understanding.

The negative consequences arising from the practice of pranayama, layaya yoga, and other methods can be prevented and corrected by mahamantras, that is, mantras containing the name of God. Such mantras themselves correct some miscalculations in practice. Anyone who systematically repeats them will be able to get rid of three types of suffering, find love for God and all beings and achieve self-realization.

The awakening of kundalini occurs suddenly and gives rise to a surge of love in a person, which encourages him to perform wonderful actions. The sages of India say that before awakening the kundalini, you need to free the central channel of the spine - sushumna - with a clean life and appropriate exercises. Such purification is necessary for spiritual growth because when the kundalini snake awakens, it begins to activate the whole mental life of a person; it's such an intense fire that it burns everything. Therefore, the path of kundalini should be free from all impurities and all obstacles, so that it can pass it quickly and without harm to humans. The system of work with the subtle energy of the human body helps to get physical and spiritual compensation for all the tensions encountered in life, so we can be healthy.

Chapter 7

Signs of Awakening Kundalini

Each experience of climbing kundalini is unique. In each case, there is its own set of criteria. In addition, signs of the awakening of internal energy can undergo significant changes, even in the same person. Nevertheless, there are some typical signs that indicate that a person feels the ascent of kundalini. We will consider them in this chapter. Some people who have experienced the awakening of the kundalini energy simply do not know what to do next. There are clear and unmistakable signs of the awakening of inner strength. First, trembling usually runs through the body, and gradually, a feeling of higher pleasure spreads. Then the temperature rises - this is a sign that kundalini passes through a certain energy center. In various parts of the body, foci of fire appear to appear; the whole body is sweating. Sometimes it seems

In any case, when the kundalini awakens, a person feels something rising up the spine. It's not necessary to feel the burning liquid: sometimes, it really looks like a snake crawling. As the awakened energy passes through the chakras, a person can spontaneously begin to perform yoga mudras, bandhas, or breathing exercises. Kundalini acts as a spiritual principle, guiding and leading a person along the path of enlightenment.

When energy goes up, difficulties can arise. From time to time, she can remain for a while in one chakra and even come back. There are three granthi (nodes) through which energy passes with difficulty. When kundalini penetrates the abdominal node, pain, or physical disruption of the body can be felt. The adept will most likely have to repeat the process of awakening the kundalini repeatedly, gradually moving it higher and higher. Raising the kundalini to the anahata chakra in the region of the heart is the most difficult task. It is believed that at this point of kundalini, a cycle passes from infancy to adulthood.

It is easy to awaken the kundalini, but it is very difficult to bring it to sahasrara through all the chakras. This requires a lot of patience, perseverance, purity of thought, and sustainable practice.

As the kundalini passes through the chakras, exciting them, a person observes specific visions and hears special sounds. He passes through the corresponding locks (cosmic plans). In mystical insights, each chakra corresponds to a lotus flower. When energy enters the chakra, the petals open.

The quality of the chakra, or its power, is expressed in the form of the corresponding deity. The Vedic tradition says that in Sahasrara, there is a union of Shiva and Shakti. This is the most transcendental and blissful state of consciousness. Individual consciousness merges with the Divine.

If you hold the kundalini at this point for longer than twenty-one days, the physical body will lose support and begin to disintegrate. However, it is usually very difficult to maintain such a state of consciousness, and the kundalini again returns to the lower chakra. Gradually, through systematic practice, the adept learns the art of controlling the energy of the kundalini and acquires the ability to control its movement at will, maintaining the state of consciousness that is most useful at this time.

As a preparation, it is useful to first study the anatomy of the human body, as well as gain control over the four aspirations (for food, sleep, sex, and self-preservation). You must have a healthy body and fully control your mind, actions, and speech. The mind cannot be allowed to fall under anyone's influence. Achieving all of this can take quite a while.

A sick body and a restless mind cannot work with kundalini energy. A healthy body and mind are two essential tools for awakening consciousness.

Exercises that are traditionally used to cleanse the body in preparation for awakening kundalini can also be used to improve health. However, it is wrong to apply powerful practices aimed at actively awakening internal energy with the goal of simply improving well-being.

How to Awaken a Dormant Kundalini

Here are the most important body cleansing methods required when working with a dormant kundalini.

Alternating Nostril Breathing (nadi shodhana)

- Reinforced expiration (kapalabhati) - Sit down. Exhale all the air from the lungs, take half a breath, and then take quick rhythmic exhalations through the nostrils. Accentuate each exhalation; inhalation occurs automatically. Concentrate on the ajna chakra between the eyebrows. Close your eyes and "look" them into the area of the third eye. This exercise clears the head area.

Fire extinguishing in the abdomen (agnisara dhauti) - Sit down. Put your palms on your knees, fingers facing each other. Bend your elbows a bit. Exhale all the air from the lungs and during exhalation, make rapid rhythmic movements of the abdomen back and forth. After that, gently inhale.

Brand of a horse (ashwini mudra) - Sit down. Take a deep breath. Perform fast and strong sphincter contractions.

Do these techniques daily.

Positive Thinking Power

There are all kinds of courses that teach kundalini yoga, mainly emphasizing its health benefits and not touching on the discussion of spiritual issues. In this way, hatha yoga is often taught in the West. It all depends on the attitude of the student. The desire to improve health is certainly laudable, but the awakening internal energy will gradually burn the ego, and a person who seeks to recover using the methods of kundalini yoga, is driven primarily by egocentric motives. Thus, internal tension is created, which can lead to a serious mental disorder.

The next stage of preparation is gaining perfect control over unconscious acts, as well as the central nervous system. During intense sadhana, one should observe perfect calm and also adhere to a certain diet. The stillness of the body and mind are two important signs of progress.

Ancient yogis depicted the development of humanity and human consciousness, in particular, as a sequence of seven steps. Seven centers are symbolically associated with the spinal column. These centers have already been mentioned above: these are chakras or lotuses. The word chakra, as mentioned above, means "wheel" and symbolizes the process of life. Slowly opening lotus, rooted in the mud, symbolizes the development from primitive consciousness to high. Chakras can be understood as levels of consciousness.

Since each chakra controls one of the five senses, the adherent must strive to develop each feeling as fully as possible and bring them all into balance. This will give him a significant advantage when working with internal energy.

Increase Mind Power

An ancient tradition says that all human actions originate in the mind. Energy is mostly neutral and takes shape as a result of the impact on it of thoughts, speech, and actions. The pollution of the chakras (levels of consciousness) occurs due to desires, selfishness, and scanning of the lower layers of consciousness. At the beginning of work on oneself, it is very difficult to abandon an entrenched system of beliefs and illusions. The need to perceive new information contrary to the usual beliefs seems unnecessarily brutal and even hurts. But any pain is caused by ignorance. A person believes that he is a victim of circumstances, while he actually creates for himself a shell of ignorance that prevents him from enjoying life. The practice of awakening kundalini leads to a proper perception of reality - instead of a false one that causes pain and suffering.

The Effects of Kundalini Activation on the Body, Emotions and the Mind

Seven signs are observed that are observed during the awakening of kundalini.

1. Pranic movements, or kriya

Prana is the Sanskrit word for life energy. When an energy flow moves through the body, clearing physiological blocks in its path, a person may experience involuntary cramps, twitches, muscle contractions. He can also clearly recall long-forgotten events, as well as moments from past incarnations.

The involuntary reactions and actions caused by the rise of the kundalini are kriya. Kriyas are designed to eliminate energy blocks within the spinal column. Kriyas also purify the mind. Blocks, known as samskaras, not only impede the movement of the kundalini, but they embody bindings, false notions, and other derivatives of ignorance that restrict freedom of consciousness. If you do not pay attention to material attachments, they lead to actions that make blocks in mind more and more insurmountable.

For example, if a person is attached to anger, then he will manifest it everywhere, even in situations that, it would seem, do not provoke aggression at all. With an increase in kundalini, it interacts with the matrix of anger, it purifies it, as a result of such purification, the corresponding kriya will occur. This can be compared with how a person's high temperature during an illness indicates an ongoing internal fight against infection. Such a perception of the kundalini as some kind of rational force may seem a little mystical, but, nevertheless, the mechanism of its action is just that.

Spoken language has many phrases with figurative meanings that reflect the state of mind. For example, about a person who has lost firm convictions, they say: "He has a confused mind." On the sincere - on the contrary: "This is a direct person." These phrases reflect a subtle understanding of the value of a human being. What seems like a good metaphor actually reflects the internal structure of the human body. Take a garden hose with which to water. If the hose is straight, then water will run along with it easily and freely. Another thing if the hose is tangled: if you turn on the water, there may even be a situation where the flow of water will be blocked, and the hose will swell in one place, unable to cope with the voltage. It can even break through. To some extent, a human being can be likened to such a hose. Kundalini rises quickly and freely along with the "direct" person; nothing holds it back. If a person is entangled in internal contradictions, there is no need to talk about a successful awakening of internal strength.

2. Yogic phenomena

Some people begin to perform yoga asanas, mudras, bandhas, which they never knew before or could not do in a normal state of consciousness. They can also pronounce Sanskrit words or sounds, hear internal music, sounds, mantras. In sacred Hindu texts, the kundalini is sometimes called Vak, the goddess of speech, perhaps because the awakened kundalini increases creativity and improves self-expression through speech. Changes also apply to breathe: it can accelerate or slow down greatly. Some people may not breathe at all for a long time.

3. Physiological signs

The awakening of kundalini often causes unusual physiological activity, as the intense movement of energy releases toxins in the body. A person may experience pain in the heart, head, and spine, digestive problems, and impaired functioning of the nervous system. Inner fever can lead to involuntary orgasms.

4. Psychological stress

Spiritual awakening challenges the consciousness of the ego. This leads to the loss of habitual mental balance. The consciousness of the ego leaves the center of the soul. A person enters into inexplicable emotional states unfamiliar before. Emotional outbursts range from feelings of anxiety, guilt, and depression to compassion, love, and joy.

5. Extrasensory experiments

As perceptions expand, people experience atypical visual phenomena, such as seeing lights, symbols, objects, or pictures from past lives. Audio phenomena may consist of hearing voices, music, internal sounds, or mantras. Even the olfactory system can begin to be sharply stimulated, and a person will begin to feel the scent of sandalwood. There may be a violation of the entire perceptual system of the body, ending with disorientation in space.

6. Mental phenomena

With the disclosure of mental abilities, a person can feel the visionary, telepathic, psychokinetic, healing abilities.

7. Mystical states of consciousness

A person can move into altered states of consciousness, where he directly feels the unity underlying the world. At the same time, he experiences a deep peace and clarity of awareness of cosmic wisdom.

In some cases, the changes caused by psychological stress are so acute that the behavior of a person becomes similar to the behavior of a mentally ill person.

What Can Be Done to Maintain the Awakened Kundalini?

When the awakening of kundalini happens to people who are not on the spiritual path of development or who are unable to realize the importance of the overturn of their mind, body, and spirit, such an experience can seriously damage their health. The question may arise: if kundalini is the Divine energy contained in a person, then why does its awakening cause some inconvenience?

All inconveniences associated with the ascent of kundalini are associated with flaws in the human subtle body. These flaws are caused by past injuries, improper lifestyles, or improper spiritual practices that weaken or damage the subtle organs, create energy blocks in the path of kundalini. A person cannot know the causes of these difficulties. All inconveniences are caused not by kundalini, but by mistakes made by the man himself. However, these errors can be corrected.

It is important not to confuse the awakening of kundalini with enlightenment. Enlightenment rarely follows from a separate experience with the supernatural. Usually, it is associated with the expansion of consciousness, which was somehow prepared for this. The intensity and duration of each enlightenment experience depend on the person's willingness to withstand them. The awakening of kundalini is not the endpoint of spiritual development, but the beginning of a transformation of consciousness. At the same time, no other technique is known than kundalini yoga, which would lead to enlightenment just as quickly.

In some people, the awakening of kundalini can be delayed for several years, even with intensive spiritual practice. It is worth noting here that the experience of mystical practices is already quite valuable in itself, regardless of whether it culminates in signs of ascending kundalini energy or not.

No one knows which impetus leads to the unfolding of spiritual potential. For some people, spiritual growth is a very delicate process that takes place over many years, devoted to prayers or meditations under the guidance of an experienced guru. Others may experience a sharp awakening of inner strength without even realizing how to work with it further.

Kundalini Climbing - Awakening Your Higher Self

According to traditional views, there are several ways in which kundalini can rise. These paths are characterized by different levels at which kundalini may linger. Thus, we can talk about the types of ascension of kundalini. This type is determined by external circumstances, the characteristics of the subtle body of the individual during the ascent. The quality of ascent is also influenced by such factors as a person's usual behavior, lifestyle, and general mental and emotional mood. Some people are already born with awakened kundalini. It is the merit of their spiritual practice in past lives.

So, in the aspect of raising the kundalini, the following categories are distinguished:

1.) No climbing occurs - This is a sign that the kundalini remains in a dormant state in the Muladhara Chakra. This is the state of an ordinary person.

2.) The awakening of kundalini - It can happen by chance within the muladhara chakra itself when stimulating vayu. Kundalini is unwound and reeled up without going beyond the root chakra.

3.) Kundalini release - Kundalini begins its ascent. This occurs under certain conditions.

4.) Partial ascents - Such fluctuations in internal strength are extremely unstable, the kundalini moves up and down the sushumna, sometimes reaching the anahata chakra at the level of the heart. In some people, it even reaches the chakra of the throat vishuddha.

5.) Indirect ascents - They are also unstable; the kundalini moves up and down the vajra-nadi or sarasvati-nadi. These two energy channels do not lead to the climax of the bindu, so the kundalini should be sent to sushumna.

6.) Intermediate ascents - They occur through sushumna-nadi to the level of vishuddhi chakra or even to the ajna chakra. These are steady ascents, as kundalini remains at the achieved level.

7.) Complete ascent - It occurs through sushumna-nadi (occasionally through chitrini-nadi) to the ajna chakra at the point of makara. After this, the kundalini enters the sahasrara chakra and brahma-randhra but still remains below the bindu point. At this level, completely spiritual life begins, and complete purification of consciousness takes place.

A complete ascent to the point of bindu, located at the end of the brahma-nadi above the brahma-randhra, the top of sahasrara. This is the culmination of an increase in inner strength, but not the final stage of spiritual development. A prerequisite is a fine cleaning of the body.

8.) Advanced ascent - involves the ascent and descent of the kundalini. This is the goal of the path of spiritual development. A person at this level can attain holiness and achieve final liberation, the complete union of the soul with God.

The goal of learning to die correctly is to investigate the nature of a non-physical posthumous state. It is recognized that consciousness is the ultimate reality and that it seeks to be structured on various planes of being, traditionally called in the Western tradition astral, etheric, causal, and so on. These structures are populated by entities, often described as beings of light, or angels. Many people who have experienced an out-of-body state talk about them. The beings of light, as claimed in occult and spiritual traditions, help the process of birth, entry into the world of higher consciousness.

Chapter 8

Mindfulness Meditation Higher levels of consciousness

The higher the released energy flows, the greater the spiritual uplift the meditator feels. Fire sparks emanating from the mouth of the kundalini snake reach the hemispheres of the brain, stimulating them more and more to vigorous activity. The meditator begins to experience the deepest ecstasy, joy, and peace. It seems that the whole body is plunged into an ocean of happiness and bliss.

With the stimulation of the right hemisphere, hidden possibilities of extrasensory perception, such as clairvoyance, clairaudience, telepathy, providence, and so on, come to the surface. Consciousness begins to expand and go beyond its borders, opening up new dimensions of cosmic unity. The sense of self-identity begins to make quantum leaps into the ever-increasing orbits of the cosmic mind. This stage of comprehension of time and space is a reward to the adept for all his efforts.

Here are a few meditations that help rise to higher levels of consciousness and control internal energy.

Meditation on the clouds of light

Find a comfortable place to relax. Let your thoughts flow freely, come, and go; you are only an observer. Take a deep breath, hold your breath. Check for tension in the body. If you find such areas, free them - and on the exhale to get rid of everything that prevents you from completely relaxing. Take a deep breath again. As you exhale, release all energy and all your thoughts from the body. Take a deep breath. Feel new energy entering the body; you literally breathe in new possibilities and allow the body to become light. Relax more and more - until you stop feeling the body.

When fully relaxed, imagine a colorful mist vibrating around you. You yourself, being light, smoothly pass into this fog, just your being has a slightly higher density. Clouds of energy slowly float around you. Relax on one of them, feel safe. This cloud lifts you up and takes you to an infinite world. The boundaries between time and space are erased. You are immersed in a world of infinite beauty and endless possibilities. You are floating in the cloud, feeling how light you have become. Suddenly you see a giant rock below; the cloud softly and easily lands, you descend on a rock.

Feel the strength of the stone, feel the power emanating from the rock. You look back, and you see a big river. You cannot make out where it begins and where it ends. You are fascinated by the water stream. It is an endless river of energy, a river of life. You come closer to the water and try to examine its color, to feel it with your whole being. What sounds do you hear? You are the light, so you can safely enter the water, cross it, rush along with the stream, and when you want, stop.

Relax and try to realize what you need most at the moment. What is your main intention? What emotions will accompany you on the way to the chosen goal? Feel the energy of these emotions, feel how it moves through your light body, burns, pulsates. Inhale energy with your whole being. Try to see the paintings, images, symbols associated with it: they will appear in front of the inner eye themselves; you can only focus on them.

When you are completely filled with this energy, enter the river, dissolve for a moment in it, purify the energy, and then release it into the water. See how the energy cloud comes out of you, touches the water, and gradually disappears in the stream. Take a deep breath. Your desire merges with the source of life. Enjoy the river of life for some more time. Take a deep breath again and exit the river. Notice that the colored fog surrounds you again, and you rise up with it. You descend to the cloud and return. With each deep breath, you return to the outside world and feel peace and satisfaction.

Sacred Space Meditation

Relax, sit in a comfortable position. Close your eyes, calm your mind. Breathe slowly and deeply; breathing comes from the diaphragm. For a while, just breathe and pay attention to the spine. It is a pillar connecting earth and heaven.

Feel the energy being concentrated at both ends of this pillar. Let the flow of earthly energy move upward, exit the crown of the head, and disperse into the Universe. Together with the energy flow, all negative emotions, pain, anxiety, tension are carried away.

Your whole being is filled with peace. Let the mind be like the ocean, and thoughts - bubbles appearing on the surface of the water. You may remember your thoughts better, but for now, remain a simple observer. Breathe deeper, gradually slow down your breathing. With each breath, relax your body and mind more and more.

Feel the cool red fog enveloping you. It is not hot, not cold: you can only feel it with your skin.

Feel yourself on a cloud firm enough to hold you on yourself, but very cozy and comfortable. Each part of your body rests on a cloud: legs, arms, back, neck, head - all organs feel calm. The cloud begins to plunge slowly into the red fog, and you plunge with it. Immersion is very slow; you go deeper and deeper and relax even more. The fog begins to change its color: from brilliant red to red-orange.

Gradually, the orange color changes to yellow-lemon. Your body is also painted in lemon color. You are floating on a cloud that carries you to the green summer lawn. You can even hear the wind shaking the grass, feel the flowing blue light from heaven.

Blue light turns into purple; moonless night comes, dark, peaceful, quiet. The cloud you were floating on gently lands.

The fog disappears. You lie on your back on the green grass. You feel light blows of the wind; you can hear the faint chatter of night insects.

Wherever you are, there is always something that pulls you toward you. It may be someplace, person, impression. What you are thinking about may appear right next to you because you are in a sacred place of fulfillment of desires. Everything can change here, but any changes will occur only at your request. You yourself built this place, inhabited it. Rise, explore the sacred space in which you are. May you meet with something (or about whom) have long dreamed of.

After a while, you yourself will realize that the time has come to leave the sacred place. Say goodbye to what you saw, leave without regret, because you can always come back here whenever you want.

Lie on your back and again feel the fog enveloping you. This time it is dark, like a moonless sky. Feel the cloud again under your feet, arms, back, neck, head. It supports you - and begins to rise very slowly.

Breathe deeply, watch the gradual change of colors: the dark color of the sky turns into blue, cyan, green, yellow. All this time, you continue to rise slowly; yellow turns to summer orange, then red. Let your mind still float, and your body will slowly return to the tangible world. You begin to feel the floor with your back, to realize the room in which you are. You are coming back.

Understanding the Benefits of a Strong Meditation Practice

The mindfulness movement is rapidly gaining popularity in the Western world. If before meditation was practiced only by people who are fond of various kinds of spiritual practices, now it is considered the most common thing. Now in Europe and here in the USA, the phrase "I practice meditation" no longer causes a wary-detached attitude, as before. So what's the point? What are some of the benefits of meditation or mindfulness? Why are more and more people doing it? I will try to answer these questions in this chapter. But let's take it in order.

What Meditation Is

In 2007, a study was published that experimentally confirmed the previously existing hypothesis that a person has two different forms of self-consciousness, and different parts of the brain are responsible for them. These two forms of self-awareness are called the narrative mode (story mode, narrative mode of self-reference), and the experience mode (empirical mode, experiential mode of self-reference).

The narrative mode is a mechanism by which we can think about the past, present, and future. Its essence is that our attention is partially or completely captured by thoughts that give meaning to what is happening. The story mode is responsible for our understanding of who we are, what is happening around us, what we are striving for, what connects us with others, and so on. The story mode connects the past, present, and future for us into one semantic picture.

The empirical mode is the ability to perceive our direct experience, what is happening to us at this second. Our direct experience consists of several parts. This is, firstly, the sensations realized with the help of the senses (hearing, sight, touch, smell, taste, balance). Secondly, these are internal sensations - thoughts, imagination, emotions, and internal states.

Meditation is the training of attention. When we meditate, we train to keep our focus on exactly what we are experiencing at the moment. That is, we train to be in the mode of experience.

Why Do We Need Each of These Forms of Self-Awareness?

Both forms of self-awareness are necessary. Narrative mode serves to perform any action. To do something, you need to make a decision. To make a decision, you need to somehow explain to yourself what is happening. Medicine knows cases of damage to the part of the brain that is responsible for the narrative regimen. In cases where this department completely loses its working capacity, a person turns into a vegetable. He does nothing more and does not say anything.

Once I read about one case when such a person fell into the pool and drowned. He could not have a motive to perform any actions for his salvation. In order for a motive to appear, one must first give the event some meaning. If the narrative mode does not work, what is happening seems pointless.

The empirical regime allows us to be in the present moment and feel what is happening to us. In addition to the fact that we get complete satisfaction from any pleasant sensations (for example, the pleasure of eating, music, sex, etc.), we are better aware of what is happening around us. That is, we can give the event meaning more accurately. The empirical mode allows us to adjust how we explain what is happening, taking into account what is happening here and now.

If the empirical regime is poorly trained, then our thoughts are more based on our ideas about ourselves and the world and to a lesser extent, on what is happening here and now.

Let's look at an example:

Victor works in sales. He is new to this business. He attended several trainings where he was told the theory. But he is not good at applying this theory in practice. When he speaks with the client, usually at some point, the client begins to close, and the contact disappears. Victor began to practice meditation. Now he notices that the contact disappears when he begins to feel excitement amid a desire to close the deal as soon as possible. Gradually, he began to recognize this sensation at an early stage and learned to behave more calmly, despite the excitement. Over time, he noticed that he began to feel more relaxed.

In this example, the practice of meditation helps Victor to pay attention to his feelings during a conversation with a client. This led to the fact that he understood the reason for the disappearance of contact with the client. As a result, over time, he first managed to adjust his behavior, and then his emotional reactions became adequate.

Awareness is a kind of feedback mechanism that allows you to adjust behavior. Without realizing what we feel, we usually act on autopilot.

Yet another example:

Andrew is a conflict person in terms of his personality. When he was angry, he could not stop. The conflict simply unwound according to a previously known scenario. But Andrew never thought about it. Each time he drew conclusions for himself and lived on. Conclusions usually came down to the fact that the other side is to blame.

When Andrew began to practice meditation, first of all, it helped him realize that he was behaving aggressively. Then he noticed that often in a conflict, he doesn't react to the essence of the issue, but to the form in which the other side answers him. This allowed him to react less emotionally. Andrew realized that from time to time, he spoke stingy, offensive phrases, the purpose of which was to offend another person. He began to learn to stop in time. The practice of mindfulness helps Andrew more often and faster turn off the autopilot in a conflict and do something for a peaceful resolution of the situation.

What Other Benefits Does Meditation Provide?

The fact is that the mechanisms of attention are the most low-level mechanisms of our consciousness. Therefore, the practice of meditation affects absolutely all aspects of our lives. Known and research-confirmed effects include:

- Increased attention span. Reducing the number of random distractions.

- Improving self-control ability.

- Increasing the pain threshold.

- Improving learning and memorization.

- Reduces irritability and stress.

Meditation to Attain Your Divine Self

As you have seen in the mediation guides, the most common meditation technique is observing breathing. Despite the fact that it is very good for training concentration, in terms of awareness of your divine self, you need to take it up a notch. For this, I recommend trying a technique called marking or mental noting.

Marking is a technique from the attention category without a choice. In other words, we are not trying to concentrate on something specific, but simply try to notice what is happening to us, whatever that is. And when we notice, we call it one word. Perhaps we feel some sensations in the body. Perhaps we are thinking about something. Maybe we want something. Maybe we imagine something. Anything. In a word.

There are various marking options without a choice. You can start with anyone. The easiest option is to use only three words: see, hear, feel. Moreover, each word can refer to both external sensation and internal. For example, the word "hear" can denote perception by the hearing organs and the thought that "sounds" in the head.

As for the time for meditation, 10-15 minutes a day is enough to start. It is advisable to find the time when no one will bother you.

While meditating, you can sit, lie, stand, or walk. Eyes may be open or closed. You can sit on a chair or on the floor. All this is not so important at first. It is important to remember that the practice of meditation is a long game. And therefore, at the first stage, it is advisable not to overdo it.

The practice of meditation is usually associated with people with Buddhist monasteries, where people come to live in order to someday achieve enlightenment. At the same time, enlightenment itself is usually not taken seriously but is used to denote a certain unattainable ideal that one will have to strive for a lifetime.

Probably, touching upon this topic, I may seem strange to some but still, take a chance. Enlightenment is an absolutely real and quite strong change in the work of the human psyche that can occur as a result of the practice of meditation. I know because it happened to me. It happens suddenly, at one point. In Buddhist texts, one can find descriptions of several stages of enlightenment. Each of these steps leads to a radical increase in the basic level of awareness.

Achieving enlightenment is no easy task. But it is not impossible. According to Daniel Ingram, whose book gave me an understanding of the technical side of meditation, it is no more difficult than graduating from a university. And for this, it is not necessary to go to live in a monastery. If you meditate an hour a day and receive personal recommendations from an experienced teacher, I think it can take from several months to several years without interruption from your usual life. If you are interested, try to find such a teacher.

Meditation has a hugely positive effect on my life. I believe that the further you go, the more you will understand what I mean. Good luck!

Chapter 9

Clearing Out Your Energy Fields - Work With Crystals

Cleansing Gemstones and Crystals

An important tool when working with kundalini energy with chakra energy is crystals. The stone or crystal you intend to work with must be cleaned. The purer energy he possesses, the more powerful he is. Crystals should be cleaned immediately after purchase. A refined, ready-to-work crystal is filled with positive energy and is cold to the touch. The crystal that needs to be cleaned is hot, heavy, unpleasant to the touch. There are several ways to effectively clean the crystals and gemstones.

Sea salt

Sea salt is a traditional cleaner; it dissipates all illnesses and negative energy, serves as a physical and mental disinfectant. Sea salt is especially recommended for the initial cleansing of the stone and when the stone is full of negative energy. Salt can be dissolved in water or used in dry form. To prepare the salt solution, take a tablespoon of sea salt in a glass of cold water. Do not use plastic or metal utensils. Put the stone in the solution and leave it in it. When using dry salt, place it in a glass dish and bury the crystal in the salt. For complete purification, it is recommended to hold the crystal in salt for a day or two. When cleaning the necklace, it is better to use dry sea salt. If you live near a pond, it is better to use water from it.

319

Moonlight

Moonlight is another traditional gem cleaner. Bring the crystal to the moonlight (choose the time of the full or new moon). If possible, hang a necklace or place crystals on a tree, exposing the surface to the moonlight. It is not recommended to expose crystals to sunlight: many stones in the sun lose their color and may even break.

Herbs

Immerse the crystal in a cup filled with dried cleansing herbs. Good plants for the purification ritual: rose petals, sage, myrtle, frankincense, sandalwood. This is a very effective way to cleanse.

Earth

Crystals can also be buried in the ground. This procedure is especially useful when deep cleansing is required. Prepare a small, the size of your crystal, recess in the ground, put a stone there, and cover it with soil above. Notice the place.

Consecration of the crystal - Using your mind to heal

After you have selected and purified the crystal, you need to perform the ritual of its consecration. The purpose of this "programming" of the crystal is to concentrate its power and protect it from negative energy. A crystal or stone that is properly sanctified becomes much more powerful and useful as a tool. Take the crystal in your hand and feel its energy. If the stone was recently cleaned, the energy would be stronger and even more attractive. When you experience this energy, calmly ask for a higher power to bind the stone to the corresponding deity. Stones, in a certain sense, are living beings, and the deity of stone gives it energy and vitality. Once you feel that your request has been granted, consider how you intend to use this stone. If a stone accepts your intention, its energy increases. Otherwise, you will feel that the stone is not being charged with the right amount of energy. So, suppose you felt the stone was full of energy; now your crystal is blessed. You can now associate it with any deity. If you intend to work with the chakras, link the stone to the deity of the corresponding chakra.

Stone laying

The technique of using crystals and gems when working with the body is called overlay. This is a powerful method of getting rid of negative energy, cleansing and balancing the chakras, normalizing the emotional matrix, and directing the flow of light into all bodies. The cleaned, consecrated stone turns into a receiver and at the same time, into a transmitter of the good vibrations of space. He releases stagnant life force, directs it to the chakras, and also heals. Stones can be used both independently and in combination with laying on of hands (reiki technique). Stones are placed in places of physical correspondence of the chakras (note that chakras are not physical objects and we are only talking about their conjugation with parts of the physical body!), Starting from the legs and moving to the head. Use gems in colors that match the colors of the chakras. Stones can be of any shape.

Lie down. Place two light crystals above your head and below your feet (this ritual is easier to carry out together, with an assistant). In the right and left hands also take a crystal. Now start slowly placing the necessary stones in the areas connected with the chakras. If you suddenly felt uncomfortable when placing a stone, then this stone is not suitable for you; choose another.

When all the stones that you were going to use are placed, begin meditation on the deity of the selected chakra (or several chakras). Begin with the first chakra, Muladhara, moving up. Visualize the deity, its strength and energy, feel its goodness. Visualize a bright color coming from a stone. Continue this visualization until you feel the need to move to the next chakra.

Lithotherapy: balancing your chakras with stones

To promote the balancing of our chakras, several methods exist, all having their own effects and influences on them. Once you have opened your chakras, it's time to rebalance them. One of the most effective methods is that of lithotherapy. So how does lithotherapy work, and what are its effects on your chakras?

What is lithotherapy?

Our body is in constant energy fluctuation, without stop, throughout our life. This fluctuation varies in intensity according to the events we live in everyday life, such as:

- Stress

- Joys and sorrows

- Cravings

- Fears

- Love

- Social and environmental interactions.

Usually, when all goes well, the energies circulate properly, and our mind keeps only the essence of our experiences (joy) to stabilize the balance of the chakras. This joy is recovered from one of the daily events. Only, when these are too intense, the chakra system can be disrupted and crash.

It is precisely to manage these fluctuations that the mineral stones can come to your aid. They are concretely the most effective to treat these dysfunctions, mainly emotional, and eliminate almost instantaneously most of the blockage.

To understand correctly, stones are always active on the same frequencies (unlike humans), which allows them to generate more good energy waves. What is called lithotherapy is the energy connection of the stones directly to the human, to balance his own energies, and to feel the benefits quickly. The virtues of crystals have been recognized for millennia because they were already present in ancient energy healing rituals.

How to Choose a Stone to Balance Your Chakras?

As noted, to choose the stone that will help to properly balance a chakra, it is very important that you have a good knowledge of yourself, your personal feelings, and especially your chakras. A simple trick to help you choose the right stone is simply to appeal to your curiosity. This is a great way to discover, as your experience with lithotherapy, the crystals that are most effective for you.

You do not need to learn them by heart: you just have to remember a few, the main preferences. For the rest, do not hesitate to check books dedicated mainly to and that talk about the subject, which will be much more detailed. Your learning must always be benevolent, never against heart.

Finally, your intuition can be an incredible engine to determine the stone you need. Generally, by instinct, you will always choose a stone that corresponds to you in the present moment, very often to harmonize the energies too present, or on the contrary, to help those who are under-effective.

Your body will always have the answer, listen to it!

What Stones Can We Associate With Your Chakras?

It would be too tedious to list all the stones and their many energy capabilities. Here is a summary of the main crystals and the different chakras associated with them.

1. The root chakra readily lends itself to easy balancing with Jasper, especially when combined with other minerals. Indeed, it relieves difficult digestion, gastric reflux, and constipation. Its beneficial actions have a very powerful impact on healing, but it also significantly strengthens the tissues and the immune system. Directly connected to the root chakra it helps to harmonize it.

323

2. To balance the sacred chakra, try an orange stone such as Carnelian, Amber, Orange Calcite, or Bronzite. The benefits of Carnelian are mainly related to the adrenal glands and the management of stress.

3. To open your solar plexus chakra with a crystal, simply use Citrine. It is very effective: the vibrations of the stone directly affect the body, counterbalancing energy variations. Its field of action is vast because it also has an impact on the intestinal flora, the kidneys, and the pancreas. The solar plexus also likes Yellow Jade or Sulfur.

4. The balance of the heart chakra can be maintained using Malachite. This one allows detoxification of the body and promotes the energies of self-healing. Likewise, Aventurine, Emerald, or Green Tourmaline also have an important role in the well-being of the heart chakra.

5. To develop the communication of your throat chakra, use rather light blue stones such as Angelite, Blue Agate, Aquamarine. On the other hand, if you want to unlock the energies of your throat chakra prefer blue-green and turquoise-blue minerals such as Amazonite or Turquoise.

6. If you are looking for the opening of your Third Eye chakra, the stones par excellence will undoubtedly be Cyclops Agate and Black Obsidian. To maintain intuition, letting go and concentration, choose Préhnite, Azurite, Cyanite, Blue Sapphire.

7. Finally, to heal your crown chakra, Amethyst and Lapis lazuli are recommended. Indeed, they clean your blood and play the role of an antiseptic for your body.

They are also full of good energies to evolve to a higher spiritual level and improve the clarity of your mind.

Once again, there is no secret: you just have to document to discover each stone one by one and learn more about their benefits.

A practical exercise in the use of stones.

As calmly as possible, lie down with your arms around your body and empty your mind gradually. If you wish, you can light incense or a candle near you. Then, gently take the stone or stones you want to use during your treatment, and place them on the site of the chakra dedicated to it. Breathe deeply and quietly; it's not a race!

Now, disconnect dark and dark thoughts that disturb your relaxation. Focus on the stones themselves. You are likely to feel a sensation of warmth: this is quite normal; it is only the energy of stones that circulates.

Congratulations, you have successfully completed your first session of energy treatment with the help of lithotherapy!

Chapter 10

Demystifying Paranormal Activities - You Can Do It!

Astral Travel: How to "Get Out" of the Body

According to many esoteric teachings, in addition to our beloved, so-called dense body, there is also a subtle, astral body. It is a kind of soul that can travel freely in time and space. But this space is special - astral. Non-physical, unearthly, light, and etheric. Material laws do not work in it, so astral travels are endless. You can find yourself in your past or future, visit the thoughts of a loved one, or even visit other planets. There is a working technique for entering the astral plane.

True, no one guarantees you that your astral body will leave the physical immediately, someone needs to train hard for a long time and hard, and someone flies out from a half kick. In order to disconnect from the physical body, it is necessary to become "easier" in the literal sense of the word. A short preparatory diet will help to "get off the ground" rather - drink plenty of water to start the cleansing mechanisms in the body. Do not overeat, increase the number of fruits and vegetables in the diet, limit or completely exclude meat: it is very grounding, but we do not need this.

Before you fall asleep or immediately after waking up, try the following: try to feel the shape of your astral body (this is not difficult, it exactly repeats your physical one) and move your toes, for example, without straining your muscles. This will be the first step towards the separation of the astral body since it is in such a dis-synchronism (the physical body is calm, and you make the astral move) that the separation of two bodies arises. When the practice of "moving the astral limbs" has already gone far enough, you can try to get out of the body, with a little effort pushing the astral out of the outlines of the physical body.

Do not worry and do not build grandiose plans - from high expectations; you often cannot get to the astral plane, no matter how clean the execution technique is. Along with the "astral movements," try to imagine what you are going to connect with and where you intend to go: your astral journey should have a clear goal, its direction.

When you feel incredible lightness and unusualness, you will see something that you have not seen before; you can safely say that you have been to the astral plane. Do not forget, by the way, to correctly return to the body - for this, just your firm intention to end the journey is enough, and remember - for any unpleasant sensations, the practice should be stopped immediately. Still, the astral is a delicate matter. Meditation helps.

Psychic Awareness

If we understand the psyche broadly, like the entire space of our inner world, then consciousness is then understood in the broadest sense - as the highest form of the psyche, namely: all those mental processes (internal information processes) in which a person can be aware of. Consciousness, in the broadest sense, is a process of orientation in the outside world and self-management, in which a person can give an account.

However, both the psyche and consciousness are often understood more narrowly, and then, if we use the metaphor of the searchlight, the searchlight of the psyche is directed outward and illuminates the outside world. The searchlight of consciousness is directed inward and illuminates the inner world: we get the opportunity to give an account of what is happening to us and in our souls.

Speaking of consciousness, it is important to distinguish between consciousness as a process and consciousness as a result.

Consciousness as a process is energy (power), which illuminates the inner world of a person and makes the management of mental processes explicit and controlled - the energy that carries light, power, and control.

Conscious - illuminated by the light of consciousness. A conscious hand movement is a hand movement that we track in detail, not an impulsive, but a controlled movement. A conscious objection is not one that accidentally flashed, unnoticed, but the one we looked at, somehow appreciated and which, as an objection, was allowed.

The unconscious is what happens in a person or with a person naturally, unconsciously: without conscious control and not requiring additional conscious effort.

Consciousness, as a result, is a person's inner world, but not closed, but open to external influences. Consciousness is an area of the psychic (inner world) available for internal vision, understanding, and control. The subconscious is a less accessible area. The unconscious is an inaccessible area.

All the functions of our consciousness at the present level of development are the result of evolution and conscious self-development.

In the early stages of his evolution, a man was far from being as intellectually and emotionally developed as it is today. His memory was not so full of information, and the ability to manage desires was not so trained.

True, in some other psychic properties - the sharpness of perception, certain types of attention that respond to physical danger, the strength of emotions, rage, which is responsible for survival, the ancient man perhaps surpassed his modern urban descendant in something.

But it should be recognized: in general, the psyche and consciousness have gone a long way in evolutionary development.

Again, meditation helps achieve this stage much faster.

Enlightening Compassion Through Your Heart Chakra

To unlock the energies present in our Heart Chakra, it is possible to use different methods and tools such as stones, essential oils, and Yoga posture. But in my opinion, it is essential to add meditation work, specific energy treatments, and reflection exercises.

It is important to know your dominant sensory channels to know how to rebalance your chakras in the simplest way.

The main sensory channels are:

The sight: the visual people will have facilities to visualize the colors during the meditations and energetic care.

Touch: kinesthetic people can use some stones, essential oils, Bach flowers.

Hearing: Hearing-inclined people will be able to align their chakra by listening to guided meditations, singing mantras, with the sound of the Tibetan bowl as well.

Conclusion

Dear reader, you and I have come to the finals of a very big deal, but I think you already realized that, by and large, this is not the final at all. Moreover, this is the beginning. I am sure that all the best in your life is just beginning because now you are the owner of a great treasure: you have done everything to open your third eye, that is, activate your intuition!

It is very important not to fight her, to listen to her prompts, not to act in defiance. My intuition tells me that we will meet again and again. So, see you soon! I am always with you and for you!

Chakra Meditation

21 Days Guided Meditation to Awaken your Spiritual Power, Reduce Stress & Anxiety and Improve Awareness of Psychic Abilities with Reiki Healing Exercises

By

New Mindfulness Lab

Introduction

Congratulations on downloading your copy of *Chakra Meditation: 21 Days Guided Meditation to Awaken your Spiritual Power, Reduce Stress & Anxiety and Improve Awareness of Psychic Abilities with Reiki Healing Exercises.* My hope is that it includes everything that you are searching for on the subject of meditation, stress reduction and building your psychic abiltities as well as helpful information which you can start to apply to your life today to bring you a deep appreciation with your natural born gifts and how to use them.

In this comprehensive guide, you will out the history and basics or meditation, Reiki and several psychic abilities that we can all tap into. There is a wide range of exercises that you can perform to strengthen your intuition, your psychic abilities as well as meditation techniques to apply to your 21 day meditation which focuses on each chakra for three days.

The book goes further to give you guidance and clarity on the purpose and responsibilities of each chakra as well as which body parts that they are associated with. This will give you a better understanding about what chakra may be blocked if you having issues with the associated body parts. Knowing where the problems lie will help you to know what direction to go after the initial 21 day chakra meditation is complete.

You will also find out more of what symptoms are experienced on a physical and emotional level with each chakra and general advice in how to balance your chakras once again. You will then have a guided meditation for the duration of three days per chakra. Following the meditations and exercises are going to help each of your chakras to become balanced and energized.

There is also a chapter dedicated to how to keep your energy levels up during the day. Using protective and counter intuitive approaches, you will be able to keep others from taking your energy as well as it bleeding out of your system.

Once you have completed the book, you have knowledge in how to start healing your body from the inside out using the meditation techniques and exercises. There are plenty of books on Chakra Meditation, and thanks again for choosing this one! Every effort was made to ensure that it is full of as much useful information as possible.

Chapter 1

Introduction to Meditation

Meditation has become more popular around the turn of the millennium, but it goes back thousands of years. The word *meditation* comes from the Latin word *meditatum* which means *to ponder*. It has been practiced in different forms throughout many different locations and traditions, but it originated in India between 5,000 and 3,500 BCE from evidence of temple and cave carvings. It was practiced first by the Vedic sages and cave yogis, with the first written evidence in the Vedas, a Hindu spiritual scripture, in 1,500 BCE after being passed down orally for centuries.

A Timeline of Meditation Development & History

The sages and yogis were the religious people who wandered around the Indian subcontinent as ascetics. Through the meditative practices, they were able to connect with universal forces and transcendental reality known as the creator of Brahman in the Vedic scriptures. From these texts, there have been hundreds of techniques and lineages of this information being shared through the generations.

It is thought that the original technique was through gazing or mantra meditation. Gazing is where a specific object is looked upon with intent whereas mantra meditation consists of a phrase of Sanskrit words which would create a specific sound and vibration depending on the purpose of the mantra. The modern movement of Yoga has basis in meditation along with breathing exercises coupled with postures and also originated in India.

Meditation continued to be practiced in the branch of Hinduism known as Buddhism. In the 6th century BCE, the prince known as Siddhartha Gautama renounced his royal life to live a life of an ascetic so that he could gain enlightenment. Through his journey, he learned philosophy and meditation techniques through the rishis, or sages. Throughout this process, he diverted from the Hindu traditions and created what is known as Buddhism today. He was successful in his goal of attaining enlightenment and became the Buddha. He then dedicated his life to teaching spiritual awakening and meditation. Over the course of decades, he was able to teach thousands of people.

In modern times, there are several lineages which have their own styles of meditation known as Walking Meditation, Loving-Kindness, Samatha and Vipassana. These types of meditations spread to the West over the centuries, and are the most widely practiced forms of meditation today.

During the same time period of Buddha, there were three religions which were created that had their own teachings on meditation. These were Confucianism, Taoism and Jainism.

Confucianism centers around morality and community. Their form of meditation has a focus on self-improvement and self-contemplation, and is name Jing Zuo. Confucianism is still popular today, but is mainly found in Asia.

Taoism is focused on creating a union with the Tao, or cosmic nature and life. Their meditation technique helps with the generation, transformation and circulation of the energy within the body, known to them as Chi. This type of meditation aids in finding inner peace by unifying with the body, spirit and Tao and quietens the mind and body.

Jainism's meditation technique uses self-inquiry, visualizations, breath awareness, gazing and mantra repetition. Their religion is based on the ascetic lifestyle and focuses on non-violence, contemplation, self-discipline and self-purification.

The Greek philosophers of Aristotle and Plato developed their own technique of meditation through the influence of the yogis and sages of India. This happened during the time of Alexander the Great's military efforts in India between 327 – 325 BCE). Meditation was not the only influence to the Greek philosopher's system as they admired the sages' immunity to discomfort and pain and their particular disinterest in pleasure and their fearlessness of death.

The meditation technique that was created by the Greek philosophers was known as navel-gazing. This involves deep contemplation of a single issue of oneself. In later years, the philosophers Plotinus and Philo of Alexandria also created a type of meditation that focused on concentration. However, once Christianity started to dominate Europe, the influence of Eastern thought was abruptly cut. However, the ideas started to resurface during the 20th century when Europe and the East started to communicate once again.

The Christians started their own type of meditation which also involved repetition of a religious phrase or word, much like a mantra, and they also would sit in silent contemplation upon God. One method of meditation practiced by the Hesychasm Christians was known as the Jesus Prayer which was developed in Greece between the 10th and 14th centuries. It is believed that this tradition of Christians were in contact with the sufis and Indian sages which influenced their type of meditation.

During the 8th century, a school of Buddhism known as Zen was founded by an Indian-Persian monk by the name of Bodhidharma. He had traveled to China to teach meditation in which the lineage of Chan was born which was adapted by Vietnam, Japan and Korea. All of these versions of meditation were known as Zen which had a massive influence on the Chinese culture and Taoism. Because of the influence from a collective of countries and traditions, Zen meditation is quite unique.

The meditation technique is known as Zazen and is still a popular method of meditation in the West today. Some lineages of Zen also have a method of meditation by the name of Koans. In this type of meditation, the teachers as their students to ponder on a puzzle or riddle in the form of phrases, questions and stories to discover the greater truths about themselves and the world.

The tradition of the Islam Sufis date back as far as 1,400 years, and they were influenced as well by Indian traditions. Their forms of meditation include gazing, the use of mantras and focused breathing exercises. Their practices are designed to solidify their connection with Allah, or God, and also include a method in which they will whirl around in circles to create this effect. In fact, this whirling method is still used in Turkey today.

The esoteric Jewish tradition of the Kabbalah had also developed their own forms of meditation during the 11th century. Their methods include deep contemplation of prayers, symbols, names of God and philosophical principles. They also would reflect upon the principle of the Tree of Life which is a representation of individual beauty, uniqueness and personal development. Similar to a tree, the branches growing up to the sky is a symbol of an individual becoming stronger as they strive for new experiences, wisdom and greater knowledge.

During the 16th century, the Eastern traditions were beginning to be translated into Western languages. The scriptures that were translated were the Buddhist Sutras, the Bhagavad Gita and the Upanishads. Two centuries later, Buddhist was a study for the intellectuals in the West with the philosopher Schopenhauer being one of the biggest admirers of the Eastern traditions and teachings. With the Transcendentalist movement in the United States, Henry David Thoreau and Ralph Waldo Emerson had deep ties to Eastern spirituality and philosophy.

During the 20th century, Swami Vivekananda had come to the United States to introduce meditation and yoga teachings. His debut of his philosophy was presented at the Parliament of Religions which took place in Chicago in 1893. This sparked great interest in the practice of meditation and was supported by the Transcendentalist movement as well. As a result, many well-known Indian babas, or teachers, moved to the United States like Swami Rama, Maharishi Mahesh Yogi and Paramahansa Yogananda to teach their methods of meditation. The

Buddhists teachers also made their way to the United States teaching Tibetan, Theravada and Zen meditation.

Due to the influx and availability of Eastern teachings, the masters were able to create a large following which laid the groundwork to the ancient traditions to be taught and practiced today. This movement was furthered due to scientific studies being released that showed that mediation practices benefited those who were not specifically seeking spiritual enlightenment. For those who were not wanting to meditate for spiritual reasons, the teachings had to be modified to remove the spiritual context. Also, the practices were adapted for the Western way of life to be more simple as most of the western disciples would not be able to follow the strict guidelines which are found in the East.

During the 20th century, scientific studies on meditation started to emerge. The first tests were conducted in 1936 and the first collection of these studies were published in 1977 by James Funderburk who was a follower of Swami Rama. In fact, Swami Rama was the first of the Indian yogis who agreed to be studied by Western scientists. These tests were conducted in the 1960s where the yogi performed different practices such as voluntarily controlling his body temperature, blood pressure and heartbeat. Before these tests were conducted, it was believed that these were involuntary actions of the body. Due to these discoveries, scientists had interests in researching meditation even further.

Over the course of the next five decades, meditation has been extensively researched. With the advances in technology, the scientists were able to dig deeper to discover other benefits that meditation can have for the mind and body. Monks and llamas from the Zen and Tibetan traditions had been also studied which demonstrated the results of mind-over-body practices. During the early years of the 1970s, Dr. Herbert Benson of Harvard University created a major shift in the thought that meditation was solely for religious purposes. Through his research, he was able to show that meditation could be used for healthcare purposes as well.

As a result, meditation during the 21st century has become widely popular and secularized. There are still spiritual meditation practices which are used today in the Western countries, but most use the secular approach to realize the benefits to the overall wellness of the mind and body. The people who meditate regularly report they have positive changes in the mental and physical wellbeing in their lives as well as having a more peaceful and calm outlook.

The Basics of Meditation

There are many different types of meditation, but they are all based upon the same basic principles. Before you start your meditation practices, you need to prepare yourself so that you are able to get the most out of your time.

Preparing for Meditation

Following these basic steps are going to help ease you into your meditation practice.

❖ Find a place which you are going to be comfortable sitting. It does not need to be completely quiet as a small amount of background noise will be fine.

❖ Wear clothing that you feel relaxed and comfortable in. If you are wearing constrictive clothing such as a scarf, belt or tie, you likely will want to loosen these ahead of time. If you are wearing shoes that are tight or heels, you will need to remove them.

❖ Whether you decide to lay down or sit in a chair, you want to have your back straight, your chin tucked in slightly and your neck muscles relaxed. You can place your hands where they feel comfortable on your knees or your lap if you are sitting. When laying down, you can lay your hands next to your body or fold them over your stomach or chest.

❖ Choose a time that you will be able to perform meditation each day by coupling it with a concrete routine such as brushing your teeth. Getting yourself in the habit of spending time in quiet contemplation will create a ripple effect of benefits in your life.

❖ Knowing your purpose and intention of wanting to incorporate a meditation practice in your life will help drive you. If you know what your motivation is to practice, you will be more likely to build your habit of practicing meditation.

❖ There is no such thing as a good or bad meditation. There are going to be some days you will not connect with the passing thoughts in your mind and others where you cannot stop engaging. This is okay. Be kind and remind yourself that this practice is to ultimately teach you patience. Continue the next day with a clean slate and do not stop because you think you are doing it wrong. It simply is not true. Over time you will find that your mind will be less distracted with thoughts and the process will be much simpler.

Basic Meditation Exercises

There are several approaches that one can take when wanting to incorporate a meditation practice. Try the following exercises to see which one works best for you personally.

Mindfulness Meditation Exercise

This type of meditation is going to strengthen your mindfulness and attention. It will help you to stay present in this given moment and anchor yourself in your purpose without judgement in the here and now.

Step 1: Lie or sit down in a comfortable position. This can be on the floor or in a chair. If you are sitting in a chair, be sure to have your feet flat on the ground during meditation. If you choose to sit on the floor, you can make yourself more comfortable with a meditation cushion or yoga mat. You can sit in a cross legged position or sitting on your bent legs. Whatever position you choose, you need to be comfortable during the entire meditation.

Step 2: Close your eyes and breathe naturally.

Step 3: While you are breathing, take notice of the movement of the body with each inhalation and exhalation. Focus on your belly, rib cage, shoulders and chest movements. Continue to breathe naturally during this process. If your mind should wander, bring your focus back on your breathing.

Step 4: Continue this practice between two and three minutes if you have never practiced meditation before. Build up the time each day to a time frame which you are comfortable.

Step 5: Slowly open your eyes and take your time moving.

There is no set time you must meditate, but it is helpful if you are able to quiet your mind for a minimum of 15 minutes each day. You will want to perform your meditation practice at the same time each day. Continuing to focus on your breathing will help to clear your mind. Once you master this technique, you will be able to perform other types of meditation with ease.

Evaluate your Meditation Practice

Especially when you are beginning with your meditation practices, it is important to evaluate when you had learned during the meditation practice. Ask yourself the following questions:

- ❖ How many breaths did it take before your mind wandered away from focusing on your breathing?
- ❖ Did you take note of how much more busy your mind was, even when you were trying to clear your mind?
- ❖ Were you getting caught up in your thoughts when this occurred?

Knowing the answers to these questions will give you deeper insight as to how your mind goes about its daily tasks. It also shows you that the mind can be overworked and full of nonsense that can take you away from focusing on what is important. Know that you are not alone. These thoughts racing through your mind is the product of not being present in the current moment, and we have grown comfortable in allowing our thoughts take over our brains.

Practicing meditation helps to calm down this freight train of thoughts and allows you to recognize these thoughts as passing ideas. Being able to see your thoughts in a different perspective will allow you to not have to become involved in every thought that comes up in your mind. They simply come and go, and the more that you practice meditation, the more the thoughts and mind will calm down.

Remedying Common Mistakes for Meditation Practice

When you are just starting out, there are many obstacles that you can create which will hinder your confidence or progress with your meditation routine. Let us go over several common ways that you are cutting yourself short from your true potential of your meditations and how to remedy or avoid them in the first place.

It is common as a beginner to feel an array of feelings such as resistant, overwhelmed, anxious, fearful, bored, restless or a combination thereof. Once you get over these initial feelings, you will notice them quickly vanish away. Remember, your mind is used to being busy all of the time. You are trying to improve that by slowing down your thought processes, and it is a result that will come with time.

You are able to help these initial thoughts by keeping to your scheduled time for meditation. There should be no excuses, and you always can make the time to sit in silence for 10 or 15 minutes a day. Doing something out of the norm can bring about these feelings, but put them aside just for these few minutes a day, and you will notice that they will not continue to come up before you meditation practice.

If you are not able to practice every single day, do not beat yourself up. Of course you are going to find the benefits of meditation much more quickly practicing each day. However, the most important thing for beginners to realize is that they are taking baby steps in creating a new habit. The time you are able to dedicate to meditation, the more you are going to get out of it, but this does not mean that you must stress yourself out in the process.

Bottom line is, you need to listen to your body. If you are in a state of stress and being overwhelmed, you are very likely going to benefit from taking the time to meditate. Setting a time 2 to 3 times a week even will be more of a benefit if you waited, let us say a month, in between meditation sessions.

Feeling sleepy is another common issue to where you may even be nodding off during your meditation. This is a very common theme for beginners. When your mind is so used to being on the go, it can confuse your stillness with relaxation, causing you to feel more tired. After you continue the meditation practices, you will start to rewire your brain so that it understands you are not resting because you want to sleep.

Three ways that you are able to help this situation is to open a window so that there is a breeze in your meditation room. You can also set your meditation time during the morning or when your mind is more alert. If you are laying down, sit up during your meditation times.

Sometimes you may find yourself expecting too much too soon from your meditation practice. Letting go of your expectations and what you should expect to happen. Simply go with the flow of where your meditation exercises take you. Find enjoyment in how you feel when you are preparing, during and after your practice. Keep a journal of your journey as you continue through the meditation so that you are able to gauge what benefits you are seeing. Find happiness in the new way that you are living your life.

When you are just beginning with meditation, it is easy to believe that you must have complete silence. However, this is not the case. In fact, if you start your meditation practices in complete silence, you will find that you are going to get distracted very easily by outside noises that you cannot control.

Instead, be more concerned with finding a space that you are comfortable. When the sounds in your environment come up randomly, treat them like you thoughts, notice them and do not get involved. It does take some practice. Over time, you will be able to hear noises during your meditation and not be distracted away from your breathing. If you are having an especially difficult time concentrating, you can use noise canceling headphones, but you will need to eventually work your way to meditating when there is background noise.

Letting go of the stereotype that meditation is only for spiritual people, a new age idea or for tree huggers. In fact, there are people from all walks of life and age young and old who practice meditation. Of course it can have a religious focus, but this is not necessary for meditation practice. Another misconception is that is has to be a serious matter with saying mantras of "om" and sitting cross legged. This is an idea that can be incorporated if you wish, but it is not necessary. So perform your meditation practice how you feel comfortable, no matter if you are 2 or 102 years old.

It can be an easy task to start something new because it can be an exciting experience. However, the trick is sticking with it when the novelty wears off. This happens because many of the meditation practices can feel repetitive. Remind yourself that you are training your mind to shift perspective on the way that you view your feelings and thoughts.

One main reason why people throw in the towel is that they do not feel like their mind is clear or empty. It simply is not working! However, like with all things that are worth achieving, there is a level of dedication and perseverance that is required so that you can push past this phase. Remember that the mind is programmed to think. Meditation is not a magical potion so that it will make your thoughts disappear completely. However, you need to learn, practice and master meditation, and the only way you are able to achieve this is to continue to build your habit of meditation.

Some are very excited about trying out a different technique each time they sit down to meditate. This is alright for a short time as you are beginning and finding the technique that resonates best with you. However, if you are continuously switching between methods, you are not going to gain the full benefits of the particular meditation you are performing.

Above all, make your meditation practice a part of your day that you look forward to. It is your way of keeping your mind balanced throughout the rest of the day, and you will help to keep you more focused and aware. Trust me, when you are able to keep up with your practices, you will start to see the benefits that ripple throughout your life. Then you will be wanting to share this secret with everyone.

Chapter 2

Introduction to Reiki

R eiki is an ancient technique which was created in Japan which centers around healing, stress reduction and relaxation. It is derived from two Japanese words. *Rei* means *higher power* where *Ki* has the meaning of *life force energy*. In full, the word Reiki means *spiritually guided life force energy*.

You practice Reiki methods by hovering your hands or lightly laying your hands in a particular area of the body to promote healing. It manipulates and transmutes the energy that is found within the body known as Chi, Shakti or Life Force. You are able to build energy if it is too low and lower it if it should be too high.

Reiki does not just revolve around the energies within the body. It has an effect on you as an entire person, encompassing the spirit, mind, emotions and the body in the treatment. You may find many benefits such as overall well being, security, peace and relaxation. In some instances, there are people who experience miraculous results. Any individual is able to use Reiki because it is not base on spiritual development of intellectual capacity.

Even though Reiki is spiritually based, it is not a religion. There is no dogma attached and you do not need to hold particular beliefs to use Reiki. In fact, Reiki will work even if you do not have a belief in the practice itself, although, it would be more powerful if you do believe that it will work for you.

Using the techniques and intention of Reiki to heal and balance your body, you will be able to help your body to heal from different illnesses. It is believed that energy is blocked and cannot flow properly resulting in illness. When this blockage is removed, you will be able to treat the illness in a more direct way than with conventional medicine. You will find with the chakra meditations that you are able to utilize this transfer of energy to heal your energy centers of the body, resulting in lasting effects felt throughout your body on a physical, mental and spiritual level.

Health Benefits of Reiki

Overall, Reiki manipulates the movement of the life force energy within the body. You will be able to realize many physical and emotional benefits to include the following:

- aids relaxation
- assists in the natural healing process
- hightens spiritual, mental and emotional well being
- helps with coping with difficulties
- relieves emotional stress

From a medical standpoint, Reiki has been successfully used to treat and sometimes cure:

- Fatigue syndromes
- Crohn's disease
- Autism
- Neurodegenerative disorders
- Infertility
- Chronic pain
- Depression
- Anxiety
- Heart Disease
- Cancer
- Stress

Reiki Healing for Anxiety & Stress

Anxiety and Stress are the most experienced medical conditions which are seen in modern society. Reiki healing can be a huge benefit to relieving the symptoms of these experiences. Let us go over the basics of these two conditions so that you can realize if you have problems with them and how reiki and meditation can help you in these cases.

Anxiety

Having occasional experiences of anxiety is a normal fact of life. However, if you are having issues with anxiety that are affecting your daily life, this is known as an anxiety disorder. This is where you are experiencing frequent amounts of persistent and excessive worry which is intense. They can involve repeated occurrence of sudden feelings, and they can also result in panic attacks which are fear, torror and intense anxiety about a particular situation.

These anxiety disorders can start to develop as early as childhood or teenage years and continue to strengthen in intensity during your adulthood. You may start to revolve your day avoid particular places or people so that you do not trigger your emotions. The common disorders of anxiety are known as generalized anxiety disorder, social anxiety disorder and separation anxiety disorder. You are able to have two of these anxiety orders simultaneously.

Common Symptoms of Anxiety

From the wide range of anxiety disorders, the most common symptoms are:

- difficulty controlling worry – this is the symptom experienced the most. It is categorized by the worry being disproportionate to the situations that trigger the worry. Usually it is connected with everyday situations. To be diagnosed with generalized anxiety disorder, you must have frequent occurrences of uncontrollable worry over the course of six months.

- difficulty sleeping – Disturbances in sleep are highly associated with anxiety disorders. This can include a wide range such as waking up in the middle of the night, difficulty falling asleep and insomnia. It is unclear what the link is between anxiety and sleeping disorders. However when the anxiety disorder is treated and under control, the sleep issues improve as well.

- trouble with concentration – This is a heavy hitter when it comes to anxiety disorders. More than 2/3 percent of the people suffering from anxiety disorders have issues with focus, short term memory and concentration. Even with this large number, it is not a surefire way of knowing you have issues with anxiety.

- overactive or feeling tired – Even though this can be a symptom for a wide range of disorders, becoming easily fatigued is a red flag for doctors when discussing anxiety disorders. Because of this reason, this symptom alone is not able to lead a doctor to a diagnosis of anxiety disorder. Alternatively, you can also experience the opposite of having hyperactivity. Fatigue is more tricky as it can be an occurrence experienced only after panic attacks or it can be chronic and experienced throughout the day.

- hyperventilation or rapid breathing – Panic attacks happen when you are under an immense amount of worry, and this leads to you not being able to physically be able to breath without hyperventilating. It is due to an intense amount of fear and can be a debilitating experience. Panic attacks usually have fear of dying, nausea, chest tightness, shaking and sweating that occur with the rapid breathing. They must occur frequently to be deemed as worthy of a diagnosis.

- feeling agitated – When anxiety hits a person, their sympathetic nervous system is sent into overdrive. With this effect, it causes a ripple effect throughout the body, resulting in symptoms of dry mouth, shaky hands, sweaty palms and a racing heart. This is in response to your brain believing that you are in danger

- overall feeling of tension, restlessness or nervousness – This is a symptom seen mainly in teens and children. It is categorized by the individual feeling like they are on edge or experiencing an uncomfortable urge to move. Even though it is a symptom that is not found in each patient, it is one of the indicating symptoms that doctors look for before diagnosis.

Causes of Anxiety Disorders

There are many causes of anxiety disorders that are not fully understood because it affects each individual on a personal level. Traumatic life experiences are going to affect people in different ways. It is thought that inherited personality traits may also be a cause of people being more sensitive to anxiety issues.

For others, underlying medical issues can be to blame as the cause for anxiety disorders. In fact, seeing signs of anxiety usually triggers an investigation which brings these medical conditions to light. Here is a list of common medical issues which are seen in conjunction with anxiety disorders.

- Chronic pain

- Irritable bowel syndrome

- Withdrawal from medications or alcohol

- Misuse of drug or withdrawal

- COPD or asthma

- Hyperthyroidism

- Diabetes

- Heart disease

You can also be at increased risk of having an anxiety disorder if you have issues with one or more of the following:

- Alcohol or drugs

- Having a family history of anxiety disorders in blood relatives

353

- Other mental health disorders such as depression

- Buildup of stress due to illness or a death in the family

- Trauma

Stress

Stress is very common today, and it is an emotional or physical response to pressures or demands that are experienced daily. Stress can be a positive part of life when experienced in small doses. It is able to help people to take action, be stimulated, develop and to grow. However, if you are experiencing high levels of stress frequently, it can be due to an imbalance in lifestyle and can include any area of your life such as illness, relationships, money and/or work.

Common Symptoms of Stress

When you having issues with prolonged stress, your symptoms can include one or more of the following:

- Irritability
- Difficulty with making decisions
- Difficulty relaxing
- Depression
- Lowered confidence levels
- Difficulty concentrating
- Sleep disturbances
- Difficulty breathing
- Decreased sexual function or libido
- Appetite changes
- Muscle spasms or nervous twitches
- Headaches
- Low energy levels
- Muscle pain and spasms
- High blood pressure
- Hyperventilation
- Heart palpitations

- Gastrointestinal issues such as irritable bowel syndrome, heartburn and indigestion
- Anxiety
- Autoimmune diseases
- Withdrawal from others
- Procrastinating or neglecting responsibilities

Causes of Stress

There are many levels of causes which can lead to stress. Most of them are extreme changes to our normal day routine. External causes of stress include the following:

- Children and family members
- Having too busy of a schedule
- Financial issues
- Romantic relationship difficulties
- School or work
- Major life changes

Internal causes of stress are the following:

- All or nothing attitude
- Perfectionism or unrealistic expectations
- Negative self-talk
- Lack of flexibility or rigid thinking
- Inability to accept uncertainty
- Pessimism

The most common life events which can cause undue stress are the following:

- Retirement
- Marriage reconciliation
- Job loss
- Marriage
- Illness or injury
- Death of a close family member

- Imprisonment
- Separation in a romantic relationship
- Divorce
- Death of a spouse or partner

These causes can lead to results or symptoms in our life that rise in a physical way. Some examples are:

- acne – This is likely the most visible way that stress reveils itself. This is due to people touching their face more often when they are stressed which leads to the spread of bacteria and the appearance of acne.

- headaches – Stress can lead to pain within the head as well as the neck. This happens in over 50% of people who experience undue stress in their lives. The pain can range in intensity and can even be debilitating.

- frequent illness – Having heightened levels of stress lowers the immune system effectiveness leading you to feel sick more often than if you did not have undue stress in your life. This leads to illnesses ranging from a runny nose to the flu. However, be sure to look at your physical exercises level and your diet to see if they are to blame first.

How Reiki Can Help

In general, Reiki helps a person to feel more calm and centered. They are able to take back control of their lives without the use of expensive doctors and treatments. In fact, you are able to use these tactics yourself, so you can heal your body when you feel out of balance. Being able to use the healing energy work of Reiki helps own to feel more in control and more confident.

Anxiety and stress symptoms are able to be dealt with on a personal level which is unique to the individual. Since both of these diagnosis stems from personal perspectives on life's events, it is important to approach the healing in a very personal way. Reiki and meditation are able to help you do just that.

As for the physical symptoms that can be experienced, being able to calm down the and make the energy flow properly throughout your body, the ripple effect is going to come down to changes in your body physically. Many of the physical symptoms of stress and anxiety are going to be erased due to the correct energy flow.

Being able to balance out the energy flowing through your chakras, it also reduces the response from the brain to go into flight or fight mode. When you are more calm and centered, you will be able to think more clearly and feel more vibrant.

In fact, more and more private practices, hospice and hospitals are incorporating Reiki sessions coupled with modern medicine. There have been many patients who have reported that they had a reduction in their symptoms, which makes it a beneficial approach to those suffering from anxiety and stress.

So Why 21 Days of Reiki?

There is an intense amount of cleansing that is occurring in the body during this process of healing. You need to ensure that you are drinking enough water and getting a sufficient amount of sleep so that your body is able to cleanse more efficiently. When you work with the meditations, you are also going to be clearing out negative energies and toxins that have built up over your lifetime. There are 7 main chakras which are worked with, and each chakra has 3 days of practice.

With the amount of new energy that is being channeled into the body, it takes a course of 21 days for your body to adjust and adapt to the new activity. From a psychological standpoint, it takes approximately 21 days for a person to form a new habit.

Even though stress is put upon the first 21 days of starting Reiki, this does not mean that the process is complete after this time. It is very important to keep up the practices so that you able to reap the best results from practicing Reiki.

Continuing to practice daily is a way to ensure that you do not have a build up of germs, emotions, negative thoughts or negativity in your life. You do not realize how much of these you pick up on a subconscious level each day. Being able to address these issues on a daily basis helps keep them at a minimum while you are reaping the benefits of living a balanced and healthy life.

Not only does daily practice keep these aspects in balance, it helps you to build up energy that has been lost throughout the day. As you continue the practice, you will continue to clear out your chakras which will lead you to see the full benefits of Reiki practice over time. Even though this book focuses on the first 21 days, it is important to keep up the practice for a minimum of 3 months so that you can see the true effects that the Reiki has on your body, mind and spirit.

Chapter 3

Introduction to Psychic Abilities

E ven though you may be unaware, every person is capable of tapping into their psychic abilities. This is because we are all immortal and infinite beings of energy and is comprised of a part of the universe known as your soul. Most of us have been conditioned to believe that intuitive and psychic abilities are not actually true because there are many charlatans out there that take advantage of people with their "powers" better known as deceptions. Using a trick of the mind for people who are desperate or in need is a powerful tool that they are able to use to their own advantage. Because of the encounters with these people in the media or in real life, society as a whole are sceptical of psychic ability's existence.

A good example is when you were a child, you may have had more psychic encounters. Children are more in touch with the energies around them, and they are more pure from the experiences of life. As a result, you likely were able to hear, dream or sense otherworldly energies or words. Because society has been conditioned to believe that psychic connections are not real, the adults in your life likely shrugged off your experiences or explained them away in a logical fashion.

However, there are some people who are fortunate enough to be able to learn about these abilities from their family members or other caretakers. These are the people that have a solid belief that there rare other energies that exist outside of ourselves, and they will support and teach the connected child so that they are better equipped to deal with all of the rare occurrences that most people will consider them crazy.

As an example, you may have had an experience with communicating with a spirit or ghost who was not there in physical form, but you were able to see and play with them as if they were real. If you confide in your parents about this person, they likely were not able to see this spirit themselves, so instead of taking you at your word, they explain it by saying that you have an imaginary friend. This is a more accepted belief in society, although far fetched for some, but most people will not think the child is crazy for making up a friend to spend their time with.

Because this experience was not defined in the proper way, you yourself most likely started to believe that this spirit was all part of your imagination as well – that you created it in your mind. However, it is very likely that you were able to see what other people could not see because of your innocence and overall trusting of the world. The magic that is experienced in the world through the eyes of a child is lost usually as you get older and start to get bogged down with tragic and emotional occurrences ranging from love to working at a job. These are not part of a child's life, and therefore, their soul is more clean for these higher energies to come through more easily.

Even if you have lost this connection as you become an adult, this does not mean this skill is forever lost. In fact, any person of any age is able to practice and work to strengthen their psychic abilities, and it requires an ample amount of self-love, exercise and patience. One of the main ways to achieve this is to switch your perspective that these abilities are a form of deception or falsehood. They are nothing of the sort, and you do not need to rely on what society has conditioned you to think through the media.

When you tap into your psychic skills, you are going to have heightened sensitivity to one or a combination of your taste, sense, feeling, hearing, vision and intuition of the energetic world. In fact in the science of psychology, there is no true definition as to how to define "normal" and as such, it is a personal scale that you base this upon. With these heightened perceptions, there are many levels of intensities. As you begin to get back in touch with your intuition and psychic abilities, you will find that the intensity will strengthen the more that you practice.

It is important to mention since you will be perceiving the world from a different perspective that you may feel more alienated as you will not be able to talk to just anybody about your personal experiences. However, there are many people just like you who have been practicing for various amounts of time that you will be able to confide in and even receive insight or guidance. Being able to tap into these extra sensory sides of ourselves, you will gain a better understanding of yourself and the world around you. The deeper you go, the most surreal your experiences to the point where you may find it difficult to put them into words. This is all part of the experience as you deepen your connection with yourself and the energies of the other worlds.

Connecting with your Intuition Again

When you are starting to work on your psychic abilities, it is imperative that you have a bond with your intuition. This relationship is going to strengthen and deepen over time as you learn to trust and truly listen to what your senses are telling you. You will start to notice the messages that your body is giving you through your intuition when you know the signs. You will need to pay close attention as we can hear a voice in our minds that we label as intuition, but it can be your ego trying to trick you that it is okay to do what you ultimately wanted to do in the first place.

One way to practice getting back in touch or strengthening your intuition is to create a visualization. See yourself a coffee shop sharing a drink with an old childhood friend that you have not seen since you were a child. You take the time to catch up on your experiences and go over all of the old stories that you shared together during your childhood. Through these conversations, you are able to remember the dynamic of the personal relationship that you had with them all this time ago, but it feels as if you had not spent so much time apart.

Even so, you feel a distance because of your different experiences you both have had and feel that you are strangers in this regard. To be able to take away this feeling of alienation, you would need to get to know your friend again as they are now instead of who they were in your memory.

This is the same way that you need to approach your intuition as if it was your old childhood friend. In this perspective, you are able to see that your intuition has always been a part of you, but you may have taken different routes and not kept in touch. However, it is always possible to rekindle this relationship with your intuition once again. Being able to take the time each day to work on this relationship just like you would with any other person, you will find that you will be able to cultivate this connection is a very personal way.

Intuition Building Exercises

To perform this exercise, you will need to evaluate your emotions and associate a color with each emotion. You can use the typical color representations such as blue meaning healing energy or red meaning angry. However, you need to pick a color scheme that resonates best with you for this exercise.

Start this practice by thinking of a situation which is straightforward, such as a text message with a potential partner or lover. You may have thoughts of love or disdain for this person. Depending on your personal feelings about this situation, assign a color to the feelings of love or disdain which may be pink or red for love and a more negative color such as black or purple for disdain. Remember there is no wrong color choice and you must choose the color that you personally would associate with your feelings.

During future interactions with this emotion and person, you will start to rewire your energy to associate this color with this particular emotion. Through this exercise, you will be able to strengthen your intuition by the color association and you will be able to communicate with your intuition nonverbally through these emotion based colors. Over time, your intuition is going to be more in tune with these color schemes and be able to signal to you through colors so that you can see the bigger picture of a situation.

As an example, if you associated love with red, when your friend is talking about a specific person, and you are able to see the color red while she is talking about them, you will intuitively know that there is a loving connection between the two without your friend needing to express this directly.

Another practice is scanning a room so that you are able to get a feel for your current environment. This is done while you have positioned yourself in the center of a room which does not have other people there. You can choose to move around the energy of the space through the movement of your eyes to witness what is going on or you can physically move about the room. Take mental notes of the scents, sounds and sights that you are taking in. Ask yourself where you are being pulled to energetically and people and places that you feel like you should avoid. Be as detailed as possible by examining the furniture, windows and corners of this space and how they make you feel internally.

The more that you practice this exercise, you will be able to do this same practice in a room of people. This is a more intense version of the exercise, and may be intense the first time depending on your level of sensitivity. Listen to your body and cease if it should become too much. However, do not let these feelings of anxiousness divert you from developing your skills. There are going to be growing pains and tests along the way, but once you push through these feelings, great benefits await you on the other side.

You can also use this exercise in other places such as subways, offices, bars and parks. Being able to practice this technique in common areas that you frequent will help you to become more familiar with the energies of your surrounds and continue to solidify your relationship with your intuition.

Another exercise that you can practice is using the subconscious and your dreams. It is through your dreams that you are able to digest and absorb the energies that you come in contact with during the day that have not been particularly resolved. Since we are not able to live balanced and healthy lives by absorbing every instance that we

363

encounter in a single day, our psyche comes into play to help us to find that balance that is required for a functional and healthy lifestyle.

Through dream work, you are able to remove the constraints of this physical plane where you are able to effortlessly move throughout spaces and other planes. It is rather common to encounter spirits of other realms, travel into the future as well as the past or explore foreign lands. There is no limit to where you can go in the subconscious which makes it an endless pool of possibilities to discover.

To be able to get the most of the knowledge that you gain through your dreams, be sure to keep a journal and pen next to your bed. It is all too common that you forget these adventures and information gathered in the dream world. You can curb this tendency by creating a habit of writing down what you remember the moment that you wake. This way it is fresh in your mind. Even if you only remember one part of your dream, write it down. You may find that you are able to remember other parts of your dreams as you writing down the one part that you remembered upon waking.

This is a daily practice which can also be used throughout the day. Strengthening your intuition requires that you are mindful of the people you surround yourself with. Make sure that you trust the people who are in your inner circle and that they are positive minded. Eliminate energy vampires out of your life if at all possible. Notice your levels of intuition while you are around certain people. If it is being strengthen while interacting with them, spend more time with them whenever possible. Guard the strength of your intuition by steering away from people who drain you, especially as you are working on building your skill.

Test your intuitive skills with your close friends by asking them about specific tips and information in which you are receiving. This will help guide you to trust your intuitive skills more when they confirm that your feelings and sensitivities are correct. As you deepen your trust in your intuition, you will learn to rely on it more fully and in effect it will strengthen.

Now that you have the basis to help you out with your daily self-care measures, you will be more ready to take on the challenges of fortifying your intuitive skills. Let us explore the other ways that you can strengthen your personal talents.

Set Challenges for Yourself

Set personal goals for yourself to continue to push yourself to your limits. Think outside of the box and expand your personal talents. This does not have to include sensitive matters. Examples include learning a foreign language, taking up a new hobby or even learning how to play a musical instrument.

This will continue to broaden your horizons, help you to come in contact with different types of people and strengthen your body and mind. This is turn will help you with your intuitive talents as you will be utilizing them to learn new things. You will also be humbled as you continue to learn and hone your skills. When you are in a humbled state, you become more empathetic and grateful.

While you are in position of challenge, these are times where you will learn more about yourself and how you interact with the world around you. You will grow in ways that you would not have without the challenge in place and end up being grateful for the experiences.

Get out of Your Comfort Zone

When you are put into new situations, it makes you rely more on your intuitive skills to help you navigate through unknown areas. Travel is especially a great way in doing this. Not only will you learn about new places, but you will come in contact with different cultures than your own. This will help to broaden your ideas and thoughts.

It will also help you to understand more types of people which will come in handy as it will aid you in helping different kinds of people. Gratefulness for the uniqueness of people will arise. Your listening skills will also be honed as you learn more about the new places and people. When you are forced to see situations in a different light, it sparks your creativity to find a solution to situations. This may help to broaden your problem solving skills while learning about new things in the process.

This will force you as well to squash any fear of the unknown. This fear is debilitating and unfounded. It is simply that you do not know what to expect that you have fear about doing certain things. However, nine times out of ten after getting through new situations, you will be better for it, and that fear will no longer exist. The less fear you have, the more you are able to thrive with your psychic skills.

Walk in Other People's Shoes

When you are able to take yourself out of the situation, it will make you a better listener and hone your intuitive skills. This forces you to place yourself in their position while thinking about what you would do in those same situations given their circumstances.

Practicing this exercise has multi levels of understanding about people. First off, it will help you to see situations from different perspectives while you are learning about their experiences. Another benefit is that you will likely be less judgmental as you will have a deeper knowledge of this person and in turn others.

At the end of the day, you will realize that each person who walks this earth has problems. No one is exempt from this fact and many times there are problems which go on for quite some time be it from complication or ignoring the fact. This may help you also to feel more grateful for the problems that you have, and, perhaps, they are not as bad as you had thought before.

As an added bonus, walking in another's shoes helps you to become more patient. Sometimes talking about issues can be challenging or it may be a complex issue which is complicated to put into words. As this person is possibly mustering up the courage and know how to express their story, you will become patient as you try to understand better what they are going through.

Find your Kindred Spirits

Many times, psychic people may feel isolated from their family members or other people who they come in contact with daily. However, it is very likely that you will have another family member who has the same talents as you. They will be a great guide in asking for the methods that they use to strengthen their own intuitive skills. They can also help you along with issues that you are experiencing as they have most likely gone through the same situation or something similar.

Also, other people who are in a deeper connection with their intuition are able to sense each other. You will likely be drawn to many of them as they will be towards you. When you create a network of people who you can relate to, this not only makes you feel more secure in being an intuitive, but it gives you a support system which is much needed. You will be able to help each other to keep you on the straight and narrow as they will let you know if you seem off or give you techniques to strengthen your skills that had worked for them.

Analyze your Thoughts and Beliefs

Take a long hard look the basis for your beliefs and thoughts as these are going to create the environment within and without you. This includes anything that needs obvious attention such as recurring cycles of unlearned lessons as well as more hidden aspects of yourself. This is the time to be honest with yourself. Only then will you be able to deepen your relationship not only with yourself but with others around you.

When you have predetermined biases and beliefs which have no foundation, this direct affects how you deal with other people. Once these issues are faced head on, you will be able to help others on a more connected nature. It will also aid you in being able to be even more objective about situations.

If you are having issues with finding items which need attention, make a point to dig deeper. We all have biases whether they are based in gender, race or age. We are all unique creatures with special characteristics that we bring to the table. Take this opportunity to learn and to grow, and it will strengthen your empathy even further.

Take this opportunity to let go of negative thoughts, feelings and beliefs which are no longer serving you. Any sort of negativity is going to impede your attitude and growth. When you are harboring these negative thoughts, you are affecting your environment even down the neurochemical level which affects your organs, overall body, your mental attitude and bleeds into your outer environment.

Keep a Curious Mind

Remember when you were a child and you could not satiate your curiosity about everything? This is the mental attitude you need to continue to possess as you grow into adulthood. There is always something to learn. Once you think you know it all, you need to take a step back. Even for talents that you already possess, there is always something that can be perfected or learned about.

There are also other instances where this will come in handy when dealing with people from different walks of life. Perhaps you are dealing with someone who has an unfaltering view which you think is narrow. Or maybe you assume that your green co-worker certain has no knowledge about life. How are you so sure until you ask and dig deeper?

Everyone grows up in different situations and sees the world with a perspective in which you probably do not share. When you delve into learning about these curiosities within other people, you will also look at yourself in a new light. It will in turn help you to understand people better.

Deepen Your Understanding

The best way to understand people better is to ask better thought out questions. The questions which bring about the most interesting insights are intellectual or even provocative. When we talk about the issues in which most people do not bring up in daily interactions, we will learn more as well as see this person perhaps in a different light.

You can practice this with family members, clients or colleagues. Not only will these conversations strengthen your relationship with them, it will give you a broader insight into people from all walks of life. The key is to never think you are ever done with improving yourself or your intuitive skills.

Become more Aware of the Details

There is no doubt that when an intuitive becomes more in tune with the environment within themselves and around them that they are able to pick up on more cues which will aid in becoming even deeply connected. There are a few ways in which someone can foster this exercise.

Firstly, you can sit in a room by yourself. This can be a place that you frequent or a totally new place. Sit quietly without any distractions and take in all the details of the space. Even if you think you know every aspect of your familiar space, make a point to look for the less obvious things. This will train your eye to keep open to new occurrences or even shifts in energy.

Another way is to come up with a mental picture in your mind which is not complex. It can be as simple as a small colored dot or a shape which is in 2D. When first starting out, try to keep your mind focused on this object for at least fifteen seconds or longer if you are able. This will train your mind to not run through so many thoughts, to slow down and to also become more present in the moment.

As you are able to consistently keep this image in your mind for the fifteen second increment, start to add form to your shape, creating a 3D object. To further escalate the exercise, start to rotate the object in your mind's eye and add more detail. Once this accomplished, set your time limit to half a minute.

The point of this exercise is to train your eyes to extract more information from your world around you. After dedicated practice, you will be able to gather details extremely quickly which will assist you in reading people and environments. It may also help you in situations where you are going to need to think very fast.

Focus on your Emotions

You can practice this same idea while focusing on a certain emotion within your heart. This exercise will not even improve your intuitive abilities; it will continue to keep positive emotion in your heart throughout the day while building your institution.

With this technique, you need to feel a deep positive emotion such as affection, joy, kindness, appreciation or love. This emotion is going to consume you first through your whole heart and then vibrate through your mind and body. It will be more powerful if you associate a bright light with this emotion so that you can both visualize and feel this emotion reverberate throughout your body.

Just like the focus exercise, you want to hold this feeling for as long as possible without getting distracted. Put all your energy and focus into this exercise so that it is more impactful. Not only will it strengthen your energy from the inside out, it will develop your visualization skills.

This is also a skill that you will need to develop if you come in contact with energy vampires, narcissists or overall negative people. When this exercise is done around these people, they will likely be aware on the outside. However, you are putting up a barrier so that they are not able to siphon your energy from you.

Deepen Your Objectiveness

When you are objective, you are free of bias and look at all the details in front of you to make a decision or to counsel someone. When you are able to listen from multiple points of view, objectiveness will come to you naturally. To strengthen this skill, you will need to be in contact with people who have different views from your own. Even if they do not think the same way that you do, it does not necessarily mean that they are taking a negative stance. Even knowing the negative side will help you to understand the full spectrum of the situation.

If you have a strong belief about a certain issue such as motorcycle safety for instance, you need to speak to motorcyclists who do not believe in wearing helmets or full protective gear. They may have a different experience than you have which will help you to see the entire picture. This will also break down your judgments of people and help you understand and perceive emotions from different types of people other than who you may be comfortable with.

Listen to Inner Guidance

The best way to strengthen your intuition is to go to the source. Your intuition is that inner voice which is in all people. The sensitive empaths have a fast track to communicating with this inner voice. It is your intuition which has all the answers that you need about your personal growth and healing. This inner voice is always going to lead you to your highest good. It will never make you feel negative feelings and only has love and compassion for you.

The only way to tap into this higher level of intuition is to quiet your mind and clear out what you think you already know. This inner voice can only be heard clearly when all of this clutter is out of the way. This can be done through several methods to include:

- Simply being silent in a space which is also quiet

371

- Meditation

- Prayer or Mantras

- Connecting with Nature

When you practice one of the methods at least five minutes a day, you will start to tap into your institution more deeply. This may appear as an epiphany, memory, sound, image, hunch or gut feeling. Those who continue to practice may actually hear their inner voice. When any of these signs make themselves known, you need to acknowledge them. It may also be wise to jot them down in a notebook so that you can expand on this knowledge that you gain at a later time.

Pay Attention to Your Dreams

Dreams are a source of intuition, and they need to have attention paid to them. During REM sleep which occurs approximately every ninety minutes each time you sleep, this is the time that dreams are experienced. These dreams can be excellent guides to show us direction in career choices, relationship, and health among others. The trick is remembering them.

The best way to do this is to keep a dream notebook by your bed. The best time to write is the moment that you wake up because you will remember the most at this time. You may even remember more of the dream as you are writing. When you make a habit of writing down your dreams, this process will become a habit, and it will become much easier to recall the dreams.

If you need some insight on a particular issue, ask a question before going to sleep. Like usual, write down any dreams that you remember, even if it does not seem to answer your question. Each night, ask the same question until you get a more solid answer to your inquiry.

Write It Down

Many times it gets very confusing in an empath's mind, especially when there are many other people's emotions and feelings wrapped up in their own. When you utilize writing down these thoughts that run through your mind, you are able to start deciphering what you are actually feeling compared to the other emotions that you are experiencing.

Not only will this help to raise your awareness, it will also help you to realize when you are soaking up people's energies when you do not intend to. The moment that you start to feel something different than what is true to you personally, you can stop the flow of energy or excuse yourself from this person's presence if possible.

Psychic Skill Development

When you have strengthened your intuition, you will be able to efficiently practice your psychic skill development.

There are many different types of psychic abilities of which I will go over a few in detail. It is possible to have one or a combination of these skills, and to have different intensities of each skill that you can further develop if you wish.

The Basics of Telekinesis

The ability of telekinesis, also known as Psychokinesis, has a certain mysitcal air as you will see this abilitiy in frequently in a sci-fi or horror movie. This is the ability to move or manipulate objects solely with your mind. Psychokinesis is translated from Greek words for motion and mind.

When you view everything in this world and the other planes based in a vibration of energy, you will be more effective in honing your psychic abilities. Items that we see as solid matter are more dense energies where as pure energies that you see and feel are lighter energies with a higher vibration point. When you are using this perspective to work on your telekinesis skills, you will be able to perceive this energy on a personal level and, through practice, be able to manipulate it with the power of your mind.

A summary of the different components of telekinesis is as follows:

- ❖ Relaxation is required so that you are able to disconnect your body and mind from the every day things that you usually process. When you are able to accomplish this task, you will be in a state of consciousness that you are able to focus and expand upon your thought processes.
- ❖ Concentration is also a required element as it is ultimately your will that will help you to be successful at manipulating these energies.
- ❖ Meditation is a process which will help your mind to accomplish both relaxation and concentration as you practice any exercise to hone your psychic abilities.
- ❖ Gratitude is the final component which will help you to strengthen your connection to the energies outside of yourself. When you are able to demonstrate any of your psychic skills, it is due to the universe for giving you these capabilities, and respect needs to be paid to these energies.

While you are practicing the telekinesis exercises, or any of the psychic skill exercises, you need to have a firm belief that these are very real abilities. When this is in place, no matter the outcome of your exercises, you know that the result was meant to be at that time. You are not always going to be successful, and that is perfectly okay. You are only trying to get back into connection with who you are internally, and there is no wrong way of following this path.

As you continue to practice your psychic exercises and gain some control over them, there will be naysayers who are going to make it their mission that you are crazy for following this dream and that they do not exist. Acknowledge what they are saying, but fall back on your ultimate belief in what you are pursuing.

Recognize that we are all at different levels of development in this soul journey. There is no point in arguing over matters of opinion with a person who is not a master at these skills. Remember, society has molded us into holding these beliefs. If you believe differently, you have this right. At the end of the day, you need to live your life how you see fit, and many people before you have done these same practices with the same goal in mind. Keep an open mind during the exercises, and prepare yourself to be amazed.

Logically thinking about this skill is going to bring about visions of you sitting in your favorite and comfortable chair as you use the power of your mind to bring you everything that you wish. However, telekinesis does not work in this way. When you have mastered the art of telekinesis, you will be able to manipulate small objects.

You must think in terms of energy. It takes an extreme amount of concentration, dedication and practice to be able to strengthen this skill, just to make small amounts of changes. Because of this fact, you are not able to move larger items such as a car or an elephant because of the sheer amount of will power and energy that it requires.

Because of this fact, scientific studies have focused on small and mundane feats such as testing the ability versus probability of a pair of dice landing on a certain number or having an effect on a computerized random number generator. The tests also rely more on complicated analyses of statistics. That is to say, scientists are less interested if a person is able to knock a glass over or bend a spoon. Rather, they would rather test if a person is able to control a coin coming up on tails at a significantly higher percentage than 50%.

Exercises to Develop your Telekinesis

Even with scientific studies resulting in mixed conclusions, there are many people who work at perfecting this skill. While you are practicing these exercises, you must have no doubt in your mind, even on a subconscious level, that you are going to be able to perform telekinesis. You will need to couple your meditations with visualizing exercises.

When you have gotten to the point where you have your mind cleared, select a small and simple object in your surrounding environment and study it so that you are aware of its every detail. Pay special attention to the scent, how soft or hard the object is, color and shape.

After some time of perfecting your visualization skills, close your eyes and visualize your object with every detail you studied. Create a connection by focusing all of your attention to your visualization of this object. Start to make the object move in your visualization how you would like to have the object moved in the physical plane.

Then you will transfer this same energy and intention towards the object in the physical plane. This is best performed by looking at the space between you and the object, then you want to take this space away. Envision you and this object as one with no separation in between.

For the objects that you want to move, it is best to start with something simple such as a matchstick or a pencil. When you are able to successfully move these items, move up to more complicated items such as a glass or lighter.

Continue to practice daily until you start to see results while refining your abilities each time. Over time, hone your visualization skills by expanding the objects that you are envisioning. Step up the objects by complexity and details. After some time of practicing, you can visualize an entire room. The focus of your visualization practices should be getting the visions as detailed as possible.

A specialized meditation practice that you can use is to sit in a comfortable position. After taking a few regular breaths, breathe in deeply for a count of 4. Hold your breath for another count of 4. Then exhale through your mouth for 8 seconds.

After a series of 3 rounds of breath have been completed, let each thought that comes across transform into a sparkle in your field of visualization as you are breathing inwards and while you are holding your breath. As you exhale, allow those sparkles to become one as bright as the sun. Repeat this process as much as necessary until you are finished with your designated meditation time. This exercise will help with both your focus and your visualization skills.

You can also work with your skills by manipulating a candle flame. Light a candle and perform your meditation exercise. Gaze at the flame and let it take over your thoughts. Watch intently and take note when the flame flickers and moves. After your mind is solely concentrated on the flame, try to manipulate which way the flame is going to move with your focused energy.

First move the flame to the left and then to the right. Then try to make the flame grow larger, then make the flame brighter and finally work on having the flame diminish.

With the practice of any of these exercises, you need to stop when you are physically or mental drained. Taking regular breaks if you are extensively practicing is important. Take at least a few hours break if you become tired during these exercises. Make sure that you drink enough water and eat a small snack to keep your energy levels risen. Even if you need a longer break, do not go back to practicing until you are feeling revived in mind and body.

The Basics of Pyrokinesis

Fire is an element which has an underlying fearsome factor, but it is also well known to garnish an impactful amount of power. It was because of fire that the cavemen were able to rise in the food chain above the animals. Likewise, fire can cause a great deal of destruction and hurt. Being able to control the element of fire is the main concept of pyrokinesis.

Pyrokinesis is derived from the Greek word pyro, or fire, and kinesis which is movement. A person who hones this skill is able to manipulate as well as create fires simply by the power of their mind. They do not use any substances to be able to create these flames. Pyrokinesis is a subset of telekinesis because people who are adept at these two practices are able to manipulate the world around them.

As an example of the skill, you can light a stack of paperwork on the floor in the living room. A master at pyrokinesis is able to light this fire with their mind. They will also be able to control that fire so that it will only continue to burn the paper and nothing else or they can dictate the direction in which the fire is going to burn and cause the whole house to burn down if they wish.

There have been no scientific tests to prove the validity of pyrokinesis, but this practice has been practiced with a handful of martial arts practitioners. These masters are able to transform their chi energy so that the heat can be felt in the areas that they choose.

Episodes of spontaneous combustion have also been recorded as far back as 1763. This is where the body of a person catches on fire without any fuel to ignite the fire. This can result in the body smoking and well as the formation of blisters and burns. Others will catch on fire completely, and is seen surprisingly in older people more often. For the firefighters who are familiar with victims of fires, they know that the injuries sustained the typical markers of a fire victim is that their trunk is usually whole while the head and limbs are incarcerated.

However, for the spontaneous combustion cases, it is the opposite with the trunk of the body being nearly gone while the feet and hands remain. It is also a curious case because the flammable items around the body will be in tact with no signs of burning. This makes those who are familiar with spontaneous combustion cases that these fires started from within the truck of their body.

Even though spontaneous combustion is not directly linked to pyrokinesis, there are some striking conclusions which have been logically discussed. One is that these people could be the victims of a person practicing pyrokinetics. Other people believe that it is possible these people were practicing exercises of pyrokinesis and were not able to control the fire completely. It is thought that with this inability to control the fire that they turned it upon themselves which resulted in them spontaneously combusting themselves.

Exercises to Develop your Pyrokinesis

When you train, you will be able to control fire. After a long time of practice, you will be able to extinguish and reignite a flame. You will only be able to hone this skill with continuous practice, unwavering concentration and meditation. Because pyrokinesis can be quite dangerous for beginners, you must be extremely careful when practicing as you will have no control of the fire at first. This is the reason why in many cases training for pyrokinesis should only be done after mastering telekinesis skills.

1. Light a candle is a space which there are no movements of the air.
2. Gaze at the flame and concentrate your focus solely on the fire.
3. Create a connection in your mind between you and the flame.
4. Close your eyes and envision the flame as vivid and detailed as possible. Feel the energy of the flame within yourself.
5. Open your eyes and gaze at the flame once more.
6. Visualize in your mind the flame moving to the right. Do not be upset if this does not occur after many days or months of practicing this feat.
7. Do not strain yourself and your energy to move the flame. You need to flow with the energy of the flame.
8. Once you have successfully moved the flame to the right, manipulate it by making it move to the left and also getting larger.
9. When you are able to manipulate the flame with your willpower, start to practice extinguishing the flame. Take a break if you are straining and stressing your energy.
10. With this same concentration, envision that the flame is extinguished. This will likely take more time than you mastering manipulating the direction of the flame, so do not get discouraged.
11. Once you are able to extinguish the fire with your mind, try to reignite the flame. It is more simple if you are able to complete this quickly after the flame has been extinguished.

Another practice you can work with is known as the Dancing Flame.

1. Light a candle in a room with no air movement.
2. Gaze upon the flame as you visualize a tunnel between the flame and you.
3. Create a connection of the energy of the flame.

4. Once the energy is connected, imagine a sphere of white energy and send it towards the flame through the tunnel.
5. Now move the sphere in different directions around the candle – higher, lower or to the sides – to manipulate the flame.
6. After you are able to accomplish this manipulation of the flame, you can move forward to extinguishing the flame.
7. Place the white energy ball over the flame to remove the oxygen so that the flame will go out.
8. Remember to take breaks if you are stressing or straining your mind.

The Basics of Empathy

There are several steps that you can take to embrace and strengthen your personal empathic skills. Here there is going to be a comprehensive set of methods to learn more about different empathic skills, way to utilize them for the greatest benefit as well as ways to continue to build up these particular talents.

Every person has the capability of deepening their intuition and empathy levels where you are able to use these God given talents to help not only you, but more importantly the world as a whole. To do this, you must put on your battle face as you are going to be strengthening these attributes by having a strong spirit.

Self-care is the number one step in making sure that you are able to not only use these talents that you have been given, but to continue to work and grow with them. It is a hard process at times, but when has anything not worth having been handed to you on a platter? These methods will take hard work and dedication. You must keep your end goals in mind which will keep your spirit strong during the tough parts of the process so that you can enjoy the full benefits and be able to help others to the best of your ability.

Your self-care is something that comes before any one person or situation. How are you able to help others fully when you are only half energized and centered? These self-care practices will keep your being strong, centered and continue to thrive. When you implement self-care daily, you will become unstoppable as your energy will be reserved for times that you are needing it. It will not continue to be siphoned away by others who are wanting to feed off your energy. You will not take on emotions and feelings that you are not willing to take on. It makes you ever strong in the sensitive world of the empath.

The following are five methods which can be used on a daily basis to continue to build up your strong spirit so that you can then work on strengthening your other empathic skills:

Be Grateful and Express Gratefulness Whenever Possible

When you wake up, start your day on the correct foot by expressing gratitude. First off, there are many people who did not get the same privilege. At the very least, you should be grateful about you breathing, your health, and other blessings including family and being able to help others.

You can continue to find gratefulness in the difficult situations that you possess. These are the greatest things to be grateful for because they are in your life to teach you the most. When you can change your perspective on these "bad" things, it will lift you up even higher in your gratitude.

When you practice gratitude on a daily basis as part of your self-care, it makes you more self-aware, keeps you in the moment and builds positive energy. It also will keep you more energized as you will not be bleeding energy by imagining things that will happen in the future or wasting worry on things that have happened in the past.

You can also utilize this method throughout the day to continue building up the positive energy. Take the time to express your gratitude to the people who you come in contact with, your pets and your family members. You can extend this idea even to strangers who you can change their attitude with a simple smile. This also shows them appreciation in a subtle way. All of these little gestures add up and will continue to strengthen you throughout the day.

Love Yourself Fully

Recognize daily that you are unique individual that has a purpose in this world. You are a gift, and you are here to share and meld with the other gifts in this world. Consider coming up with a phrase or mantra which is special to you that will help you lift yourself up. If you are coming up with your own, try to incorporate all aspects of you in a short sentence which is powerful and impactful to your spirit and well being .

Other ways that you can love yourself is to listen to your body and adjust your day accordingly. Do not try to push yourself to the point where you are breaking when you are just waking up in the morning. Just like you need to stretch to warm up your body before exercise, you must allow yourself to wake up properly so that you are centered and focused on the tasks of the day.

Whatever makes you the happiest in your soul whether it is reading a certain book of inspiring quotes or drinking your favorite tea while watching the birds play out in your yard, take the time to nurture your spirit in the morning times, especially, even though this also can be applied throughout the day.

The properly love yourself, you must be quiet and listen to yourself so that you will know what your needs are. Once these needs are met, you will be able to be your full self to be able to share your healing energy with other people in a more impactful and helpful way.

Aware and Mindful Breathing

At some point during your morning routine, likely coupled with the meditation exercise, you need to empty your energy and spirit of any negativity and stress. This will not only help to calm your inner self, it will give you a sense of clarity and strengthen your energy throughout the day.

You are going to want to try to do this at the same time of the day and you can do this exercise at any time that you are feeling stress build up in your body. This will help you to keep your focus throughout the day as well. The morning exercise should be a minimum of ten minutes, but you can do whatever time length you feel comfortable as long as your stress and negativity is melted away.

The mindful breathing exercise is as follows:

1. Find a place in which you feel comfortable and shake the extremities of your body before you sit or lay down to help with the process of relaxation.
2. Breathe in deeply and long in through your nose while allowing your stomach to fill with air.
3. Hold the air for a few seconds.

4. Slowly let the air out through your mouth.

5. Do this practice for a minimum of three breaths before moving onto the next part of the exercise.

For the next section, you need to visualize a situation, place or phrase which brings you to a place of relaxation. Once you find this calm, continue on.

1. Close your eyes and continue to breath in through your nose.

2. As you are breathing, visualize the air you are breathing is full of calm and peace. Allow this feeling to immolate throughout your body.
3. Then breathe out slowly through your mouth while visualizing any tension   or stress in your body leaving with the breath.

4. Continue to breathe in and out using the visualizations for the remainder of your breathing exercise time, for a minimum of ten minutes.

5. Continue on to the meditation practice if you wish for your daily self-care.

Exercises to Develop your Empathy

The Basics of Astral Projection

This is a skill that can be perfected which will allow you to have an out of body experience or a state of consciousness which is altered. It is experienced when your spirit is able to physically leave your body so that you can travel through different dimensions. Your spirit is not entirely detached from your body as there is a silver cord similar to an umbilical cord which keep the two connected. This cord is not able to be detached except through death, so there is no possibility of this cord breaking while your spirit is out of your body.

There is not simply one experience that you have when you astral project. Some people says that you can experience sensations of floating or flying in the sky while you are able to look down upon the world. You can also experience the world as if you were standing in the room, yet no one would be able to see and interact with you. Lucid dreaming is a type of astral projection since you are conscious of your activities during the sleep state.

Exercises to Develop your Astral Travel Skills

Like all of the other physic abilities, you need to use meditation to keep your mind focused and quiet. You will need to remove any doubts that you are able to accomplish and hone this skill, as these doubts will surely keep you from experiencing an out of body experience. You need to ensure that the space that you choose to astral project from is a comfortable temperature. It is also important to make sure that you are not going to get hungry, but do not eat a large meal ahead of time, otherwise you will likely go to sleep.

1. Sit or lay in a spot where you will not be disturbed. All the muscles in your body to relax.

2. Take deep and slow breaths in through your nose and out through your mouth.

3. Concentrate your focus on creating a white light which will cover your entire body.

4. Once you envision your body is covered in white light, imagine that it is floating up slowly.

5. As you see your body rising, your spirit and body will separate in your mind, leaving the physical body where you first started. The spirit body is going to rise above the physical body.

6. Remove any fear or doubt in your mind. Choose a destination you would like to experience.

7. Once you have projected to another location and you want to return back, simply think of your physical body, and envision your spirit entering your physical body slowly.

Another method that you can use is known as The Rope

1. Envision yourself laying down with a rope laying on top of you.

2. Then imagine that you reach your hands out to the rope and start pulling yourself upwards.

3. Continue to pull upwards on the rope until you start to feel a vibration throughout your entire body.

4. As you continue to pull on the rope, you will start to feel the sensation of flying. This is when your spirit has separated from your physical body.

5. Let the rope go, and look downwards to see yourself lying down.

6. Return to your body by thinking of your spiritual body slowly entering your physical body once again.

One last technique was created by Muldoon, and it is known as his Thirst Technique. For this exercise, you need to refrain from drinking water throughout the entire day you want to practice. You will be using your want and need for water as an emotion which will drive you to bartering for an out of body experience.

1. Pour yourself a glass of water in a clear cup. Place it on a table in front of you.

2. Gaze at the glass of water as you imagine yourself drinking the water. Continue this practice for three hours.

3. Before you go to sleep, set the glass of water within a few feet of you and eat a pinch of salt. This will cause you to be craving water more.

4. As you lie in bed, continue to imagine yourself getting up out of bed and drinking the glass of water.

5. You will know this exercise is successful if you are able to astral project and drink the water in your spirit form.

The Risks and Benefits of Psychic Skills

There are some perks to being tapped and connected with your psychic skills. Once you start to delve deeper within this connection, you will realize that these benefits will touch on all areas of your life and bond you closer to yourself, your environment and those close to you.

It is important to note that these skills also come with their own responsibilities because if you use them for your personal benefit of an ill intention, they can quickly start to cause havoc in your life as well as others. An example of this would be someone who is able to see future events. Remember that the future is not static and is based upon possibilities. Refrain from telling people that something is sure to happen because their personal choices may change the outcome of your vision for their future.

You will start to see the world from a unique and different perspective. You will also have more clear insight into how to make decisions which will be for your greatest benefit and choosing the correct path for you. You will also feel more tapped in and find there is a natural flow of energy that takes you through life. You will be able to feel more at peace knowing that you have nothing truly to worry about because it is all part of a larger plan.

When you tap into these psychic energies, you need to be aware that they can come at a cost. They are meant to connect you to something much greater outside of yourself, but it must be respected. If you are wanting to strengthen these skills just to get personal gain, you are likely going to see a ripple effect of terrible things infiltrating your life and those surrounding you. Let me go over the main difficulties that you may face when you are learning about your skills and if you should use them for the wrong purpose.

There is a limit to the storage space of the energy within your system. While you are cultivating your skills, these energy levels will rise. Your body is able to adapt to these fluctuations in energy, and your space is going to grow over time. However, if you try to take on too many energies before your body adapts, it will result in overload of your system. You will simply will not be able to handle above and beyond the space that you body has dedicated to handling these energies.

The symptoms when you take on too much energy will be dizziness and headaches. You may feel like you have ADHD because you will lack the ability to focus, resulting in you loose your psychic skills temporarily. You may feel lost as you are swimming through the heightened amount of energy flowing through your body. If this should occur, consciously bring yourself down by grounding and centering yourself so that your energy will naturally neutralize. Take some time to nurture yourself by taking some alone time to revitalize your body.

In this same effect, you may be in the position where you are taking on too much information as you are developing your psychic skills. As you delve deeper into the process, you may come across information which may be an epiphany which your mind is not able to fully handle or comprehend at the moment. It may completely negative a firmly held belief you have had your entire life.

This is usually the case if you are working to build your psychic skills each day as a beginner. Be sure to listen to your body and your mind as you are going through this process. Do not push yourself if you should be feeling tired or hungry. If you are feel particularly stressed, take care of your physical self before you venture into your spiritual side.

If you are gifted with the vision of spirits, this may be an interesting and wanted experience, when it happens occasionally. However, the more that some people deepen their connection to the other side, they are able to see spirits all of the time as they mingle with living people. It may get to the point where you are not able to determine if they are spirits or living people, which can pose a problem.

If this should happen, be sure to talk to your other psychic friends to get support. They may also have some very good advice as to how to handle this. Grounding yourself on a daily basis will help this from occurring. Meditation is also very helpful to help continue to calm and focus your mind.

As you strengthen your intuitive and empathic skills, you may find that you are able to experience other people's pain and emotions. This can drive a person a bit mad if they are unaware that this wide range of symptoms and emotions that they are feeling are not actually their own. When you have other people's emotions mixed with your own, they can be conflicting, which makes you feel confused within yourself.

If you find that you are empathic in this way, make sure that you learn how to shield your energy from other people so that they are not able to meld with your own. Essentially you are building a protective bubble which cannot be penetrated. This will also help you in the case that other people are trying to drain you of your own energy.

Chapter 4

Root Chakra Reiki Meditation for Day One Through Three

Overview of the Mooladhara Chakra

Root or 1st Chakra

Associated with the earth element, the purpose of this chakra is to give a firm foundation, support, stability and safety. It is associated with the sciatic nerve, bones, legs, feet. It is the location of the energy of existence. It connects our energy to the material world as well as primal survival. The color which is connected with the root chakra is red.

When this chakra is clear and balanced, you will feel happy to be alive as well as worthy of your existence. However, when this chakra is in need of work because of it being blocked, our perspective changes. We feel entitled to occupy our space or we may feel a lack of love or value. This negative thinking leads us to resent our existence as well as compare ourselves with others.

As you work on balancing the mooladhara chakra, you will start to trust in the flow of prosperity in all forms in your life. You will also strengthen your overall wellbeing and health along with your sense of security. Exercises based on opening and charging the 1st chakra contains the pranic energy. It also is the place in which our hidden or darker sides of our nature are concealed, sometimes even from ourselves.

Responsibilities of the Root Chakra

It is extremely important to pay special attention to the 1st chakra because making sure that it is healed, cleared, opened and balanced is key for the other chakras to do the same. This is the energy center where all of your basic needs are addressed. The term *Muladhara* translates into *base* or *root support*. The main influences of the root chakra are the following:

- ❖ You confidence levels
- ❖ Your survival
- ❖ Your sense of security and safety
- ❖ Your drive for basic physical needs like rest, shelter and food
- ❖ Your feeling of being grounded

Imbalance Symptoms

A root chakra imbalance can easily throw your entire system out of order. When your base chakra is in alignment, you will feel an overall peace while also feeling comfortable with your life, relaxed and stable. However, when this chakra is misaligned or blocked, you will feel quite insecure as well as worried about your basic needs. It will also raise your anxiety and stress levels as you continue to worry. You may also have problems with one or a combination of the following:

- ❖ Feeling overwhelmed easily by bright lights, loud noises or crowds
  Major illness plague you such as depression,fibromyalgia, fatigue and chronic pain
- ❖ Overly care for people who are physically and mentally able.

- ❖ Heightened feeling of panic or being threatened which can lead to racing heart, hyperventilation and panic attacks.
- ❖ Overall feeling of uncertainty
- ❖ Lack of concentration due to preoccupation with worry.
- ❖ Cold extremities
- ❖ Low energy levels
- ❖ Sore lower back
- ❖ Pain in the legs
- ❖ Digestive upset
- ❖ Negativity towards yourself and other people
- ❖ An unhealthy relationship with food such as purging, binging or starving.
- ❖ Low self-confidence levels
- ❖ Extreme reliance on external feedback for validation

These imbalances and blockages can happen due to a singular event such as a conflict with a friend of family member, financial difficulties or losing a job suddenly.

Day 1 Root Chakra Physical Meditation

It is important to have your chakras straightened and centered before performing grounding and meditation practices. This ensures that your energy is flowing properly throughout your body and will bring the best benefit to your grounding and meditation exercises. **Be sure to perform this each day before you start your meditation practice.**

To center yourself, you will simply:

1. Stand up straight with your hands down by your side. You can stand against   a wall to ensure your body is straight. Alternatively, you can do this exercise while sitting down with your feet flat on the floor.

2. Visualize a line going from the top of your head down through your back   straight down to the ground.

You can now move onto the practice of grounding. It is a simple practice that can be done practically anywhere. It is best to do this outside where you are able to place your bare feet on the ground. However, the same principle can occur anywhere, even with shoes on. The point of this exercise is to make you feel more connected with the earth as well as being fully present in the moment within your body.

To ground yourself:

1. Stand outside on the dirt, grass or sit in a chair with your feet firmly planted on the ground.
2. Breathe deep through your mouth. As you are breathing in, visualize white light encompassing your body.
3. As you breathe out through your nose, direct the breath visually down through your feet.
4. Continue with this cycle of breathing until the sense of calmness overtakes   you again which usually takes a minimum of three breaths.

The follow through to the physical root chakra meditation:

1. While starting this mediation, breathe with intent while focusing your attention to the base of your spine, the location of the root chakra.
2. While standing in a comfortable position, make fists out of your hands and   hold them tight for two to three seconds.
3. Continue to clench your fists for five rounds.
4. Shake your hands to release the energy and allow them to become relaxed.
5. Then rub your hands together for several seconds until you feel them become warm and electrified.
6. Clap your hands together forcefully once the point has been reached that your hands are full of electric pulses.

7. Put one foot out in front of you while pointing your toes. Hold for a couple of seconds.
8. Move your foot up and down vertically to stretch out your ankles while   holding in both positions for a couple of seconds.
9. Repeat the last two steps with your other foot.
10. Set your hands on your knees and quickly rub your thighs up towards your hips and then back to your knees.
11. Repeat this step a few times or until heat is generated in your thighs.
12. Now stand straight with your hands resting by your side.
13. Raise one hand above your head as high as you can as you breath in through   your nose.
14. Then lower your hand slowly as you breath out through your mouth.
15. Repeat with your other hand and practice this for a few rounds.
16. Once complete, leave your arms loosely at your sides as you rest for a   moment.
17. During this rest period, intently pay attention to your energy levels in the root chakra as you mindfully breathe in and out.
18. Continue to release any negativity and stress in your 1st chakra with each breath out. Breathe in healing and positive energy.
19. Now take a walk in the park or in nature for a period that you set so that you can recharge and balance your first chakra.

Day 2 Root Chakra Mental Meditation

1. Sit on the floor in a cross legged or kneeling position. Alternatively you can sit in a chair with your feet flat on the floor.
2. Keep your shoulders, back and your spine straight.
3. Relax all your muscles, closing your eyes and take a few normal breaths.

393

4. Inhale deeply and fully through the nose. Pull the breath as far down into your body as you can. Exhale slowly through the mouth. Repeat for 3 breaths.

5. Then turn your focus to the area of the root chakra. Take note of any tightness in the area.

6. Envision a ball of red energy at your root chakra. Manipulate this ball in your mind so that it expands. Then start to see it spin.

7. As the red ball of energy grows, feel the sensation of your root chakra as it becomes relaxed and warm.

8. Once your 1st chakra feels warm, continue to meditate while feeling this sensation of warmth between five and ten minutes.

9. With every breathe in, see and believe that you are breathing in positive and healing energy. While you breathe out, envision you release the negative, stagnant and stale energy.

10. When you have completed, slowly open your eyes.

11. Rest in this space for a few minutes before trying to get up.

Day 3 Root Chakra Spiritual Meditation

Each chakra has what is known as a beej mantra which is a word from Sanskrit. Chanting these mantras create a specific sound and vibration which resonates with each chakra in a unique way, helping to clear and balance your energy centers as well as connecting you to the higher power outside of yourself.

1. Sit comfortably in a meditation posture which is comfortable for you. This can be on a yoga mat, cushion or a chair.

2. Close your eyes and take in three normal breaths, focusing on the flow of the air throughout your body.

3. Concentrate upon your root chakra as you envision red throughout your sight of vision.

4. Take note how the color makes you feel.

5. Place the tip of your tongue on the back section of the upper palate on the roof of your mouth.

6. Focus the red into a sphere at the base of your spine.

7. As you breathe in, focus your concentration on the sphere.
8. Chant the sound "loom" for each slow release of breath as you envision the red sphere vibrating.
9. With each breathe, see the sphere getting larger and more vibrant.
10. Continue chanting between three and five minutes as you continue to concentrate on the root chakra sensations.
11. As you breathe in, fill yourself with positive energies. Allow the breath as it exits your body to take away any of the blockages and tension that you feel.
12. When the exercise is complete, slowly open your eyes and take your time moving when you are comfortable to do so.

Chapter 5

Sacral Chakra Reiki Meditation Day Four Through Six

Overview of the Svadhisthana Chakra - Sacral or 2nd Chakra

The sacral chakra is associated with the element of water. The purpose is to allow pleasure, emotional wellbeing, expansion, flow and movement. The areas of the body which are connected with this chakra are the joints, inner thighs, sex organs, lower abdomen, sacrum and hips. The color of orange is associated with the sacral chakra. It is also responsible for helping us to trust our sensation. As we are drawn to the things that make us feel good, this chakra is starting to open up. When we trust our instincts, we are able to surrender to our highest consciousness and allow nature to work her creative force through us.

When this chakra is blocked, which means the pranic energy is not able to freely flow, we no longer have the trust as we have lost the connection to our intuition and source of our feelings. As we are separated from our higher power, we start to feel negativity, lethargy and depression. If you are a person who must be in control of their lives, it is usually because the 2nd chakra is out of balance as you feel as if everything is out of control. The truth is, you must accept that much of everything is out of your control. Only when this thought of control is surrendered will you feel more at peace.

Responsibilities of the Sacral Chakra

The 2nd chakra is related to anything to do with creation and creativity. It also has an association to personal growth, imagination and sex drive. It is located in the middle of the abdomen about two inches below the belly button. It influences your feeling of:

❖ Feedback of artistic pursuits
❖ Your confidence level in what you create
❖ Pleasure you feel in life
❖ Satisfaction in romantic relationship
❖ Ability to be playful with others
❖ Inspiration level you experience

Imbalance Symptoms

When this chakra is open, you have an overall feeling of being stimulated as well being full of ideas. You will also feel heightened confidence to proceed with significant changes in your lifestyle. However, when this chakra is out of balance, your life will feel stifling, repetitive and boring. Your sacral chakra can become quickly closed if you have any negative feedback about sexuality or creativity. Other common symptoms are:

❖ Losing sleep while worrying too much or heightened anxiety level
❖ Suffer from passive aggressiveness and resentfulness when others only take from them
❖ Isolating themselves from other people and normal activities
❖ Becoming addicted to substances such as alcohol, medications or illegal drugs
❖ Lack of creativity
❖ Cyclical dysfunctional relationships
❖ Lack of motivation

397

- ❖ Diminished sexual appetite or unpleasant sexual intercourse
- ❖ Emotional confusion
- ❖ You feel unimportant and thinks that no one loves you
- ❖ You cannot take care of yourself or you feel you do not know how
- ❖ You tend to hang your shoulders bent forward
- ❖ Easily offended
- ❖ Fear of change
- ❖ Massive amounts of guilt about the past
- ❖ Low self-worth
- ❖ Frequent bouts of jealousy
- ❖ Heightened issues with allergy symptoms
- ❖ Bladder discomfort
- ❖ Low energy
- ❖ Gambling, shopping addiction and eating issues

Some common causes of these symptoms are based on associations with sexuality, creativity and change. You may find that you have sexual incompatibility in a relationship, rejection of your creative words, reproductive issues or rejection from a crush or love.

This chakra is associated with water which means that any activities in body of water will help balance the energy. If you are not around any sources of water, a long and soothing bath will do the trick as well. When you eat foods which are orange such as mangoes, melons, oranges or carrots, you will clear this chakra.

Day 4 Sacral Chakra Physical Meditation

To enhance this meditation, you can perform it by a body of water such as a lake, river or ocean. If these are not available and you would like to incorporate this idea into your meditation, you can also draw a bath.

1. Sit comfortably in a meditation posture which is comfortable for you. This can be on a yoga mat, cushion or a chair.
2. Close your eyes and take in three normal breaths, inhaling through your nose and breathing out through your mouth.
3. Envision a stream of light shining down on the top of your head and having the light flow through your body all the way to your toes.
4. This light is going to wash away any tension that is present in your body as you allow your muscles to loosen and relax.
5. Now imagine that light slowing moving up your legs up to your waist. Pause it there for a short time, as you feel comfortable.
6. Then push this light up to your chest and covering your shoulders and back.
7. Allow this light to flow down your arms to the tips of your fingers.
8. Push this light up your neck, throat, face up to the top of your head.
9. Sit while focusing on your breathing as well as the sensations that are felt throughout your body for a minimum of 10 minutes.
10. When you are ready, slowly open your eyes and take note of your quality of your mind afterwards. Make an intention to keep your mind in this space throughout the day.

Day 5 Sacral Chakra Mental Meditation

1. Sit in a comfortable and quiet place. Keep your back and neck straight with your limbs relaxed.
2. Take ten slow, deep breaths in through your nose and out through your mouth.
3. Envision a spinning orange sphere at your sacral chakra.
4. Imagine the orange light rippling outwards until it covers your entire body.
5. Feel the sensation that your body is warming up.

6. Continue to focus on your breath and keep feeling this orange energy for a minimum of five minutes.
7. When you are ready, slowly open your eyes and take your time getting back up on your feet.
8. Do this for as long as you like (preferably for at least five minutes), then open your eyes when you're ready.

Day 6 Sacral Chakra Spiritual Meditation

1. Sit comfortably in a meditation posture which is comfortable for you. This can be on a yoga mat, cushion or a chair.
2. Close your eyes and take in three normal breaths, focusing on the flow of the air throughout your body.
3. Concentrate upon your sacral chakra as you envision orange throughout your sight of vision.
4. Take note how the color makes you feel as your body starts to warm up.
5. Place your upper set of teeth on the inner section of your lower lip.
6. In this position, you will sound similar to a car revving up when you breath out.
7. Focus on the orange sphere, as you breathe in. Focus your concentration on the sphere.
8. Chant the sound "vahm" for each slow release of breath as you envision the red sphere vibrating.
9. With each breathe, see the sphere getting larger and more vibrant.
10. Continue chanting between three and five minutes as you continue to concentrate on the 2nd chakra sensations.
11. As you breathe in, fill yourself with positive energies. Allow the breath as it exits your body to take away any of the blockages and tension that you feel.
12. When the exercise is complete, slowly open your eyes and take your time moving when you are comfortable to do so.

Chapter 6

Solar Plexus Chakra Reiki Meditation Day Seven Through Nine

Overview of the Manipura Chakra - Solar Plexus or 3rd Chakra

T his chakra is associated with fire and has the purpose of change, transformation, willpower, strength and energy. The ribs, adrenal glands, digestive organs and upper abdomen are associated with the 3rd chakra. When there are any issues with these parts of the body, this chakra is in need of attention and energetic cleansing. The navel was where everyone was once connected to their mothers through the umbilical cord. Of course we relied in this cord for our connection and nutrients from our mother. Even after the umbilical cord is cut, this connection will always be present in the navel.

On an energetic level, this chakra holds the power and consciousness of our spiritual selves. As the prana flows through our manipura chakra, is gives the sustained energy the same as the sunshine. This is why the color yellow is associated with this chakra. It also gives us the capability of manifesting with confidence on this plane.

In the case of Kundalini awakening, the 3rd chakra is where the true awakening happens as this is the location where the internal fire is ignited and sent through to the other chakras. It is also the seat of our gut instinct as we feel if something is off in this chakra. These messages are extremely important to listen to as this is the connection to our internal guidance system.

If this chakra is out of balance, you will feel uncertain about your choices as well as your day-to-day decisions. As you work on opening and clearing the navel chakra, you will feel a sense of balance and you will be more sensitive to the messages from your gut instinct. Once you start to practice listening, you will be able to feel as if you are in the correct flow with the universe.

Responsibilities of the Solar Plexus

The 3rd chakra is in direct alignment with your ability to cultivate your skill and make the best decisions because you will be able to see the bigger picture of a situation. You will also experience heightened confidence and self-esteem levels. It is located in the stomach area at the top of your abdomen and is commonly known as the personal power chakra. The solar plexus is responsible for the following:

- ❖ How you define your purpose
- ❖ Your level of independence
- ❖ If you learn lessons from difficult situations
- ❖ Self-discipline levels
- ❖ Your ability for self-forgiveness
- ❖ Whether you envision yourself as being good enough
- ❖ Your response to criticism from others.

Imbalance Symptoms

With the 3rd chakra in balance you will be certain of the steps needed to succeed, you are sure of your identity and are self-assured. When this chakra is out of balance, you will find that you will have difficulty with sudden changes or moving from your past mistakes. You are also able to have an oversensitive chakra when out of alignment which may lead to anxiety issues or mania. Symptoms you may experience when the solar plexus is not open are:

- ❖ Not exercising personal boundaries or standing up for themselves
- ❖ Attracting energy vampires and negative people
- ❖ Cannot let things go and soak up toxic and negative energy
- ❖ Low self-esteem levels
- ❖ Lack of direction or purpose
- ❖ Feeling helpless
- ❖ Feeling the need to control everyone and everything around you
- ❖ Feelings of worthlessness
- ❖ Nausea
- ❖ Bloating
- ❖ Short-term memory issues
- ❖ Digestive cramps

The element for this chakra is fire. Create a bonfire and sit around it while basking in the fire. Alternatively, sit in the bright afternoon sunshine for at least twenty minutes. Changes in the diet should include yellow foods such as corn, pineapple, turmeric, ginger and bananas.

The element for this chakra is fire. Create a bonfire and sit around it while basking in the fire. Alternatively, sit in the bright afternoon sunshine for at least twenty minutes. Changes in the diet should include yellow foods such as corn, pineapple, turmeric, ginger and bananas.

Day 7 Solar Plexus Chakra Physical Meditation

1. Sit in a comfortable position and take note about your mental and physical state.
2. Take a few deep breaths while inhaling through your nose and exhaling through your mouth.
3. As you exhale, release the tension and pressure within your body and mind.
4. If there are any tense areas of your body, focus you attention by relaxing them on each exhale.
5. Envision a place in your mind where you are completely calm and at ease.
6. Be detailed about your picture of your happy place with all of the smells, sounds and sights you can experience.
7. Continue to breathe slowly and deeply as you continue to envision and enjoy this space you have created for a minimum of five minutes.
8. Create a space where all of your dreams and aspirations are true for you. Take note of how this space makes you feel as you build yourself higher.
9. When you are ready, slowly open your eyes and reflect on your feelings towards yourself.
10. Take your time getting back up on your feet.

Day 8 Solar Plexus Chakra Mental Meditation

1. Sit in a comfortable spot where you will not be disturbed.
2. Take in a few deep and long breaths in through your nose and out through your mouth as you clear your mind.
3. Focus your attention on your solar plexus chakra.
4. Envision a sphere of yellow at the center of your chakra. Take the time to grow the sphere in size and intensity.
5. Manipulate the sphere to spin as it is growing. You will find that your body is going to grow warm during this process.
6. Sit in this space while controlling your breath between three to five minutes.

404

7. Take notice of how the energy makes your body feel inside and out.
8. When you are ready to open your eyes, take three additional deep breaths before doing so.

Day 9 Solar Plexus Chakra Spiritual Meditation

1. Sit comfortably in a meditation posture which is comfortable for you. This can be on a yoga mat, cushion or a chair.
2. Close your eyes and take in three normal breaths, focusing on the flow of the air throughout your body.
3. Concentrate your attention of the lower middle section of your back. Envision yellow throughout your sight of vision.
4. Take note how the color makes you feel.
5. Place the tip of your tongue on the front section of the upper palate near your teeth on the roof of your mouth.
6. Focus the yellow into a sphere at the spine where you have focused concentration.
7. As you breathe in, focus your concentration on the sphere.
8. Chant the sound "rrahm" by rolling the "r"for each slow release of breath as you envision the yellow sphere vibrating.
9. With each breathe, see the sphere getting larger and more vibrant.
10. Continue chanting between three and five minutes as you continue to concentrate on the root chakra sensations.
11. As you breathe in, fill yourself with positive energies. Allow the breath as it exits your body to take away any of the blockages and tension that you feel.
12. When the exercise is complete, slowly open your eyes and take your time moving when you are comfortable to do so.

Chapter 7

Heart Chakra Reiki Meditation Day Ten Through Twelve

Overview of the Anahata Chakra - Heart or 4th Chakra

The air is associated with the heart chakra. It is commonly known to have the purpose of union, connection, relationships, expansion and love. The parts of the body that are associated with the 4th chakra are the shoulder blades, respiratory system, heart, ribs, diaphragm, lungs and chest. This is an important chakra to have cleared and energized as it helps you to relate to others outside of yourself.

The color which is connected with this chakra is green and it is the most powerful chakra center in the human body. When Kundalini energy is released from the navel to the heart chakra, it brings a cascade of spiritual, emotional and physiological changes. We are able to resonate with the truth of our feelings when this occurs as the heart has the capability of transcending everything.

When we are doing anything based in emotions, they are based in the heart chakra. It could be a memory, vulnerability or even when we are speaking to others in a heartfelt way. It is through the 4th chakra that we are able to inspire other people. When this chakra has been activated, it is not solely depending on outside sources. In fact, internally you need to experience empathy which is self-sustaining and deep to fully connect with yourself and others.

When the anahata chakra is out of balance, you do not pay attention and ignore your own needs. You may also start to cling to others and become codependent for the support that you require rather than giving that support to yourself. Of course when you start to clear and charge this chakra, you will become more compassionate and giving to yourself and others.

The heart chakra is positioned directly above the heart. So, slightly to the left at the center of your chest. Sometimes called the Anahata, it both responds to and helps to shape your capacity for compassion, affection, and love.

Responsibilities of the Heart Chakra

The 4th chakra is located in the middle of your chest next to your chest. It is a type of bridge between your spirituality, emotions and thought. You heart chakra has a connection with:

- ❖ How much peace you feel
- ❖ Your capacity to self-reflect
- ❖ Knowledge of self
- ❖ Emotional openness
- ❖ Intensity that you are able to care about others
- ❖ Your level of empathy

Imbalance Symptoms

When your heart chakra is balanced, you are a giving and compassionate person who is also calm and loving. This is directed towards yourself and others, and you keep boundaries well for your own well-being. When it is not open, you are going to feel emotionally hurt for anything that does not happen your way. It can also quickly drain your emotional resources. Other symptoms include:

❖ Putting other people's needs first and showing codependent tendencies
❖ Staying in an abusive or negative relationship
❖ Attract bullies and narcissist personalities lack of empathy
❖ Irritability or impatience
❖ Difficulty in trusting other people
❖ Restlessness
❖ A decrease in the effectiveness of the immune system
❖ Raised or high blood pressure
❖ Insomnia
❖ Struggle to relate to others

Toxic and difficult romantic and non-romantic relationships can quickly close off the heart chakra. You might be dealing with an intense amount of emotions that you do not know how to deal with, loss or grief, cutting ties with someone or a lover who does not reciprocate. You can also be having a hard time accepting a specific truth about yourself.

The air is associated with the heart chakra. Deep breathing exercises will eliminate the blocked energy. You could also take a boat ride, fly a kite or open the windows of your home, office or car. Green foods will clear this chakra. Examples include spinach, kale, avocado and broccoli.

Day 10 Heart Chakra Physical Meditation

1. Sit on a cushion or a chair with your feet flat on the ground. Relax your muscles as you take a few deep and long breaths. Breathe in through your nose and out through your mouth smoothly.

2. Close your eyes slowly and envision a flame within your heart chakra as you continue with your smooth and long breaths.

3. Keep the flame burning steady. You will notice that any distractions to your thoughts or otherwise is going to cause the flame to flicker and waver.

4. Keep this meditation and concentration on keeping the flame constant for a minimum of ten minutes, but no more than half an hour.

5. When you are ready, slowly open your eyes and continue to breathe steadily until you are ready to stand up.

Day 11 Heart Chakra Mental Meditation

1. Sit in a comfortable, relaxing place where you will not be disturbed.

2. Breathe in through your nose and out through your mouth for three minutes. Continue to relax your muscles as you breathe.

3. Envision green energy flowing up through your body towards the heart starting at the 1st chakra.

4. Picture the green energy creating a sphere at your heart chakra. As you inhale and exhale, see that ball becoming larger and more vibrant.

5. Focus on tuning into feelings of love for yourself and others as you allow the green energy to permeate your whole body.

6. Continue this meditation between three and five minutes.

7. Carefully open your eyes slowly and take your time getting back to your feet.

Day 12 Heart Chakra Spiritual Meditation

1. Sit comfortably in a meditation posture which is comfortable for you. This can be on a yoga mat, cushion or a chair.

2. Close your eyes and take in three normal breaths, focusing on the flow of the air throughout your body.

3. Concentrate upon your heart chakra as you envision green throughout your sight of vision.
4. Take note how the color makes you feel.
5. Focus the green into a sphere on your spine behind your heart chakra.
6. As you breathe in through your mouth, chant the sound "yum" as the air fills your mouth and throat.
7. With each breathe, see the sphere getting larger and more vibrant.
8. Continue chanting for a minimum of 10 minutes up to half an hour as you continue to concentrate on the heart chakra sensations.
9. As you breathe in, fill yourself with positive energies. Allow the breath as it exits your body to take away any of the blockages and tension that you feel.
10. When the exercise is complete, slowly open your eyes and take your time moving when you are comfortable to do so.

Chapter 8

Throat Chakra Reiki Meditation Day Thirteen Through Fifteen

Overview of the Vishuddha Chakra - Throat or 5th Chakra

The element of sound is associated with the throat chakra where refinement, purification and communication is the purpose. The body parts which are associated with the 5th chakra are the ears, mouth, tongue, throat, neck and shoulders. If there is any sort of imbalance with these areas of your body, you are in need of clearing and charging of the vishuddha chakra.

Because the 5th chakra corresponds to the throat, it is the energy center in which we are able to speak with our authentic voice. It is where choices turn into actions and allows us to make focused choice on how we want to communicate with others. The color which is used with this chakra is blue. It is where our true self originate as we express who we are with the outside world.

When you realize that this chakra is not receiving pranic energy, you will have expressing emotions or true thoughts. You will put out a kind face to the world and try to be polite at all times when in truth it is not resonating with how you feel in your heart. This is a form of denying your truth which is what causes the blockages in this chakra. When you start to work on opening the throat chakra, you will be able to express your true feelings and thoughts without fear in a loving way.

If everything in your life is going well, all of these chakras will be aligned and in harmony. You'll be happy, healthy and at peace. In contrast, a blockage in one or more of the chakras can make you feel profoundly unsettled.

Responsibilities of the Throat Chakra

The throat chakra is located in the middle of your throat and is connected to your communication and self-expression skills. It will have an impact on:

❖ Awareness of your needs
❖ Your capability to be heard
❖ The quality of your relationships
❖ How you react to confrontation or conflict
❖ If you live your life authentically
❖ Your emotional honesty

Imbalance Symptoms

When this 5th chakra is open, you will be able to communicate clearly and be able to express any of your views with tact. You will have an understanding of what you need and be able to put your words across in ways that people will want to listen. When the throat chakra is out of balance, you will find that you feel that people do not listen to you and you will have difficulty communicating with others.

❖ Unable to stop listening to someone who is venting or spouting off   with   negativity Listening to people's problems even when it is inconvenient
❖ Feeling like people do not know the real you
❖ Feel like you have many secrets
❖ Lacking the words to describe your emotions

❖ An achy or stiff neck

❖ Drastic changes in hormone levels

❖ Sore throat

If you are having problems with the throat chakra closing, try not to be so hard on yourself. You may have past experiences where it was painful to communicate such as a harsh argument that has stuck with you. You could also have difficulty with opening this chakra is you were told as a child to keep your feelings to yourself.

Ether is the element for the throat chakra. Sitting in a space where you can enjoy the clear sky will remove the blocked energy. Alternatively, eat blue foods such as dragon fruit, currants and blueberries.

Day 13 Throat Chakra Physical Meditation

1. Sit in a comfortable position on a yoga mat, cushion or chair. Place your feet flat on the floor if you are sitting in a chair.
2. Close your eyes and breathe in three smooth and deep breaths in through your nose and out through your mouth.
3. Focus your concentration on your breathing and the flow throughout your body.
4. As you exhale, pay special attention to the sound of the breath entering and exiting your body.
5. Continue your focus on your breath between three to five minutes, noting the sensations of the air in the throat.
6. When you have completed your allotted time, slowly open your eyes and get up slowly to your feet.

Day 14 Throat Chakra Mental Meditation

1. Sit down in a comfortable chair with a straight back in a place you will not be disturbed.

2. Inhale and exhale ten times smooth and deep. Breathe in through your nose and exhale through your mouth.
3. Starting at the top of your head, mentally scan down the body and imagine your muscles relaxing as pass your body over.
4. When your muscles are relaxed, envision a spinning, vibrant blue ball at your throat chakra.
5. Imagine the sphere is growing larger and brighter.
6. As it grows, imagine your throat chakra expanding and clearing at the same time.
7. Allow the blue energy to take over the energy of all your body.
8. Sit with this energy, continuing to focus on your breath between three and five minutes.
9. When you are done, slowly open your eyes and take your time getting back to your feet.

Day 15 Throat Chakra Spiritual Meditation

1. Sit comfortably in a meditation posture which is comfortable for you. This can be on a yoga mat, cushion or a chair.
2. Close your eyes and take in three normal breaths, focusing on the flow of the air throughout your body.
3. Concentrate upon the spine at your neck as you envision blue throughout your sight of vision.
4. Take note how the color makes you feel.
5. Focus the blue into a sphere at your throat chakra at the spine.
6. As you breathe in, focus your concentration on the sphere as you say "hum" pronounced like humming.
7. Release the breath as you envision the blue sphere vibrating as the air passes through your throat.
8. With each breathe, see the sphere getting larger and more vibrant.
9. Continue chanting between three and five minutes as you continue to concentrate on the throat chakra vibrations.

10. As you breathe in, fill yourself with positive energies. Allow the breath as it exits your body to take away any of the blockages and tension that you feel.
11. When the exercise is complete, slowly open your eyes and take your time moving when you are comfortable to do so.

Chapter 9

The Third Eye Reiki Meditation Day Sixteen Through Eighteen

Overview of the Ajna Chakra - Third Eye or 6th Chakra

The 6th chakra is associated with the element of light and gives the person imagination, vision, wisdom, guidance and insight when it is clear and charged. The pineal gland, forehead and eyes are associated with the third eye chakra. It is where our sixth sense and intuition reside and is associated with the color of indigo.

The ajna chakra is the seat of the hormones for wakefulness and sleep are released as the area between your eyebrows is sensitive to the light of day and the absence of light in the darkness. When you continue to work with the 6th chakra, you will become more empathic and sensitive towards the feelings of others and also the universe.

Continued work to clear and charge this chakra will also the Kundalini Shakti to open and close your third eye to give you insight into situations as needed. When it is balanced, you will know all the answers that you need to know when you need to know them. There is no need to search outwardly for answers. You will simply know intuitively as you will trust your higher consciousness fully. However, if this chakra is not balanced, you will have a difficult time of making decisions which are clear and to your highest benefit.

Ranging from the root chakra at the bottom of the spine to the crown chakra at the top of the head, all seven chakras are powerful energy centers.

The aim is to use chakra exercises to keep all these energy centers open and balanced. If you can achieve this, you'll be better able to fulfill your full potential and live a happy life. In contrast, the more chakras are blocked or misaligned, the more you'll sense something is wrong.

Responsibilities of the Third Eye Chakra

Your third eye chakra is situated between your eyebrows and is your direct connection to your spirituality. It has an affect on the following:

- ❖ Your feeling of being stuck, stagnant or moving forward
- ❖ Your balance between reason and emotion
- ❖ Your ability to see the bigger picture of life

- ❖ Your capability to form accurate gut feelings

Imbalance Symptoms

With your 6th chakra in balance, you will be able to make big decisions based on a balance of logic and emotions. You will have a solid trust in your intuition and know that you are living your purpose in life. Because you trust your intuition, you will naturally flow towards opportunities which are right for you and to your highest purpose. You will also be more mindful about yourself and the world around you. When the third eye is closed, you will doubt your intuition or the existence of it which will make you question everything. Other common symptoms include:

- ❖ Feel as if the weight of the world is on their shoulders alone and feel responsible
- ❖ Mood swings due to taking on other people's moods
- ❖ Paranoia
- ❖ Believing that your life or career is insignificant
- ❖ General indecisiveness
- ❖ Lack of faith within yourself or your purpose
- ❖ Sinus pain
- ❖ Leg and back pain
- ❖ Eye discomfort
- ❖ Migraines or headaches
- ❖ Trouble sleeping or insomnia
- ❖ Struggle to learn new concepts
- ❖ Clumsy
- ❖ Cynicism
- ❖ Overly logical or emotional
- ❖ Often lost in your thoughts
- ❖ Frequently escape into daydreaming to avoid reality
- ❖ Addicted to external things such as shopping, status, money, sex, food or relationships which you believe will bring you happiness
- ❖ Interactions with other people are very trivial or superficial
- ❖ Mistrust or dislike people easily
- ❖ Stubbornness
- ❖ Suffer from delusions or mental illness

You may find that your chakra becomes closed after someone belittles your passion or career. Also instances of transitions in life such as divorce, job loss, death or illness will cause a misalignment.

This chakra is coupled with light. To heal this chakra, sit in a sunny window or in the direct sunlight. Indigo foods such as blackberries, grapes and purple kale will help as well.

Day 16 Third Eye Chakra Physical Meditation

1. Go outside in a place you will not be disturbed where you are able to see the moon clearly.
2. Sit down in a comfortable position and take a few deep and long breaths. Breathe in through the nose and out through your mouth.
3. Relax the muscles in your body and sink into the earth.
4. Gaze upon the moon for as long as possible without blinking your eyes. As you gaze, envision the moon as an experience occurring within you.
5. Become one with the energy of the moon as you feel it reverberating within you.
6. Once this occurs, close your eyes slowly and focus your eyes upwards to the third eye. You should still see an image of the moon. If not, take in 5 long and deep breaths and focus on the movement of air in your body.
7. When the image of the moon disappears from your mind's eye, open your eyes once again to gaze upon the moon.
8. This is one round. Keep repeating as many times as necessary to practice this exercise for a minimum of 15 minutes until you are feeling too much strain in your eyes.

Day 17 Third Eye Chakra Mental Meditation

1. Sit comfortably and close your eyes. Inhale and exhale ten times, slowly and deeply.
2. Focus your attention on the location of the third eye chakra, imagine a violet sphere of energy in the middle of your forehead. Remember, purple is the third eye chakra's color.
3. As you continue to breathe slowly and deeply, picture the purple ball of energy getting bigger and warmer. As it does, imagine it purging negativity from your body.
4. Think of yourself of absorbing the third eye chakra's energy— allow yourself to feel it all over.
5. Open your eyes when you feel ready.

Day 18 Third Eye Chakra Spiritual Meditation

1. Sit comfortably in a meditation posture which is comfortable for you. This can be on a yoga mat, cushion or a chair.
2. Close your eyes and take in three normal breaths, focusing on the flow of the air throughout your body.
3. Envision a white colored disk of energy rotating slowly at the top of your head.
4. Imagine a violet ray of light reaching up to the sky.
5. Then envision an additional violet beam coming from the sky to your white disk.
6. Allow this violet beam to flow downwards through each chakra down to the muladhara and into the earth.
7. Concentrate upon the light and let it envelop your entire body.
8. Chant "Shaam" as you are exhaling.
9. Meditate on this energy for 20 minutes.
10. When you are done, slowly open your eyes and take your time getting back to your feet.

Chapter 10

Crown Chakra Reiki Meditation Day Nineteen Through Twenty-one

Overview of the Sahasrara Chakra - Crown or 7th Chakra

The crown chakra is located at the very top of the head and encompasses the elements of all of the chakras. It is associated with spirituality, communication with the Divine, union, ideas, awareness, thought, consciousness and nothingness which includes everything. The part of the body which are affected by the 7th chakra are the nervous system, brain and head.

Since the sahasrara chakra is where Kundalini Shakti reunites with infinite wisdom, it is the last element in completing your Kundalini awakening. When the prana and Kundalini flow through to your 7th chakra, there is a blossoming of your consciousness. The color of this chakra is violet and leads to love-infused prana. As this energy is flowing, the pineal gland is further activated which leads to a vibrating feeling at the top of the head.

When this chakra is open, clear and balanced, Kundalini Shakti is able to freely flow and you will be connected to the divine source within you. It is the final step of the process. However, you will need to continue to work on keeping your chakras clear and charged to allow this prana to continuously flow. However, for this state of being, it is rather difficult to keep up with daily tasks in the West as we know it.

Responsibilities of the Crown Chakra

The 7th chakra is located at the top of your head, which is why it is known also as the crown chakra. It is your source of spiritual connectivity and has an influence on the following:

- ❖ Self-worth
- ❖ Capability of finding peace
- ❖ Restful sleep
- ❖ Motivation to reach goals
- ❖ Excitement levels
- ❖ The level of beauty you see in the world around you.

Imbalance Symptoms

When your crown chakra is in alignment, you will experience a high level of pleasure in life. You will experience joy and gratitude along with spiritual awareness. When your 7th chakra is out of balance, you will likely experience issues with restless, melancholy, boredom and disillusionment. Other symptoms of an overactive crown chakra are the following:

- ❖ Self-destructive habits
- ❖ Disconnect from your spirituality
- ❖ Apathy
- ❖ Cynicism
- ❖ Desire to oversleep
- ❖ Lack of inspiration
- ❖ Confusion on which direction you should take in life
- ❖ Exhaustion
- ❖ Chronic tension headaches
- ❖ Poor coordination
- ❖ Depression

There are several reasons why your crown chakra can become blocked. Some common ways are coined as mid-life crises when you are reevaluating components of your life such as your relationship or career. Other ways are conflict in family relationships and negative feedback on projects that you are proud of.

Because this is the top chakra, it incorporates all of the aforementioned elements of earth, water, fire, air, ether and light. To balance out the energy of the crown chakra, spend quiet time in prayer, chanting mantras and meditation. There are no necessary changes needed for the diet.

Day 19 Crown Chakra Physical Meditation

1. Sit in a comfortable position where you will not be disturbed. Keep your back straight and your legs uncrossed. Place your hands on your your upper legs with your palms facing upwards.
2. Close your eyes and breath in through your nose and out through your mouth in three long and deep breaths.
3. Ponder upon a problem or personal blockage that needs attention. Visualize this problem in your mind.
4. Start chanting "Om" as you exhale. Become one with the energy that you start to feel.
5. Envision a white ball of flame in the heart chakra. With each breath, see this light get brighter and larger to envelop your entire body.
6. Continue to focus on the breath as this white flame spreads at a minimum of three feet from your body on all sides.
7. Now visualize a small violet colored flame by starting in the same fashion as you created the white flame. You will cover this white flame with the violet flame when you are complete.
8. Repeat the intention "I AM the Violet Flame of presence, blazing and transforming whatever within me that needs to be healed." Repeat this intention as many time as you need.

423

9. Feel the sensation of the energy throughout your being and continue to focus on your breath.
10. When you have finished, slowly open your eyes and stand slowly back on your feet.

Day 20 Crown Chakra Mental Meditation

1. Get comfortable while sitting in a chair with your back straight and your feet on the floor.
2. Put your hands in your lap overlapping each other and turn your palms to the sky.
3. Close your eyes and inhale through your nose and exhaling through your mouth.
4. Envision a lotus flower at the top of your head.
5. Continue to breathe slowly and evenly and see the lotus petals unfurling. There is a vibrant violet light in the middle of the lotus.
6. Focus on your breathing as you see the light getting brighter and more vibrant.
7. Feel the sensation of warmth at the crown of your head.
8. Allow the warmth to flow downwards throughout your whole body.
9. Sit with the sensations of warmth and continue to focus on your breath for ten minutes.
10. Slowly open your eyes and sit quietly for a few minutes before you get back up on your feet.

Day 21 Crown Chakra Spiritual Meditation

1. Sit comfortably in a meditation posture which is comfortable for you. This can be on a yoga mat, cushion or a chair.
2. Close your eyes and take in three normal breaths, focusing on the flow of the air throughout your body.

3. Bring your hands up to your face and cover your closed eyelids with the middle and ring fingers.
4. Place your index finger on your eyebrows and your pinky fingers on your cheekbones.
5. Breathe in deeply through the nose. As you exhale, chant "Om" with the "m" being drawn out, creating a buzzing sound.
6. Continue meditating and chanting for five minutes.
7. When the exercise is complete, slowly lower your hands and open your eyes. Take your time moving when you are comfortable to do so.

Chapter 11

Daily Practical Tips

It can seem like a daunting task at times when you get into a negative cycle of thinking to snap yourself out of it. Many times empaths feel like they need to rant to express the pent up collection of emotions that they are feeling. Sometimes there just does not seem like any other way to feel balanced and sane again. However, this is not always the best approach.

Ideally, you will try to keep negativity out of your life altogether as you realize that it does not serve you and only brings your mind and energy down to a low level. How are you able to be the best you can be when you are feeling miserable? Of course you can use the self-care tools which are in chapter 4. However, there are further measures you can take to ensure that negativity does not cloud your energy and ultimately your day.

Center Yourself in Love and Truth

When you are not centered in your energy, this gives the person that you are interacting with the perfect opportunity to take advantage of syphoning your energy from you. The ego in the other person is driven to be fed and will drain you of your energy at any given moment as the ego is very selfish.

Signs that you are not centered are you will start to react to things that happen either in a conversation with another or a scenario that has happened in your environment. When you realize that you are reacting, especially out of emotion, you need to take a moment to recenter your energy.

426

Deep breathing exercises and meditations will help you to continue to stay in your calm, loving and true center. When you start to practice these daily, you will notice that you will not be as reactive with people or situations, and you will not become as drained and drawn to the negativity.

When you practice these centering activities, you are noticing your actions and thoughts from an impartial standpoint. It is as if you are seeing yourself from outside of your body. You are in a higher place and can see things for what they are. When you are in this state, you have achieved a balance based in love and truth. The longer you stay in this space, the deeper the connection will be with your inner voice and intuition.

Do Not See the World in Black and White

When you try to figure out what is "right" and "wrong" you are fighting a losing battle. The ego comes in to play and makes you think that everything that you are doing everything right, even if your gut tells you otherwise. When you just accept things as they are and not try to figure out what is right from an intellectual standpoint, you will be able to listen to what your intuition is trying to tell you to do.

This also means that you should not try to figure out the reasoning for negativity in another person's ego. When you start down this path, it will only start to feed your ego or their ego will start to drain your energy. Instead, continue to focus on your true purpose and determine if this person needs to be spending any more time with you.

If their ego is starting to go in a negative way by extending guilt, shame, blame or even start attacking you and your purpose, simply take note. Do not engage or react. This is exactly what the other person's ego wants as it will take the opportunity to take more energy from you.

Save Your Energy

When you are navigating through another person's emotions while you are not centered, you will certainly start to feel depleted of your energy. When you start to feel your energy start to dip, fill yourself up with light in every way possible. This should be done on an emotional, mental and physical way. Not only will it protect your energy from continuing to be drained, it will lift your spirits higher. Soon, your energy will be one that does not resonate with the energy vampire, and they will likely leave.

When you are able to save your energy from people who are trying to take advantage of you, this leaves you available for the people who need your help and will appreciate it. They will not willing take your light and energy away; they will welcome it. You will also see the benefit in helping and talking with people who are only wanting to lift each other up higher.

You Come First

Allowing yourself to come first is quiet effective when utilized on a regular basis. When you make sure that you practice your self-care each day and you ensure that your needs are met each day, this will prioritize your energy to where it needs to flow.

Remember, you are only able to be an effective psychic when your energy is centered and balanced. When you do not put your needs first, your time and energy will likely be spent on other people's needs. You will not be able to find the balance that you need while experiencing the world as a psychic or sensitive person in this way.

Effective Practices to Protect Yourself from Negativity

When you have negative energy attached to your body, there are several signs to warn you which are:

- Negative thinking
- Mood swings and emotions being uncontrollable
- Uncharacteristic impulsiveness
- Headaches and stomachaches that will not go away

- Inability to sleep
- Feeling of restlessness
- Feeling of depression, anxiousness or simply down
- Suddenly feeling drained or tired
- Not feeling like doing your regular routine

No matter where we go, there is negative energy which can infiltrate our energy levels and bodies. They can come from people or environments and it makes you feel more negative even when there is no immediate cause. When the dense energy affects your energy levels, you may feel a dip in your alertness and productivity. When it is found in your body, you will start to have physical symptoms such as headaches or pains throughout the body which cannot be readily explained.

Luckily, there are many different methods that can be used singularly or in combination to help you to rid yourself of the negative energies and get you back into a good place.

Herbal Smudging Stick - You can utilize an herbal smudging stick which can be used on yourself and your immediate environment. They usually come small hand tied bundles of Sweetgrass, Cedar, Mugwart, Rosemary or the most popular White Sage. They can also be in the form of incense sticks as they are a more concentrated form of the herbal bundles.

Light the top of the herbal bundle or incense stick and move it in a circular motion so that the fire is put out and it is just smoking. Continue to circle around the body by motioning around each of your seven main chakras and then around your whole body. The power of intention is necessary to clear out any negative thoughts or energies. Just thinking about the dense energy leaving your body will free its grasp on you.

If you want to smudge your house, simply walk around each room and permeate the rooms with the smoke. Pay special attention to where stagnant energy will rest underneath furniture and in corners. It is helpful to open the windows so that it invites the negative energies to vacate the house. Again, visualize these energies dissipating from your space while you are performing the smudging.

Saying a Mantra or Protection Prayer - As there are many choices as to what prayers or mantras to say, choose one that resonates with you and stick with it during the times you are clearing your energy. When you switch back and forth between different mantras during a clearing session, it confuses the energy.

Recite this mantra with emphasis and belief. When you think that it might work, it will not gain the power that it requires to work. You must absolutely believe these prayers are going to work with no doubt in your mind. This is when they are able to do their most powerful work.

Before you start to say the mantra, ask for your higher power to protect and aid you in ridding your body and environment from this negative energy. Ask for the energy to leave your body and remind that it does not have any power over you. Then start to take deep and deliberate cleansing breaths while visualizing a bright white light in a bubble around your body.

Start to say the prayer or mantra while visualizing the negative energy leaving your body and space. Say this prayer until you feel a general peace about you. Continue to keep the white light around you during and after the session to continue to strengthen your energy field to protect against the negative energies coming back into your body.

Dissipate the Energy with Noise - Everything in the Universe is comprised of vibrations. Some are denser than others, but this also means that it can be affected by other vibrations. When the energy in the environment seems too dense, make noise with your hands or start drumming if able to dissipate this energy. It will introduce a new vibration and will force the denser energy to break apart. You can simply clap your hands three times or you can incorporate this clapping exercise into a dance if you choose to continue to raise your spirits.

Physically Remove the Negative Energy - Use your hands to physically take the energy out and off of your body. This is something that can easily be done anywhere and will work quickly to help rid yourself of the negativity. Simply place your hands with your fingers together and move your hand across your body in a diagonal fashion. While you are doing this, visualize dusting this energy off of your body.

Use Protective Visualization - In the middle of your chest, picture a ball of golden light while you are taking deep breaths in and out. While you are breathing, imagine this ball of light growing larger with each breath you take in. Expand this golden light until it covers your entire body and then approximately three feet away from the body on all sides to protect your aura.

Take a Bath or Shower - You can soak in a bath to release these dense energies from your body. Use a combination of 1 cup of baking soda with 1 cup of sea salt. You can mix this combination into a full bath or utilize this remedy while performing a foot bath by cutting the recipe into a quarter. Both will be effective in making your feel calmer, grounded and cleansed. If you are taking a shower, you can bundle some lavender or rose at the shower head to create a sweet and calming effect.

The Power of Thought - What you think becomes your life. When you focus and stress about all the things that are not making you happy in life, then you will only bring more stressful events into your life. Instead, shift your thinking to be more grateful for the things that you do have which make your life that much easier. Even look at the simple things as they will compound much easier. When you shift your thinking, you will automatically clear the negative energy in your body and around you as these two types of energy cannot coexist.

Remove the Negative People - When you find that you are constantly feeling drained about a certain person or group, you need to think about the positive benefits these people are bringing to your life compared to the negative effects. Usually the good will not outweigh the bad in these instances when the negative effect is very great. Instead, find more positive and happy people to spend your time with as you become like the four people you are closest to your life.

Take A Walk - Dense energies literally drain away your energy and make you want to stay stagnant. When you become active, the negative energy will have less of a hold on you. It can be as simple as going for a short walk to help clear your head or going on a day trip to your favorite place to spend some me time.

Mindful Meditation - When you are feeling stressed out or pulled in too many directions, find a quiet place to sit and start breathing in several deep and intentional breaths. With each inhalation, imagine you are taking in the power of your higher source and then breathing out the negativity you want to rid yourself of. When you are feeling more grounded, start to clear your mind of all random thoughts until you find peace. This may take a few minutes or an hour, but it will calm your energy as well as clear the negativity away.

Just Let it Go - When you hold grudges or negative ideas about places and people, it takes a toll on your body. These emotions will attach onto you if you allow them to. However, if you simply let these emotions go when they appear, they will not have this hold on your and not infiltrate your energy field. Acknowledge how you are feeling but do not internalize the emotions. Simply breath and visualize these emotions floating away if they do get attached.

Get Moving - This can include any type of exercise to include running or even dancing. Moving your body helps to invigorate the organs in the body as the blood starts to flow. Stagnant energy cannot be present when you are on the move which will keep negative energy from clutching onto you. Also, you are getting a little healthier each time you get out while doing something that you enjoy.

Music Cures Everything - Put on your favorite tunes which help to lift your spirit. Try to refrain from any depressing music. Feel the pulsing go through your body as it energizes your system and start to feel more upbeat. Find some new music who are similar to other artists that you enjoy to broaden your music collection and find songs that have positive lyrics and messages.

Sincere Gratitude - Just as positivity and negativity cannot exist in the same space, if you practice gratitude for what you have in your life, this will dissipate negative thoughts and energy. Consider writing down the people and events that you are thankful for. If you are having difficulty coming up with things to write, ponder about how there are many people in the world who are much worse off than you. When you understand that everyone in life goes through ups and downs, it helps you realize the bigger picture.

Inner Child Nurturing - Act and play with your inner child by putting your favorite happy song on the stereo system and sing at the top of your lungs. Even better if you dance along as if no one is watching. When you let yourself go in this positive way, the negative energy will lift very quickly. If singing is not your thing, find some silly jokes online or a favorite funny video.

Let Nature Shine - If your house or office is feeling negative and stagnant, open the windows or doors and let the breeze bring some new air and energy into the space. The sunshine will also couple well with the new air and you will feel revitalized, keeping negativity at bay.

Conclusion

I hope you enjoyed your copy of *Chakra Meditation: 21 Days Guided Meditation to Awaken your Spiritual Power, Reduce Stress & Anxiety and Improve Awareness of Psychic Abilities with Reiki Healing Exercises.* Let us hope it gave you all of the information that you were searching for about how to use Reiki and meditation techniques to heal yourself as well what you needed to get started in delving into the psychic abilities that we all posses.

The next step is to start working on the exercises which are going to strengthen your intuitive and psychic skills which will continue to compound into enjoyed benefits. There is no reason to be discouraged about your particular talents. When you continue to work with embracing and appreciating yourself for being a unique human being, the more confident and comfortable in your skin you will become.

When you are starting to apply the knowledge in this book, it is best to write down what your particular goals are so that you will have direction and not be side tracked. When you start to work with each goal individually, you will come to master your skills and goals at a higher rate. It will also help to keep you motivated towards the reasons you started in the first place.

Remember to keep your energies and thoughts balanced so that you do not feel overwhelmed. Utilize the methods in having more control over what emotions and sensations that you experience so that you are able to continue to fortify your skills. When you use this book to have more understanding about yourself, you will become your greatest self which will be able to help others much deeper than what you are capable of now.

Once you make it through the initial 21 days of the reiki meditation, be sure to keep it going. Take note where you body is still having issues, and work with the corresponding chakra. Keeping your energy clear and clean is an ongoing process, but you will know where and what to do now when a problem arrises.

When you finally start to embrace yourself for the beautiful soul that you are, you will start to realize all the benefits and gifts that come with living your life truly connected. Other than growing into a strong, deeper and connected individual, you will make a large impact in your family, community and even the world with your talents. The sky is the limit, and only you are limiting yourself in this matter.

I wish you luck while you continue down your paths in your journey. Remember to always trust your intuition as it will never steer you wrong, and have faith that you will be able to master all aspects of your psychic abilities so that you will shine at your brightest at all times. Also keep up with the meditation practices as they will continue to benefit you for some time to come.

Finally, if you found this book useful in any way, a review on Amazon is always appreciated! Thank you!

Reiki Healing

An Essential Guide For Beginners To Learn To Self-Healing With Positive Spiritual Energy By Using Traditional Techniques Of Yoga Therapy And Chakras Meditation.

by

New Mindfulness Lab

Introduction

Each object of animate and inanimate nature that surrounds us has energy: the soil has energy, natural rocks, and people radiate energy. In fact, the whole world is a huge field of energy, in which an exchange of energies constantly takes place between smaller fields. It is thanks to the exchange of energy that such treatment as healing from a distance is possible.

Since energy is unlimited in time and space, it can travel any distance and be used in healing.

Experts believe that the healing energy associated with a person can be used for healing. Thus, the physical presence of the healer near the patient is not a necessary factor, since healing energy can reach anywhere on the planet. You just need to apply the necessary techniques to help use the healing energy for healing.

Prayer is the best example of healing from a distance. When you pray, you appear before God; your prayers are a form of energy, and the answer will be the improvements you or the person you are praying for shall get. Both in prayer and in meditation, there is a consistent exchange of energy with your soul (inner world) and, thus, people who meditate and pray are most likely calm, balanced, and in harmony with their soul.

I will teach you all of this in this book...

Whatever happens,
In any situation
I want my spirit
To always be free.
Japanese Emperor Meiji (Mutsuhito).

439

Chapter 1
The Definition of Healing

What is Energy?

Energy, as you know now, is all around us. Every day we come into contact with Energy in space. It carries great potential for us, but unfortunately, only a few have opened up to realize its capabilities.

The Divine energy of the Universe can be used to maintain health, for spiritual growth, to feel joy from life, but unfortunately many only come to know their inner, powerful essence when there are so many problems that it is impossible to deal with them in the usual, traditional ways. The ways you knew and that you were used to.

But we came to this world in order to grow, improve, and there always comes a moment when you are faced with something new, with something that you never did and did not know. This begs the questions - what is healing? How can energy influence my healing and that of others?

Simply put, in one word - "Reiki."

What is healing energy, and how does it work?
Since energy healing surrounds the whole concept of Reiki, let me rephrase - what is Reiki? How does this work?

This name itself consists of two Japanese words - Ray and Ki. It is difficult to accurately translate them since Japanese words have many meanings: each word takes on a special meaning depending on the

441

context. Since we are going to talk about spiritual healing, the word "Ray" we should probably translate as a divine spirit, wisdom permeating everything - both living and inanimate, and the word "Ki" - as non-physical energy that nourishes all living beings.

Universal wisdom (Ray) can be a source of guidance in our lives and help us improve. Energy (Ki) is present in all living things - in people, animals, and plants. A person filled with energy feels confident in his abilities. He is ready to enjoy life and overcome difficulties. With a lack of energy, a person loses strength and becomes more vulnerable, which is prone to the development of various diseases.

According to ancient Eastern philosophy, the Universe consists of Three Circles (Three Forces) - Heaven, Earth, and Man. The energy of Heaven's Ki (Heavenly Ki) always goes down, while the Earth's Ki always goes up. Human Ki is formed as a result of the collision of Heavenly and Earthly Ki. The human energy Ki created our world: minerals, plants, and living things.

It turns out that we experience the influence of Ki energy of two types - Heavenly and Earthly. Heavenly controls morality and Earthly desires, and understanding this system help balance these two types of influence. Thus, the concept of Reiki can be interpreted as non-physical healing energy, consisting of the energy of a life force controlled by a higher intellect (consciousness). So, at least, those who directly practice it determine the meaning of the Reiki technique. These people believe, or rather, feel that Reiki's energy is inherent in the intellect, which, in fact, directs it to where it is most needed. This energy creates in the body special healing conditions necessary for the individual development of the individual.

Do not confuse: it is about intelligence inherent in energy, and not about human intelligence in general. A person is not able to control this energy with the help of his mind, so it is not limited to his experience or abilities. Probably for the same reason, it cannot be used incorrectly or to the detriment. No, it always has a healing effect.

By the way, try to avoid one more mistake: do not confuse Reiki with the energy of a vital force, which can very well be radiated by the mind and create both favorable consequences and problems, including diseases. Here, we discuss positive energy.

The Energy Body

Let's talk in more detail about the energy of Ki. Where do we get it from? From the air, from food and water, from sunlight and sleep. And if she is not enough, we can help ourselves by using breathing exercises and meditation.

Ki is rightly considered a source of health. Passing through all organs and tissues, she revives them and supports them. It is clear that any violation of the flow of Ki is the main cause of the disease.

Interestingly, Ki is sensitive to thoughts and feelings. From the quality of thoughts and feelings, its flow intensifies or weakens. Negative thoughts and feelings can limit it, disrupt the healthy and harmonious flow of Ki.

By the way, Western doctors also admit that 98% of diseases are caused by our thoughts - directly or indirectly.

And if you think that thinking exists only in the brain, then you are mistaken. Like the nervous system, thinking permeates every organ and every tissue of our body. Moreover, it extends beyond the physical body and is located in a subtle energy field called the aura. The body and mind are closely connected, and only with their interaction is thinking created.

Now it becomes clear why negative thoughts, originating in the brain, gradually gather in various parts of the body and penetrate the aura. They block the flow of energy, preventing it from entering the tissues and organs as a result of which the latter begins to function worse. Our task is to remove negative thoughts and feelings, if, of course, we want to protect ourselves from illness.

But there is one problem. Yes, we can try to get rid of those thoughts and feelings that interfere with us and of which we ourselves are well aware. But what about the thoughts and feelings stored in the depths of the unconscious? How can we remove or change these thoughts and feelings, even if we are not aware of them?

This is where Reiki comes to our aid. Thanks to this method, we can unlock energy by working directly with the unconscious part of our brain. The Reiki stream, passing through a weakened or diseased area, as it wears out all negative thoughts and feelings. Sick organs and tissues again begin to receive a full supply of Ki energy. The energy balance in the body is restored, and disharmonious energies are supplanted.

The basis of Reiki, perhaps, should be considered our involvement in all of humanity. The idea that we are separated from the rest of the world is just an illusion. The wisdom we strive for is endless and accessible to all. Our task is to learn how to connect to the collective mind. How to do it? First of all, we must abandon the thought that we are all allowed. Thinking in this way, we contribute to the dispersal of the forces of goodness and love, and as a result, we feel lonely. Sometimes we do not want to consider ourselves part of a great whole for fear of losing personal freedom. This is wrong: we do not lose our freedom, combining it with a sense of integrity. Moreover, it is this combination, the ability to see in ourselves that which is one and the exclusive, which will allow us to find the right way to correct ourselves and the whole world.

Chapter 2
Energy Healing

The Reiki Story

In one of the districts of Tokyo, there is the Saihoji Temple, next to which is a memorial dedicated to Mikao Usui, the creator of the Reiki method. The memorial was erected in 1927 by students of Mikao Usui, who founded the Reiki Society for the Treatment, a year after his death. This method is still popular today in Japan and in other countries.

The spiritual basis of the Reiki method was revealed by Mikao Usui during his three-week prayer and fasting on Mount Kurama, located north of the city of Kyoto, the former capital of Japan. Apparently, the very atmosphere of Kurama, covered with centuries-old trees, surrounded by pagodas and tall stuff all around, contributed to the emergence of the idea of sacred art associated with the spiritual healing of all diseases and the achievement of happiness.

The story of Reiki began in the mid-80s when Dr. Mikao Usui began to search for the ancient healing system, which, according to legend, was used by Christ and Buddha. Legend has it that this idea arose for a reason: his students moved the doctor to search. Having adopted Christianity, the Japanese scientist and philosopher became a priest, as well as the director of the Christian school for boys in Kyoto. The disciples, doubting the teacher's true faith, asked him to prove their faith in the Holy Scriptures in the same way as Jesus Christ did. In other words, they suggested that Usui perform one of the miracles that Jesus performed. The teacher could not do this, and then the students said that his faith was not enough to support faith in someone else.

Dr. Usui was so amazed at the depth of their approach to the issue of faith that he decided to immediately go to the West, where Christianity reigned. Mikao Usui was determined to learn how to perform miracles and, on his return, to demonstrate to his students' new evidence of his faith.

Mikao arrived in America, where he became a student at the University of Chicago. However, having deeply studied the Holy Scriptures of Christians, in particular, the description of miracles of healing, he realized that he could not put them into practice.

Nevertheless, giving up was not in the character of Mikao Usui: he began to study the sacred texts of other religions of the world. After ascertaining that the Buddha and his first disciples also performed miracles of healing, Dr. Usui carefully studied Buddhist manuscripts for seven years. He did not stop researching Buddhist sutras even when he returned home to Kyoto.

Mikao Usui tirelessly traveled around the country, visited temples and monasteries, talked everywhere with monks. From them, he learned that the Buddha did indeed often heal the sick, but this practice was lost by the Buddhists. The monks admitted that they focus mainly on their spiritual health, and consider physical healing to be the business of doctors. In short, Dr. Usui still could not find the answer to his question. Once, the abbot of a Zen Buddhist monastery invited him to live in a monastery to continue his research. After some time, Mikao Usui became a Zen Buddhist monk. After familiarizing himself with the sutras translated into Japanese, he began to study Chinese for a more accurate translation, since Buddhism penetrated Japan from China.

Then Dr. Usui began to study Sanskrit in order to read the sutras in the original. He found the required symbols but did not know at all what to do with them. It was then that Mikao Usui went to Mount Kurama, located a few kilometers from Kyoto, which the monks considered sacred.

For three weeks, Dr. Usui fasted and meditated in the expectation that he would reveal the meaning of mysterious symbols. He did not want to return to the monastery without receiving the right answer and even asked the rector to send monks for his remains if he did not return in 21 days.

As soon as he climbed the mountain, Dr. Usui piled 21 pebbles at the entrance to the cave, which became his shelter, and daily removed one of them so as not to lose track of time. Thus, 20 days passed, which Mikao Usui spent in a state of deep meditation, but nothing happened. And then came the last morning of the deadline set by him. In the dark predawn hour, Dr. Usui saw a sheaf of bright light directed directly at him. The first desire was to escape as far as possible from here, but Mikao Usui did not move. He suddenly realized that this was exactly the moment he had been waiting for so long. And if he once devoted himself to searching for many years, then he should not refuse to unravel the mystery even in the face of death. The experience was so strong that Dr. Usui lost consciousness.

When he came to consciousness, he suddenly realized he'd dreamed of "millions and millions of bubbles of all colors of the rainbow," and Reiki symbols loomed against the background of these bubbles. And not just symbols, because they were previously known to him: their meaning was revealed to him, and information was given on how to activate their healing abilities. This is how the first Reiki settings appeared in the modern world - the repeated and completely supernatural discovery of the ancient method of healing.

What do Energy Healers do?

Having made the discovery, Dr. Usui, the first energy healer, immediately went to Kyoto. He was in such a hurry that he stumbled and bruised his toe. Mikao Usui took this annoying incident as an opportunity to put his healing system into practice.

With a hand on his bruised finger, Dr. Usui took advantage of Reiki's energy and immediately felt that the pain had passed. This was the first proof of the truth of his discovery. Satisfied, he set off on. The path was not short, and after some time, Dr. Usui was very hungry. He went to the house by the side of the road and asked for food. The meal was taken out by the owner's granddaughter. Mikao Usui turned his attention to her swollen cheek. It turned out that the girl was tormented by severe toothache. But, as soon as he touched her cheek, the pain immediately disappeared, and the tumor began to subside right in front of their eyes. This was the second confirmation of his discovery, which led to the conclusion that Reiki can be used not only for self-medication but also for healing other people.

Returning to the monastery, Mikao Usui found the abbot completely sick. The unfortunate came down from a severe attack of arthritis. Needless to say, Mikao Usui immediately relieved him of pain and received another confirmation that the secret of the ancient healing art, which was used by all the great teachers, was revealed.

For the rest of his life, Dr. Usui practiced Reiki in Japan and taught others this art. The learning process was quite long: the students for a long time lived next to the master, learning Reiki. Dr. Usui considered training completed only when he was convinced that his students could put into practice everything that he himself knew about Reiki. Students gradually became masters themselves and went to society to heal people on their own. True, some followers of Dr. Usui, like the apostles of Christ, continued to live and work alongside their teacher.

Our Dynamic Multilayer Energy Field

For many centuries, healing work has been a mystery behind seven seals that defies any explanation. However, at present, some aspects of healing work can be explained from a scientific point of view. For example, the effectiveness of Reiki is explained by the theory of electromagnetic fields generated by all living things. This book is devoted to the book of Doctor of Philosophy James Oschman, "Energy Medicine, a scientific basis."

The presence of electric currents in the body has been known for a long time. One of the methods of self-regulation of the body are currents passing through the nervous system. The nervous system is associated with every organ, with every area of body tissue. It is through her that the brain sends its signals to regulate the activity of the body.

Another network through which electric current flows is the circulatory system. Blood passing through the blood vessels transmits "cardiac electricity" to every particle of our body.

Electric currents flow in each cell and between cells. Many of the cells actually contain liquid crystals. Living crystals are found in cell membranes, in the myelin sheaths of nerve fibers, and in many other places. All crystals have a piezoelectric effect, which manifests itself when exposed to pressure. Therefore, the liquid crystals of the body constantly generate an electric current. Currents are often coherent, which means that next to this area, there are always frequencies similar to those of the laser. These laser-like vibrations can propagate within the body and also radiate outward.

Scientific Studies That Prove That Energy Healing Works

Today, the studies of many foreign and American scientists have experimentally proved the existence of special energy-information processes that are fully consistent with Reiki's teachings on universal life energy.

Under the influence of research in this area, the point of view of Western scientists has changed. One of the reasons for this change was the invention of sensitive instruments to detect energy fields around the human body.

Subsequently, it was discovered that all tissues and organs produce certain magnetic pulsations, which became known as biomagnetic fields. Conventional electrical recordings, such as electrocardiograms and electroencephalograms, are now complemented by a biomagnetic recording called magneto cardiograms and magnetoencephalogram. For various reasons, mapping magnetic fields around the body often provide a more accurate definition of physiology and pathology than traditional electrical measurements.

Back in the 1920s, Harold Saxon Burr, an outstanding researcher who worked at the School of Medicine at Yale University, suggested that diseases could be detected in a person's energy field before their physical symptoms appear. In addition, Burr was convinced that diseases could be prevented by exposure to the energy field.

These concepts were ahead of their time, but are now validated in medical research laboratories around the world. Scientists use various instruments to determine how diseases alter the biomagnetic fields around the body. Others use pulsating magnetic fields to stimulate healing. Sensitive individuals have described these phenomena for a long time, but there was no logical explanation for how this could have happened.

In the early 80s, Dr. John Zimmerman, while conducting research at the University of Colorado in Denver, discovered that a strong biomagnetic pulsation emanated from a Reiki practitioner. The ripple frequency was unstable; it ranged from 0.3 to 30 Hz (cycles per second), most often in the range of 7–8 Hz. Biomagnetic pulsations emanating from the hands were in the same frequency range as his brain waves. Further scientific studies have shown that the entire frequency range has healing properties.

Confirmation of Zimmerman's research appeared in 1992 when Dr. Seto and his colleagues (Japan) began to directly examine masters practicing alternative healing methods. The energy emanating from their hands is so strong that it can be detected by a simple magnetometer, consisting of two coils with 80,000 revolutions of the wire. Subsequently, the experiments were expanded and transferred to sound, light, and thermal fields emitted by healers. The most interesting thing is that the ripple frequency changes all the time. Moreover, doctors investigating the therapeutic effects of pulsating magnetic fields have found that these frequencies are effective for healing both soft and hard tissues. Certain frequencies stimulate the growth of nerves, bones, skin, capillaries, and ligaments.

Reiki practitioners and their patients receive daily evidence of the effectiveness of this system (sometimes - even in hopeless cases!), and modern medicine is beginning to recognize this therapy as yielding results, which has been confirmed by new scientific studies.

Recently, research has been stepped up directly related to Reiki energy. During treatment, the internal and universal energies are combined in the hands of the practitioner, and this unity, regardless of philosophical, religious, or esoteric views, contributes to the healing process.

Scientists have conducted many experiments proving the effectiveness of the effects of Reiki energy at the cellular and other levels and even on inanimate objects. The objects of scientific research were unicellular organisms, plants, insects, laboratory animals, and such laboratory material as blood cells, neurons, cancer cells, water molecules, and, of course, the effect of energy on humans was studied in the most detailed way.

For example, the effect of Reiki energy on an open wound has been investigated. At the same time, two people were treated with the same damage to the skin, but one of them was exposed to the Reiki conductor hidden from him every day for 10 minutes. Doctors who observed the healing process also did not know about this effect. Four independent experts carried out monitoring measurements of the healing processes after five and ten days. The results were very different from each other. When a person was exposed to Reiki energy, the healing process went 50% after five days and 85% after ten. The second investigator stopped at the days of control measurements on the following results: 15% and 40%, respectively.

The presence of electric currents in the body has been known for a long time. One of the methods of self-regulation of the body are currents passing through the nervous system. The nervous system is connected with every organ, with every part of the body tissues, and it is through it that the brain sends its signals to regulate the activity of the body.

Another network through which electric current flows is the circulatory system. A saline solution of blood that travels over more than fifty thousand miles of blood vessels transmits "cardiac electricity" to every particle of our body.

The body has a secondary nervous system formed by perineurium, which is a layer of connective tissue surrounding each nerve. More than half of the brain cells are perineurium cells. Perineurium work on direct current. They control brain vibrations and are directly involved in the treatment process. If any part of the body is damaged, the perineural system generates an electrical potential in the damaged area, which puts the body in a state of readiness. Using these electrical potentials, the perineural system directs regenerative cells, such as white blood cells, fibroblasts, and motile skin cells, to the damaged area. When the treatment for the damaged area is completed, the electrical potential changes. The perineural system is also very sensitive to external magnetic fields.

When an electric current flows through a conductor, a magnetic field is created around it. The electric currents circulating in the human body generate magnetic fields, called biomagnetic, that permeate and surround the body. Sensitive magnetometers allow you to measure these biomagnetic fields. Dr. John Zimmerman of the University of Colorado College of Medicine, Denver, used a device called SQUID (superconducting quantum interference device) to measure biomagnetic fields in various parts of the human body, including the brain, heart, and many other organs. The measurements of the biomagnetic field made it possible to better understand how the body works and to improve the diagnosis of diseases.

The heart has the strongest biomagnetic field; it can be measured at a distance of 4-5 meters. The brain and all internal organs of the body are surrounded by their own biomagnetic fields. All fields have their own frequencies and interact with each other. When an organ is healthy, the frequency of its field is a well-defined quantity that changes if the organ's health is impaired. Adding together, all biomagnetic fields form a large aggregate biomagnetic field surrounding the body. This is very reminiscent of what we call an aura. Therefore, the biomagnetic field can be one of the main components of the aura, although other aspects are possible here.

Fields interact with other fields that are close to the body, including the fields of other people. The basis of this interaction is induction, that is, one magnetic field can affect another, as a result of which both the field itself and the strength and frequency of the currents passing through the conductor change. Thus, the biomagnetic field of one person affects the biomagnetic field of another person, which can affect the well-being of each of them, as well as the functioning of organs and body tissues. From this follows a completely definitive explanation of the concept of "magnetic personality." The same interaction of fields allows us to scientifically explain the therapeutic effect of one person on another.

So, from a scientific point of view, a human being does not end with skin, it extends beyond the physical body. We know this from personal experience, as we all sense the presence of other people. Now it has been proven and explained scientifically.

When Will Energy Healing Help Me?

Hands are also surrounded by a biomagnetic field - especially in people involved in healing. The healing energy of the hands, at least in part, is generated by the perineural system. This system surrounds nerve fibers, and it is through it that direct currents pass. Currents are modeled by vibrations emitted by the brain.

In addition to biomagnetic hands, other types of energy can also radiate, which also has a therapeutic effect. There is some evidence that infrared rays, microwave waves, and other types of photon radiation emanate from the hands of healers and that biological systems respond to them.

When a person is sick, the biomagnetic frequencies of some of his organs differ from their frequencies in a healthy state. Herbert Fröhlich, a researcher who discovered many interesting aspects in human biomagnetic fields, explains this process: "The association of cells forming a section of tissue or organs has a certain general frequency that regulates some important process, for example, cell division. Usually, these control frequencies are very stable. If for some reason, the cells change their frequency, the signals attracted from neighboring cells will tend to restore the correct frequency. However, if the frequency of a sufficiently large number of cells changes, the strength of the general vibrations of the system may decrease to the point where stability is lost. Loss of coherence leads to disorders and illnesses.

When the healer puts his hands next to the diseased organ and begins to heal it, the biomagnetic field emitted by his hands becomes much stronger than the field emitted by the diseased organ. In this case, the frequency of the biomagnetic field of the healer's hands approaches the frequencies that the diseased organ needs. Since the field of the healer is much stronger than the field of the diseased organ, it induces healthy frequencies in the field of this organ, forcing it to adjust its frequencies so that they again correspond to the healthy range. This regulation, in turn, affects the characteristics of electric currents flowing in the cells and the nervous system of the diseased organ and around it, as well as biological processes, as a result of which healing occurs.

The process can work in the opposite direction when the healer scans the patient's biomagnetic field or tries to find an area of disharmony in him. In this case, he slowly moves one or both hands at a distance of several centimeters from the body, paying attention to the sensations in his hands. The healer feels the changes radiated by the patient's field in the field of his hands. This allows him to determine where in the patient's biomagnetic field, there is an area with disturbed vibrations.

Hence, energy healing will help you to diagnose illness. Secondly, it will help you treat yourself and others. However, as you shall see, one of Reiki's unique qualities is its ability to come from tuning. The healer does not guide Reiki using his mind - the energy of Reiki itself finds the right direction.

Chapter 3
Levels of Energy Healing - Different Established Energy Healing Modalities

In Reiki, healing takes place on two levels - physical and spiritual. And it happens thanks to our connection with the very high spiritual vibrations of the Universe. This is precisely the secret of miraculous healing: the soul and body are healed not by human energy, but by the spiritual (vital) energy of the Universe. The healer passes it through himself while not spending his personal energy. The main task of the healer is not to bring his negative vibrations into Reiki's energy, to be as pure a conductor as possible. Only then can Reiki be used not only to cure diseases but also to achieve enlightenment and spiritual growth. When we ask Reiki for healing, we must be aware that help comes from the highest level.

The origins of the Japanese Reiki tradition can be found in the teachings of Yamabushi (holy hermits) on self-improvement, superpower, and the extension of life, dating back to the 7th century. Tradition is always connected with the culture of the people, but one must understand that tradition and culture are not the same as spiritual teachings. The essence of spiritual teachings is to know the nature of man.

To practice Reiki, you do not need to become a Shinto or Buddhist. You just need to be able to incorporate this spiritual teaching into your own culture. In order to better understand the spirit of Reiki itself, it is very important to have an idea of the culture and traditions of Japan, but not be limited only to their external form. True spiritual values - spiritual growth, self-improvement, the

455

ability to be oneself, and to reveal one's inner creative abilities, comprehension of one's own depths — are accessible to every person, regardless of the culture in which he is brought up.

From ancient times, the qualities known to people who embarked on the Path of spiritual growth have been known. The past masters are perfect, skillful mystics, insightful and mysterious, were too deep for their time.

The principles of Energy Healing

On the memorial plate, erected by students of Mikao Usui, the basic principles of Reiki are carved, which their teacher called to follow. As a matter of fact, these instructions were stated in poetic form by the Japanese emperor Mutsuhito, who made every effort to give his people a truly spiritual orientation.

The wise and subtle poetry of Emperor Mutsuhito was recited daily by members of the society created by Mikao Usui. The basic principles of Reiki became a guide in life, an inexhaustible food for the mind of those who grasped their deep meaning.

Agree, these are rather short, but very important instructions for development. After all, it was no coincidence that the ancient sages followed them, never ceasing to strive for self-improvement.

Mikao Usui believed that it was these principles that helped him to clearly and accurately formulate the purpose of his teachings, as well as to find the easiest and simplest ways to achieve this goal.
According to Mikao Usui, there is nothing complicated in mastering the Reiki method; everyone can master it. You just need to say the basic principles of Reiki every morning and every evening, sitting in a comfortable position and joining hands in prayer so you can develop a clean and healthy mind. This is, in fact, the essence of daily practice. Let's try to understand the principles of Reiki.

Let's start with the words that apply to each of them, and therefore by themselves become some kind of principles.

456

Being Connected to the Energy Field Awareness

The first words are, "Exactly today!" In fact, these words are the key to the secret of spiritual awakening. This key, which psychologists call "Here and Now," allows us to dissolve in the present and, breaking beyond the material world, get into the realm of love and light. This truth was revealed by Mikao Usui after 21 days of meditation and fasting on Mount Kurama.

Deep enlightenment, based on knowledge and experience accumulated throughout his life, allowed him to create a "System of Natural Healing" and transmit it to people. Thus, the main message of the mystical path of Reiki can be formulated as follows:

"Let your consciousness be here and now. This is the only way to come to the Great Divine Light. This is the only way to change your life for the better and give it a more spiritual meaning." The following principles are the other important steps to energy healing practice:

Principle 1 - Don't be Angry

You yourself know how often we are overcome by feelings such as anger, resentment, and hatred. Experiencing such emotions, we not only destroy ourselves but also cause irreparable harm to those around us. Where does so much hostility and annoyance come from?

Reiki meditative practices help us understand the true causes of negative emotions, get rid of them and harmonize our spiritual life.

Principle 2 - Do not Worry

The anxiety we experience affects us as destructively as anger. This state also has certain reasons, which meditation, contemplation, and intuition help to understand. With Reiki's help, we can translate basic energy, blocked by anxiety and fears, into constructive, meaningful actions.

457

Why are we even worried? It happens like this: one of the unconscious aspects of our senses ceases to control the important points necessary for survival. In other words, a sense of danger or threat is rooted in the subconscious. How to fix the situation is unknown. We cannot solve the problem, because we don't know what we are afraid of, and we begin to worry. However, in most cases, after realizing what is happening, the cause of fear turns out to be frivolous and easily eliminated.

The Reiki method is precisely able to free us from anxiety - both justified and completely far-fetched.

Principle 3 - Be Filled with Gratitude

How often do we forget about such a simple feeling as gratitude! But this is the energy of higher awareness, which exists only in man. Gratitude breeds trust and makes us part of a great whole. Forgetting gratitude, we seem to be losing ourselves. We leave unnoticed a helping hand extended to us by the Creator because we only strive for a specific kind of happiness and success. Thus, we deprive ourselves of all happiness and success. Showing gratitude, we recognize the greatness of creative power, its divine spark. So let us be attentive to any assistance provided to us, let us rejoice at everything that we receive.
It's not difficult to take this rule into your heart: you just need to understand that the right things always come to us at the right time, and not demand more.

Principle 4 - Work Hard

Performing any work, you need to try to maintain a meditative state of mind, completely immerse yourself in the workflow precisely "here and now." This, perhaps, will be the best application of accumulated spirituality in real life.

Principle 5 - Be Kind to Others

Imbued with love for other people, that is, to recognize and honor the Divine in them, is not an easy task. To make it easier, you need to try to feel yourself a part of the Universe, a part of the great whole. This does not detract from personal freedom. On the contrary, only a combination of freedom and involvement in the common allows us to gain the strength of goodness and love. Anyone who is not capable of this is doomed to loneliness.

Primary Awareness Exercise

As you can see, the life principles of the "System of Natural Healing" by Mikao Usui is not a strict set of rules that must be strictly observed; it is rather a call to more carefully examine your own behavior and try to get rid of senseless habits. These principles make us think once more about our own lives. They can also be perceived as some spiritual riddles mobilizing our rational mind, used to control everything to the smallest detail, to learn something new in life. Finally, mastering these principles can significantly help in a practical approach to the Reiki method.

Energy Healing Practices

Reiki practices can change a person's life and teach him a lot. They allow you to better know yourself, make life joyful, and happy.

Reiki is a system of natural healing. It is very simple - this, perhaps, is its secret. To many, this seems strange - after all, we are used to living by the principle: "The more difficult, the better the result." Overcoming obstacles instill a fighting spirit in us, arouses interest, provides food for the mind, and satisfies our Ego.

However, what is attractive to the Ego does not lead to spiritual growth, and a simple technique can give real growth. So choose for yourself what is more important and more valuable for you.

Meditation

Osho Meditation is a system of meditative techniques. She is not called to teach or give anything. It grows from within, from your wholeness. This is observation, or rather, the quality of observation, the quality of a conscious, alert state, a state of no-mind. This is the joy of life, affirming, and causeless. The constant dying for the past and the birth of a new quality of being, openness to this new. And the technique itself is just a way to create the right conditions for a positive energy flow.

Who is Osho, and why has Osho meditation become known all over the world? Osho (Bhagwan Sri Rajneesh) was a spiritual leader and mystic; he was born and raised in India. Osho created a system that combines religion and philosophy, and involved followers in it.

Osho Philosophy

There is a misconception that meditation is a way to come to harmony and change what you don't like. Beginners think that the problems will disappear, and silence will reign in the head.

Osho proposed a new approach. He believes that meditation does not need a goal. To eternally hurrying residents of megalopolises, it seems that everything that has no purpose is a waste of time.

Everything that we should gradually wean from gives the philosophy of Osho meditation. No race for results, exhausting goals, and the opportunity to practice without preparation. A space free of obligations, apart from the main thing, is to enjoy the practice.

Since emotions and the mind live in the physical body, you need to start first with this. Subtle matters can be started when the body is ready and open to practice.

Imagine a three-year-old child who seriously expects to pick up a bag of potatoes. He is not physically ready for such a load. Also, working with the inner subtle plans is the next level of growing up. To begin with, let's take care of our own body, nourish it with our forces and let it be understood that we remember about it.

The essence of Osho's meditations is to allow energy to flow freely throughout the body. If you are already tensed by reading the word "energy," then I hasten to reassure you - energy is a force that is born at the junction of calm and relaxation. When you start the practice, you will feel how this energy washes away, like water, the husks of fuss and habitual anxiety. Imagine the crabs that the wave washed ashore. The next wave will take the animals back to the ocean and wash their tracks. Also, the practice of meditation helps restore inner purity and silence.

Osho practices begin with the active part because it is familiar to the mind. The mind is unlikely to resist if you are dancing or running. At the active stage, we release anxiety and suppressed emotions, prepare the mind for practice.

The active stage can be different - dance, laughter, running, breathing. The most unusual technique is gibberish. During this practice, you release your body on all sides and do whatever you want. Angry - stamp your feet, clench your fists and scream. Sad - hug yourself, cry, stand motionless. Rejoice - laugh, jump. You can do literally anything. The main thing is to give vent to emotions through the body, let go of yourself and throw out everything.

Next to the active stage is the stage of silence. The more emotions you release in the first part, the quieter and deeper the second part of the practice will turn out.

What meditation should a beginner choose?

Osho developed one hundred and twelve methods of meditation. I recommend that beginners learn two basic meditations - Dynamic and Kundalini. With experience, proceed with the rest of the methods. I discuss these in the chapter "Reiki Meditations."

461

The main morning technique is Osho Dynamic Meditation. It relaxes the body and gives it strength for the coming day. Meditation lasts an hour and consists of five stages: chaotic breathing, thoughtless movements, jumping with arms raised, complete stillness and silence, and spontaneous flowing dance. For beginners, we recommend that you go to a quiet spot and master the techniques.

Evening Meditation - Kundalini Meditation. It helps to digest what happened during the day, relax the body, and release control. Meditation consists of erratic body shaking, smooth dance and complete immobility. Each previous stage releases even more energy, calming the body and mind.

For beginners to meditate, we suggest choosing for yourself the methods by which you will meditate in the morning and evening. It is better to invest your forces gradually, without immediately embracing 112 methods.

Awakening the Body Response

Imagine you are walking along an empty street and towards you - a cat. You see a cat, and at that moment, an observer wakes up in you. Then your internal observer steps aside and sees both you and the cat on an empty street. The essence of meditation is to separate the inner observer from the physical body and look at the sides. The bonus of this approach is that you can practice anywhere. Walking down the street, talking with colleagues, reading a book. After some time, you will be able to take a neutral position. The next stage of practice is to learn to observe your emotions and mood.

Osho teaches us to watch constantly. If we practice only an hour a day, sitting still in meditation, then for the remaining twenty-three hours, we will do exactly the opposite.

To watch is to look in the inner mirror. When you observe your thoughts and acknowledge the existence of everything that happens, an extraordinary silence sets in. There is no one to argue with. No one is attacking, so no need to defend. Saying "I'm angry" to ourselves and stepping back two steps to the side, we give ourselves the opportunity to feel the situation without experiencing toxic guilt for the "wrong" emotion. There is no internal censor who decides which emotions are good and which are bad. Then the energy of observation returns and gives all the accumulated power to you. Like natural elements.

What to remember: In the Osho tradition, there is no term "novice." You can practice without preparation. Practice does not require special equipment, and you can perform it at any time of the day. Although it is accepted that the best time to practice is dawn or dusk.

The main rule of Osho - let meditation bring pleasure and joy. Practicing for pleasure does not mean that on difficult days, you need to give up everything, though. Remember to practice every day and meditate no matter the circumstances.

Deep Touch

Deep Touch is a practice that harmoniously combines work with the body, energy, and attention. It would seem that we all know how to walk, sit, lie down, and get up. But are we doing it right? Admittedly, no.

Due to improper walking, we lose a huge amount of energy and gain health problems, especially with the spine. But our body is the only thing that indisputably belongs only to us. Only through the body do we work with our consciousness.

Deep Wave

All surrounding space, the whole world is riddled with waves. Of course, we don't even notice it. This state of affairs is so usual and familiar to us that we simply do not pay attention to it. Meanwhile, the waves penetrate everything, often without colliding with anything and without stopping at anything.

In the practice of the Deep Wave, technology has been developed that allows us to create an environment in our physical body that can catch the subtlest vibrations and in which their energy can settle.

Deep Sound

In the world around us, everything sounds without exception, including man. However, far from everyone knows how to sound competently. The practice of Deep Sound allows you to learn to tune the body so that it becomes a high-quality sound resonator, and use certain forms of internal attention. This effective technology of working with yourself and with your voice leads to real growth - the emergence of Deep Sound.

Deep Gymnastics

Also referred to as yoga, this is another way to work individually with your body. The difference from ordinary gymnastics, at first glance, is very small: a slower movement and a different focus of attention - not on an external object, but inside your being. But no wonder they say that everything ingenious is simple. The technique gives an amazing effect. It has a general healing effect on the whole body - thanks to it, not only the quality of muscles and tendons improves, but also a feeling of holistic perception of oneself arises.

Chapter 4
Energy Healing Initiation and Steps

Today, there are a large number of different areas of Energy Healing. Some of them are called traditional, some - non-traditional. One of the traditional destinations is Reiki Usui Shiki Ryoho.

It should be noted that the Reiki tradition in the form in which it is now, did not arise immediately. It was formed, changed, and developed. Actually, it continues to develop today. Such is the natural property of a living tradition - the desire to develop in changing living conditions. At the same time, there is something unchanging - the basis without which tradition would cease to exist.

In Reiki Usui, Shiki Ryoho, this form is defined by nine elements and four aspects. Thanks to their existence, it is possible to transmit the mystery that Reiki is.

What is a tradition for? Primarily for security. In Reiki Usui, Shiki Ryoho, this security is realized in a natural way - in all the actions prescribed by tradition. Reiki is transmitted through initiation, and at the same time, can be transferred to any person. And as a result, a person receives what he now most needs, what is most capable of supporting his life. The second important role of tradition is that it gives a person the opportunity to do with ourselves, and sometimes with another person, something that in ordinary life we never do. More precisely, it gives permission for this. What a person does is not that he just suddenly wanted to, but that which is sanctioned by the subtle world. This sanction in Reiki was given to Mikao Usui (remember - on Mount Kurama?).

The third merit of tradition is that it gives a feeling of reliability. The fact that Reiki Usui Shiki Ryoho is already about 100 years old and over the years hundreds of thousands of people have studied this practice (or maybe more) is a definite test of time.

When a person regularly practices Reiki Usui Shiki Ryoho, then he really gets the best and necessary for his life. And even if he does not always immediately understand this, tradition does its job. It honestly fulfills its role, providing primarily efficiency, reliability, and safety.

The elements and aspects that describe the Reiki tradition of Usui Shiki Ryoho did not arise immediately - not from the first years of Reiki's existence. However, knowing them will allow us to understand a little better what we get from Reiki and how best to transmit it to other people.

Listed below are the elements and aspects of Reiki Usui Shiki Ryoho:

1. The mystical order
2. The technique of healing
3. Spiritual discipline
4. Personal growth

Mikao Usui, in his book "Usui Reiki Ryoho Hikkei" wrote: "From time immemorial, it often happened that one who comprehended the ancient secret teaching, either kept it for himself or shared it only with his heirs. This secret was not passed on to any of the outsiders. However, this tradition of the last century has already gone out of fashion. In our time, the happiness of mankind is based on the joint work of people and their desire for social progress. That is why I will never allow a single person to possess this knowledge only for themself. Our Reiki healing is a completely original method, and it cannot be compared with any other method in the world. That is why I would like to make this method available to the people for the prosperity of all mankind. Each of us has the potential to receive a divine gift, which leads to the unification of the soul and body. Through Reiki, a great many people can feel a divine blessing. Our Reiki healing is an original therapy that builds on the spiritual energy of the universe. Through it, a person first gains health, and then a calm mind, and joy in life will increase. Today we need to improve and rebuild our lives so that we can free our loved ones from illness and emotional suffering. This is the reason why I dared to freely teach people this method.

Today we need to improve and rebuild our lives so that we can free our loved ones from illness and emotional suffering. This is the reason why I dared to freely teach people this method."

You are about to learn all about it...

Initiation

Initiation is an ancient way of transferring energy and sacred knowledge from one person to another. This method has long been used by spiritual teachers and masters of the whole world in cases where energy or knowledge cannot be transmitted through words.

In almost all spiritual traditions, symbols and mantras are used for meditation, working with energy, healing, and personal development. Some of them are capable of causing subjective changes; others are objective. Symbols and mantras include symbolically significant objects (cross, Yin and Yang symbols, light, various shapes, and colors). With their help, certain moods and associations are created.

For energy healing, this consists of Reiki symbols and mantras, runes, and magical amulets. In order to work with them, it is necessary to receive instructions from someone who has already dealt with them and is capable of initiating, that is, transferring the energies acting in them. If we cannot receive such instructions, or simply want to achieve the goal with our own efforts, we must first spiritually set ourselves up for the corresponding system of symbols and learn how to use them correctly.

You can, for example, turn to Tantric Buddhism - the spiritual path from which Reiki arose. Here, the exact rituals and recitation of mantras during favorable astrological periods are connected with the sequence of visualizations of the mantras and the evocation of a certain deity in a state of deep meditation.

It is these opportunities that Mikao Usui used on Mount Kurama. He managed to establish a connection with the spiritual traditions behind the symbols and mantras. He gained the ability to connect with Reiki energy and began to use symbols and mantras for subsequent initiation.

However, we have already said that Kurama is known as a place especially favorable for meditation and spiritual practices. And since not everyone is able to be there, it becomes obvious that initiation, that is, the transfer of human knowledge to man, is a simpler, more accessible, and less demanding path.

First, you need to understand that symbols and mantras are not Reiki yet. They can only be used within the Reiki system after traditional initiation. Otherwise, they will remain signs and words, no different from any others. Even with Mikao Usui, the symbols and mantras found by him in Sanskrit manuscripts made no impression until he made a certain spiritual setting.

We must also understand that relying on the power and influence of symbols and related mantras within Reiki is possible only if used correctly. Only after receiving personal initiation, symbols, and mantras from simple hieroglyphs turn into an accurate and powerful tool for working with energy.

Steps

The traditional Reiki system has always consisted of three levels - Shoden (entry), Okuden (immersion), and Shinpiden (sacrament). Today, the fourth step has also been added to them - the Workshop, aimed at "teacher training."

As a result of initiation at each of these steps, the student receives "settings" for Reiki energy, theoretical knowledge and learns meditative and healing practices.

At whatever stage of Reiki comprehension, you may be, you should know some rules:

- Reiki method can be used simultaneously with other methods of treatment.

- The more you practice Reiki treatment, the more powerful and sophisticated it becomes.

- You should not complicate Reiki too much.

- Reiki can be used in everyday life. This method should become part of your existence, and then you can apply it in any situation.

- Reiki can help even in one minute with just a touch or a close look.

- Treatment should only be given to those who wish to receive it.

- Using the Reiki method, you can heal yourself, other people, animals, plants, energize any objects, including stones and amulets, purify energy and fill it with rooms, food, and drink.

- One of the important conditions for healing is the purity of intent.

The Reiki stepped system allows you to calmly and smoothly climb to the top at an individual pace. To improve healing abilities, of course, constant practice is necessary.

The first step

Shoden (entry) - understanding the basics of the spiritual method of healing Reiki.

- "Settings" on Reiki energy.

- An explanation of the Reiki method.

- Basic meditative and healing practices.

- Hand positions during healing.

At the first stage, you learn to work with energy, to feel its flow. The healer's experience is gaining - how the energy goes, what resonance is felt in the hands when healing a person, animal, plant, inanimate object; how quickly it is possible to calm thoughts, emotions during meditation, the depth of immersion in oneself.

This is a kind of preparation for the transition to the second stage, in which treatment occurs not only through the hands, through touching the object of healing, but mentally, at the level of awareness and intention. By regularly performing meditative and healing practices, you heal the mind and body, emotional state, purify and harmonize the energy flows in the body and prepare yourself for a new, higher level of work with Reiki energy.

The second step

Okuden (immersion) - an increase in the strength of Reiki and the expansion of the possibilities of using Reiki.

- Settings for three Reiki characters.

- Theory: remote treatment; the study of symbols (their origin, purpose, and practical application).

At the second stage, you learn to transmit healing energy in time and space; use Reiki symbols to transfer energy to any distance (into the past, present and future); to heal not only people, animals, objects, but also situations, relationships with other people; You can also protect yourself, objects; heal habits, behavior; work with emotions; successfully implement a plan and so on.

In the second stage, you learn to work more deeply with yourself and with other people. People begin to become more aware of the processes that happen to them and their loved ones, to work more consciously with the healing energy of Reiki.

The third step
Shinpiden (sacrament) - further spiritual growth, increased intuition, healing abilities.

- Setting for the fourth Reiki character.

- Theory: on the origin, meaning, and practical application of the symbols.

- The technique of energy amplification - Reiju.

In the third stage, further spiritual growth occurs. After the student has gained enough experience in distance treatment, in meditative practices, learned to better control his thoughts, emotions and much more, he is ready to move on to the third level of training, that is, to an even higher level of energy work. At this level, the ability to heal and self-clean with Reiki is markedly increased.

The third step is the threshold of the Workshop. Not everyone feels the desire or willingness to devote themselves to the work of the Master. After all, this is a completely different level of work with energy, a great responsibility to students, high requirements for personal qualities.

In the Japanese tradition, you can go through the third step and continue your spiritual growth by taking the fourth, very powerful symbol for personal spiritual growth - a symbol of spiritual enlightenment. Indeed, many people turn to Reiki in order to learn how to treat themselves, their friends and relatives, to learn how to meditate, to control themselves in difficult situations, to purify themselves from negative energies, to cultivate oneself spiritually, to recognize the causes of failures and ailments, to successfully solve life problems, to learn the laws of the Universe etc.

And advancement to the third step allows them to more effectively and successfully improve in this.

The fourth step

The level of the Master (Teacher) is the level that gives the right to teach others the Reiki method.

First, you need to go through the initiation to the level of the Reiki Master (Teacher). Only then can one gain the right to initiate at the first stage of Reiki and begin to gain relevant experience.

In parallel with this practice, training takes the form of classes in which you study:

- make settings for the second, third and workshop stages;

- conduct a theoretical course of each step;

- conduct meditative and healing practices in a group.

As already mentioned, the level of the Master (Teacher) is an even higher level of work with energy. You re-comprehend the essence of the first, second, third, and Workshop of Reiki steps. In addition to owning theoretical and practical teaching material, the Master should be able to control himself, constantly improve, and be able to help students on their spiritual Path. No wonder they say that there is no better way to learn something than by starting to teach it. Each initiation or lesson you take in a group opens up new possibilities for understanding the Reiki method and energy. And there is no limit to this perfection.

Circle Training

One of the conditions for receiving initiation is compulsory training. The training takes place on the Reiki circle, conducted by the Master. During the training, skills are transferred on how to use what was received during the initiation. The master also answers the student's questions.

During training, the first step is passed on how to do a Reiki session for yourself and another person. Learning takes the form of oral transmission. At the same time, it is clearly stipulated that the training takes place (first stage, second stage, third stage). A certain amount of information and a "key" are transmitted, allowing you to use it correctly.

Oral Tradition

Reiki is an oral tradition. What is written in the book is just information, not a Reiki broadcast. Reiki practice is transmitted by the Master personally to the student, in person. Information can be distributed widely and accessible to everyone. And the sacrament can only be transmitted to a person personally.

With oral transmission, in addition to information, something else is transmitted that cannot be transmitted without personal contact. The story of Reiki is a story about people's lives, thanks to which we now have the opportunity to learn this practice and practice it. In Reiki sessions, both the narrator and the listeners live some of their internal events. And this residence gives an invaluable experience of touching the mystery of what happened in the mind of Mikao Usui when he went to get Reiki. And then to pass it on to people.

Each of us goes his own life; each carries out his search and makes his own choice. The example of Mikao Usui allows us to decide for ourselves what to do in similar situations. And history gives a chance to feel, catch what Mikao Usui relied on when the people around him were ready to accept his gift. And if he had not achieved this, Reiki would not have reached us. But he managed to achieve this by doing a great job not only outside, but also inside himself.

Reiki Symbols

There are four characters in Reiki Usui Shiki Ryoho. These symbols are not a secret - they are passed on to everyone who receives the second stage. But at the same time, they are a mystery; that is, they not only have an external form but are also endowed with something more.

We will not give an image of these symbols here, since these are just drawings, and their essence, filling through a book cannot be transmitted. If you decide to do Reiki, then you will be introduced to them by the Master - the person who will teach you. And then you yourself will begin to build your relationship with symbols and with Reiki through symbols.

Here is a quote from the book of the Japanese Master Reiki, a member of the Usui Reiki Ryoho Gakkai (Tokyo) society, Mr. Hiroshi Doi, "The Modern Method of Reiki Healing":

"The symbols presented in Reiki for working with higher energy techniques are easily applicable. In the Japanese Reiki tradition, symbols are not given as much importance as in the Western tradition, where the number of symbols is increasing.

In the Japanese tradition, the role of Reiki symbols is exactly the same as the supporting wheels of a bicycle when you learn to ride. Anyone can ride a bike with support wheels. The shape of the support wheels can be different as long as the "support" function is satisfied. The same can be said of Reiki symbols.

Symbols facilitate the use of Reiki energy. The symbols are useful, convenient, and enjoyable to use, but Reiki healers should leave them when they have grown enough as healers (supporting wheels are also removed when a person has learned to ride a bicycle well). Symbols need to be used as a tool. You should not have a misunderstanding of the function of symbols. It's pointless to look for new additional characters or consider them sacred.

Usui-sensei did not use symbols but said: "Use symbols well. Use them more and more, and you will find yourself at a level where you no longer need symbols. The human mind can instantly reach anywhere in the universe. You need to grow so high that you no longer need symbols."

In other spiritual practices, symbols are mostly of religious significance or given as a revelation for spiritual growth. But the symbols used in Reiki do not have that meaning. They are designed to facilitate the implementation of higher Reiki techniques with the help of vibrations and resonance characteristics of symbols.

When using characters, two effects occur:

- The shape of the characters has its own vibration, the resonance of which can be used.

- Mental energy vibration occurs when you understand the action of a symbol. Then there is a resonance between your energy and the energy of the symbol.

First, the first effect occurs, and then you can get the second. When you learn to control the energy of your mind, you can no longer use symbols.

You should study all the characters and learn how to use them correctly. Then you will need to achieve a level of non-use of characters. You decide when to use the first three characters, and then the fourth character. After that, you will understand that you are ready to rise above the symbols.

If you have any doubts or misconceptions or you do not feel any effect from moving to the next stage, you can use all the symbols as before. If you practice long and long enough, you are so filled with Light that one day, you yourself become a symbol of Light. But it is you who decide (feel) when to make this transition.

So, in the second stage of Reiki, you apply three characters. At this stage, the flow of Reiki energy for healing doubles compared to the first stage, you become able to better use Reiki energy in various ways.

1st character
The meaning is to heal and purify at the level of matter and body. The first symbol is called the symbol of increasing power and can be used in various ways since it contains a higher power. It is used alone or with other symbols - to increase their strength. It may also have protective value.

2nd character
The meaning is to heal and purify at the level of spirituality and the subconscious. The second symbol is a symbol of love and harmony. It is sophisticated and full of harmony. A distinctive feature is that it sends the energy of balance and harmony precisely to an object that does not have a form, for example, to feelings. Harmonizes the emotional and mental energies. It is used both independently and together with the first character.

3rd character
The meaning is to heal and purify from a distance, in the past, present, and future. This symbol is a conductor in space and time. It helps transfer energy from a distance. It is effective when used together with the first and / or second character. Directs energy directly to the center of the essence, located outside of time and space - this is its distinctive feature. It is mainly used for healing at a distance, cleansing karma and injuries, and for creating a beautiful future.

4th character
In the third stage of Reiki, one symbol is used, which replaces all previous ones.

Chapter 5
Learning to Read the Energy Field

The main practice in Reiki Usui Shiki Ryoho is a Reiki session. You can do a Reiki session for yourself or another person, or you can get it from another person. Anyone conducting a Reiki session must have Reiki initiation and undergo training.

During the session, open palms are placed on the human body. This is done by the one who is conducting the session. He does nothing else. He only puts his palms, and Reiki does the rest.

Each person feels the session differently, and each one receives something of their own in the session. That which is most necessary for him at a given moment in time. That which has his inner consent.

Thanks to Reiki sessions, even quite serious illnesses are sometimes cured, a life situation or a person's attitude to it changes. However, there a few things you must learn. That is what this chapter of this book is dedicated to.

Increase Positive Energy and Avoid the Negative Energy

With the help of Reiki, we can cleanse, heal, and harmonize the energy centers - chakras. Agreeably, we are often overreacting to difficult life situations. No matter what we feel - anger, fear or aggression, we feel at this moment completely unprotected. At the same time, we don't even realize that we ourselves are the source of such

477

sensations. External life only provokes us to manifest our inner imbalance.

The situation can be corrected by learning to be distracted from external problems and concentrate on internal energy - the energy of the chakras. After all, it is her imbalance that is the cause of the violation of our internal balance.

Energy movement and the Chakra

In order to heal with the help of Reiki the seven main chakras, it is necessary to know their location, and the properties of the energy flow passing through them. Then you can meditate with each of the chakras until you reach a feeling of complete balance.

Unlocking and Balancing the Chakras

Unlocking the chakras is to determine the causes of the blocks and the malfunctioning of energy centers, and their subsequent elimination. However, preventing the blocking of energy nodes is much easier than working with closed chakras. Unlocking energy centers requires determining the causes of blocks for each energy center.

- Fear is the cause of the Muladhara blocks.

- The second energy center of Swadhisthana is destroyed by guilt.

- The center of self-realization of Manipura is exposed to the emergence of blocks as a result of shame.

- Grief is the cause of the destruction of the Anahata love center.

- Lies, including to oneself, block the Vishuddha chakra.

- Unlocking is necessary for the center of intuition of Ajna if a person lives in a world of illusions.

478

- The divine center of the Sahasrara is destroyed by strong earthly attachments.

When energy is Unbalanced or Blocked?

Is it possible to unlock the chakras yourself, you may ask? Self-unlocking of the chakras is possible as much as a person's desire. Working with the energy system requires a serious and responsible approach. One-time meditations and periodic visits to yoga centers are not sufficient efforts. Unlocking the chakras in a person is a rather painstaking work that requires daily exercise.

Meditative practices help but also involve difficult work with one's own mind. The results may not come very soon, which, of course, often deprives enthusiasm. Yogic asanas aimed at activating certain chakras may seem too difficult for beginners to perform physically. The development of the body, as well as the improvement of the energy system, does not tolerate haste. Unlocking the chakras on your own will require your self-control and seriousness.

How can chakras be unlocked on the human body? Before you unlock the chakras, you need to find out the cause of the blocks. As we have already found out, each energy center has its own reason for blocking. Therefore, each energy node requires a specific approach to unlock.

- Chakra Muladhara is destroyed by fears. To cope with them, they need to meet, look at them, and feel.

- Guilt blocking Swadhisthana is subjected to the same method. Feelings of guilt must be analyzed, accepting the real reasons for it and removing the illusory.

- The same applies to shame that destroys Manipura.
- Unlocking the Anahata chakra, blocked by sorrow, requires a lot of willpower and sometimes time.

- Working with Vishuddha has a basic rule - do not lie. Speaking a lie to others, we begin to do the same in dialogs with ourselves. This blocks the speech center.

479

- Ajna opens and loses blocks if reality is added to his perception of the world.

- The Sahasrara is cleansed by letting go of earthly attachments.

Is there a universal practice for unlocking chakras?

As I already mentioned, unlocking the chakras requires a serious and high-quality approach, including working with each energy center. The best practice is to unlock the chakras in turn. The universal technique is the practice of working with the middle Anahata chakra. The heart center connects the lower chakras with the upper. Charging this energy center, we supply energy and open all the others. Again, this technique of unlocking the chakras is not sufficient. Despite its versatility, it requires additional work with each energy center.

First Chakra

The first chakra - Muladhara (root) - is located at the base of the spine. It is the source of our existence because it closely connects our body with the Earth. The first chakra is responsible for our survival - for food, clothing, shelter, protection, and procreation.

The first sign of imbalance in the first chakra is a sense of danger.

Go for a walk just to mingle with nature. Take a closer look at the life boiling around you. Feel how it is imbued with life force. Nature fills everything that exists with life - trees and grass, animals and birds, rivers, and mountains. Her power pervades you, feel it. Realize that you are not living life, but life is living by you. Understand that there is a force that gives you life, makes your heart beat, your lungs breathe, and blood runs through your veins. Recognize yourself as part of nature, and a sense of fear will leave you.

Second Chakra

The second chakra - Swadhisthana - is located in the pelvic area. Its main driving force is the search for pleasure. The main desire is a sensual and sexual activity, the desire to plunge into the ocean of sensations, to feel attractive and to be able to get whatever you want.

With the unbalanced second chakra, the pursuit of pleasure never ends with a sense of pleasure. Remember the feeling of satisfaction that made you feel guilty. Restore the object of pleasure in your memory and try again to experience all the sensations, but this time fully aware of them. Describe your feelings. Did this experience bring you pleasure? In what place of your body are the experienced sensations concentrated? Realize them fully. Surely you will find that your ability to enjoy has become much wider. Now it's much easier for you to achieve it.

Third Chakra

The third chakra - Manipura - is located in the solar plexus. It is a source of self-confidence, self-awareness. Thanks to her, we are able to distance ourselves from the influence of the outside world and at the same time, exert influence on it.

The main signs of instability of the third chakra are guilt that embraces us when someone refuses something, fawning over others, a constant sense of ourselves as a victim, a feeling of helplessness and an inability to fend for ourselves. Once in a conflict situation, we can balance the third chakra by asking ourselves two very important questions.

1. Is something really threatening me? (Is my safety or even survival in jeopardy?)

2. Do I really care about the outcome? (If I win the fight, will it mean something to me?)

Fourth Chakra

The fourth chakra - Anahata - is located in the region of the heart.

The "path of the heart" is not a life strategy, but joy in all its manifestations. It allows you to live your life and influence the material world.

The main manifestation of the unbalanced fourth chakra is sentimentality. When our heart is broken, we are not able to separate our problems from those of others. The imbalance of the fourth chakra is also manifested in an exaggerated immersion in love and dependence. Learn to listen to your heart, and soon it will become a habit with you! You will gain a sense of comprehensive calm. Accept with gratitude what people want to give you. Let them feel the joy of doing a good deed.

Fifth Chakra

The fifth chakra - Vishudha - is located in the neck. Having opened it, we begin to perceive our own giftedness, no matter what manifests itself. The main property of the fifth chakra is the awakening of your inner voice, capable of telling you the truth.

With the unbalanced fifth chakra, we realize our right to independent thinking, but we cannot put its manifestation in order. We are in a constant struggle for personal freedom.

Analyze everything you believed in before. What were your ideas about life? After all, it was this which influenced your life. It was this which shaped your point of view. Try to consciously change and expand your range of beliefs; this will give a powerful impetus to your discovery of your uniqueness.

Concentrate on your breathing, as it is through it that energy comes to you. Focus on the depth of breathing; try to make it even deeper and slower.

You will feel that your anxiety disappears. You are immersed in a state of peace and tranquility.

Sixth Chakra

The sixth chakra - Ajna - is located in the forehead, at the point between the eyebrows. The ultimate goal of the sixth chakra is inspiration and grace. This is a world of images that arise in our thoughts. However, she also has the opposite extreme - the desire to escape from reality into the world of illusions.

The unbalanced sixth chakra allows fear to completely absorb our personality. But if we realize that we are in an unbalanced state, if we can look inside ourselves and find the source of this fear, then we are able to overcome it.

Try to answer the following questions:

- What are you dreaming about?

- What is your imagination striving for?

- What images dominate your fantasies?

- Do you seek to plunge deeper into the world of fantasy, or is the mind overpowering your imagination?

Become a witness to your own life. This will mean that you have taken the first step towards the development of the spiritual will. Describe your feelings and try to understand in which direction your imagination is moving - healthy or pathological.

Seventh Chakra

The seventh chakra - Sahasrara - is located at the top of the head. It is also called the "crown chakra." It represents pure, unclouded cosmic energy. Our desire to feel God is the main desire of the seventh chakra.

483

The unbalanced seventh chakra is a dangerous business. There is a threat that we will begin to live in an independent reality that has nothing to do with the outside world.

Surrender completely to the will of providence and submit to the Higher power. You should no longer wonder about your path. You simply live, abide in this world, and your consciousness is on a divine level.

At this level, we come to the realization that we will have to answer for our actions in the face of Eternity.

Chapter 6
The Chakra Meditation
Opening Chakras in
Meditation

The simplest method for identifying chakras and nadis is to simply concentrate on them, which then automatically goes to Dhyana and, at the last stage, to Samadhi. Relaxing and closing your eyes, you concentrate on one of the chosen chakras.

In all cases, the eyes should be closed at all stages of the exercise. Closing his eyes, the one who is engaged in the inner gaze directs all his attention to the area where the chakra or Nadi that interests him should be located. No other thoughts, except about this chakra (its localization, form, and properties), are unacceptable. At first, you will not see anything. Then, some heaviness, burning, or elasticity will begin to be felt in the area of the chakra. Then the chakras will begin to be felt in the form of some dense clumps. Finally, the success in the exercise will be accompanied by the "lighting" of the chakra, when the chakra chosen for today's class begins to be seen as a bright ball, glowing with the corresponding color.

In any case, the first week of classes may not even lead to the sensation of the chakras as dense clumps. You should not be upset and increase the time of your studies yourself (5-10 minutes for the first week are the limit) and even more so - you should not consider yourself unsuitable for such practice. In the first months of training in one session, you should not concentrate on more than one or a maximum of two chakras. Do not rush. When all the chakras feel like luminous

485

and emitting balls, it makes sense in one lesson to "look through" all of them. This is the control of the successful completion of this exercise. Such a procedure to fully identify all the major chakras along Sushumna can take 20-30 minutes. In no case should you concentrate more, since an overload of your mental and physical capabilities may occur. Over time, this restriction disappears.

The second version of the practice of exercises to identify the chakras is as follows. Having taken the initial position and relaxing, the student does not close his eyes but meditates on the graphic image of the corresponding chakra in the form of the yantra. This is the first stage of practice. It lasts no more than 5-10 minutes, similarly to the Trataka described above. All thoughts are excluded, and those that will one way or another relate to the search for bodily localization of the chakra should be preserved. At the second stage of the same exercise, the student, without rising from the mat, closes his eyes and focuses on the place where the chakra should be.

After spending as much time with his eyes closed, how much he practiced with visual fixation of the picture with the chakra, he opens his eyes again. This makes up one cycle. In one lesson, you can do from two to three such cycles. This practice option can be somewhat complicated by the fact that when closing the eyes after visual concentration in the figure of the chakra, the student tries to mentally transfer and immerse its graphic analog into the corresponding chakra.

This third option of practicing the exercise is as easy as the first two. In this case, it is advisable to open the AUM mantra with a voice or mentally at least 3 times before opening the eyes. After opening your eyes, it is useful to read some prayer formula or perform the Octagon of the Buddha. Anyway, some hard work, requiring well-known physical or intellectual efforts immediately after exercises in the identification of chakras, is categorically excluded.

I recommend reading the scriptures (for example, the Bhagavad-gita) or any other literature that is pleasant to the soul and ennobles thoughts. You should also not take a bath or go to the shower. It should be noted that the colors of the chakras that you see during successful meditation may not coincide with those colors that are given in the drawings - their graphic counterparts. The color of the revealed chakra depends both on the purity of your astral body, and on what part of the chakra you selected during the concentration process.

It should also be remembered that the exercise is called meditation, and not concentration due to the fact that in addition to highlighting the chakra itself, an attempt is made by the practitioner to determine all the related properties.

Effects of Chakra Meditation

1. The astral body is cleansed, which leads to greater mental poise. This helps strengthen intellectual abilities, creates the conditions for unlimited growth of the mind and knowledge of the properties of the universe.

2. The psyche becomes more flexible and controlled. At the same time, the student acquires basic prerequisites for controlling internal energy and developing the capabilities of a psychic.

3. The ability of the sense-perception of objects of the external and especially the internal world is heightened.

4. Eliminate the negative consequences of past mental activity. This primarily refers to meditation on the Ajna Chakra. Even in its simplest form, having not yet achieved complete success, the student receives mental rest.

Things to note
Once again, I draw your attention to the importance of observing the conditions preceding and following meditation. In addition, compliance with the principles of Yama and Niyama should be analyzed. If all these conditions are not observed, the effect may be the opposite: the psyche becomes aggravated, the consciousness becomes unbalanced and excessively nervous.

487

If you experience any negative feelings, proceed to reading the mantra. Until that time, when you can freely "light" the chakras, that is, during the development of the technique of exercise, you should take breaks in classes and meditate on the chakras no more than 2 times a week. The rest of the time, do lighter exercises. In any case, special attention should be paid to the Trataka, especially to the flame of a candle.

The recommended sequence for identifying chakras can be slightly modified in accordance with the principles of A. Ghosh Integral Yoga, the main of which is a ban on the activation of the lower chakras (that is, first of all, Muladhara and Swadisthana) without appropriate readiness for that from the higher chakras: Sahasrara, and Vishuddha Chakras. One way or another, the main significance here is the consolidation of the principles of Yama and Niyama in the subconscious of the practitioner, and one should always return to them with any variant of practice.

The identification of chakras and other meditative procedures of higher yogis can awaken the Kundalini. The translation of at least part of the body's static energy into a dynamic form is usually accompanied by a sensation of heat along the spine. The spine becomes hot from the inside. This sensation can be considered as a sign of the manifestation of Samadhi (the last phase of the octal ladder of the "means of achieving yoga") on the physical plane: oncoming warm and cold "waves," a cloudy veil in front of the eyes, slight dizziness, slow speech, etc. Here these processes are very probable and should not get you scared: they are objective and must pass quickly. If they do not pass, the OM mantra will help you.

In this case, the student, having adopted a meditative pose, be sure to sit cross-legged (it is very important to observe the requirement to keep your back straight!), relax and, closing his eyes, concentrate on one of the chosen chakras.

Chapter 7
Energy Healing
Application

Hand Positions for Energy Healing

In the Reiki system, there are 12 main positions of the hands and 4 additional. Each of them has its own purpose in terms of healing from various diseases.

The main positions of the hands are located in the head, back, and front of the body.

The main positions for the head

The first position - Hands close the eyes
Relaxes and relieves fear and tension. It helps with problems associated with sinuses, diseases of the eyes, nose, teeth, and jaws.

Balances the pineal gland and the pituitary gland corresponding to the 6th and 7th chakra.

The second position - Hands cover the head
Synchronizes the left and right hemispheres of the brain, improves memory. Used for headaches and otitis media.

The third position - Hands cover the back of the head
It relaxes, relieves stress, and relieves mental fatigue. It is used for problems associated with the cerebellum and spinal cord, as well as headaches.

The fourth position - Hands cover the neck

It gives a feeling of joy, instills self-confidence, and enhances creative abilities. Used for tonsillitis, tonsillitis, and thyroid diseases. Corresponds to the 5th chakra.

The main positions for the front of the body

The fifth position - Hands just above the chest, at heart level

It creates a feeling of love, trust, and spiritual harmony. It affects the thymus corresponding to the heart chakra.

Useful for the lungs and cardiovascular system.

The sixth position - Hands at the level of the solar plexus

Relieves from fears and worries caused by stress. Affects the solar plexus corresponding to the 3rd chakra. It is used for diseases of the liver, stomach, gall bladder, spleen, and digestive tract.

The seventh position - Hands on the stomach

It helps to get rid of stress and unfounded fears. It affects the 2nd and 3rd chakras. It is used for diseases of the liver, stomach, gall bladder, spleen, and digestive tract.

The eighth position - Lower abdomen

Relieves of sexual impotence and relieves stress associated with insecurity in sexual capabilities.

It has an effect on the 1st and 2nd chakras. It is useful for women for the ovaries and uterus, for men - for the prostate gland.

It helps with diseases of the digestive tract.

The main positions for the back

The ninth position - Hands at the base of the neck
It relieves stress and promotes relaxation. It helps with problems in the spine and neck.

The tenth position - Arms at shoulder level
It has the same effect as the ninth position for the front surface of the body.

The eleventh position - Hands on the back
It has the same effect as the seventh position. It affects the 2nd and 3rd chakras.

Useful for the kidneys.

The twelfth position - Hands at the base of the spine
It has the same effect as the eighth position. It has an effect on the 1st and 2nd chakras.

Useful for tailbone injuries.

Additional positions

First position
One hand is on the forehead, the other on the back of the head. This position is also called the "cosmic plug" because it helps to "recharge" your energy or the energy of the person you are healing.

Second position
One hand is on the heart chakra; the other is on the face. This position helps with insomnia: it allows you to calm down and fall asleep.

Third position
Both hands are on the heart chakra. This position also contributes to rapid falling asleep.

Fourth position

One hand is on the heart chakra; the other is on the solar plexus. It acts the same as in the first position.

Experiencing Presence - Treatment Session Conditions

Ventilate the room well before starting a treatment session. It should be clean, bright, and quiet so that you can relax well. If the room you choose does not particularly meet these requirements, before starting treatment, clean the energy in it using the Reiki method.

Prepare a blanket in advance in case you feel cold during relaxation. You can also use soothing music.

Wash your hands in advance if you have to touch the person you are healing. In addition, you need to cleanse yourself of the low vibrations of energy in your hands.

Rub your hands to warm them.

Both you and your patient must remove the watch if you do not want the time displayed on it to change under the influence of Reiki energy.

You, as a person transmitting energy, remove everything from your hands so as not to injure the patient during touch.

The healed must take off what constricts his body — a belt, tie, and bra. As for jewelry: it is better to remove chains and bracelets. Removing rings and earrings are not necessary, as they are charged with good energy.

The patient should lie or sit comfortably. You must definitely relax. Do not cross arms or legs and try to free yourself from tension.

If you cannot touch the healed, keep your hands above the person. Keep your hands 3-5 cm above body areas that should not be touched due to burns or skin diseases. You can put your hands on top

492

of clothes or a wool blanket. If it's uncomfortable to touch some areas, put your hands on this area over the hands of the recipient.

Tell the patient in advance about the changes that may occur after treatment. He should know that immediately after a healing session, his condition may worsen, unpleasant symptoms such as fever, nervous excitement, more profuse discharge, eczema or pain may appear. These phenomena are called an improvement reaction, indicating that the process of restoring health has begun.

Reiki exercises

Those who are just starting to practice Reiki can be advised on simple exercises that are directly related to the teachings of Mikao Usui. They will be very helpful in the preparatory phase. Basically, they are associated with relaxation, by learning which, you can at any moment, barely feeling tired, fully relax.

The state of rest does not occur on its own. It may seem strange to you, but you need to learn this. Without the ability to relax, Reiki may seem to you too complicated a practice - not getting rid of fatigue, but, on the contrary, an excessive waste of strength and energy.

You can contact the complex below at any time as soon as you feel tired. You can also use it as a protective gymnastics to recover from a Reiki session you do for someone else.

Exercise 1
Sit on a comfortable (medium-hard) mat. Cross your legs. Keep your back and head straight. Cover your eyelids and look in front of you. The abdominal muscles are tense, and the upper body is relaxed. Keep your hands on your stomach - one slightly higher than the other. The breathing is even calm.

Your task is to direct energy to the area just below the navel and mentally focus on this point.

493

Exercise 2

Cross your fingers and hold them by the head, hold on the back of the head. Press lightly on the back of the head. As you exhale, relax. Perform the exercise for 5-10 minutes. It not only helps to relax but also relieves dizziness.

Exercise 3

Release your fingers and pinch your auricles. Press with your index fingers on the points located just above the auricles. Place your thumbs in position behind the ear. Do this exercise 5 times.

Exercise 4

Slowly lower your arms down. Then place them near the abdomen so that the palm of one hand touches the back of the other. Cross your legs. Tilt your head forward a bit. Swing your head from side to side. Do this about 10 times.

Shaking your head has a powerful healing effect. It leads to the massage of points located behind the ear. This exercise is an excellent prevention of various diseases of the eyes, ear, throat, nose, as well as neurasthenia.

Exercise 5

Performing the previous exercise, you can feel an unpleasant heaviness in the back. The reason is the stagnant processes. In order to get rid of negative feelings, you need to give the spinal and lumbar muscles the necessary tone. This is done by rubbing the points located on the lower back.

A massage is performed in a sitting position. Cross your legs and keep your back straight. Take a few deep breaths. Mentally direct energy to the navel. Then hold your breath. At this point, you will feel the heat spreading inside the abdomen. Spread your hands, as before self-massage, and with warm fingers touch the lower back. Lightly stroke the points near the lower parts of the spine. Do this 10 times.

Exercise 6

Stay in a sitting position. Keep your back and head straight. Pull the legs forward so that the heels touch and the toes point up. Bend your arms at the elbows - so that the palms are pointing down. Do not strain.

Describe the circle in the air as if you were spinning a wheel. Hand movements begin in the lower abdomen and then to the hypochondrium. Fingers should be free.

This exercise relieves fatigue in the legs and at the same time, has a therapeutic effect on diseases of the lower back.

Exercise 7

Sit with your legs extended and touching the heels on the floor. Squeeze your fingers into a lock and raise your hands above your head with your palms up. Stay in this position for a few seconds, and then touch the crown of your head with your fingers. Keep your head straight, slightly extend the spine up. Relax your hands and touch your toes. Try not to bend your knees, but do not strain. Repeat exercise 5 times.

It is aimed at relaxation and rest, and in addition, when it is performed, the muscles of the chest, legs, and arms are filled with energy.

Exercise 8

Take a sitting position. Keep your back and head straight. Look in front of you with your eyes half-closed. Keep your hands in the lower abdomen, one palm over the other. Take a few full breaths. Calm down and tune into contemplation. Concentrate on the point in the navel. Abdominal breathing. Thanks to this exercise, you will feel an influx of heat into the abdomen, which means restoring the balance of yin and yang.

And here are a few more exercises aimed at restoring the balance of elements and relieving stress. They are performed in the famous yoga position "Lotus."

495

Exercise 9

Sit on the floor. Stretch your legs. Keep your torso straight. Imagine your spine is the axis from earth to sky. Keep your hands on your lap. Bend the left leg at the knee, turn its foot with the sole upward, and place it on the thigh of the right leg at the groin. You need to touch the back of the foot. Bend the right leg at the knee, and put the foot on the thigh of the left leg in the groin area (backside). Both knees should be pressed to the floor.

If it doesn't work right away, don't worry. Achieve perfection gradually. When you take the desired position with ease, know that you are at the goal. In this case, the effect of breathing exercises will increase significantly; rhythmic breathing will appear. You will stock up on creative energy; you will feel its surge in your body. If your breath is directed towards enlightenment, then you can hold back the energy that overflows you. Then it will serve only for your good - it will create a barrier to illnesses, bad thoughts, and deeds.

Exercise 10

Lie on your back. Stretch your legs, and place your hands along the body. In succession, relax all the muscles, starting from the legs - feet, lower legs, knees, hips, and then - the trunk, arms, shoulders, neck, head.

Breathe smoothly, calmly, without straining. At some point, you will stop feeling your body. Consciousness will concentrate on the inner workings of the heart. You will feel that you are immersed in a state of absolute peace and joy. Try to breathe as slowly as you can, but do not do it too consciously. The right pace will come on its own.

Exercise 11

Take a sitting or standing position. The eyes are half-closed. The breath is even measured. Focus on the point just below the navel. Hands up. As you inhale, feel the life-giving energy approach you. As you exhale, lower your arms - so that the palms are turned toward the body. In this case, mentally imagine the channels of energy passage and remove all blocks from its path. The spent energy will go to the ground through the legs.

496

As you inhale, let the energy rise again. Hands up. Repeat the exercise several times. It opens the chakras, which is necessary for the effectiveness of Reiki.

Learn How to be Mindful During Energy Healing

All of the above exercises allow you to fully absorb Reiki and make the most of the opportunity open to you to improve your condition - both yours and other people.

The practice of Reiki involves a special attitude towards the purification of the soul. This allows you to distance yourself from all situations and emotions that distract the mind. You may well resort to such mindfulness practices at the end of the day when you feel tired.

Chapter 8
Practical Classes For You!

Dr. Mikao Usui's Reiki's natural healing method is based on three pillars - Gassho, Reiji Ho, and Tiryo.

Gassho

At the end of each meditation or healing technique, Gassho's position is used, which in Japanese means "two hands joined together." Keep your palms at chest level, or rather, at heart level, which will be an expression of gratitude to God or the Universe.

Take a lotus or half lotus pose.

Close your eyes and relax. If you can, keep your eyes closed all the time to save energy inside and not be distracted by external stimuli.

Try to keep your back as straight as possible, but do not strain. If it's hard or uncomfortable for you to sit like that, you can put something under your back.

Do not regulate breathing; just let air in and out. Inhale deeply into the stomach.

Concentrate all your attention on the tips of your middle fingers (or on the tanden) and forget about everything else.

Do not drive away thoughts. Look at them from the side, be aware of them, and then again focus on your fingertips.

If you feel that your hands are tired, then slowly, without opening your palms, put them on your knees, and then return them to their original position.

At the end of the session, open your eyes and shake well your hands.

Thanks to gassho meditation, an increase in energy and an addiction to a meditative state of mind occur. Gassho should be performed every day - in the morning and/or in the evening - for 20-30 minutes.

Reiji ho

Translated from Japanese, the word "reiji" means "definition of the spirit," and in our case - "definition of Reiki energy." This technique teaches us to follow our intuition. It is to follow, not develop because intuition as a divine gift is given to us at birth. Our business is only to learn to hear her voice and act as he tells us.

As for the Reiji technique, just let the energy live freely. Feel like an empty vessel, which itself, without any participation from you, will be filled with vital energy. Do not think about where, when, and how it enters you; everything will happen by itself.

Sit or stand in front of the person you want to heal from some kind of ailment. Close your eyes and fold your hands in Gassho.

Focus your attention on tanden. Get rid of any stress and relax. Feel how your body is filled with Reiki energy and how you become part of this energy.

Ask your patient to be aware of the causes of his ailments, failures. Then ask for his healing at all levels. Slowly move your hands to the "third eye" area and ask Reiki to bring your hands where you need to. Problem areas will call your hands for help themselves.

Now you just have to wait a bit. You will certainly feel where your hands should go. This can happen in different ways. If visual images are closer to you, then you will see that part of the body that needs to be treated. If you tend to perceive the world by ear, you will hear this information. If you are a kinesthetic, that is, you perceive the world as if it were pores of the skin, then you just feel where you should touch the patient.

You can receive a "message" immediately or after some time. In order to speed up this process, place one or both of your hands on the patient's crown chakra and tune in to the energy of his body. If you still can't feel the problem area, use the Beesen technique (we will talk about it a bit later).

However, you must be assured that regular training will do the trick: you will learn to identify problem areas much faster, and when practicing Reiki for several years, you will see them with a bare glance at the person.

"How do you recognize this answer?" you ask. It comes to everyone differently. You yourself will feel it by a slight tingling sensation in your hands, a feeling of warmth or magnetism, or maybe you simply realize that the answer is received.

The art of Reiji Ho is akin to creativity: starting to use it for healing, you can extend your skill to any other areas of your life.

Tiryo

Translated into English, the word "tiryo" means "treatment." The patient lies on the floor or on any bedding. The healer kneels next to him and holds his dominant hand over his parietal chakra until there is an impulse or inspiration, which is followed by a hand.

The healer gives his hands complete freedom. It refers to the painful areas of the patient's body until they cease to hurt or until the hands themselves are detached from the body and find a new area for treatment.

Reiki Meditations

To elevate the spirit and heal the body in Reiki, special techniques are used that use the energy of higher dimensions and the accumulation of light.

Meditation (in the lane with Latin. - Reflection) is an internal concentration and concentration of the mind, control of one's own thought processes. Historically, meditative techniques have appeared in various religious practices (Buddhism, Sufism, Judaism, and Taoism). Nowadays, they are widely used in psychotherapy as a method of mental relaxation.

Along with the direct healing effect, meditation affects the deepest spiritual layers of human life. It opens up access to those innermost depths of the personality that are buried in everyday life under everyday worries and problems or are carefully covered with all kinds of social masks. With the help of meditation, we seem to establish a dialogue between consciousness and the subconscious; we allow the content of the subconscious to "surface" and manifest itself in consciousness. Meditative practice contributes to the development of intuition, which will undoubtedly be useful to any of us in everyday life and in creativity.

The method of meditation can also be used to combat stress.

Meditative techniques give both quick psychotherapeutic results and long-term ones. Experience shows that even short classes in meditative practices have a positive effect on human health. With long classes, of course, a greater effect is obtained. People who use the method of meditation both independently and under the supervision of a specialist have a more stable nervous system. They are less anxious and better manage stress.
In order to master the method of meditation, you need to practice regularly; then, it will become a familiar tool in self-medication.

In this case, it is necessary to control breathing, muscle tone, emotions, the flow of thoughts, and attention - the psychophysical components of meditation.

Muscle Tone Control

You can determine the depth of stress by muscle tension: the stronger the stress, the higher the muscle tension. With depression, the tone of the respiratory muscles decreases, and with anxiety and fear, the tone of the occipital muscles and muscle groups associated with speech increases. In other words, in order to relieve stress and normalize the psychophysical state, it is necessary to achieve relaxation of the muscles that affect the state of rest and rest.

Deep muscle relaxation leads to the release of substances with anti-stress action and stimulating the centers of pleasure of the brain - endorphins. Activation of the pleasure mechanism not only gives a pleasant feeling of relaxation but can also be considered as a preventive measure against stress.

Breath Control

First, learn how to regulate inhalation and exhalation. This will help you when you start practicing Reiki. To do this, take a regular, natural breath. Mentally pass your life energy to the navel area, as if deepening into the intestines. Hold your breath for a couple of seconds. Exhale - continuously, slowly, making the sound "Ha." The mouth is slightly ajar. Relax. Repeat this cycle 10-15 times.

A person in a stressful situation is characterized by superficial (shallow), fast or intermittent chest breathing, and slow abdominal breathing in a state of rest and comfort. Typically, the breathing process is automatic, and through meditation, you can learn to carefully monitor your breathing and be aware of it. Thanks to meditation, we can maintain abdominal breathing and mentally direct it to the desired area of the body, thus neutralizing anxiety, agitation, and outbreaks of negative emotions. In other words, we ourselves are able to give ourselves the opportunity to calm down in a situation of sudden short-term stress.

In meditation, breathing through some part of the body is often used. What does this mean? How can you breathe through some part of the body? It goes without saying that this is not about physiological breathing, but about the imaginary, existing only in our view. And if, as a result of meditation, you have a feeling of "extrapulmonary" breathing. A temporary connection has been established between two parts of the brain - the one that receives information from the respiratory tract and the respiratory muscles, and the one that receives information from the corresponding area of the body that is not connected with breathing.

As a result of changes in sensations in a selected part of the body, in particular, rhythmic fluctuations in their intensity occur synchronously with the phases of the respiratory cycle (attenuation of intensity - by inspiration, amplification - by exhalation). Such a temporary connection between different foci of excitation in the brain helps us fight pain, control our own pulse or blood pressure, and improve our mood.

How to understand whether you are doing the meditation exercise correctly? The criterion is the synchronization of breathing and sensations in a selected part of the body. As we have said, this is an increase in inspiration and a decrease in exhalation. With excitement or sudden fear, the ratio of inspiratory time to the time of the respiratory cycle increases as the inspiration becomes longer. Accordingly, a person in a state of relaxation is characterized by an inverse relationship. In meditation, the function of a longer expiration is used to more fully relax and calm emotions - muscle relaxation exactly at the time of exhalation.

In many meditations, the method of breathing through the hands is used. The fact is that palms and fingers play a very special role in our bodies. The area occupied by the projection area of the hand is larger than any other part of the body. Therefore, focusing on the sensations associated with the hands captures a much larger area of the cerebral cortex than for any other part of the body, and accordingly has a greater effect on the state of the brain and consciousness.

Emotion Control

With the help of breathing, we can not only monitor our emotions but also manage them. Our task is to learn to control our emotions. This is not so difficult: you need to feel your own body and grasp any changes associated with emotions. Our mistake lies in the fact that we often perceive only the information that comes from the outside, and completely ignore the signals coming from the inside. We do not seem to notice that we live in our own bodies.

Self-observation is, in essence, the ability to stay in the "here and now" state, on which the Reiki method is based.

Thought Flow Control

With the help of directed attention, calm breathing, and muscle relaxation, you can control the flow of thoughts. Decreased muscle tone reduces the flow of information from the muscles to the brain, allowing it to rest. Partial liberation of brain neurons from information processing leads to a special, or, as they say, altered, state of consciousness, which, in fact, plays a healing role.

How does this happen? In a state of altered state of consciousness achieved through deep meditation, the asymmetry between the hemispheres disappears. There comes a kind of condition without time and space, where the most controversial internal problems of the body are resolved - both psychological and physiological.

To enter an altered state of consciousness, you must do the following:

- Focus on inner feelings. This will reduce the influx of external stimuli to the brain, thereby helping to escape from the outside world and plunge into the depths of the inner world.

- Breathe in a measured rhythm, forcing attention to follow yourself and helping to direct it to certain parts of the body.

- Achieve muscle relaxation to reduce the flow of information from the muscles to the brain and help it sink into a state of rest.

As a result of immersion in this altered state, the roles are redistributed between consciousness and the subconscious. In the ordinary, awake state, our subconscious mind is suppressed by consciousness. In an altered state, consciousness, as it were, goes by the wayside, and the subconscious, on the contrary, is sharply activated.

Unexpectedly mobilizing reserves of the subconscious helps us solve important external problems. Due to the formation of new ties that expand the narrow framework of stereotypic response, the resolution of internal psychological problems also occurs.

An altered state of consciousness gives us the opportunity to relax, relieve the effects of stress. The body's natural regenerative processes are activated to help cure stress-related diseases.

Meditation is sometimes called the gap between thoughts. It seems that the internal dialogue ceases, there is a "stuck" on unresolved problems, a state of inner peace sets in, allowing you to know yourself, listen to the voice of the subconscious. This path to the inner wisdom that helps us find a way out of a difficult situation at first seems very difficult. But as you master the meditative practice, it becomes easier and comes to automatism.

Breathing Techniques

Many underestimate the role of breathing in Reiki practice. It is not right. After all, breathing is not just a process of inhaling, exhaling. It is directly related to vitality. In order for the energy to work for the good, you need to master several methods of proper breathing. You can choose one of them that will not cause difficulties.

What is "proper breathing"? It is distinguished by naturalness, measuredness, concentration, and evenness. In this case, you can breathe in different ways: inhaling and exhaling through the nose, or inhaling through the nose, and exhaling through the mouth, or inhaling and exhaling through the nose and mouth. Consciousness, at the same time, should concentrate on deep and rhythmic breathing. The mind prevails in this case. Every movement and every breath is controlled by it.

Remember that breathing exercises should not cause tension or dizziness. If this still happened, stop doing the exercise and breathe normally. Never allow violence against yourself! Remember that your breath is one of the sides of the whole being created.

Cleansing Breath

Stand up straight. Legs together. The palms are pressed to each other. The wrists are slightly pressed on the stomach so that the palms are perpendicular to the body. Take a deep breath through your nose. Hold your breath for a moment and start exhaling. In this case, the lips fold into a tube. Then, rhythmically, with strong, but sharp exhalations, throw out the air. Make sharp sounds. Do not puff out your cheeks.

This method of breathing cleanses the lungs and refreshes the body, gives it a reserve of vigor and health.

"Ha" - Breath

"Ha" breathing cleanses the respiratory system and helps improve blood flow. It also helps to keep calm and eliminate feelings of depression.
Stand straight - legs together, toes slightly apart. Take a deep breath. As you inhale, slowly raise your arms above your head, palms forward. Hands should be relaxed. Hold your breath. Then lower your hands and swiftly lean forward - so that your hands almost touch the floor. Exhale sharply through the mouth, saying "Ha" without the help

of the vocal cords. Sound is produced by exhaled air. Thus, you are freed from negative energy - it goes down through the hands. Stay in the tilt position for a few seconds - until the next breath. As you inhale, slowly straighten up, raising your arms above your head. With an exhalation through the nose, take the starting position. Repeat the exercise again.

Breath for Clarifying Thinking

This breathing exercise improves brain activity, increases the clarity of consciousness, and activates the thought process. The main role here is given to the diaphragm. Everything is built not on inhalation, but on exhalation.

Accept the Lotus position. If this is difficult for you to do, take any sitting posture. First, exhale sharply and quickly through your nose. After that - a full breath, just as fast and strong. No breath holding is required. Exhalation is done through the movement of the abdominal muscles and diaphragm (similar to the work of blacksmith bellows). Air fills the middle and lower parts of the lungs.

After exhaling, relax your abdominal muscles. The diaphragm will also be relaxed, and the lungs will be able to go down. First, do the exercise 10 times, and gradually bring it to 100.

Calming Breath

Soothing breath - smooth and deep. It can also be called natural. It usually complements the complete relaxation of the body. During such breathing, all your anxieties go away. You begin to feel that living is easy and enjoyable. You learn to mentally direct energy as you need.

Stretched breathing is also natural, but you should try to extend the breathing cycle a bit. On inhalation, touch the palate with your tongue. Lead energy to the lower body (just below the navel). Then hold your breath for a couple of seconds. Take a long exhalation, freeing the lungs. Do all this and mentally. Mouth ajar. Hold your breath again for a couple of seconds and exhale.

Deep Breathing

Deep breathing stimulates all endocrine glands, especially the thyroid gland. Metabolism improves. Such qualities as the ability to concentrate, the speed of reaction, and thinking develop.

Attention! This exercise cannot be performed at high pressure.

Accept the Lotus position. If it not yet comfortable for you to take this position, you can stand, sit, or lie. Concentrate on the thyroid gland. Take a full breath through your nose for every 8th pulse beat. Hold your breath for the same length of time. Then exhale completely through your mouth, making a whistling sound. Do not tighten your lips. The duration of exhalation is twice as long, so the proportion "inhale-hold of breath-exhale" is 1: 1: 2. Repeat exercise 5 times.

Abdominal Breathing

Abdominal breathing leads to the active work of the diaphragm, which means that it becomes easier to work with the lungs. It is also beneficial for blood flow to the spleen and pancreas. Cells are actively enriched with oxygen, which has a positive effect on the brain.

The first way - Take a breath - as you feel comfortable. The tongue should be located in the mouth so that the middle part slightly touches the palate, and with the tip - touch the teeth. Mentally direct life force below the navel. Focus on this area and hold your breath. On inspiration, try to maximize the size of the lower abdomen. Open your mouth slightly and exhale. The lower abdomen is compressed, and your attention is focused on the area below the navel.

The second way - Take a breath, as in method one. Also direct life force to the lower abdomen. The abdomen does not protrude, but contracts. Focus on the bottom of it. Hold your breath for a few seconds, and then exhale according to the same rules as in the first case. Hold your breath again. Focus on the navel.

These exercises can be complicated with the help of meditative phrases such as: "I feel good and calm,"; "I am in peace and harmony,"; "I am balanced," and others. Mentally pronounce the first part of the phrase when the tongue touches the palate. The lower abdomen increases in size. As you exhale, touch the tip of your tongue to your teeth and speak the second part of the phrase. The stomach is compressed and remains a couple of seconds in this position.

There is a variant of exercise when inhalation is done through the nose and exhale through the mouth. Repeat the exercise slowly and measuredly.

Primal Breath (Fetal Breathing)

A person's breathing is usually a reflection of his lifestyle. People who are in a hurry all the time breathe shallowly. Those who have the opportunity to contemplate breathe deeply. But each of us had a period of maximum comfort and protection from the stresses of the outside world - a period of stay in the mother's womb. Therefore, exercises that restore initial breathing are very effective.

Focus on the area below the navel. Send life energy there. Its penetration is controlled by a thought that is focused on it. As you inhale, squeeze your stomach, hold your breath and exhale slowly. As you exhale, relax your muscles. Hold your breath out and take a breath again. Such breath is given to us by Nature.

You can combine complete breathing, covering all body parts, with the conduit of energy. This will allow your body to get the maximum energy necessary for healing energy and for life.

Take a full, deep breath. Move vitality from the navel along the legs to the main point, which is located between the pads of the foot. Hold your breath and then exhale - slowly and completely. The energy at the same time rises up - from the feet to the lower abdomen.

This method of breathing will lead to the maximum enrichment of your body with oxygen and the removal of processed products. The work of the heart is normalized. The functioning of the respiratory and circulatory systems will improve. This breath can be called the "breath of youth."

There is also a method that includes the whole body in a breath-exhale cycle. Focus on the area below the navel. On inhalation, vital energy spreads throughout the body. Hold your breath for a couple of seconds. On exhalation, vital energy is carried out from the area below the navel throughout the body. As you exhale, hold your breath. With this method of breathing, all cells of the body are filled with life-giving force, which leads to their rejuvenation.

Full Breath

Full breathing activates the entire respiratory apparatus. With this method of breathing, energy consumption is significantly saved. All muscles work, the diaphragm is completely free, is not clamped by anything, and, therefore, actively helps air exchange processes.

Full breathing allows you to accumulate a large amount of energy in the body, increases the useful volume of the lungs. It calms the nervous system and promotes the development of will and determination. The functioning of the endocrine system improves, and hence the metabolism, which leads to the rejuvenation of the body.

Accept any position - lying, sitting, or standing. Exhale, trying to do so as fully as possible. Inhale through the nose.

Inhalation should be done for every 8th pulse beat, so that in a cycle of inhalation - breath-holding - exhalation, a proportion of 2: 1: 2 is observed. In this position, hold your breath for 4 heartbeats. Then start exhaling - slowly, following the same sequence as when inhaling. First, air goes through the nose, the abdominal walls are drawn in, then the ribs are compressed, and the shoulders and collarbones are lowered.

Directed Attention

Thanks to the ability to direct attention to various parts of the body, the appearance of a stable "image of oneself," or, speaking the language of physiologists, "body patterns" is achieved. This awareness affects both the person's self-esteem and his relationship with others.

Focused exercise has more than a healing effect. They provide an opportunity to quickly recover after sudden stress, at a time when emotional balance and self-control are lost. These exercises free us from panic and all kinds of fears.

The essence of the exercises is to mentally move to certain boundaries, which we will now mention. We can say that we are, as it were, attached to reality by both ends of the body: below - through contact with the ground, above - through the crown of the head.

In Taoist meditation practices, special attention is paid to the following boundaries: the crown - to enhance the sensation of ascending flows of "energy" (the border "man-sky"); palms - to reproduce the feeling of emphasis in the fingers and palms (the "man-man" border) and feet — to enhance the feeling of downward flows of "energy" (the "man-earth" border).

Exercises come down to taking a few deep breaths and exhaling and switching attention alternately to each of the indicated boundaries, starting with the "earth."

You probably already understood that all the psychophysiological components of meditation are closely related. Calm, slow breathing, muscle relaxation, and directed attention lead to calming thoughts and normalize the psychophysical consciousness of a person.

Meditative practices can be applied in everyday life. If you conduct them constantly, you will develop self-regulation skills that will give you peace and well-being. You will learn to control emotions and thoughts, and therefore, will adequately respond to any events.

From the foregoing, it follows that meditation is an integral part of the Reiki energy healing method.

Chapter 9
Unique Reiki Healing
Practices

B efore meditation or healing begins, it is necessary to activate three energy centers, or, as they are called in the Taoist tradition, three Dan-tien. This is necessary in order to further focus on its connection with the energy of the Earth and the energy of the Universe. Indeed, at the initial stage, you are not accustomed to energy flows, and you need to learn how to train the state of deep immersion of attention "inside yourself." Then this will happen automatically: in a split second, you will feel your connection with the Earth and the Universe.

In general, the concept of the three main energy centers (reservoirs) of a person is one of the basic concepts in Reiki. The philosopher from the sacred mountain of Kurama, Dr. Usui, teaches that in the Universe there are three main forces - Light, Love, and Power, for the harmonious functioning of which it is necessary to observe their balance. Light, Love, and Strength are represented in man by three Tributes (Tribute is concentrated energy). If you live in harmony with Love, Light, and Power, you will find happiness.

The upper Dan-tien is in the head. Using the power of the Spirit, it provides the interaction of the microcosm with the flows of Universal and Cosmic energy.

Middle Dan-tien is located in the middle of the body, at the level of the heart center. It provides an internal interaction of forces, is a container of love and virtue.

Lower Dan-tien, which is also called the "internal battery," is located between the navel, kidney and sexual centers. In Japanese tradition, this place is called tanden. With its help, the interaction of the microcosm with the flow of Earth energy is provided. In the lower Dan-tian, energy from all sources is mixed and converted into life force. This area contains many large lymph nodes, such as the lumbar lymph, common ileal, main drainage canal in the lower abdomen. An increase in the amount of energy in this area enhances blood flow, the movement of lymph and hormones, and saves the heart from unnecessary work.

Here is the area of the kidneys, which is also very important. The normal functioning of the kidneys in eastern folk medicine is given great attention since their condition affects the functioning of other body systems.

Thus, the physical health of a person, his sexual abilities, life expectancy depend on the quantity and quality of energy in tanden.

Concentrating on tanden is used in all Reiki techniques. By focusing on the tanden area, we can gradually restore our core energy.

Kenyoku

Translated from Japanese, "kenyoku" means "dry shower." The purpose of Kenyoku meditation is to cleanse the soul and body of negative thoughts and emotions in which we are immersed so much that we have no opportunity for self-disclosure.

We worry about all kinds of problems - both our own and others' - and miss the moments in life that will never happen again. But Kenyoku just allows us to feel the real, only moment.

This original technique should be performed every time you return home to free yourself from everyday fuss. Kenyoku meditation is carried out before each healing session, energy exercise, and at the end of the healing session.

It is performed in a sitting, standing, or lying position. The hand either touches the body or is located at a distance of 10 cm from the body.

In Reiki practice, three variations of this technique are used.

Option One
1. Place the open palm of your right hand on your left shoulder. The fingertips are opposite the top of the shoulder, where the collarbone meets the shoulder. Run your open palm in a straight line through the sternum to the upper right thigh. Repeat this action on the right side using your left hand, and then do the same thing on the left side again.
2. Place your right hand on top of your left shoulder. Slide your open palm on the outside with your straight left hand to your fingertips. Repeat this with your right hand, and then, if you want, again with your left.

Option Two
1. See paragraph 1 of the first option.

2. Sweep the open palm of one hand with the open palm of the other hand.

Option Three
1. See paragraph 1 of the first option.

2. Swipe movements with the open palm of one hand on the inside of the other hand, from the shoulder to the tips of the fingers.

Any of these options for Kenyoku ends with Gassho's position.

Joshin Kokyu Ho

Translated from Japanese, "Joshin Kokyu Ho" means "breath that cleanses the soul." The main goal of this meditation is complete relaxation, which will help you absorb cosmic energies with all organs and harmonize them. Only in this way can the best results in recovery be achieved. Joshin Kokyu Ho meditation is primarily aimed at relaxing the "third eye" area (the eyebrows).

This original technique is performed standing, sitting, or lying down.

Breathe slowly and naturally. Allow your body to relax and allow Reiki energy to flow completely freely.

Activate energy centers.

Put your hands on your hips with your palms up and breathe naturally through your nose. Focus on the lower energy center (tanden). As you inhale, imagine the white light entering the crown chakra, which will descend into the tanden, accumulate there and begin to gradually spread throughout the body, dissolving all tension. As you exhale, imagine how the white light that fills your entire body radiates through the skin, saturating and strengthening your aura.

A light flow of thought, minimal involvement of consciousness, and focus on sensations will appear, and Reiki energy will enter the body through the crown and exit through the pores.

This exercise takes a few minutes, but you can do it as much as you want. Finish it in the Gassho position and shake afterward, your hands.

Zakikiri Zoka Ho

This original technique of "cleansing objects" (this is how Zakikiri Dzoka Ho is translated from Japanese) allows you to remove strong negative energy and restore vibrational order using Reiki energy. Usually, this technique is used to charge crystals, amulets, and other items.

Your task is to activate the three energy centers.

Put the selected item on the palm of your left hand (and if you're left-handed, then right). If the subject is too large and does not fit in your palm, then the technique should be applied at certain points.

Say out loud: "I am starting Dzakikiri Dzoka Ho."

Constantly focus your attention on the lower Dan-tien.

Swipe your right palm at a distance of 5 cm from the subject, and then abruptly stop movement and hold your breath.

Do this manipulation 3 times, and then let Reiki fill this item through your hands.

When finished, set aside the item you were working with. Fold your hands in the position of Gassho and say: "I have finished Zakikiri Zoka Ho." Shake your hands well.

If you want, you can repeat this meditation again. In general, carry out such cleaning of objects as necessary.

Reiki Undo

The Japanese word "undo" means "exercise." In this case, we mean an exercise that frees the body from blocks and tension, allowing it to move without restrictions. This technique is performed while standing or sitting.

You will have to make circular motions for about 35 minutes, and therefore, for a start, you need to find a suitable place where no one will bother you and where there are no sharp corners that can cause injury.

Fold your hands in Gassho and mentally say: "Reiki Undo begins." So you allow Reiki energy to flow freely into your body.

Activate the three energy centers (Tribute).

Take a deep breath and exhale completely relax. Now take another deep breath and as you exhale try to let out as much air as possible.

By conducting such inhalations and exhalations several times, you may feel that your body has begun to move. If movement is difficult, be patient and continue to do this exercise daily for 3 months. If you find it difficult to completely relax, try to imagine that you are not an adult, but a child who can act the way he wants. Forget about self-control and remember that no one is looking at you. Throw all thoughts out of your head and indulge in a children's game.

If any sounds fly off your lips, do not shut up. If any memories come or emotions flow, do not drive them back, but rather, be aware of them and feel them. If tears flow from your eyes, do not hold back - cry as much as you want. You kind of open up and let off steam: letting your body clear. Do not worry, it itself knows what and how to do it. The main thing is not to limit your healing, to eliminate all prohibitions. Continue until your movements stop themselves.

When this happens, sit down or lie down. Immerse yourself deeply in yourself and observe the movement of energy within you. You may feel like you have stopped feeling the boundaries of your physical body. Fold your hands in Gassho and mentally say: "I graduated from Reiki Undo." Thank the energy of Reiki, and shake it well with your hands.

Reiki Shower

This technique is very simple and effective. You can apply it when you need to quickly cleanse yourself, restore energy balance, and fill up with Reiki energy.

Stand up or sit back. Close your eyes. Breathe easy and relaxed. When inhaling, raise your hands up, and as you exhale, slowly lower them with your palms towards you.

Activate the three energy centers (Tribute).

When you inhale, you absorb the energy of Reiki, and as you exhale, it passes through the whole body, purifying and healing it. At the same time, unused energy, together with our negative energy, goes to the earth.

We can say it another way: when you inhale, you raise the energy of the Earth and pass it through the body, and when you exhale, you give it to Heaven. By completing the exercise, you transfer the energy of Heaven to Earth.

Repeat the exercise several times, joining hands in Gassho.

Reiki Mawashi

The word "mawashi" in translation from Japanese means "current." Reiki mawashi is a group exercise with the current Reiki energy that passes through the bodies of the participants in the exercise.

Sit in a circle and hold your hands a few centimeters above or near the hand of each of your neighbors left and right.

If it's more convenient for you to touch your hands, then, please.

Turn your left palm up and the right palm down. The teacher sets the flow of energy to the left. Left hand, palm up. The receiver takes energy with his right hand, palm turned down, conducts energy through his body, and gives it to the next participant through his left hand. Interestingly, the energy of the group often exceeds the sum of the energies of all participants. It spontaneously heals at all possible levels.

The technique is performed within 10-15 minutes.

Healing Practices

In addition to the meditative practices of Reiki, there are also healing practices.

When self-meditating, you need to put your hands on your body in the indicated order (or hold them above the body). You will go through all the main positions or those that you consider necessary. To touch places that are hard to reach, such as those located on your back, simply put your hands nearby and imagine that they are in the correct position. Then the energy of Reiki will go exactly to the place you are thinking about. After all, it is able to pass either through the hands or through the realization that healing is directed to a certain position.
The time for transferring Reiki energy to the main positions for those who have passed the first stage is basically 5 minutes. Thus, in an hour, you can go through all 12 positions. However, do not get hung up on just this time: determine how much you personally need it.

After you have sent Reiki to all the main positions, put your hands on the sore spots. If you do not have enough time, put your hands on the sore spot immediately after directing energy to the head area. Remove your hands when you feel some effect - healing or at least relief. You can carry out such treatment at any time and in any place. If you have no time, you need not fulfill all 12 positions of Reiki treatment, but do them separately at different times. However, if you want to achieve complete harmony, you will have to complete all 12 positions.

It's all about self-healing. But you can treat other people with Reiki's help. To do this, put your hands on each of the positions on the other person's body and keep them there for 5 minutes, that is, the same way as in self-treatment.

If you want to direct energy to any one position or to a place that causes concern to your patient, first direct Reiki energy to the head area, and then to this position.

With the help of Reiki energy, you can also heal animals. First, put your hand on your pet's forehead, and then move on to other positions on his head and body. If you cannot touch any place or hold your hands firmly, hold them just a short distance away. The animal will feel calm and comfortable when during the transfer of energy, you gently put your hands on his head or neck.

If you want to cure a bird, carefully grab it with both your hands or keep your hands above the cage. You can even treat your aquarium fish with your hands on the aquarium!

To treat a plant, place your hands on its leaves, trunk, or roots. Flowers heal as follows: the stems or roots are held with both hands. You can send Reiki vital energy to the seeds of plants or vegetables, or you can send it to the soil and water.

To purify the atmosphere and heal the air in the room, send Reiki energy with both hands to every corner of the room, on the walls, floor, and ceiling.

If you want to "recharge" your food with Reiki energy, direct it to the ingredients before cooking or to cooked food before eating it. Keep your hands above the food or touch the dishes in which it lies with your hands and direct energy there.

As a matter of fact, you can apply the Reiki method daily in relation to any object - to medicines, perfumes, and even to your wallet. It takes a little time - just one moment, and the effect will be amazing.

Now, let's move directly to healing techniques.

Beesen

The Beesen technique is also called the "scanning technique." Translated from Japanese, the word "bee" means "treat," and the word" sen "means" determine," establish."
Activate the three energy centers.

Join hands in Gassho. Ask Reiki for energy to enter you and direct your hands to the part of the patient's body that needs

521

treatment. Follow your feelings. If no sensations have arisen immediately, place your dominant hand on the patient's crown chakra.

If you still do not feel the "direction," slowly move your hands along the patient's body, from top to bottom and at a small distance. Feeling a tingling sensation in your hands, warmth, attraction, pressure, know that you have found the right place on the body. You will be able to see or hear the necessary information.

There is a feeling of unpleasant pain in the hands, rising to the elbows and even to the shoulders, at the moment when you reach the problem area of the patient. In this situation, you can't remove your hands; on the contrary, you need to continue to hold them until this sensation leaves your hands through your fingertips. After that, you can move them to another position. It is believed that this unpleasant sensation called "hibiki" (resonance) occurs when Reiki's positive energy is directed to a negatively charged area of the body.

With Beesen, sensations vary depending on the type and stage of the disease, as well as on the personality of the patient. Using the sensation of movement, pulsation, tingling, heat, or cold, you can determine the disease, its stage and the time required for healing.

In any case, each person has his own ailments (even if he is not aware of them), so you need to be very careful when performing Beesen technique. With this approach, you will be able to heal the disease before it manifests. If, during the process of Reiki's influence, you got rid of the sensations of Beesen, then you prevented the disease.

The sensations of Beesen can be manifested not only in the problem area, but also in some other area: for example, with a disease of the stomach - in the forehead, and with problems with the liver - in the eyes, etc.

In general, the ability to beam in different people manifests itself in different ways. And if you do not rush, then you can develop this ability in yourself. You just need to give yourself time to get used to the sensations in your hands and thoughts. The best assistant in this process is your intuition.

The technique ends in the position of Gassho.

Gyoshi ho

Gyoshi ho's technique is called "eye healing." The Japanese word "gosh" means "sight." Dr. Usui argued that energy is emitted by all parts of the body, but especially by the hands, eyes, and breathing. And this technique teaches us to use the energy emitted from the eyes.

First, try to do this technique not with a person, but, for example, with a flower. Take the flower in your hand or place it two steps away from you, at eye level. Defocus your gaze and look through it. After some time, you will find that you can see almost 180 degrees.

Look at the flower and let the image come closer to you. Soon you will feel a very subtle form of breathing emanating from your eyes, associated with inhaling and exhaling. This exercise should be performed for 10 minutes every day until you understand that you can use your gaze to treat people.

Defocus your gaze. In other words, make sure that it is not intently in a stare. The fact is that in the gaze, there is certain aggression, and this is contraindicated for treatment.

Gently focus your eyes on the part of the body that you want to treat, and look there for several minutes. Then stop "actively" looking at your patient and let his image "enter your eyes." Notice how a circle of energy is created between you and the patient: its energy enters your eyes. You can put Reiki symbols on the part of the body that you want to treat.

If you liked this technique, you could also try Trataka meditation:

Sit back and look at a candle for 45-60 minutes. Try not to blink your eyes, even if after a few minutes they begin to watery. Keep your gaze on the candle. By practicing this technique regularly, you can safely perform it for an hour. Your consciousness will become like a laser beam - as sharp and focused.

Practicing with a candle can scare you: then do a Trataka meditation with a photograph or a lit statuette. You can do this while in a dark or dark room with your reflection in the mirror or with a person sitting opposite.

Affirmations

If you work with yourself, make affirmations - positive judgments. If you are working with a patient, help them compose affirmations. Affirmation should be short, accurate, and positive. It must be compiled in the present tense, in the words of the person who uses it, and in his native language. It is important that you do not limit it to anything. Of course, it will take time to understand what a person really wants in life. After all, our desires are not always obvious. Activate the three energy centers.

Place the non-dominant hand (left, if you are right-handed) on the patient's forehead (or on your forehead), and the dominant one on the back of the head. Keep them like this for about 3 minutes, mentally repeating the composed affirmation. Then forget about affirmation, remove the non-dominant hand from your forehead, and simply give Reiki energy to the patient with the dominant hand lying on his head. Fold your hands in Gassho at the end of the exercise.

It is known that Dr. Usui used the five principles of Reiki and the verses of Emperor Meiji as affirmations. You can do the same.

Joshin Kokyu Ho

This technique is aimed at healing the Tanden. We have already said that the word "tanden" in Japanese means a place located two to three fingers below the navel. Thus, first, you need to correctly determine the location of the tanden.

Put your feet shoulder-width apart. Take a deep breath several times. Relax and think about something nice. Open your mouth a little. Hold your tongue against your palate and inhale through your nose. Exhale through the mouth, allowing the tongue to naturally lower. Bend your knees and focus on the lower abdomen. Take a few steps very slowly.

Suddenly, you will become aware of a point in the lower abdomen, two to three fingers below the navel: it is in this place that your life force lies.

You have found your tanden and now you can start the breathing technique of the Joshin Kokyu Ho.

Place one or both hands on the lower abdomen and breathe in the place you touch.

Activate the three Tributes.

Place one hand on the tanden and the other across from the back. Hold your hands until you feel the effect is achieved. Fold your palms in Gassho.

Joshin Kokyu Ho is used as the main technique for creating energy. This technique can also increase willpower - both yours and your patient.

Hishiryo

Hishiryo is a navel healing technique. Translated from Japanese, the word "hizo" means "navel."

Activate the three energy centers.

Bend the middle finger slightly and lay it on the navel, gently press down; when you feel the pulse, you can start the exercise.

Let Reiki energy flow through your middle finger into your belly button. Perform this exercise for 5–10 minutes while your pulse and energy are in harmony. If you want to use this technique to treat another person, first make sure that he does not mind that you touch his navel.

Perform the technique very gently. At the end, slowly and smoothly remove your finger from the navel. Fold your hands in Gassho, then open your eyes.

Ge Doku Ho

Ge Doku Ho is called a detoxification technique. The word "ge" in Japanese means "conclusion," and the word "doku" - "poison" or "toxins." Using this technique, you can remove toxins from both your body and the patient's body. Thanks to this, you can get rid of the side effects of drugs.

Activate the three Tributes.

Place one hand on the tanden and the other on the back. Stay in this position for about 30 minutes until you imagine that all the toxins have left your body (or the patient's body) through your feet to the ground.

Fold your palms in Gassho.

Hanshin Koketsu Ho

The Hanshin Koketsu Ho technique is aimed at purifying the blood. The word "hanshin" in Japanese means "half the body," and the word "koket" means "purification of blood." The technique is used to return the patient to planet Earth after healing; helps people with mental disabilities.

Activate the three energy centers.

Ask the patient to lie with their back and to bend the knees slightly.

Putting your left hand on his shoulder, use your right hand to move from the left shoulder to the right buttock, from the right shoulder to the left buttock - 15 times.

Swipe down with two fingers of the right hand from the seventh cervical vertebra down to the third lumbar vertebra. Press on the third lumbar vertebra and slightly restrain movement. Do this 10 times.

Swipe with two hands from the spine to the sides, from top to bottom, 10-15 times.

Fold your hands in Gassho.

Syu Chu Reiki

Syu Chu Reiki is a group Reiki concentration exercise. Translated from Japanese, "syu chu" means "concentrated." This technique is performed in a group.

Activate the three energy centers.

All members of the group send energy to one person, wishing him health and happiness. Participants practicing the first stage of Reiki put their hands directly on the patient, and those who practice the second and third stages use symbols. This exercise can only be done with an emotionally balanced person, as it can have a very powerful effect. If the group is large, the exercise should be performed for 1-2 minutes with each.

If the group is so large that there is no way for everyone to put their hands on the patient, form several rows. The first healers lay their

hands on the patient, and those behind them lay their hands on their shoulders.
Finish the exercise in the Gassho position.

Chapter 10
Yoga Therapy

T his chapter is special. Why? This is due to the fact that people often start to engage in some kind of technology or activity precisely because of health problems, and are limited to these goals. Such limits personal freedom by binding. In this chapter, the principles and basic mechanisms will be set forth, on the basis of which everyone will be able to build a sufficiently self-sufficient and holistic system of healing for himself - and for others.

To begin with, we should remember that before the organism is living, it possesses really unlimited resources for restoration, it is important to properly distribute the efforts and do not leave any stone unturned.

Step one: create a goal and adjust the background

It has already been said about the need for a correct and clear goal-setting: the person must know what they want from it. Intuition will then help direct the hands and in which direction it should go. However, abstract efforts will lead to abstract results. Those resources that will be released during the practice should be directed to something specific. Otherwise, the effect will be evenly distributed across all organs and systems, especially without emphasizing any organ. You must form an extremely clear, lively, "convex" image that carries information in itself simultaneously for all senses.

Let's see what happens in the life of an ordinary, normal person over time. A person is born, being the owner of a conditionally defined health potential. From the first moment of life, he is exposed to environmental factors, often not the most favorable ("... from the moment of birth, a person's life turns into a continuous process of dying."). A body part peel when unintentionally struck against a stone, and any virus that enters the body, even if it does not cause a disease, every meal, every breath, every heartbeat, every disease is inevitable, step by step, brings a person closer to the natural finale - the body runs out of safety and starts inevitably collapse. This often happens because an ordinary person simply does not imagine what should be his body and how it should be felt "from the inside" in optimal condition. It turns out that a person lives on the resources of his body, often ineptly squandering the potential of vitality and health, allotted to him by nature.

In general, the aging process of the body and the mechanism of the development of the disease can be described as follows: under the influence of external factors, even with strong body resistance, there remain many adverse effects. "Malfunctions" gradually accumulate in the body, some defects in the work of first small groups - cells, and later organs and their systems that are increasingly diverting the body away from the optimal - that is, its normal working condition. The "specific gravity of errors" is accumulating in cells and tissues, and the processes of degeneration of tissues and organs begin. In fact, if you look at it, the majority of diseases are based on degenerative-dystrophic tissue changes: gradually, sections of a healthy organ become denser for one reason or another, their normal structure is replaced by dense tissues, respectively, the total percentage of healthy working cells decreases.

This can be very clearly explained by the example of heart diseases: all of them basically have impaired blood supply and myocardial trophism, as a result of which changes in the structure of the heart begin. This is especially clearly seen in heart attacks: dead tissue is replaced by a scar, which significantly reduces the contractility of the myocardium, against the background of this compaction, rhythm and conduction disturbances appear. Then the process begins to develop at an increasing rate. So the body gradually degenerates. In fact, similar processes occur in the human mind: unused qualities - the structural organs of consciousness, gradually die out as unnecessary, the general structure of consciousness is simplified, becomes primitive and degenerates, reducing the set of functions to the minimum necessary. Consciousness gradually "condenses" loses mobility.

This process can be compensated by a clearly constructed intention uniting all levels and structures of a human being, aimed at creating the most powerful and clear image-state of oneself in an ideal form. This is a kind of matrix of our optimal state, on which our whole body, emotional sphere, and sphere of consciousness are built. It is necessary to constantly maintain and develop this state, constantly adding as many shades to it as possible, making it more and more real and alive. So, gradually, we will be able to learn not to lose our own energy in the process of life, but rather, gradually draw to our center - the force that we once lost.

Creating a Goal for the Whole Body

This is the stage of creating a holistic strategy for a further, more or less long period of life. Our task now is to note for ourselves our initial state. Keeping this in mind, we try to see ourselves from the side, noting all our weaknesses - the self-diagnosis system in our body always works, we just don't need to stop it from reporting all detected damages. The principle is simple: on our internal "virtual" screen, without straining and not expecting anything, we try to see ourselves. The picture that we will see will give fairly clear information about the real state of our organs and systems.

To begin with, it is worth turning to the anatomical atlas in order to at least, in general terms, imagine where which organ is located and how it looks.

The next stage is the search for the image of the ideal state of the whole body as a whole. You can turn to childhood memories (in early childhood, as a rule, we are much closer to our ideal state, we just do not have time to find all that number of masks that now make up our "alien" roles and identities) or just come up with a new image of ourselves anew. When a lively and clear image is created, we "try it on ourselves," enter it. If this is really what we need, we will immediately feel it - we will be comfortable, and the world around us will seem more vibrant and rainbow. In any case, we try to revive the feeling of childhood; this alone will greatly stimulate recovery processes.

Take this as a rule: if the body "believes" you, your image, it completely reorganizes its functioning mode. For this, you just need to return to it more often and get used to your new state more and more.

The last step at this point is to replace the old image with a new one. We combine the picture of the old image and the new ideal state; we try to make it so that all the components of the old image: colors, sensations from the other senses organically transfer to a new image, reinforcing it, making it even more bright and convex. We do this as often as there is enough "survivability" of the old image - until it once completely disappears.

As a possible option, here is one of the options for restoring your optimal initial state of feeling like a child: imagine yourself as a small child. Look into his eyes. What will you see there? Perhaps it will be sadness, longing for love – perhaps a love for you? Take the child in your arms, hug him. Let him feel how much you love him. Promise him that you will always be near and will be able to help him if necessary. Now make this image very small and place it in your heart. Let it be there so that you can give is such necessary love. Pass this feeling through yourself; let it go outside. Let it begin to change your own life.

Creating a Goal for a Specific Organ

This stage is the stage of constructing tactical, less global goals. It is no different from the previous one, except that here we are rebuilding the ideal state matrix for the organ that we are currently interested in. Here we simply specify the task.

Optimal Background Tuning

The optimal background is that the psycho-emotional state in which the body will recover as efficiently as possible, which, in fact, will start the recovery processes in it, and the overall level of its energy, respectively, will be maximum. In many psycho-training systems, such a state is called the state of the winner or something similar. It is important that the maximum rise is felt in this state. Everyone has their own best way to enter this state, and perhaps the most difficult in the initial period is to learn how to create this state and then constantly maintain it. We are trying to use all possible and accessible methods for this: films, music or any technological techniques.

It's convenient to use the following as a possible technique for entering the "activated" state: we release attention, evenly distributing it throughout the body, try to feel how the whole body is drawn into the breathing process, how the pores on its surface open, tissues begin to come to life. If there are no such sensations right away, then we create them. It already exists in us; it is important to learn how to distinguish it from the general background and maximize it. We are looking in the space inside the body for the zone that is currently at the peak of its activity. When we enter it with our attention, there is a surge of strength and freshness.

We begin to breathe in this place, with each inhalation-exhalation, increasing the volume of this zone, we try to fill the entire body from within with this sensation, to impregnate all tissues and organs. We saturate with this sensation the part of the body that interests us, create in it a kind of epicenter of this sensation. We enter this state in the morning; we try to start with it every day. Now our task is not to lose this feeling, as far as possible we try to strengthen it even more.

This is the core of the entire recovery system; without this state, it is hardly possible to cause radical changes in the established distorted relations between organs and systems. Even if you do, in this case, the efficiency of such activities will be significantly lower.

Step two: optimize your lifestyle

Another necessary element on the path to health is the introduction of certain adjustments to the mode of life. One of the most basic elements related here is nutrition. So many worthwhile books have already been written on this subject, that it hardly makes sense to dwell on this issue in detail. In the most general terms, the following should be said:

We exclude all heavy proteins and fats of animal origin from our menu: meat, replacing it with soy and products from it, and minimize the use of butter, replacing it with ghee. Also, exclude coffee and black tea. These products are acceptable in rather "extreme" situations - during periods of severe cold, for example, when sufficiently tough external stimulants are needed.

Meals - only when the body insists on the need for it. We do not overeat, always leaving empty space in the stomach after eating, there should remain a feeling of slight hunger. In fact, with the relatively efficient operation of body systems, the amount of food needed is minimal. If you are a constitutional "meat-eater" - it happens, such people are basically not able to do without meat - we try, at least.

Food is not only a source of building materials for the body but also an element that irritates the immune system. In addition, each serving of food passing through the intestine has an effect on its walls, similar to the action of sandpaper - food masses desquamate the intestinal epithelium; this is necessary for normal digestion. That is, for the normal functioning of the same immune system or intestines, on the one hand, an influx of energy and "building materials" is necessary, and on the other, what we eat has a destructive effect on these systems. All body structures should be able to fully recover.

In addition, in the conditions of constant intake of nutrients, decay products that are not completely eliminated are constantly accumulated. All that was said is to justify the need to periodically arrange for yourself the so-called fasting days. This is not starvation; hunger for the body is a condition in which it is forced to break down its own tissues. A few days without food, under no circumstances, will lead to this.

There is always a certain amount of nutrients in the body - as if put aside "in reserve." These "stocks" must be periodically updated: products, even when stored in the refrigerator, deteriorate. A pause in food intake for 24-36 hours approximately once a week may well help. Traditionally, it is recommended in yogic literature to do such periods of "food abstinence" on the new moon, full moon, 11th, 26th, and 29th days of the lunar month. On such days, we drink little, but often: herbal infusions (if you used to drink herbs and you know which ones are right for you) or just green tea. If, for the first time, pesters hunger, the more we try to drink more often: water leaches the gastric juice, which in many ways causes hunger. However, gradually, the body will get used to it.

All of the above rules regarding the restructuring of the diet are the simplest elements in the recovery system, which, however, are amazingly effective. In just a week or two, you will notice how much the perception of yourself and your body has changed: it becomes more relaxed, flexible, obedient, and movement becomes easier and more pleasant, and perception becomes more clear and bright. The severity and inertness gradually and imperceptibly disappear completely.

The optimal set of products for each person is different, if you want to rebuild your diet "as science says", you should turn to books on Ayurveda, although by and large it will be absolutely simple to pay attention to your own feelings about the time of eating, diet, quantity, etc. likewise, a simple understanding that all internal organs need to be cleaned of accumulated waste products over the time is necessary.

In addition to periodic "food abstinence," it is advisable to use special cleansing procedures, their technology has already been described many times in other books: from those devoted exclusively to healing to books entirely about yoga. In hatha yoga, importance is attached to techniques for cleaning the nose (neti), eyes (trataka), tongue, stomach, intestines (basti). However, before mastering these techniques, it is advisable to consult with an experienced yoga instructor.

By and large, there is no need to use all of them: it's worth choosing a few that are most suitable for the situation and use them regularly, when these organs are unloaded to some extent, the rest will become more active, and the effect will increase exponentially.

To facilitate the task of constantly maintaining an optimal state, we adhere to, at least the first time, a certain mode of life: we go to bed early, get up early, twice a day - water cleansing procedures (bathing). We avoid any negativity in relation to myself; as much as possible, we support the inner feeling of strength and self-determination, the state when you reach "I can achieve everything." As often as possible, if possible several times a day, we actively load the body with physical exercises, without which, ideally, it should not receive food.

Step three: work with the body

Firstly, to constantly maintain the optimal level of activity of consciousness and the body, all the usual types of physical activity are necessary: swimming, running, etc. Secondly, specific activity is highly desirable: the so-called gymnastic part of yoga therapy, which, in many respects, determines its truly amazing effectiveness. Here at this point, it is worth stopping in more detail.

The practice of asanas in the therapeutic version makes it possible to work out all internal organs, activating the blood flow and nerve plexuses, leveling the hormonal and psycho-emotional background.

In general terms, this mechanism can be described as follows. Most of the diseases can be relatively arbitrarily characterized as a disruption in the functioning of the body systems, accompanied by a violation of blood flow in the tissues of various internal organs (vasoconstriction due to edema with inflammation or for other reasons) and a violation in the innervation of the affected organs. Several of the parts of the nervous system are responsible for this. Cells that have lost their normal energy levels partially or completely lost their functions, simply cannot recover in the absence of a full connection with the

536

body and its regulatory systems. Accordingly, it is possible to restore the normal function of an organ by increasing the blood flow in it and activating the nearby nerve plexuses and higher sections of the nervous system.

The most important thing to remember during training is what you started to do. This has already been discussed in detail above. There must always be a clear awareness of the goal, its bright and strong image. When stretching the ligaments, the main principle of work is: we take a breath from those areas that are now "stretching" - from the joints and ligaments in which tension is felt, as if we are sucking it out, lifting it along the spine into the head, "impregnating" it with our image of ideal condition, and we return back, pumping joints and ligaments to the limit with breath.

In case of diseases of the abdominal organs, all asanas where the abdominal cavity is squeezed will be useful: by reducing its volume, intra-abdominal pressure rises, and blood from the aorta is squeezed out under increased pressure directly into all abdominal organs, activating metabolic processes in them and saturating the tissues with oxygen. This includes all the deflections and especially the deflections lying on the stomach, various twists, inclinations to one, and two legs from different positions, mayurasana, as well as all asanas, where the muscles and ligaments of the legs are actively stretched and the hip joints open.

Here it is necessary to carry nauli - band techniques, where work is actively used the front wall of the abdomen and all the breath at inhalation and exhalation, accompanied by bandhas (mula bandha, jalandhara bandha, and uddiyana bandha). All this works equally well for diseases of the liver, stomach and intestines, pancreas and kidneys, and pelvic organs. Also, in this situation, asanas will be useful in which the main load (stretching and tension) is on the legs and especially the hip joints. All standing asanas, all types of twine, butterflies, asanas with one or two legs under the arm, behind the head and all lotus elements are also effective.

In diseases accompanied by congestive processes in the organs (many diseases of the intestine, internal genital organs, etc.), all inverted elements will be very effective, especially all versions of the so-called "Egyptian" inclinations and twists, adding as much as possible to all inclinations during the fixation of the position of uddiyana bandha and nauli to strengthen the body.

For diseases of the organs of the chest cavity, it is worth using those exercises in which the chest is deformed, and the pressure in it increases accordingly. This group also includes, first of all, bends and all kinds of tilts to the sides, as well as those asanas where we are actively forced to use our hands and shoulder girdle. Dynamic practices will also be useful because of their training effects on the organs of the chest cavity. In inverted asanas, blood is redistributed and in the abdominal and chest cavities. There is a relative overflow of blood vessels, which also favorably affects the state of organs. In the case of heart disease, one should be extremely careful and build up the load very gradually. In any case, we focus on well-being.

All bandhas affect the state of the chest organs. When working with them in this case, it is especially important not to pinch the chest, leaving its internal volume as free and straightened as possible.

For diseases of the visual and auditory apparatus, all inverted positions, as well as asanas where the cervical spine is pulled or twisted, will be useful. If the brain is pulled into the pathological process, one should work extremely carefully and, rather indirectly: the main impact is on other departments with the simplest exercises, and through the normalization of the main functions, the state of the brain is corrected. All bandhas used in pranayama also affect intracranial pressure.

In diseases of the spine, it is first necessary to restore the correct position of the vertebrae relative to each other. To do this, you first need to stretch the spine. For this purpose, it is convenient to use various forward bends, rolls on the back, asanas where the legs rest on the hands. However, the simplest option is the usual bakasana.

Further, it is advisable to use twisting. Here, the possible set of these exercises is very large. After this, you need to strengthen, fix the newly rebuilt spine with a muscle corset. The possible and affordable set of asanas here is also very large: these are various face-ups with arms behind, and back deflections, which in themselves have a pronounced training and restorative effect on the intervertebral joints and stimulate the spinal cord, nerves, and plexuses adjacent to the spinal column, which is extremely beneficial for the condition of internal organs. Deflections, in turn, must be compensated by stretching the spine forward and twisting.

With spinal instability do not particularly zeal with stretches, so as not to stretch the intervertebral ligaments even more. Without a strong working muscle corset that fixes the spine, it will not be possible to fully restore it: the vertebrae simply will not be able to remain in an optimal position for a long time. The muscle corset is not only the back muscles, but also the oblique muscles of the abdomen and, in general, the muscles of the abdominal press. Accordingly, you should definitely include exercises for these muscle groups in your training. Such an approach will make it possible to deal with many problems, including severe injuries, in which surgical treatment or Reiki healing can be used. As the main principle of working with the spine, it is worth noting its constant stretching; any movement is made on a well-elongated spine, which should be followed in everyday life.

In general, it should be noted that many diseases of the internal organs are caused by just spinal problems.

In diseases of the joint-ligamentous apparatus of the extremities, it is especially necessary to carefully approach the development of damaged zones. If there is damage to the joint of a rheumatic nature or the type of osteoarthritis, when the joint surface is damaged, so as not to damage it, even more, do not immediately begin to actively load this joint. You need to start with tensile loads, and you need to select exercises so that there is no significant load on the body weight or stress on this joint.

539

If the joint or a group of joints are unstable, which sometimes happens after ruptures of the ligaments, or there is any other pathology associated with damage to the ligamentous apparatus, the approach should be the opposite: the joints should be actively loaded with power work, not really trying to stretch them at first. It is worth using both dynamic and static loads: this develops various groups of muscle fibers, and ligaments are strengthened more efficiently.

A sufficiently universal asana in this sense is a properly performed ordinary slide (uttan adho-mukha-svanasana). The technique of internal work in it has already been described above. The full practice of this asana in this version will make it possible to deal with problems of the spine, disorders in the central nervous system, organs of the chest and abdominal cavity, especially the lungs, heart, liver, kidneys, and in general the genitourinary system, joints and ligaments of the arms and legs. There is also a pronounced harmonizing effect on the endocrine glands. The effect can be enhanced by alternating a series of hyperventilation methods like kapalabhati or bhastrika with uddiyana bandha and nauli.

In diseases of the endocrine glands, all deflections tilts, and twists are very effective, especially those in which the main effect is on the spine at the level of the gland of interest to us. For the pancreas and adrenal glands, the same principles in work will be effective for other pelvic organs.

If there is a general weakness and lack of tone, hypotension, a tendency to depression, then it is necessary to focus on the practice of standing and power asanas, deflections mainly by the type of bridges and work in a dynamic mode. If the situation is the opposite - there is a tendency to hypertension, emotional instability, with a feeling of general tension, then we focus on stretching asanas. It is better to do them on the floor, with long relaxing fixations in order to minimize stress.

In any case, the body sooner or later begins to prompt itself on when what, and how best to do. It is important to simply understand that the real master of the situation is you yourself, and take responsibility for everything that happens in your life for yourself.

As the effect increases, it is important not to stop there, but to constantly increase the load and the degree of complexity of the exercises. Thus, the body will be forced to constantly be in a state of complete mobilization, which will help to quickly return the lost power potential to the body.

At the end of each lesson, check the effectiveness of work. Again, as already described above, we are trying to see our body on the virtual screen, as if from the outside, tracking the changes in the "diagnostic" image that we managed to achieve. It is necessary to carry out the correction again, now the final one: again, we check the image obtained with the standard and try to remove all inconsistencies, maximizing the state that is our standard.

Thus, from time to time, step by step, rebuilding your body, re-creating ourselves as we want to see ourselves.

Conclusion

As I had said at the beginning of this book, you must admit that often we react too sharply to difficult life situations, lose energy, and feel completely unprotected. But everything can be fixed by studying Energy Healing, Reiki meditation, and Yoga.

You have learned the simplest and most effective exercises of these methods, which will help you gain health, amazing grace, and beauty for many years. However, these are just theoretical until you decide to take action.

Make a move. Take a step. Ennoble your mind. You will surely find the light at the end of the tunnel! I wish you all the best.